JEEP

THE POWER CENTER about which the world-wide service record of the Jeep fighting car revolves ... the *reason* for every motorized miracle it performs for the Allied forces ... and the *sole source* of Jeep power, Jeep speed, Jeep flexibility, dependability, and fuel economy, is the Willys "Go-Devil" Jeep Engine, designed and perfected by Willys-Overland Motors, Inc., "Builders of the Mighty Jeep".

The power and stamina of the versatile Jeep will serve many needs in the years of reconstruction ahead.

THE SUN
NEVER SETS
ON THE
MIGHTY JEEP

WILLYS *Builds the Mighty* JEEP

JEEP

The 50 Year History

Robert C. Ackerson

Foulis

Haynes

A **FOULIS** Motoring Book

First published 1988

© Robert C. Ackerson and Haynes Publishing
Group.

Published by:
Haynes Publishing Group
Sparkford, Nr. Yeovil,
Somerset BA22 7JJ, England

Haynes Publications Inc.
861 Lawrence Drive, Newbury Park,
California 91320 USA

**British Library Cataloguing in Publication
Data**
Ackerson, Robert C.
Jeep.
1. Jeep military vehicles, to 1980
I. Title
623'.74'722'09
ISBN 0-85429-533-X

Library of Congress Catalog Card No.
88-81065

Editor: **Robert Iles**
Design: **Mike King**
Printed in England by: **J.H. Haynes & Co. Ltd**

Contents

Introduction   7

Chapter One: Origins   9

Chapter Two: The post-war CJ–2A, CJ–3A, CJ–3B   33

Chapter Three: America's first all-steel station wagon   51

Chapter Four: The first generation post-war pick-ups   85

Chapter Five: The Jeep goes to college   101

Chapter Six: The Kaiser-Frazer/Willys merger   111

Chapter Seven: The CJ–5, CJ–6, CJ–7: The Jeeps that
                      wrote the book on four-wheel-drive   117

Chapter Eight: The forward control models   165

Chapter Nine: The Jeep Jeepster/Commando: 1967–1973   177

Chapter Ten: The Jeep Wagoneer: 1962–1988: From
                      Pioneer to Grand Dame   185

Chapter Eleven: The J–Series trucks   215

Chapter Twelve: The Jeep Cherokees: 1974–1983   237

Chapter Thirteen: The Jeep Scrambler   255

Chapter Fourteen: The Cherokee/Wagoneers: 1984–1988   261

Chapter Fifteen: The Comanche pick-ups   283

Chapter Sixteen   The Jeep Wrangler   295

Chapter Seventeen: International Operations   311

Chapter Eighteen: Merging and converging: 1954–1987   319

Introduction

When American automotive production resumed in late 1945 only the foolhardy assumed that it would be "business as usual". The war years represented a break with the past that soon became institutionalized. Among today's automobile enthusiasts the term "postwar" carries as much validity as does "classic", "antique" or "vintage".

Initially, the American manufacturers sought to fill the void left by four years of war when their plants were devoted to the production of military equipment with cars that were moderately facelifted 1942 models. But it wasn't long before plans that had been put aside after Pearl Harbor were resurrected to become reality. Thus it was that Detroit soon was producing cars with tailfins, overhead valves, V-8 engines, automatic transmissions and all sorts of power accessories.

In the midst of this headlong rush into a brave new automotive world it was easy to ignore the Jeep. True, it emerged from the war as one of the best known symbols of modern mechanized warfare. But somehow its virtues as a utilitarian vehicle seemed too mundane for a nation infatuated with wraparound windshields and three tone color combinations. Yet, as the years passed the Jeep and its truck and station wagon siblings gradually gained an intensely loyal following that found their virtues of honest design and go-anywhere capability a refreshing alternative to the gloss and glitter that characterized other American automobiles.

While this bastion of market strength was gathering strength a phenomenon known as the recreational vehicle market began to emerge in the early 1960s. Americans with plenty of discretionary income and a love of the outdoors joined farmers and sportsmen in discovering that a four-wheel drive Jeep filled a niche in their lifestyle far better than a conventional automobile.

While the Jeep's popularity steadily increased, the forces leading to greater consolidation within the automobile industry lead to the acquisition of Willys-Overland by Kaiser Frazer in 1953. By 1970, with all the independent producers gone except for American Motors Corporation, which itself was the result of a Nash-Hudson merger, the timing was ripe for AMC to acquire Willys from Kaiser. Ironically, this move, bitterly opposed by many within AMC was to prove one of the most incisive moves ever made by AMC's management. During the darkest hours of American Motors' existence one of the few bright spots was the popularity of its Jeep products.

Indeed, it can be argued that AMC, if it had to rely upon the sales of its passenger cars would never have survived into the 1980s. It's hardly a secret, in that context, that the primary force behind Chrysler's purchase of AMC in 1987 was to bring Jeep into its corporate fold. This development was bittersweet to many longtime AMC/Jeep advocates who, like this writer, saw in AMC a certain tenacity and rugged individualism that was seldom evident in the Big Three.

But as part of Chrysler Jeep has a bright future. With resources that dwarf those available to AMC in the best of times, the Jeeps that will replace today's models are likely to be nothing less than sensational.

This volume traces the heritage of those vehicles from the Jeep's prewar genesis through the 1988 model year models. Over that time span, which comes close to a half century, the basic Jeep character traits of honest design, versatility and a penchant for hard work remained intact. This book celebrates that achievement. Contributing to its final form were many individuals who gave willingly of their time and knowledge. A sincere thank you is extended to the members of American Motors Public Relation Department, including Rita McKay, Ben Dunn, Alan McFee and Lloyd Northard. Louis Halverson of the Philadelphia Free Library and Andrea Gerberg of the State University College at Oneonta Library staff helped locate numerous items that proved invaluable in the preparation of this book's content. Special thanks go to Ed Shultis and John Barlow who loaned the author many items from their personal collections. All of these good people are in effect co-authors of this volume. Like the Jeep they were as good as any and better than most.

Chapter 1

Origins

The last military Jeep of the World War Two variety was produced by Willys-Overland in Toledo, Ohio on 20 August, 1945. Earlier, on 17 July, the first civilian CJ–2A model left the assembly line. Although initial plans called for the output of approximately 20,000 CJ–2As in 1945, actual output was only 1824 units with serial numbers ranging from 10001 to 11824.

Three years earlier, automotive designer, John Tjaarda, whose credits included the Lincoln-Zephyr, proposed a daring plan to Willys-Overland board chairman Ward M. Canaday that, if successfully implemented, would have Willys-Overland become part of the world's first multi-national automotive producer. In essence, Willys-Overland, two British firms; Daimler and Briggs, the French Mathis company, the Swedish Automobile Company and the Industrias Basicas Mexicanas of Mexico would form the International Car Company. The vehicles to be sold by the participants would be of three types: a civilian Jeep, a larger station wagon with Jeep running gear and a 2-wheel drive sedan also utilizing Jeep running gear.

Willys-Overland was in a solid financial position as the war came to a close. At the start of 1945 company assets were $72 million, with a net profit of $4 million for 1944 and working capital of $14 million. Back in fiscal year 1940 the company had lost $800,000. This was turned into an $800,000 profit in 1941. The following year Willys did even better, reporting a $1,265,000 profit in 1942. In 1943 net income more than doubled to reach $3 million. From 1941 to the end of the war Willys produced over $760,000,000 in military equipment of which the sales of Jeeps and Jeep parts represented $456,019,176.

This was an impressive achievement but Willys-Overland remained a David in the midst of a tribe of Goliaths. For example, General Motors, from 1933 to 1941, netted $1,454,279,000. Most of those years Willys-Overland lost money. Furthermore, it took a long look back in history to see a time when Willys-Overland was what could be regarded as a volume automobile producer. In 1927, for example, Willys-Overland sales exceeded 314,000 cars. But in the 1937–1941 time span its production had averaged only 35,000 cars a year.

Clearly, Willys-Overland had to proceed into the postwar era with a mixture of caution and audacity, helped by a pinch or two of luck. It was to be an age when the pent-up demand for cars, due to both the long depression and the war years would create an immense seller's market. But these good times would be tempered by the great battle between Ford and General Motors for industry supremacy and the growing sophistication of buyers accustomed to new styling and engineering features appearing on an annual basis. In such an environment a small company could get seriously bruised!

The International Car Company never made it to the starting gate, yet, Willys-Overland eventually did produce a fine little sedan, the Aero Willys, that was powered by a Jeep-derived engine. In addition, one of the greatest Jeep civilian vehicles of all-time was the Jeep station wagon. Furthermore, Willys-Overland, by 1946, had adopted a two-pronged strategy that enabled it to sustain profitable operations on a relatively modest production basis by entering market sections that were either overlooked or ignored by the large companies while avoiding costly year-to-year model changes.

Yet, none of this would have allowed Willys-Overland to survive if its basic product had been merely average. To the credit of everyone involved in its design, creation and production the vehicle that Willys-Overland offered the postwar world was not merely adequate. Instead, it was one of the truly outstanding mechanized products of the modern age, a vehicle that aroused the best of human emotions, generated feeling of immeasurable loyalty and assumed a personality of its own.

The prime catalyst for the development of what was to become the Jeep was the release of specifications for a new military vehicle by a Quartermaster Corps Ordnance Technical Committee on 27 June, 1940. The major requisites consisted of 4-wheel drive, seating for three passengers, room for a .30 caliber machine gun mount, an empty weight of 1300 pounds, wheelbase of 80 inches, body height of 36 inches, front and rear tread of 47 inches, minimum ground clearance of 6.5 inches and a payload capacity of 600 pounds. The vehicle's operating speed range was to be from three to fifty miles per hour.

The Quartermaster Corps set a deadline of 9:00 a.m., Monday morning, 22 July, 1940 for plans and bids for a $175,000 contract for the construction of an initial batch of 70 vehicles. The first vehicle was to be ready for testing in only seven weeks and the remaining 69 examples (including eight with 4-wheel steering) were to be delivered just 26 days later.

Although the horse and mule had provided the bulk of the energy required to move the American Expeditionary Force's equipment in World War One, there was graphic evidence both before and after that conflict that the age of mechanized warfare was underway. Before the start of the 20th century French military officials had observed civilian vehicles in military maneuvers and in 1899 the French Army had purchased three civilian vehicles for reconnaissance and communication purposes. When the French equipped a Panhard in 1904 with a Hotchkiss machine gun the implication for extended use of motor vehicles in combat situations became obvious.

During World War One Cadillacs with their new 70 horsepower, 314 cubic inch V8 engines were used extensively by both American and Allied forces for staff and ambulance use. Shortly after the United States had entered the war the U.S. Army tested a number of passenger cars at Marfa, Texas which resulted in the purchase of over 2000 Cadillacs for use in Europe. More widespread was the use of Model T Fords as ambulances, patrol and reconnaissance purposes.

In their skirmishes with Pancho Villa, American forces commanded by General John Pershing and Lieutenant George Patton had used standard production model automobiles. In Europe there were numerous cases when the use of motor vehicles made the difference between victory and defeat during World War One. The best known of these was the transportation of thousands of French troops to the front in Renault taxis where they stopped the German advance upon Paris. Both the French and British forces also used the Nash Quad 4-wheel drive truck during the war.

With the end of the war and the return of the United States to an era of normalcy and isolationism, progress towards the creation of a versatile, lightweight vehicle capable of performing a multitude of tasks was not a top priority of an army in a diminishing state of combat readiness.

Nonetheless, the army did maintain an interest in the use of motor vehicles and on 17 July, 1919 assembled 60 trucks, 12 touring cars, several motorcycles and 235 men for a transcontinental convoy from Washington D.C. to San Francisco. One of the revelations of this two month operation was the atrocious condition of American roads and bridges. Another was the inability of the participating motorcycles to cope with the deep sand and glue-like mud all-too-often encountered enroute to the West Coast. This shortcoming, plus their poor stream fording performance made motorcycles unattractive in the view of many Army officers as scout vehicles.

On the other hand the trucks that didn't break down were regarded as too large and cumbersome for reconnaissance use. What was needed was a vehicle with the maneuverability and speed of the motorcycle, the stamina of the truck and of a size that was large enough to carry three soldiers but small enough to avoid making it a tempting target to the enemy. Of prime importance was an ability to traverse all sorts of terrain and, for that, 4-wheel drive was mandatory.

As a result, the Quartermaster Corps, in 1920, began development of a multi-wheel drive vehicle whose primary purpose would be for reconnaissance and scouting. The initial project was a ¼ ton farm tractor-type vehicle with the advantages of excellent traction and road clearance. Less attractive was its great height and low speed.

The following year the United States Army Ordnance Technical Division, via the head of its automotive engineering section, William F. Beasley, proposed the conversion of medium-duty standard trucks into cross-country vehicles. The machines, totalling 15 in all, with a track traction system were tested in 1921 at the Aberdeen Proving Ground.

Becoming more and more apparent to the objective (and perceptive) observer were the difficulties inherent in converting any existing product into the type of vehicle desired by the military for all-terrain operations. Among the observers of the Ordnance trials of 1921 was Major L.H. Campbell, Jr. who, while appreciating this problem, was also aware that a cost-conscious bureaucracy would turn down any "start from scratch" project. As a result he directed his attention to existing inexpensive passenger cars that could serve as the foundation for multi-purpose military use. Major Campbell might have been accused of believing he could create an automotive purse from a sow's ear by proposing to the Ordnance Technical Committee that a production automobile could be modified to serve a variety of functions including off-road vehicle, scout car, light cargo carrier and as a general purpose military transporter.

The result of Campbell's interest was a series of "Cross-Country Cars" based on the Model T Ford and Series K Chevrolet. The first of these was a Model T Ford modified by William F. Beasley and Army Captain Carl Terry to accept huge, oversize balloon tires and 4-wheel drive. The total number of these vehicles was under 100 and in 1932, without additional funding, the project came to a close. A criticism made of the final "Cross-Country Cars" was their heavy weight which was due in part to the inclusion of machine guns, munition boxes, tools, etc. In contrast, the early models with weights of around 1100 pounds had only a basic body (canvas stretched over a wooden frame was used for bodywork on some models), cycle fenders and exposed fuel tanks. A very important achievement of the "Cross-Country" project was the clear-cut superiority of 4-wheel drive over track propulsion for high-speed operations over varied terrain.

The winding down of the "Cross-Country" activity did not, however, bring an end to the Army's interest in that type of vehicle, nor did it discourage the efforts of independent manufacturers to create a product that would land a large government contract. In 1933, for example, the Army evaluated an American Austin roadster equipped with oversize tires. Its performance aroused the interest of Captain Robert G. Howe. Four years later at Fort Benning, Georgia, Howe, along with Master Sergeant Melvyn C. Wiley used an American Austin chassis converted to front-wheel drive as the basis of a vehicle capable of carrying two men in prone positions plus a 0.30 caliber machine gun.

This creation, which was examined by Willys-Overland Engineering vice president, Barney Roos, was found, after approximately 4000 test miles, lacking in several important areas including ride quality and ground clearance. This would not be, however, the last time the Army would evaluate a vehicle produced by the American Austin Company or its successor.

The Austin Seven, on which the American Austin and the future Bantam were based was also built under license in Japan and Germany whose armed forces (as did the British Army) used them for military purposes. In addition, the Italian Army adapted the Fiat Balilla Spider for its use beginning in 1932.

Back in the United States the Marmon-Herrington Company, which had been founded in 1931 by Walter C. Marmon and Arthur Herrington and specialized in the production of 4-wheel drive trucks, built a number of 4-wheel drive Ford ½ and 1.5 ton trucks that the Army evaluated in 1936. These were capable and durable machines, the forerunners of the heavy-duty trucks and transporters Marmon-Herrington produced for the Army during World War Two. They were not, though, the small, maneuverable and inexpensive vehicles envisioned by Major Campbell back in 1922. Nonetheless the ½ ton model, which was nicknamed the "Darling", impressed Army test drivers with its ability to operate in difficult conditions. One result was an order for 64 additional ½ ton models from Marmon-Herrington.

In the late thirties the Quartermaster Corps' procurement planning office in Detroit took a number of preliminary steps that provided the basis for the output of military vehicles in the event of a major armament program. Among the activities carried out was a review of existing plant facilities, the filing of allocation requests with the Army and Navy Munitions Board, and the preparation of estimated production needs. The three major producers: General Motors, Ford and Chrysler were expected to assume most of the wartime production, but also in line for military work assignments, if they were made, were International Harvester, Mack, Willys-Overland and American Bantam.

This prewar planning failed to establish a realistic basis for the mass production of the special components required by tactical vehicles or for substantially increased output of heavy trucks. Yet, it stands as an example of forward thinking that was substantiated by the nature of land operations that took place during World War Two. Also reflecting an enlightened outlook was the earlier mentioned release of specifications for a 4-wheel drive General Purpose Vehicle in June, 1940 by the Quartermaster Corps.

Since a grand total of 135 companies were invited to respond to this design competition the field appeared to be wide open. But, of these, only two companies, American Bantam and Willys-Overland, submitted bids. American Bantam appeared initially to have the inside track in landing what could blossom into a large and lucrative, multi-thousand unit contract.

This company, which had originated as the American Austin Car Company on 28 February, 1928, began the following year producing cars closely based upon the British Austin Seven which had been a sensation in England since its introduction in 1922. American automotive tastes, however, were not those of England and regardless of the economic impact of the Great Depression and the American Austin's low cost (this really wasn't as much as a factor as may be thought since at $445 the Austin was five dollars more than a Ford Model A) there was little interest in mini-car motoring in America. As a result, only 8558 American Austins were sold in 1930. The next year was even more disastrous with an output of only 1279 cars.

Two years later American Austin was in receivership and apparently headed towards extinction. But more than one automobile company during those times attracted an individual whose self-confidence, optimism, perseverance and vision either postponed that day of reckoning or banished it forever. For American Bantam that man was Roy S. Evans. In the late twenties Evans had become the most successful automobile dealer in the Southern United States. Purchasing 1500 unsold cars at the Austin plant in 1932 and then selling them at $295 each reinforced Evan's view, based on prior sales success with the American Austins, that a market did exist for a small car in the United States.

For a short time under Evan's supervision the company appeared to be recovering, but, after sales of 3846 in 1933 American Austin faltered badly in 1934. Output fell back to approximately 1300 cars and the American Austin receiver had little choice but to file a petition of bankruptcy.

The decision marked the third phase of the company's struggle for survival. Evans paid a mere $5000 for the company's Butler, Pennsylvania factory (which was valued at $10 million), created a new firm, the American Bantam Car Company and, through the sale of preferred and common stock had $2 million available for design and development purposes.

What followed next was a mixture of financial moves by stockholders depriving Bantam of this badly needed money, the creation of vehicles far superior to the old American Austins (One example was a ¼ ton truck that found a customer in the form of the U.S. Army. The Pennsylvania National Guard also field tested three Bantam roadsters in 1938), and sales that remained disappointingly low. In this environment the news from the Quartermaster Corps was regarded as offering American Bantam's best chance for survival.

As early as 1938 Charles H. Payne of American Bantam had attempted to interest the military in his company's products but it wasn't until 17 July, 1940, just five days before the Quartermaster bid due date that Bantam president, Charles H. Fenn, contacted Karl K. Probst, who, in the view of some automotive historians was the "Father of the Jeep".

Karl Probst was born on 20 October, 1883 in Point Pleasant, West Virginia and had studied mechanical engineering at Ohio State University under Charles Kettering who eventually became head of General Motors engineering. Although illness prevented him from graduating, Probst, in the early years of his career, displayed an excellent grasp of the essentials of small car design. Forced for a time to leave the automobile industry because of his health, Probst had, by 1940, amassed an impressive list of credentials, including the position of chief engineer at both Milburn and Reo. He also worked on small car projects considered by both GM and Ford. In addition, Probst had been involved with Arthur Brandt and Frank Fenn in a small car and

truck program that envisioned sales through Sears and Roebuck outlets. In 1940 Probst was operating an independent engineering firm – Probst, Shoemaker and Merrill, Inc. with an office on Grand and Woodward in Detroit.

Prior to approaching Probst in July, 1940 Fenn enlisted the help of Arthur Brandt who had been his predecessor as American Bantam president in persuading Probst to work on the Bantam military contract. Brandt also approached William Knudsen, the former General Motors president who was then serving as head of the National Defense Advisory Commission. Knudsen appealed to Probst's sense of patriotism to overcome his hesitation about working for a company with no money under conditions that promised nothing if the Quartermaster bid was not successful.

The vehicle that Fenn originally envisioned would not be a new, from the ground-up vehicle, instead it would be based on the production Bantam. This type of thinking was also found in Germany where plans were being made to modify the original Volkswagen into a general purpose military vehicle. When a committee from the Army Quartermaster Corps spent several weeks testing Bantam roadsters and considering their conversion to 4-wheel drive hopes soared at Bantam that the U.S. military might adopt the German plan.

When Fenn first called Probst on 15 July, 1940, he had not yet received the official bid specifications from the army. Thus he was, as noted, asking Probst to modify an existing vehicle, not create an all-new vehicle. This perspective was completely shattered less than 24 hours later when Probst learned that the minimum horsepower requirement had been raised from twenty to forty. This would require use not only of an engine other than the Bantam's, but replacement of nearly every other essential component. Probst had initially held Fenn off, asking him to call when these specifications were delivered. On 17 July, when he learned the specifics, Probst, to his great credit, put his sense of patriotism ahead of his valid professional concerns and accepted the assignment from Fenn.

Probst left from Detroit for Butler, Pennsylvania the same day. What followed was an 18 hour stint, broken into two segments by eight hours off for sleep by Probst at his drafting table that resulted in the needed layouts for submission to the government. The next two days were spent completing blueprints, bid forms and finalizing supply specifications.

From the beginning Probst decided to ignore the Quartermaster Corps' requirement that the final product had to weigh 1300 pounds empty. He regarded this weight limit as completely unrealistic and out of the reach of any manufacturer. This assessment, in spite of its validity, was vetoed by Charles Payne, a retired Navy Commander who worked as Bantam's military sales representative. Knowing that Probst's stated weight of 1850 pounds for the prototype would automatically throw Bantam out of the race before it really began, he had new bid forms typed stating the dry weight of the Bantam as 1273 pounds.

The moment of truth for this issue came later during a field conference of the Bantam prototype. Sources disagree as to the precise weight of the Bantam, placing it between 1840 and 2030 pounds. In either case it was well over the specification limits. Among the military brass in attendance was a six-foot senior cavalry general who took the view that if the Bantam could be hauled out of a ditch by two men it met his criteria as far as weight was concerned. He settled the issue by lifting the car's rear end off the ground without assistance. Eventually, the Jeep's production weight was set at 2160 pounds.

To meet the 49 day time limit for the delivery of the prototype (if

Bantam won the bid competition) Probst had no choice but to use components already in production. At the bid opening, held at Camp Holabird at 9:00 a.m., 22 July, 1940 were Probst and Fenn as well as representatives from Willys-Overland, Ford and Crosley. But the only companies submitting bids were Willys and Bantam. Compared to the complete set of blueprints prepared by Probst, the Willys' presentation has been depicted as little more than a crude drawing. Willys also fared badly in this initial round since it requested the 75 day time limit for the delivery of the prototype to be extended to 120 days. This was rejected. As a result, Willys' lower bid was negated by a penalty of five dollars for each day beyond the 75 day limit that its prototype would fail to appear. Therefore, when the $171,185 contract was announced on 5 August, 1940, it was assigned to Bantam.

Bantam didn't have to wait until the contract was officially announced to begin work on the pilot model since it had been informally told it was the winner just a half-hour after the bid presentations were completed. The 70 vehicles built by Bantam contained little of importance from the Bantam roadster that a Quartermaster Corps committee (which included Major Howie) had attempted to convert to 4-wheel drive. Indeed, all that linked the Bantam prototype with that car was its speedometer, engine temperature, amps, fuel and oil pressure gauges, and horn button.

Its frame and suspension was far stronger, and the Bantam 50 cubic inch, 22 horsepower engine was replaced by a Continental BY-4122, L-head 4-cylinder with a 3.1875 inch bore and 3.5 inch stroke. Its peak horsepower was 46 at 3250 rpm. Maximum torque was 86 lb.ft at 1800 rpm. A single Stromberg 1-barrel carburetor was used and a compression ratio of 6.83:1 was specified. A 6 volt, 70 amp battery was installed.

Front and rear suspension was via semi-elliptical springs and Gabriel telescopic shock absorbers. The axles were modified Studebaker Champion full floating units supplied by Spicer with a 4.88:1 ratio. On his drive from Detroit to Butler, Probst had stopped in Toledo to meet with Spicer chief engineer Bob Lewis who assisted in working out the details of these modifications. Also of Spicer origin was the transfer case providing both 2 and 4-wheel drive.

The transmission, with three forward gears and one reverse was supplied by Warner Gear. Stamped steel, 5-bolt wheels measuring 4 × 16 inches were used with 6.00 × 16, 6-ply tractor tread tires (some models used 16 × 5.5 inch tires). Nine inch diameter drum hydraulic brakes were used at all four wheels. A Ross worm and lever steering system with three turns lock-to-lock and a ratio of 12.0:1 provided a turning circle of 29 feet. Frame construction was of channel section steel with four cross members, a single K-member and double-drop side rails. The wheelbase of the Bantam BRC-40 (Bantam Reconnaissance Command-40 horsepower) was 79.5 inches, overall length measured 127.5 inches and front and rear tread was 49.5 inches. Maximum body width was 59 inches and ground clearance was 9 inches.

In appearance the initial Bantam BRC had a more rounded front end than did later models, but the essence of what was to become the classic Jeep look was apparent. All four wheels and their primary suspension elements were fully exposed and the front fenders were shaped for function, not style. The door-less body was constructed of steel, sturdy bumpers were fitted along with a folding, one-piece windshield, a single windshield wiper and a canvas top.

Before delivering the first Bantam BRC-40 to the Army at Camp Holabird on 23 September, 1940, where formal testing would cover 3410 miles over a thirty day time span. Bantam plant manager Harold Crist (whose career spanned years at Duesenberg and Stutz and who

played a major role in producing tools and parts for the BRC) and Probst drove it a little more than 400 miles. The bulk of these, 250 miles, consisted of the drive from Butler to Camp Holabird. This was a long trip, with both men observing a 25 mph break-in speed. When they finally arrived at their destination, it was 4:30 p.m., just 30 minutes short of the deadline.

The arrival of the Bantam naturally attracted considerable attention, not only from military personnel working on the base, but from drivers employed by General Motors, Ford and Chrysler who were on hand with larger vehicles. The first military driver to operate the Bantam was Major Herbert J. Lawes, who had earlier opened the 22 July bid.

Lawes, having test-driven virtually every vehicle purchased by the U.S. military in the past twenty years was arguably the world's foremost authority on military equipment. Before he drove the Bantam, Lawes asked Crist to drive it up a 60 percent slope in second gear. This was accomplished without difficulty. Lawes' first drive consisted of a wild and rough 15 minute run. The result was an extremely impressed Major Lawes who predicted that the Bantam would make military history.

One of the more notorious components of the Camp Holabird test ground was the "Hell-Hole" measuring approximately 300 feet in diameter and some three feet deep. Its bottom consisted of a muck called "gumbo" by knowledgeable drivers. In the past the only vehicles capable of traversing the "Hell-Hole" had been 6 × 6 trucks and tanks. The Bantam failed in its first run only because its carburetor was flooded with mud and water. When the deepest part of the pond was avoided the Bantam sucessfully travelled across the quagmire.

The objective of the military test drivers was to abuse the vehicles placed at their disposal in order to discover any shortcomings. Some of the tortures meted out to the Bantam included a drive off a four-foot freight loading platform at 30 mph, full speed runs down log roads and plowed fields and through sand traps and forests. It took twenty days of brutal mistreatment to finally crack the Bantam's side-members.

As expected of critics intent on doing their job, the Army evaluators pointed out areas where they believed change or improvement was needed. Although the final report noted the Bantam had sufficient power to operate as intended, some officers were critical both of its weight and engine output. Other negatives included the Bantam's need for frequent maintenance and its excessive height. None of these, however, detracted from the Bantam's overall outstanding level of operation. The Army had found its limits of endurance and they were impressive.

Although Willys had lost the first round of bidding to Bantam, it had not abandoned efforts to offer the Army its version of a general purpose vehicle. One reason for this stubborn behavior was Willys' precarious financial position. It wasn't, however, as economically moribund as American Bantam which, in mid-1940, was broke, shut down and had a grand total of 15 people on its payroll.

Willys-Overland history dated back to 1909 when John North Willys took control of the Overland Motor Car Company, which had been in the automobile business since 1903. Renaming the firm the Willys-Overland Company, Willys became the nation's second largest automobile producer by 1912, outranked only by Henry Ford. Willys was caught up in the midst of a grand expansion scheme by the depression which followed World War One. After a span of time when Walter P. Chrysler ran the company as general manager, John North Willys regained effective control in 1922. By 1925 his company was turning out 215,000 cars annually. In 1927 he introduced a four-cylinder Whippet model which joined a line-up of sleeve-valued Willys-Knight automobiles. The Whippet four was soon followed by a six-cylinder model and both versions were seen as key factors behind Willys-Overland's third place sales position with an output of 320,000 cars (behind Chevrolet and Ford) in 1928.

The following year Willys sold his Willys-Overland stock to a syndicate headed by C.O. Miniger of Electric Auto-Lite for approximately $21 million. Willys remained the company's chairman while he also served as the United States Ambassador to Poland. The stock market crash and the depression that followed soon made shambles of Willys' belief that his company's future was secure. In the Autumn of 1932 he returned to Toledo to attempt to restore Willys-Overland back to health. By this time Willys-Overland had lost $35 million and Willys, along with many other automotive executives sensed that the only way to survive the depression was to concentrate on the low-priced car field.

The automobile that resulted was a good one; the Willys 77. The only American car priced under its $385–$475 range was the American Austin and with a 4-cylinder L-head engine displacing 134.2 cubic inches it was an impressive performer. A top speed of 71.5 mph was possible and a Willys 77 averaged 65.5 mph for 24 hours in a run conducted at the Muroc dry lakes in California.

Unfortunately, Willys' effort to avoid receivership was unsuccessful. Committing $12 million of his money to the company's cause, John North Willys arranged for a $1 million loan from a Detroit bank. The day the transaction was to take place, 3 February, 1933, the bank failed. What followed was a time of sporadic production under receivership, and as expected, a struggle for control between various factions for the company's assets. In the midst of these contretemps Willys organized a triumvirate with George Ritter, a Toledo attorney who handled his local legal affairs, and Ward M. Canaday, whose advertising agency had the Willys-Overland account.

After John North Willys died of a heart attack on 26 August, 1935, Canaday and Ritter joined with Willys' first wife (he had remarried in 1934) to create Empire Securities, Inc. which eventually purchased 70 percent of Willys-Overland bonds and 97 percent of its unsecured claims. In 1936 Willys-Overland was reorganized into two companies; Willys-Overland Motors, Inc. and Willys Real Estate Realization Corporation. While the former was to produce automobiles, the later was to acquire all Willys real estate that would hinder automotive output and either sell it or make it available for rent.

Since the new Willys-Overland Motors was set up to produce only 70,000 cars per year, the Willys Real Estate Realization Corporation acquired control over most of the old Willys-Overland physical assets. Eventually, Empire Securities gained control of the real estate company which in turn, put Ward Canaday and George Ritter in power.

What they controlled was a company whose products, while not very costly, failed to make much of a sales impact. But whether it was the sheer size of the giant six-story Willys-Overland administration building (of which the motor company used only two floors) and the memory of past glory that it symbolized, or the opportunity for future success that some visionaries saw in Willys' small car tradition, Willys-Overland had little problem attracting talent to its ranks.

In 1938 and 1939 two men, Delmar Roos and Joseph Frazer, who would be vital both to Willys' ultimate success in gaining the lion's share of the military Jeep contract, and in peacetime, capitalizing on its unparalleled reputation for ruggedness and versatility responded to this siren song.

Delmar Roos, in 1938, when he became Willys-Overland's vice president and chief engineer, was at the peak of his powers. He began his engineering career at General Electric after graduating from Cornell University. From that point he moved, in succession, to Locomobile, Pierce-Arrow, Marmon and Studebaker. At each of these automobile producers Roos demonstrated a genius for engine design. At Locomobile he developed a new straight-eight with overhead valves and his straight-eight Studebaker engines with their nine main bearing crankshafts were used to power official Studebaker teams in the Indianapolis 500 race in 1932 and 1933. Roos was also involved in front suspension design and while spending a year in Europe in 1937 after a divorce settlement with his first wife, Roos adopted his planar (transverse leaf spring with upper and lower links) independent front suspension to the Hillman, Talbot and Humber cars produced by the Rootes Group in England.

When Roos joined Willys-Overland it was enjoying a modest sales revival. In 1934, sales had been a mere 6576. The next year they had risen to 10,439 and in 1938 reached 24,083. These figures were a far cry from 1928 when sales had exceeded 314,000 units. Clearly Willys-Overland, although to a far less degree than American Bantam, could benefit from a major government contract.

Thus, as earlier noted, Roos had been part of a Willys-Overland delegation that had watched the American-Austin-based "Howie Belly Flopper" be put through its paces. This gave Roos the opportunity to learn first-hand from Army officers about its shortcomings and what they wanted from a vehicle of that type. Never a shy violet, Roos unabashedly told them that he could build the machine they desired.

Ironically Roos' first assignment at Willys-Overland, the redesign of the Willys 4-four cylinder engine which had originated back in 1926 as the Whippet Four was to play a decisive role in making Roos' boast to the military a reality. Included in the changes Roos made in its design were smoother intake ports, a larger intake manifold equipped with a 1.25 inch Carter carburetor (in place of a Tillotson single barrel model D–IEO), a stronger crankshaft, cam-ground aluminium valve-seat inserts, thin-wall insert main and rod bearings plus vastly improved oil control piston rings. The engine displacement remained unchanged at 134.2 cubic inches but horsepower increased from 49 at 3200 rpm to 63 at 3800 rpm.

Just a year after Roos joined Willys-Overland, its board chairman, Ward M. Canaday, scored another coup with the announcement in January, 1939, that Joseph W. Frazer was leaving Chrysler Corporation to become Willys-Overland president. If Roos was an engineer of extraordinary talent, Frazer was a salesman of unparalleled talent. In his early days (Frazer was born in 1892) he was involved in sales with such diverse firms as Saxon and Packard before joining, in 1919, General Motors where he was a participant in the development of the General Motors Acceptance Corporation. After working at Pierce Arrow (on loan from General Motors) and Maxwell-Chalmers, Frazer joined Chrysler Corporation where he played major roles in the sales success of Plymouth and the organization of DeSoto. In the process he served as a vice president of Plymouth, DeSoto and Chrysler.

Frazer's first big impact upon Willys-Overland fortunes was felt with the introduction of the 1941 Model 441 Americar which was promoted as "the lowest-priced, full-sized car in the world." But his long term legacy to Willys would be his vision of the Jeep as a vehicle for civilian use.

As early as 1939 Willys board chairman Canaday had discussed possible war material production by Willys-Overland with military officials. One of his proposals involved modification of the Willys passenger car for Army use. This idea was definitely passé, but Willys' interest in securing a government contract continued to grow in intensity.

When the first Bantam BRC was tested at Camp Holabird a

contingent of observers from Willys-Overland as well as Ford were on hand. Both groups made numerous notes and drawings of the Bantam. Most importantly, since they were now government property, copies of the Bantam blueprints were supplied to observers.

The decision of the Quartermaster Corps to allow Bantam's competitors this type of unrestrained access to what was obviously very useful information was an early tip-off that the military, which had viewed the Bantam plant first hand, had doubts about its ability to produce large numbers of the BRC. As a result, both Willys and Ford were encouraged by Colonel H.J. Lawes to develop alternatives to the Bantam model.

At stake initially was a contract for an additional 1500 4-wheel drive vehicles. Bantam had won the first round and was busy assembling the 70 examples called for in its successful bid of 23 September, 1940. With Ford and Willys nearing completion of their proposals some high ranking members of the Quartermaster Corps pushed for them to share the 1500 unit contract with Bantam. This naturally aroused the ire of Charles Payne who with considerable justification argued that since Bantam had been the only company that had judiciously conformed to and met the Army's initial specifications, it alone should be the recipient of the first volume contract. At the same time Payne didn't ignore the issue of Bantam's limited production facilities. It would, he maintained, share all technical data and co-operate fully with other companies to enable large scale production to take place if in the future Bantam was not capable of fulfilling orders it received.

The first order did go to Bantam as directed by Secretary of War

Henry Stimson, but Payne's comments failed to mollify Bantam's critics. The military's concern over Bantam's production capability plus the willingness of Ford and Willys to produce pilot models at their own expense resulted in yet another contract announced on 14 November, 1940 calling for Ford and Willys to also receive orders for 1500 vehicles if their prototypes conformed to Army specifications. Willys had delivered its pilot model, then called the Quad, to Camp Holabird on 11 November, 1940. Fords proposal, the Pygmy, arrived on 23 November, 1940.

This development appeared to pull Ford and Willys aside with Bantam in the race to win a really large government contract but Willys' proposal was, at 2423 pounds, well over the revised limit of 2160 pounds. If Willys couldn't reduce the Quad's weight it would produce 1500 vehicles and no more.

In three-way comparisons between Bantam, Ford and Willys models each had revealed certain strengths and weaknesses. Willys' forte was its overall performance, power and ride. If Willys used a smaller and lighter engine it would most likely lose these advantages. Furthermore, the Willys engine was a point of great pride at Toledo and to abandon it was out of the question.

In contrast to the outstanding performance of the Willys Go-Devil

The original Jeep "Quad." (Courtesy American Corp.)

engine, the powerplant of the Ford entry, renamed the GP (General Purpose), a 119 cubic inch 4-cylinder Ferguson Dearborn tractor engine developing 45 horsepower at 3600 rpm was clearly inferior. Neither it nor the Bantam's Continental engine equalled the Willys' power output.

In order to reduce its weight Roos and his staff re-examined every component (except the engine) and production aspect of the Willys, ferreting out ounces of unneeded weight that soon accumulated into pounds. At one time Roos had walked out of a Willys-Overland board meeting when he was ordered to meet the original 1300 pound limit. But this time he was working within the realm of possibility and his achievement was outstanding.

By using a lower gauge, higher grade steel Roos reduced body weight by 115 pounds and that of the frame by 35 pounds. The front seats lost 18 pounds while the fuel tank shed 11 pounds. A simpler fender form saved another 12 pounds and a redesigned windshield lightened the Willys by 14 additional pounds. In addition to examining every unstressed part to determine if its weight could be reduced, Roos also adapted a new paint spraying procedure for the Willys that by using only a single coat provided a 9 pound saving. The net result of these efforts was a vehicle weight of 2154 pounds, just six pounds over the limit.

The revised Willys, known as the MA (its serial number range was W–2019832 to W–2020431) squared off against its Bantam and Ford rivals for the "Service Test" finals. All three contestants had to conform to the "U.S. Tentative Specifications, U.S.A.–LP–997A" which called for the following:

1. A maximum level road speed of at least 55 mph at an engine speed not above the rpm level for the peak horsepower output.
2. A minimum level road operating speed of no more than 3 mph.
3. A fording capability of at least 18 inches at a minimum speed of 3 mph without suffering any adverse affects from the water.
4. The ability to operate with tire chains installed.
5. A weight of no more than 2100 pounds including lubrication and water but without fuel, tire chains or payload. (The military was still studying a 4-wheel steering model and specified a 2175 pound limit for this model.)
6. A payload capacity of 800 pounds.
7. The vehicle's approach and departure angles were to be 45 and 35 degrees respectively.

The test results plus reports from the field of the Bantam, Ford and Willys made it evident that the MA Willys was the cream of the crop. Army drivers liked the power of the Willys, which with 60 horsepower, easily outpaced the Ford and Bantam. The Ford engine was essentially a Fordson Model 9N tractor engine minus its governor and with a downdraft rather than the updraft carburetor as used on the Ford tractor. Since all vehicles had to ford an 18 inch stream the Ford's distributor had been raised approximately 12 inches. This engine's weakness was simple; it wasn't intended for use in a general purpose military vehicle. Down on the farm it would last for ever, but without a governor its bearings rapidly wore and required frequent tuning.

The Willys gave nothing away to its competitors in terms of rugged construction and durability. After what was depicted as ranking among the most difficult evaluation procedure ever held by the U.S. Army, Willys-Overland signed a contract with the Quartermaster Corps on 23 July, 1941 calling for the production of 16,000 revised MB models at a unit price of $739.

1941 Willys MA Jeep. (Courtesy American Motors Corp.)

The Jeep calls them Daddy...

THE QUARTERMASTER CORPS OF THE U. S. ARMY AND THE CIVILIAN ENGINEERS OF WILLYS-OVERLAND

We pay public tribute here, to the Engineers of Willys—the most highly lauded automotive engineering staff that the pressure and inspiration of war have brought to light.

These are the men whose engineering skill and creative minds, added to those of the Quartermaster Corps of the U. S. Army, gave birth to the amazing Jeep of today. No other single mobile unit is so typical of modern mechanized war.

And it *proves*, beyond question, that the Willys Go-Devil *Engine* and the defense-time Willys *Americar* were no "door step" babies, but legitimate offspring of fine engineering practice that is both fundamentally sound and reliable.
Willys-Overland Motors, Inc., Toledo, Ohio.

TODAY do your part. Conserve rubber and other materials vital to war equipment. Buy defense stamps and bonds. Pay taxes with a smile. Whatever the total price you pay, it will be as nothing compared to the value of continued Freedom. . . . . . TOMORROW, make your first new post-war car a Willys—"The Jeep in Civvies."

WILLYS

MOTOR CARS   TRUCKS AND JEEPS

U. S. ARMY JEEP

AMERICAR
the People's Car

THE GO-DEVIL ENGINE—power-heart of WILLYS CARS and all JEEPS

It was only 30 May, 1942 when this advertisement appeared but the Jeep was already a wartime legend. Note the comment: "TOMORROW, make your first new post-war car a Willys – The Jeep in Civvies'." (Courtesy of author's collection)

18

THE SUN NEVER SETS ON THE MIGHTY JEEP

A JEEP'S-EYE VIEW OF THE SEABEES IN ACTION

A true incident from the battle of the South Pacific (with Jeeps from Willys-Overland)

IN the essential and dangerous *work* of war, the Navy Seabees—those busy, buzzing worker-fighters—are writing heroic history today.

The incident illustrated here is typical of war as the Seabees find it, and as a Seabee whose buddy made the supreme sacrifice, actually saw it:—

★ ★ ★

"We had occupied this little island in the Solomons a few days before. All our equipment—our cranes, steam shovels, graders, bulldozers, trucks, a fleet of Jeeps, guns, materials, tools—everything needed to do our job—had been put ashore without opposition.

"In fact, we had the runway of the new air field leveled off, and about a third of the steel mat laid, before anything happened. It was really beginning to *get* us—just waiting.

"Then one day hell broke loose. An 'alert' brought us to our feet with a jerk. We could hear the roar of low-level Jap bombers. It had been raining and they were coming over the air field right out of the glare of the sun. Bombs began falling

and machine guns popping. Then there was a crash and we could see that a direct hit had blasted a big hole right in the middle of our steel matting.

"That was bad. It would keep our own fighters from going aloft to intercept the Japs. Larry—that's my buddy—and some more of us, piled into a couple of Jeeps with our repair stuff, and tore for the still smoking crater.

"Just as we got there we heard the Japs coming back. We were caught flat-footed—all but Larry. He dove into a nearby machine gun pit. Two Zeros with their machine guns blazing were headed straight for him. He could have ducked, but he didn't. He just trained his gun on the lowest of the Japs and let her go. We could see his bullets cutting a pattern in the Jap's fuselage. Then there was a puff of black smoke, a burst of red hot flame, and the Zero crumpled, and crashed in the cocoanut palms at the end of the runway.

"Larry saved our hides that day. We made the repair, our planes were able to go up and control the sky, and the base was completed in record time.

"But they got Larry a few days later when they bombed a

pontoon barge loaded with gasoline, on which he was working. *He* had what we call 'Seabee guts'!"

★ ★ ★

The records show that "Larry"............, Seaman Second Class, in recognition of conspicuous gallantry above and beyond the call of regular duty, was posthumously awarded the Silver Star Medal. He was the first Seabee to receive this citation.

It is a great satisfaction to us that Willys-built Jeeps are considered an essential part of the equipment of the Seabees (Construction Battalion). These courageous men—the newest branch of Navy service—contribute their skill and experience as surveyors, electricians, carpenters, iron workers, masons, riveters, welders, plumbers, etc., etc. and risk their lives day after day, to *build, maintain,* and *protect* when necessary, air bases, docks, barracks, roads, etc., for our fighting forces—anywhere. Our hats are off to these courageous builders—these "busy bees of the Seven Seas."

WILLYS

JEEPS, MOTOR CARS AND TRUCKS

The heart of every fighting Jeep in the world—and the source of its amazing power, speed, flexibility, dependability and fuel economy—is the Willys "Go-Devil" Engine, the design of which was perfected and is owned exclusively by Willys-Overland.

A graphic advertisement of November 1943. (Courtesy of author's collection)

19

Bantam quickly faded out of the scene, eventually producing a total of 2643 BRC–40 models and receiving contracts for trailors, torpedo motors and aircraft landing gear. During 1942 Ford produced another 2150 GP models.

Much more significant was the contract Ford signed on 10 November, 1941 in which it agreed to manufacture the MB according to Willys' specifications. For a time the Quartermaster Corps had pushed for Ford to receive the entire 16,000 unit order given to Willys because of Ford's far greater production capacity. Fortunately for Willys, William Knudsen, then heading the War Production Office, vetoed this move, maintaining that Willys, by virtue of its low bid, was to be the recipient.

Even before Willys delivered any of these MBs the Jeep's reputation was well established. In its 3 November, 1941 issue *Times* magazine quoted Lieutenant Colonel Ingomar M. Oseth as saying, "Transportation in the U.S. Army is at least 50 percent superior to that of any other army in the world, and the Jeep can grab a big share of the glory." The chief of infantry, Major General Courtney H. Hodges added, "It is the most versatile motor vehicle we've ever had." *Time* prophetized that "in war or peace, the Jeep appears to have a long future ahead of it as a stouter resurrection of the old flivver. Some agricultural experts expect the Jeep to be an invaluable asset to the farmer, and many a soldier is firmly determined to get one after the war for his personal use."

At this point not everyone was certain what to call this revolutionary vehicle although "Jeep" had the inside track. Willys-Overland president Joseph Frazer, who claimed to have coined the phrase as a derivative of G.P., had the foresight to register Jeep as a Willys-

A May, 1944 advertisement paying tribute to Barney Roos' achievement – the Jeep engine. (Courtesy of author's collection)

THE POWER CENTER about which the world-wide service record of the Jeep fighting car revolves ... the *reason* for every motorized miracle it performs for the Allied forces ... and the *sole source* of Jeep power, Jeep speed, Jeep flexibility, dependability, and fuel economy, is the Willys "Go-Devil" Jeep Engine, designed and perfected by Willys-Overland Motors, Inc., "Builders of the Mighty Jeep".

WILLYS *Builds the Mighty* **JEEP**

Inset: **A common sight in Europe in 1945: liberated civilians, happy GIs and an MB Jeep. (Courtesy of author's collection).** *Below:* **An MB Jeep in company with a Sherman tank. (Courtesy of author's collection)**

The Sun Never Sets On the Mighty "Jeep"

JEEP-PLANNING!

" 'Will she pull a plow?' . . . 'What's her draw-bar horse power?' . . . 'Bet she'd be great stuff on a hay loader or a hay hook!' . . . 'Can she do 60 on the highway?' . . . 'How about pulling a binder and running a separator?' . . . 'How about road grading and snow plowing?' . . . 'Will she buzz wood?' . . . 'Will she haul a corn picker and fill a silo?' "

Not only farmers but men in all walks of life and in all kinds of businesses are eyeing the amazing "Jeep", with postwar uses in mind.

On every battlefront and in every country touched by this war both soldiers and civilians link the names "Jeep" and *Willys* together. Are *you* Jeep-planning? Willys-Overland Motors, Inc., Toledo 1, Ohio.

★ ★ ★

A Michigan Farmer says:—

"From where I sit, the tough 'Jeep', with its great war record, has already set a standard for postwar transportation and work. This 'Jeep' is *new, modern*—the kind of equipment that can be made to serve both farm and city at work or at play. Willys has done an *historic* job."

With the war almost over, this advertisement from May, 1945 shows the Jeep back home in rural America. (Courtesy of author's collection)

The Sun Never Sets On the Mighty "Jeep"

JEEPOTENTIALITIES

Tough, irrepressible, battle-stained—the mighty "Jeep" is today doing its appointed task on the battle fields of the world, *as planned.*

That this mighty "Jeep" is speedy enough, powerful enough, versatile enough and rugged enough to meet the stiffest demands of war is not an accident.

The "Jeep" was designed, powered and strategically engineered expressly as a *war* machine—to perform and *keep going* no matter *when, where* or *what* the demand—and to stand up.

The same skilled craftsmen who were able to produce a "Jeep" equal to the harsh and unremitting demands of a world-wide war, have developed plans to adapt it to greatly expanded usefulness on farms, in industry, in small businesses and among individuals with many widely diversified needs. Have you considered Jeepotentialities—after the war?

★　★　★

We have received many letters asking us about buying "Jeeps" after the war. Among the numerous "Jeep" uses suggested in these postwar plans are, operating farm implements, towing, trucking, road work, operating power devices and many personal business and pleasure uses. Does the "Jeep" figure in *your* postwar plans? Willys-Overland Motors, Inc., Toledo 1, Ohio.

In this advertisement from July, 1945 Willys' plans for the peacetime Jeep are apparent. (Courtesy of author's collection)

23

Overland trademark. Other names suggested at the time included Beep, Peep, Bug, Chigger, Gnat, Midget and Blitz Buggy. One of the earliest, if not the first, uses of the Jeep name in print in reference to the Army's new General Purpose Vehicle has been credited to Katy Hillyer of the *Washington Daily News*. Other sources of the Jeep name have been traced back to a 1936 Popeye comic strip which contained a creature with magical talents called Eugene the Jeep. The Minneapolis Moline Company, in 1937, called tractors it supplied to the government Jeeps and an experimental bomber, the Y–17, that lead to the B–17 was also identified as the Jeep.

But what really mattered for Willys-Overland was that it owned the trademark to a name that would soon be associated world-wide with toughness, durability and strength. Not since the Model T Ford would a motor vehicle become so famous and well known as the Jeep.

The MB Jeep differed in many ways from the MA. The bulk of changes were established at Camp Holabird shortly after Willys received the 16,000 unit order. In general, the goal was to increase parts interchangeability of the Jeep with other military vehicles and to improve the Jeep's operation under field conditions. To satisfy the former objective Willys adopted a different air cleaner conforming to Bureau of Standards specifications. The carburetor was also redesigned to enable the Jeep to operate on a tilt of 20 degrees on either side and on front or rear tilt of 55 degrees. Also installed was a 40 ampere capacity QMC (Quarter Master Corps) generator already in production and used on many military trucks. For the same reason the MB used a Type 2H 6 volt battery and 5 inch sealed beam, double filament headlamps. Small front and rear black-out lamps were also used. An additional black-out headlight was added later.

These changes made the MB not only more of a standard military vehicle but also contributed to a revised front end appearance. Whereas the MA's headlights were fender-mounted, those of the MB were positioned within the iron bars of the grille. Also altered was the

Somewhere in Asia; a trio of MB Jeeps. (Courtesy of American Motors Corp.)

Even 4-wheel drive had its limits in WW II. (Courtesy of author's collection)

hood which was flatter on the MB. Eliminated was the Willys lettering across the front hood edge. Also removed were the faired-in regions of the front fenders and the Willys name stamped on the rear panel. On the first 25,808 MBs built a barred radiator grille was used. Subsequent models had the definitive Jeep look; a steel stamping that angled outward to enclose the head and black-out lights. Whereas the MA fuel tank had a 10 gallon capacity, the MBs carried 15 gallons. To accomplish this the tank was L-shaped and positioned beneath the driver's seat. A box was placed below the tank that had trench holes and removable sealing caps. The larger fuel tank necessiated the re-routing of the exhaust system which now exited on the right-side. Provision was also made to carry another 5 gallon fuel can on the MB's rear deck.

Other MB features easily seen included a floor-mounted shifter in place of the MA's steering column unit, provision for carrying an axe

and shovel on the driver's side, the location of the dash-mounted handbrake between the front seats rather than on the driver's left side and the use of a double, rather than single bow canvas top. The MA dash gauges were standard Willys Americar units. The MB used conventional military versions consisting of a large speedometer and gauges for the oil pressure, engine temperature and ammeter. The first 20,698 MBs did not have dashboard boxes. This feature was found on MBs starting with serial number 120698.

Compared to the MA the MB had higher mounted steering tie-rods, additional protection for the hydraulic brake hoses and sealed spring shackles. Also fitted was a power take-off. With the exception of the MA and a few early model MBs (which used 5.50 × 16 tires) Jeeps were equipped with 6.00 × 16 tires and split rim rather than drop center wheels. This revision allowed a Jeep to travel on a deflated tire. Early in MB production provision was made for a government standard plug connector socket. This modification enabled a ¼ ton trailer pulled by the Jeep to have operational tail lights. Ironically, these changes (the use of standard combat wheels and 6.00 × 16 tires increased the Jeep's weight by 60 pounds) returned the weight that Roos had so laboriously sweated off the old MA. The gross weight of the MB as finally accepted by the Army was 2450 pounds. The last MBs weighed 2554 pounds.

From 1941 through 1945 Willys built 361,349 MB Jeeps while Ford, whose first contract in November, 1941 was for 15,000 Jeeps, turned out 277,896 GPWs (General Purpose Willys) which were in most respects similar to the MB. The Ford-built Jeeps were easily identified by their inverted U-section front chassis cross-member which differed from the tubular cross-member used by Willys. In addition, most Ford parts were stamped with a capital letter F.

The MB's basic design, which became a matter of intimate knowledge to millions of allied soldiers during World War Two, was straightforward. With an 80 inch wheelbase, 62 inch width and a 132.75 inch overall length (two inches longer than the MA's) the Jeep's compact dimensions belied its role as the GI's workhorse. Front and rear tread measured 48.5 inches. Height to the top of the windshield was 63 inches.

Few, if any, soldiers gave much thought to the Jeep's styling but in 1951 the New York Museum of Modern Art included a 1941 Jeep in its display of nine cars regarded as "works of art". The other vehicles displayed were a 1931 Mercedes-Benz SS, 1948 MG TC, 1937 Talbot Lago, 1946 Cisitalia, 1941 Lincoln Continental, 1937 Cord, 1938 Bentley and 1937 Bugatti. From any perspective of the Jeep it was a case of form following function. In essence, this made the Jeep a classic design. The front fenders were simple angled affairs while there were none at all for the rear wheels. Unlike the early postwar American cars that with just a couple of exceptions maintained the pretense of a rear fender line, the Jeep simply tucked its rear wheels in circular body recesses. The spare tire was mounted on a bracket at the rear of the body.

President Franklin D. Roosevelt reviewing a contingent of U.S. Army Infantrymen from an immaculate MB Jeep. (Courtesy of author's collection)

The simple, flat glass, two-piece windshield could be folded flat or removed entirely simply be removing two wing nuts at the end of the lower support rods. This feature necessiated the use of a hand-operated windshield wiper since electric or vacuum wipers would have required detachable wires or tubes.

Seating for four occupants was provided in the form of two tubular-framed front seats and a single bench seat at the rear with a fold-down back rest. A small tool locker was placed directly behind the driver's seat. The framework of hinged tubular struts for the top could be folded flat and clamped to the body sides when not in use. The top was stowed under the passenger seat when not needed.

The MB suspension system consisted of front and rear semi-elliptic aluminium-alloy springs. The front springs had eight leaves measuring 38 inches in length. Those at the rear had nine leaves and were 32 inches long. In order to compensate for the unequal weight distribution caused by the off-center location of the engine the left front spring had two heavier leaves. Bendix hydraulic shock absorbers were used for all four wheels. A Lockheed hydraulic braking system with Bendix two-shoe, double anchor drums was used. Initially the handbrake operated an externally contracting brake band mounted on the end of the transfer box mainshaft. This was not known

for its effectiveness and was subsequently replaced by a drum brake unit.

The Jeep chassis was built by Midland Steel and consisted of box-section side members that arched over the front and rear wheels. Five cross-members were fitted. Those used on Ford and Willys models differed in details such as the previously noted front cross member shape as well as different shock absorber mounts.

A variable ratio 14- 12- 14:1 Ross cam and twin lever steering unit provided just over three turns lock-to-lock. The Jeep's clockwise turning circle measured 38 feet while the opposite direction circle measured 37 feet.

Fully floating, hypoid bevel axles supplied by Splicer were used front and rear. The rear wheel hubs were mounted in bearings positioned outside the casing tube ends. This made it possible to remove a damaged axle or rear drive shaft in an emergency and still retain front-wheel drive. Similarly, the Jeep could operate with rear-wheel drive if the front axle was damaged since the front driving places could be easily removed.

An MB Jeep with 1942 Ohio registration plates. Photo taken 9 October 1943. (Courtesy of author's collection)

A single 7.875 inch Borg and Beck Model 11123 clutch was linked to a 3-speed Warner Model T–84–J transmission with synchromesh on second and third gears. Its ratios were 3.55:1 (reverse), 2.665:1 (first), 1.56:1 (second) and 1.0:1 (high). A two-speed transfer case supplied by Brown-Lipe or Spicer provided either a direct drive high range or a 1.97:1 low range which could be engaged only when the Jeep was in 4-wheel drive. This provided six forward and two reverse gear ratios that made for some interesting performance capabilities. For example, the high range reverse ratio was 17.3:1, in low range it became 34.2:1. Similarly the forward overall ratios in high range of 4.88, 7.63 and 13:1 became 9.61, 14.99 and 25.6:1 in low range.

An intensive on-site maintenance operation in China during WW II. (Courtesy of author's collection)

Controls for the front axle drive and low-high range were placed adjacent to the floor-mounted shifter. Their operation was not difficult for the typical motor-minded soldier to master. The transmission required double clutching for a clean entry into first gear and most drivers soon found engagement of low range was best accomplished at a speed under three mph. The change into 4-wheel drive had to be made with the Jeep brought to a complete stop.

In direct drive the Jeep's top speed was 62 mph. In Low range this dropped to 32.8 mph. The Jeep obviously wasn't intended for vigorous standing start acceleration runs but it was capable of a zero to 50 mph run in high range of under 19 seconds.

The 4-cylinder Willys engine, which was instrumental in the MA's victory over the Bantam and Ford was tightly squeezed under the Jeep's 40 inch high hood. With a bore and stroke of 3.125 inches and 4.375 inches respectively it displaced 134.2 cubic inches. Peak horse-power was 60 at 3600 rpm. Maximum torque of 105 lb.ft. was reached at 2000 rpm. The compression ratio was 6.48:1. For military use a

29

governor was installed limiting engine speed to 3800 rpm. The crankshaft rode in three steel-backed babbit lined bearings and was equipped with four integral counterbalancing weights. Forged steel connecting rods were joined to LO-Ex Lynite aluminium alloy, three-ring pistons. The initial Type 441 engine had its cam driven by a chain from the crankshaft. The subsequent Type 442 had a gear driven cam.

The Willys engine had a very efficient cooling system with an eleven quart capacity. The water jackets were very large and extended to the base of the cylinder. Roos also had paid close attention to cooling the valve seats, arranging the water passages to increase flow over them.

The end of the road, almost. (Courtesy of author's collection)

External components included an AC Model HF mechanical fuel pump and filter and a Carter Model W0539S single-barrel carburetor equipped with a large oil bath type AC air cleaner. The exhaust and intake manifolds were cast as a single unit and a bimetallic thermostat operated an exhaust deflector valve to heat the intake manifold. A 6 volt electrical system was used with a 110 ampere-hour battery installed under the hood. Autolite supplied the generator, starter and voltage regulator.

Numerous variations of the Jeep appeared during the war. For example, Jeeps were modified for desert use, deep water crossings, amphibious operations and, with 12 volt electrical systems, for radar operation. In any and all forms the Jeep made military history. General Eisenhower commented that "The Jeep, the Dakota and the landing craft were the three tools that won the war". His boss, George C. Marshall, described the Jeep as "America's main contribution to modern war."

When the war began to draw to a close it became more and more apparent that the Jeep would also be the main contributor to Willys' postwar program.

Chapter 2

The post-war
CJ–2A, CJ–3A, CJ–3B

Willys-Overland, quite naturally, was immensely proud of emerging as the ultimate victor in the contest with Ford and Bantam for the Jeep contract. Adding more luster to this pride was that the Jeeps built by Ford during the war were constructed according to Willys-Overland blueprints.

During the war the exploits of the Jeep attracted world-wide attention and interest that one publication, *Business Week*, 8 April, 1944, regarded as equal to that which accompanied the introduction of the Model A Ford in 1927. Willys-Overland president Joseph Frazer recognized the value that the linkup of the Willys and Jeep names would have in the postwar years and virtually every Willys advertisement made this connection very clear. This lead to a complaint registered with the Federal Trade Commission in June, 1943 charging Willys-Overland with misrepresentation in claiming that it had created and perfected the Jeep in cooperation with the Quartermaster Corps. Eventually, in 1948, the FTC ruled that the Willys ads constituted an unfair method of competition and issued a "cease and desist" order.

By that date the FTC decision had little or no impact. Willys had been building civilian Jeeps for several years along with its Jeep-inspired trucks and station wagons and was about to introduce the sporty Jeepster. Those early Jeep ads, however, seem more balanced in content than the FTC decision suggests. For example, one that appeared in many major magazines in mid-1942, headlined "The Jeep Calls Them Daddy ... The Quartermaster Corps of the U.S. Army And The Civilian Engineers Of Willys-Overland", seemed to make a reasonable assertion given the Quartermaster Corps' long interest in a GPV as well as Willys-Overland's determination to secure a government contract. "We pay public tribute here", the ad continued, "to the Engineers of Willys – the most highly lauded automotive engineering staff that the pressure and inspiration of war have brought to light.

"These are the men whose engineering skill and creative minds, added to those of the Quartermaster Corps of the U.S. Army, gave birth to the amazing Jeep of today. No other single mobile unit is so typical of modern mechanized war.

"And it proves beyond question, that the Willys Go-Devil Engine and the defense-time Willys Americar are no 'door-step' babies, but legitimate offspring of fine engineering practice that is both functionally sound and reliable."

Willys-Overland, as expected, denied that ads of this nature were in violation of any FTC provisions. Instead it noted that the Willys-Overland Jeep ads had been submitted to the Army prior to publication. In addition, Willys-Overland stoutly defended its view that Willys' cooperation with the Quartermaster Corps had originated the Jeep's design and it had not been copied from another source.

Nonetheless Willys did tone down its ads for the duration of the war. For example, a November, 1943 ad showing Jeeps in action in the South Pacific avoided any reference to the Jeep's origin. Instead it noted that "The Sun Never Sets On The Mighty Jeep". After the ad text mentioned the accomplishments of Willys-built Jeeps, its writer took a swipe at Ford by reminding readers that "The heart of every fighting Jeep in the world – and the source of its amazing power, speed, flexibility, dependability and fuel economy – is the Willys 'Go-Devil' engine, the design of which was perfected and is owned exclusively by Willys-Overland."

A similar theme was used for a May, 1941 ad depicting super-sized Jeeps riding around the Eastern and Western hemisphere. It noted that "The power center about which the world-wide service record of the Jeep fighting car revolves ... the *reason* for every motorized miracle it performs for the Allied forces ... and the *sole source* of Jeep power, Jeep speed, Jeep flexibility, dependability, and fuel economy is the Willy's 'Go-Devil' Jeep Engine, designed and perfected by Willys-Overland Motors, Inc., Builders of the Mighty Jeep."

Most of these wartime ads made some sort of reference to the years after the war, often suggesting "Tomorrow, make your first new postwar [sic] car a Willys – the Jeep in Civvies". One ad predicted that the "power and stamina of the versatile Jeep will serve man's needs in the years of reconstruction ahead."

As the war came to a close Willys began to seriously promote not merely a Jeep-powered vehicle but the Jeep itself as a viable source of postwar transportation. These ads noted; "To millions of people all over the world 'Jeep' means Willys ..." and had such titles as "Jeepotentialities" and "Jeep-Planning". The illustrations were of Jeeps in peacetime, distinctly rural environments plowing fields or transporting a farmer's goods to and from market. A Michigan farmer was quoted in one ad as saying, "From where I sit, the tough 'Jeep', with its great war time record, has already set a standard for postwar transportation and work. This 'Jeep' is *new*, modern – the kind of transportation that can be made to serve both farm and city at work or at play. Willys has done an *historic* job."

Responding to inquiries about the purchase of Jeeps after the war, Willys suggested they would be suitable for such activities as operation of farm implements, towing, trucking, roadwork, operation of power devices as well as numerous personal and pleasure uses.

Public opinion surveys supported this view that the Jeep was the answer to just about every automotive need of the postwar era. In the midst of this euphoria there were a few discordant notes. Naysayers were quick to note that interest and enthusiasm stirred up by war-time attitudes and values might quickly dissipate in a time when war memories soon fade and desires for creative comforts come to the forefront. Supporting this contention was a report from Cincinnati, Ohio in December, 1945 that ex-servicemen in that area weren't terribly interested in purchasing surplus military Jeeps for civilian use. In the first five days of a nation-wide sale of 10,000 Jeeps available at prices ranging downward from $782, just seven veterans had applied to the Regional Surplus Property Office in Cincinnati. In the Chicago region only eleven veterans signed up for a military Jeep. In other parts of the country there was more interest. Fort Worth, Texas reported receiving 1387 applications; Atlanta, Georgia's total was 742; Denver, Colorado had 229, New York, New York recorded 725, and Boston, Massachusetts had 507 responses.

Reconditioned Jeeps were also used as prizes in a contest that brought the Victory Loans campaign to a close in New York State. The top sellers of Series E bonds in the state's rural, urban and New York City areas were each to receive one of three Jeeps named Anzio, Normandy and Leyte. To drum up enthusiasm for this campaign fifty flare-carrying Jeeps took part in a torch light parade down New York

City's Seventh Avenue to the Statue of Liberty model in Times Square.

As suggested by its war-time ads, Willys-Overland envisioned a large market among farmers for its civilian Jeep. An effort by Willys-Overland to supply the Department of Agriculture with eight Jeeps for farm machinery tests was first vetoed by the Army which expressed concern about the psychological effect of applying a military vehicle to peacetime use. Other critics of the Jeep's applicability to farm use

A CJ-2A with a Willys Station Wagon. (Courtesy of author's collection)

cited the Jeep's low 8.75 inch axle clearance (as compared to a tractor's 22 inches), its 49 inch tread (corn planting required a 40–42 inch tread), high, 23 inch, hitch height (tractors usually had a 17 inch height) and its relatively high speed operation.

Willys-Overland did not, of course, allow any of this to go unchallenged. Ward M. Canaday expressed the view that the Jeep, while "mainly for the farm market (a comment which, in the light of the Jeep's evolution into a recreational vehicle is quite remarkable) was not intended as a replacement for the tractor but rather, to take care of the numerous tasks that abound down on the farm."

In July, 1945 when production of the civilian Jeep had started, Willys-Overland president Charles E. Sorensen outlined the peacetime uses for the Jeep. In his view, it would, in addition to appealing to hunters, fishermen, farmers, contractors and oil drillers also be used for

hauling goods, road construction plus endless types of repair work performed in isolated areas.

Sorensen's 2000 acre Michigan farm was the location of a demonstration of the civilian Jeep's multi-faceted versatility. The Jeeps were kept busy plowing fields, cultivating, threshing, digging post holes, spraying orchards and operating as a power source for an electric power plant.

The Jeep's reputation as a farm utility vehicle had already been enhanced by the results of testing by the United States Department of Agriculture in 1943 at its Tillage Machinery Laboratory at Auburn, Alabama. The chief of the Department's Farm Equipment and Research Division, R.B. Grayson, concluded that the Jeep was "highly useful in plowing, harrowing and other field work."

Specific achievements of the Jeep included the ability to plow an acre of cotton bottom land to a depth of seven inches with a 16 inch plow in an hour and 43 minutes, while consuming 2.32 gallons of gasoline. The CJ-2A was equipped with a drawbar with nine horizontal positions and two heights. The Department of Agriculture reported that under these conditions the Jeep's drawbar horsepower was 8.51, its drawbar pull was 862 pounds and that a speed of 3.7 mph was maintained. In a dynamometer test the Jeep demonstrated an ability in 4-wheel drive to pull 1300 pounds without slippage.

Results of another test session on a farm near Toledo also boded well for the Jeep's postwar career as a utility vehicle. In this case the Jeep consumed only 20 gallons of fuel while discing 20 acres of a muddy field. The field was in such poor condition that the Jeep required both 4-wheel drive and tire chains. The Jeep's performance in discing another 20 acre field with a 16 disc drill compared very favorably with that of a heavy tractor which typically consumed 66 gallons of gasoline to complete the same task. In contrast, the Jeep's gas consumption totalled just ten gallons. Perhaps its most impressive achievement was the hauling of a 1700 pound wagon with a load of 4500 pounds 13 miles on a single gallon of gasoline.

This performance and the Jeep's wartime accomplishments attracted the attention of *The New York Times* which devoted a substantial part of its 28 July, 1945 editorial to the Jeep. *The New York Times* summed up its review of the Jeep's world-wide service in World War Two and potential for peacetime use by concluding: "The Jeep is no limousine for long hauls, but it will carry the farmer and his family to market and the movies or a hundred and one errands speedily and with reasonable comfort. It will also serve as a useful workhorse for many specialized applications as well, in field or barn yard. The unusual degree of traction developed by its 4-wheel drive makes it one of the most interesting motor vehicles to appear in many years."

Aside from its presence on the farm, the Jeep was put to use in other environments in the early postwar years. In Toledo, the police force found the Jeep practical for traffic control, parking meter servicing and removing illegally parked cars. In New York City they served in that city's highway patrol fleet to tow disabled vehicles out of traffic lanes in the bridges and tunnels leading into Manhattan.

In Bountiful, Utah, a group of 20 Jeeps, organized into the Bountiful Posse, gained world-wide recognition for their work in fire and rescue operations. Fire equipment for the Jeep was made by the Howe Fire Apparatus Company of Anderson, Indiana. Among the items it offered was a front-mounted centrifugal pump capable of delivering 375 gallons of water a minute at a pressure of 120 pounds. Outfitted as a fire vehicle the Jeep was popular both domestically and on the export market. Bogota, Columbia ordered 30 units and the Toronto, Ontario fire department made use of Jeeps as auxiliary equipment.

Additional examples of the Jeep's versatility included their use in painting traffic lines in Charlotte, North Carolina, and powering a swinging crane for emergency use by the Los Angeles Department of Water and Power.

Willys-Overland, as early as December, 1943, had expressed concern about the possible impact the sale of MB Jeeps might have upon the domestic market. On 12 December, 1943, George W. Ritter, Willys-Overland vice president and general counsel told a congressional committee that unless the Jeeps were geared down before they were sold to civilians, they would be too dangerous because of their rapid acceleration. Ritter also disclosed that while Willys-Overland anticipated that the postwar Jeeps would be capable of performing 36 different tasks on the farm, they would not, in MB form, be expected to plow fields. He did concede, however, that the MB could be modified for farm use.

Nonetheless Ritter suggested that surplus Jeeps be returned to Willys-Overland to avoid ruining the market by "junk price" Jeeps that were not suitable for civilian use. Ritter opposed any plan that would give Jeeps to former servicemen because it would ruin the automobile industry which had done so much for the war effort.

Ritter was unduly concerned about the latter point since the supply of surplus Jeeps was miniscule in comparison to the size of the pent-up demand for new cars. He also was disregarding the public's taste for luxury and comfort in a new postwar car. Even the Jeep's strongest advocates admitted it was lacking in those two areas!

Willys-Overland began serious development work on the civilian Jeep about 18 months before the war ended. Most objective observers agreed that the result was a vehicle that was stronger, more versatile and, in general, superior to the MB. The first civilian Jeep, the CJ-2A, was priced initially at $1090 FOB Toledo. It differed in many ways from its military predecessors by having a power take-off and revised transmission, transfer case and axle gear ratios.

Key physical dimensions included an 80 inch wheelbase, front and rear tread of 48.25 inches, and an overall length, from front bumper to spare tire, of 130.125 inches. This shorter length compared to the MB was due to the relocation of the spare tire mount to the driver's side. Maximum body width was 57.125 inches with body height to the top of the windshield of 64 inches.

The front suspension consisted of eight leaf semi-elliptic springs measuring 36.25 by 1.75 inches. Their compression rate was 225 lb./in. The standard rear spring arrangement used nine leaf semi-elliptic springs measuring 42 by 1.75 inches. They were rated at 190 lb./in. Also available was a heavy-duty rear spring option with eleven thicker (2.407 inches to 1.973 inches) springs rated at 225 lb./in. as well as ten heavy-duty front springs.

The channel steel used for frame construction had a maximum depth of 4.125 inches with maximum width being 1.937 inches. Five

Ready for peacetime; a 1946 CJ-2A. (Courtesy of author's collection)

A 1947 CJ–2A (Courtesy of Old Cars Weekly)

cross members were used with the rear member being "K" shaped. Overall frame length measured 122.656 inches. Willys continued to use Monroe double-acting, telescopic shock absorbers but mounted those at the rear to incline forward.

Major steering specifications were unchanged from the MB. They included a 17.25 inch diameter steering wheel, a 36 foot turning circle, a Ross Model T–12 cam and lever steering system with 14- 12- 14:1 steering ratio. Standard Jeep tires were 6.00 × 16 inch 4-plys mounted

on Kelsey-Hayes 16 × 4.50 steel disc, five-bolt wheels. Willys recommended front and rear tire inflation of 26 and 28 pounds respectively. Optional were 7.00 × 15 inch 4-ply tires on 4,50 × 16 inch rims. Hydraulic brakes measuring 1.75 by 9 inches were fitted front and rear with a total braking area of 117.75 inches. These differed in small details from the MBs. For example, the linings on the civilian model were fractionally longer and thicker.

The CJ–2A L-head, 4-cylinder engine retained the same bore and stroke measurements of the MB. Although the compression ratio was unchanged at 6.48:1, a revised combustion chamber shape altered the power curve slightly. Maximum horsepower was 60 at 4000 rpm. Peak torque was 106 lb.ft. at 2000 rpm. SAE horsepower was stated at 15.63. The cast aluminum pistons had three (two compression, one oil) rings and their surface was either tin or brass plated. Normal oil pressure was 35 lbs. at 2000 rpm. Oil capacity was four quarts. Carburetion was by a single one-inch Carter Model WO–596S downdraft unit (some CJ–2As were fitted with the MB military carburetor). The Jeep engine crankshaft ran in three bearings while the cast steel cam was supported by four bearings. Maximum lift of the cam was 0.351 inches. The intake and exhaust valve heads measured 1.53 inches and 1.458 inches respectively.

The CJ–2A drivetrain initially consisted of a Spicer Model 23–2 semi-floating, hypoid gear rear axle with a 5.38:1 ratio and a full-floating, hypoid front axle with the same ratio. Beginning with serial number 13413 Willys used a semi-floating Model 41–2 front axle. It had the same drive ratio but provided 8.75 inches instead of 8.625 inches of road clearance.

The CJ transmission, a Warner Gear Model T090A, was of a larger size than that used for the MB. It had a special rear mainshaft and side-mounted shifting levers to allow for a column-mounted shift lever. This arrangement didn't last long. CJ–2As built after serial number 38221, in early 1946, reverted to a floor mounting. Other changes introduced at this time included pressure lubrication of the mainshaft pilot bearing, a more durable rear bearing oil seal and needle bearings for the countershaft. Accompanying this development was use of a larger, 8.5 inch rather than 7.875 inch Borg & Beck clutch with a torque capacity of 144 lb.ft.

37

The 3-speed transmission had ratios of 2.798:1 (first), 1.551:1 (second) and 1.00:1 (first). Reverse ratio was 3.798.

Additional specifications included a 6 volt electrical system and an 11 quart cooling capacity. A radiator shroud was also installed to improve engine cooling at low speeds. During the production life of the CJ-2A numerous changes were introduced. Up to serial number 27926 and Serial Number 48658 through 48707 the shock absorbers could be disassembled for refilling. After serial number 27926 and the interval noted they were sealed. The CJ-2A engine's 4-bearing camshaft was driven by a silent type timing chain up to Serial Number 44417. After that point all CJ-2A engines as well as all engines installed in the 463, 2WD and 4WD models were equipped with gear driven camshafts. CJ-2A engines with timing gears had a J prefix added to their engine numbers. Beginning with CJ-2A engine number 62054 a double baffle was added to the timing cover case, and the oil seal was changed from braided asbestos to a spring loaded leather seal. The fan pulley was also changed to provide a polished surface at the seal contact. This change was made to more effectively prevent dirt and grit from entering the engine. Up to CJ-2A engine number 55137 the Jeep's drop forged steel crankshaft was built with its four counterweights forged as an integral part of the shaft. After that point the counterweights were independently forged and attached to the shaft with a dowel and cap screw. Initially an AC model 153886 fuel pump was used on CJ-2As up to Serial Number 16965. Subsequently a combined fuel and vacuum pump, AC model 1537409 was used. Effective with serial number 24196 oil circulation was provided between the transmission and transfer case by the addition of drilled passages between the two units.

A CJ-3A used by the Philadelphia Police Department. (Courtesy of author's collection)

Former G.Is marvelled at the civilian Jeep's color choices of gray, tan, blue and brown; its new vacuum-powered windshield wiper (a second wiper was provided for the passenger but it was manually operated) and padded seats. Also welcomed was the relocated gas filler which was positioned on the outside of the body just behind the driver's seat. No longer did the operator have to hop out of the driver's seat before he could "fill her up". A pressure type fuel tank filler cap was used in order to prevent fuel leakage when the Jeep was positioned on a side slope.

CJ-3B. (Courtesy of author's collection)

These weren't the only visual changes taking place in the Jeep's transition to civilian life. Veterans quickly noticed the re-routed exhaust which now exited behind the rear wheel and used a transversely-mounted muffler. Not installed on the CJ-2A were the MBs side body-mounted pioneer tools. Corcoran-Brown 7 inch sealed beam headlights with chrome rings were installed on the grille's outer surface as were circular parking lights. The side hood panel carried Willys lettering. At the rear a chain-supported tailgate was used which allowed, with the rear seat removed, a loading space of 10 square feet to be used.

Willys offered a selection of both basic farm implements and industrial tools for use with the CJ-2A "Universal" Jeep. For field plowing either a single 16 inch or double 12 inch mould board plow was available along with a two-disc, 26 inch plow. For harrowing a choice of brush and bog, tanden disc or 8.5 inch spring tooth harrows were produced. Rounding out this group of optional equipment was a six foot field and pasture cultivator, a six foot farm mower and a terracing blade.

The basic industrial equipment intended for use with the CJ-2A included either 60 or 105 c.f.m. compressors, a 12.5 k.v.a generator, 300 amp D.C. arc welder, a Hydro-Grader and Terracer, and a lift-type overland scraper.

These items were in addition to many other options that enabled a customer to virtually custom order a Jeep for very specific purposes. The rear power take-off had a standard 1.375 inch, six-splined shaft suitable for driving a power-operated implement towed behind the Jeep. In addition, a pulley-drive unit could be attached with an eight inch diameter pulley. Its speed was governor-controlled within a range of 225 to 2,674 rpm.

The center power take-off, mounted on the rear of the transfer case could be equipped with a pulley for a V-belt drive of one to five belts. Among the pieces of equipment Willys suggested could be operated from this location were air compressors, electric welders and generators.

The front power take-off drive came from the front end of the crankshaft and, said Willys, "provides for plenty of war-proven 'Jeep' power for such useful implements as the capstan or drum winch, suction pumps [and] booster pumps."

In addition to the drawbar, the CJ-2A could also be fitted with a Monroe hydraulic implement lift controlled from the driver's seat. One of its attractive features was the accessibility of its working parts and non-interference with other Jeep accessories such as the power take-off and tow bar hitch.

Since many farm and industrial operations for which the Jeep could be used required a constant engine speed, the CJ-2A was available with a centrifugal-type King-Seeley governor. The unit was controlled by a dash-mounted switch with nine notched positions, the first of which set engine speed at approximately 1000 rpm. Each successive position increased engine speed by 200 rpm up to a maximum of 2600 rpm. These nine engine speeds in conjunction with the Jeep's six forward gear ratios provided for 54 controlled forward speeds.

Since the Jeep would obviously be operated in off-road sites, Willys offered brush guards for the front and rear propeller shafts and a baffle plate for the transfer case. These reduced the possibility of fire or damage to the oil seals resulting from grass, hay or weeds matting up on the drive shafts.

During the war American soldiers had created numerous schemes of weather protection for their MBs that served as the basis for the CJ-2A's two canvas top options. Both were constructed of 10 oz. soldenized mildew-resistant duck with double-sewn seams. Kit no. 667888 enclosed the front cab region while Kit no. 667826 (which could not be ordered separately) enclosed the rest of the body. In this form the Jeep had what Willys claimed was "adequate protection from the weather in most climates".

Although Ward Canaday did not represent the Universal Jeep as a replacement for the tractor, Willys promotional literature often compared the CJ-2A to the typical farm tractor. The Jeep's conventional 4-wheel brakes, driveability and low, 21 inch, center of gravity were cited as important safety factors. Willys also pointed out that whereas a tractor had only seasonal use, the Jeep was, in its view, a year-round workhorse. Furthermore, the Jeep's shock absorbers, springs, and seats fitted with backrests, as well as its top, doors and heater gave it "field comfort" far beyond the reach of a tractor.

Of course the Jeep's 4-wheel drive was its main attraction and Willys enthusiastically told potential farm customers that the Jeep "was carefully designed for 4-wheel drive ... has its weight distributed equally on all four wheels ..." These factors enabled the Jeep to be

40

driven over terrain and to climb hills impassable with conventional 2-wheel drive vehicles. At the same time the CJ–2As fuel economy was respectable in either 2- or 4-wheel drive. A CJ–2A operating in high gear on a level paved road with a 3250 pound gross weight and tires inflated to 28 psi could average 19.8 mpg at a speed of 30 mph. As its speed increased, the Jeep's gearing had a severe impact upon its fuel consumption. For example, at its maximum speed of 60 mph, the Jeep's fuel consumption moved up to 8.8 miles per gallon.

That the Jeep was almost all things to almost all people was demonstrated by its sale by Hearn's Department Store in New York City. The Bronx was far removed from the rigors of rural farm life, but when Hearn's put two Jeeps on display in early October, 1945 with price tags of $1195.59; their cushioned seats, column-mounted shift lever and body/wheel paint schemes (green-yellow and yellow/orange) in place of Army olive drab and Navy battleship gray attracted considerable attention from urban dwellers.

By early 1946 as this advertisement indicates, the CJ–2A was touted as a multi-purpose civilian vehicle. (Courtesy of author's collection)

Willys-Overland, along with other American automobile producers found the road back to full production anything but smooth. On 17 July, 1945, when it built the first CJ–2A, Willys-Overland announced that "The plan we have evolved for the manufacture of the civilian Jeep and other motor vehicles is designed to keep our employment at a high level through the reconversion and into the postwar period as the curtailment of military production makes civilian materials available. We plan to furnish our dealers with the vehicle which we know will be greeted by a large waiting market."

This proved to be no easy task. Although its initial production plans for 1945 called for the output of approximately 20,000 Jeeps during the rest of the year, Willys-Overland was able to turn out only 1823 units with a serial number range of 10,000 to 11,824. Nonetheless, Willys-Overland ended its fiscal year on 30 September, 1945 with a net profit of $2,711,332.

Making that announcement was Charles E. Sorensen, who had replaced Joseph Frazer as Willys-Overland president in June, 1944. Frazer, who left Willys-Overland in September, 1943, had engaged in a lengthy dispute with Ward Canaday over both the company's operation and its future direction. One of the key points of dispute between them involved the resumption of Willys-Overland passenger car production with a suitable successor to the prewar Americar. When Frazer had accepted the Willys-Overland presidency in January, 1939, his options for immediate change were limited. He dropped the Overland name from the 1940 models and the following year introduced the Willys Americar. Whereas the emphasis in 1940 had been on the Willys' low price (one ad bragged: "You can buy *two* full-size Willys cars for the price of one heavier car."), the Americar was restyled and updated in 1941 to become not just a low-priced automobile but one with a wider appeal than the older model. Its appearance was refined, a two inch longer, 104 inch wheelbase was used along with a stronger chassis, wider rear tread and lower overall height. The result was a model year sales of 30,100 cars.

While Frazer recognized the importance of the Jeep to Willys-Overland, he also envisioned a postwar expansion by Willys into the passenger car market based upon the success of the Americar. Willys did eventually produce a postwar passenger car, but not until 1952. In the intervening years Willys released numerous statements and arranged displays of sedan prototypes to the press.

Note the column shift of the CJ–2A used in this ad of June, 1946. Most models had floor-mounted shift levers. (Courtesy of author's collection)

Ward Canaday was less eager than Frazer to jump back into competition with larger companies in spite of the temptations offered by the lucrative seller's market. Instead, he regarded as a higher priority the strengthening of Willys' production base. Thus, after an effort to gain control via an $8 million bid by Frazer and a group of eastern investors failed, Frazer left Willys-Overland (in the process exercising his options on 75,000 shares of Willys-Overland stock which provided him with approximately $200,000) to eventually become chairman of the board at Graham-Paige and thereafter, a key force in the Kaiser-Frazer Corporation.

In the meantime, Canaday, who owned 75 percent of Willys-Overland common stock, went shopping for a new company president. The man he finally selected was 64 year-old Charles Sorensen. For forty years Sorensen had worked at Ford. A man with an international reputation as a production genius, he had become a victim of one of Henry Ford's periodic and irrational purges. During the war Sorensen had designed the massive Willow Run plant where some 8800 B-24 Liberator bombers were built. Ironically, Willow Run would eventually be the site of Kaiser-Frazer automobile production.

Sorensen had a solid understanding of the Jeep's assembly having produced them at Ford. This expertise was often cited as a key factor in Willys' rapid conversion to peacetime CJ production. To lure Sorensen out of semi-retirement in Florida Canaday offered an attractive financial package – a $52,000 annual salary for ten years (payable whether Sorensen lived or died), plus an option to purchase 100,000 shares of Willys-Overland stock for $3 a share between 1945 and 1950. Its price when Sorensen signed his contract was $12.50 a share. By mid-1946 it stood at $26.50.

Sorensen's arrival at Willys-Overland renewed speculation that Willys might be on the verge of a merger with another automobile manufacturer. The company most often mentioned was Hudson. This idea, which was based on the contention that having Sorensen's talents at Toledo made Willys-Overland an attractive merger partner, never had a chance to be put to the test since Sorensen resigned his position less than two years later, on 15 January, 1946. Both Sorensen and Canaday had strong wills that clashed over the issue of modernization of the Willys operations. Sorensen regarded it as essential for the company's future growth. Canaday, who reflected Willys-Overland's long dominant "salesman-at-the-top" leadership, contended that emphasis should be placed on strengthening the dealership structure and sales network. Since Sorensen couldn't be maneuvered out of his ten year contract he was appointed to newly established vice-chairman of the board and chairman of the finance positions. This move, which reflected Canaday's clout, was based upon a provision of Sorensen's contract which stated that whenever Canaday deemed it appropriate, another man could be elected president, with Sorensen taking a new position with the company.

Replacing Sorensen was James D. Mooney, who from January, 1942 to March, 1945 had served as a captain dealing with the construction and tooling of production plants in the U.S. Navy. In his civilian career Mooney, who had been trained as an engineer, had risen to become a General Motors vice president in charge of exports (which he raised from 22,000 in 1922 to 282,000 in 1928) and overseas operations. Until he joined Willys-Overland he was also a member of the General Motors administrative committee. At Willys-Overland, Mooney not only succeeded Sorensen but also replaced Canaday as board chairman.

Although Mooney would also become a victim of Canaday's tendency to sack chief executives before their programs had a chance to jell, his arrival at Toledo added another exciting dimension to

Willys-Overlands' postwar expansion plans. Soon after assuming his duties Mooney explained that "Our philosophy begins with platitudes: we have to pay for the war. Money, credit and prices will all express that in one way or another in the next few years. You can't devitalize a country's industry for six years – four years of war and two of active preparation for war – and not pay for it someway. For a while we'll all be poor. We'll have a complexion of being richer – in paper dollars – but with taxes and higher prices we'll actually be getting along with very much less. At this very moment price is no object to the public, but we're shaping our programs for the larger economic picture, for what you might call the middle-term pull between the time when the first gush of spending exhausts itself and the point when there is a more general production and distribution of luxury goods. It's during that middle period that we feel there'll be a broad opening for this company with its appealing utility design.

The CJ-2A, by May, 1947, when this advertisement appeared, had become a common sight on American farms. (Courtesy of author's collection)

"Our program is in line with the Willys tradition. Before the war, Willys always produced a lighter-weight, smaller capacity automobile. During the war – in a short period – we established the tradition of the Jeep. By keeping both, by capitalizing fully on our fame, and by maintaining our realistic relationship to the economics of the country, we'll have a sound and successful program."

Mooney followed up his appointment as Willys-Overland president and board chairman with a bit of headhunting. Brought in to take charge of public relations, advertising and sales promotion was Robert R. Thiess who had previously served as general sales manager of the General Motors Export Corporation. Another GM expatriate, Arthur J. Wieland, the former vice president of General Motors Export Corporation arrived in Toledo to serve as executive vice president of the newly created Willys-Overland Export Corporation.

By 1947 Willys had increased the Jeep's payload from 800 to 1000 pounds. (Courtesy of author's collection)

These appointments took effect just before Willys-Overland announced an ambitious financial plan to provide funds for its postwar expansion. The five major development proposals were:

1. Production by Willys-Overland of its engines from original castings to finished product.
2. Expansion of body stamping and assembly lines along with the construction of ultra-modern body trim facilities.
3. Enlargement of the four motor assembly lines to supply increased capacity for a vehicle program built around Jeep motors.
4. Creation of a completely new six-cylinder motor production line for use in passenger car models.
5. Reopening of the Los Angeles assembly plant with enlarged capacity to meet the growing market of the Pacific Coast and the Orient.

To finance these activities, Willys-Overland would issue 250,000 shares of preferred stock and increase the amount of authorized common stock to 4,100,000 shares from 2,850,000 shares. Of the $21,000,000 realised, $14,300,000 would be spent on new machinery, tooling and expansion of the Toledo plant.

WILLYS-OVERLAND'S
4-WHEEL-DRIVE FARM VEHICLES
Work in Any Weather . . . Any Place . . . the Year 'Round

THE 4-WHEEL-DRIVE 'JEEP' DOUBLES AS TRACTOR AND ALL-PURPOSE VEHICLE

You get more than a tractor when you get a Universal 'Jeep'—you get a general-utility vehicle for towing and transportation over the toughest roads, in the worst weather. With 4-wheel-drive, six forward speeds and an operating range from 2½ to 60 mph, the 'Jeep' serves you every season —handling pull-type or hydraulic implements, hauling in the field, hustling a trailer to town in a hurry. No other vehicle spreads its cost over so many jobs. Ask your Willys-Overland dealer for a free demonstration on your farm.

4-WHEEL-DRIVE UNIVERSAL Jeep

THE 4-WHEEL-DRIVE 'JEEP' TRUCK ANSWERS A LONG-FELT FARM NEED

Much of your hauling must be done off the road, over ground that strains ordinary trucks. Many a job can't wait because of weather or bad road conditions. The one truck that exactly fits your needs is Willys-Overland's 4-wheel-drive 'Jeep' Truck. Its all-wheel traction means all-year service, on the road or off. It is the right size—5300 lbs. GVW. Sturdy construction and its thrifty 'Jeep' Engine give low operating costs. See it at Willys-Overland dealers in pickup and platform-stake styles.

4-WHEEL-DRIVE 'Jeep' Trucks

WILLYS-OVERLAND MOTORS • TOLEDO • MAKERS OF AMERICA'S MOST USEFUL VEHICLES

In 1987 the Jeep Wrangler was one of America's top recreational vehicles, but in 1947 as this advertisement indicates, the CJ–2A was the farm workhorse. (Courtesy of author's collection)

Put 'Jeep' Power to Work on Your Farm

IT SAVES YOU TIME...IT'S DEPENDABLE...THE 4-WHEEL-DRIVE

You get more for your money when you invest in a Universal "Jeep".

You get a truly modern tractor—engineered for steady pulling at speeds of 2½ to 7 mph, with 4-wheel-drive traction, powered by the famous 60 hp "Jeep" Engine. The "Jeep" will operate pull-type implements, or you can equip it with the new hydraulic lift that raises, lowers and controls 3-point-hitch implements at the touch of a lever by the driver's seat.

You get more comfort and less fatigue

—a full-back, cushioned seat, windshield, car-size lights, mudguards, easier steering.

You get more than a tractor, for the "Jeep" helps out at other jobs. With power take-off, it operates shaft-and belt-driven equipment. It gives you highway speeds in 2-wheel drive, and helps with your hauling and towing. The "Jeep" will get you through deep mud or take you cross-country.

See this versatile farm vehicle at Willys-Overland dealers now.

'UNIVERSAL' Jeep
with Hydraulic Lift

TWO GREAT LINES OF 'JEEP' TRUCKS FOR THE FARM

THE 4-WHEEL-DRIVE 'JEEP' TRUCK gives you the pulling power of the "Jeep" Engine and all-wheel traction for hauling on bad roads, in the field and on steep grades. Drive this great new truck before you buy. Pick-up and platform-stake bodies. 5300 lbs. GVW.

THE 2-WHEEL-DRIVE 'JEEP' TRUCK gives you low operation and maintenance costs for ordinary farm hauling. Note the common-sense fenders and full-opening hood, designed for farm use. Comfortable cab. Pick-up and platform-stake. 4700-5300 lbs. GVW.

SEE YOUR WILLYS-OVERLAND DEALER
WILLYS-OVERLAND MOTORS, Toledo, Ohio, MAKERS OF AMERICA'S MOST USEFUL VEHICLES

The arrival of the Jeep trucks in 1947 strengthened Willys-Overland's position as the world's largest producer of 4-wheel drive vehicles. This advertisement is from February, 1948. (Courtesy of author's collection)

Willys-Overland would also purchase, for $3,700,000, the Wilson Foundry Company of Pontiac, Michigan, which was the largest gray iron automotive casting plant in the United States. The new machinery and equipment intended for use in the Los Angeles plant was priced at $700,000. The remaining $2,300,000 was to be paid to the Willys Real Estate Corporation for the purchase of land and buildings in Toledo.

Later, in October, 1946, Willys-Overland followed up release of its ambitious plans with the first of its "Institutional Days" at Toledo. Although initial reaction to Willys' offering of $100 par preferred stock had been lukewarm, Mooney, by predicting Willys would earn approximately $10,000,000 in 1946, presented an optimistic view to the bankers and financiers on hand.

An April, 1948 advertisement. (Courtesy of author's collection)

In announcing Institutional Day on 25 September, 1946, Mooney expressed his frustration about the problems of labor, management and production that were still dogging the industry because "People are talking instead of working. Labor, management and government", he said, "are so busy arguing about their various viewpoints that nobody has a chance to see that we are all in the same boat."

Mooney's comments were apropos to the current mood of the country's labor-management relations but they had little meaning to the status of Willys-Overlands' product line. It was already the most unique in America and in the years to come it would become even more distinctive.

Production of the CJ-2A, which ended in 1949 overlapped that ot its successor, the CJ-3A which was introduced in late 1948. To the uninformed the CJ-3A was, at least at first glance, very similar to the CJ-2A. But as this chart indicates they differed in many physical dimensions:

A trio of hard working CJ-2A and CJ-3A Jeeps (Courtesy of author's collection)

	CJ-2A	CJ-3A
Front overhang	20.75 in.	20.59 in.
Rear overhang	22.31 in.	22.31 in.
Passenger compartment length	68.5 in.	68.31 in.
Tailgate height	19.25 in.	19.71 in.
Cargo bed length	35.62 in.	32.0 in.
Overall body length	123.12 in.	123.0 in.
Steering wheel to seatback distance	14 in.	15.12 in.
Steering wheel to seat distance	7 in.	7.37 in.
Height (open, to top of windshield)	64 in.	66.37 in.

Visually the domestic model CJ-3A was identified by its one-piece windshield (a two-piece windshield was available for export) and dual windshield wipers positioned on the windshield base. Viewed head-on the CJ-3A was seen to have a new air intake set in a panel with three indented sections.

A advertisement from November, 1948. (Courtesy of author's collection)

The two CJ models also differed mechanically in a number of areas. The CJ-2A used a Carter 596S carburetor. The CJ-3A had a Carter 636SA carburetor. In place of the Jamestown J-161 radiator, the CJ-3A used one supplied by Harrison. Cooling system capacity remained 11 quarts without heater and 12 quarts with heater. The thermostat on early CJ-3A Jeeps was unchanged from that used on the CJ-2A. It started to open at 150 degrees F. and was fully open at 180 degrees F. Subsequent models used a thermostat that operated at 180 degrees F.

and 202 degrees F. The fan-to-crankshaft ratio of the early CJ-3A was 1.83:1. It was then changed back to the 1.18:1 ratio used on the CJ-2A. The length of the engine drive belt used on the CJ-3A was 44 inches as compared to the 42.34 inch length belt installed on the CJ-2A. The angle of the belt "V" also differed between the two models. The CJ-2A's had a 42 degree angle; the CJ-3A's had a 45 degree angle.

Replacing the Auburn clutch of the CJ-2A was either another Auburn unit or a Rockford version. Their specifications were as follows:

	CJ-2A Auburn	CJ-3A Auburn	CJ-3A Rockford
Spring pressure	180–195 lbs.	220–230 lbs.	170–180 lbs.
Torque capacity	144 lb.ft.	165 lb.ft.	140 lb.ft.

Another Auburn clutch was offered as an option for the CJ-3A which had 160–170 lbs. of spring pressure and a rated torque capacity of 145 lb.ft. Replacing the Spicer Model 41-2 semi-floating rear axle of the CJ-2A was a Spicer Model 44-2 on the CJ-3A. Engine changes were limited to a piston clearance of 0.003 in. instead of 0.004 in, a valve tappet clearance of 0.016 in. instead of 0.014 in. and use of a different flywheel.

FRONT POWER TAKE-OFF

REAR POWER TAKE-OFF

(With center P.T.O., Willys-Overland Kit No. 640726)
(When including pulley drive, Kit No. 646452)

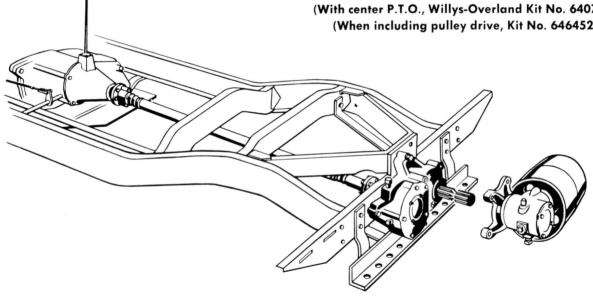

A sampling of Jeep options. (Courtesy of author's collection)

Key dimensions of the CJ-2A and CJ-3B Jeeps.

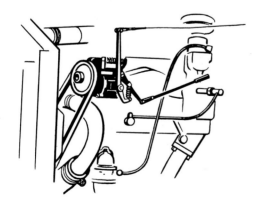

CENTRIFUGAL-TYPE GOVERNOR

(Willys-Overland Kit No. 645313)

48

PROPELLER SHAFT BRUSH GUARDS

(Willys-Overland Kit No. 641760)

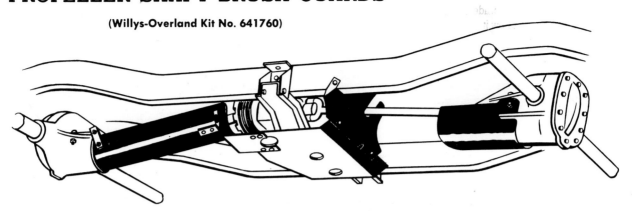

BODY-BUILDER'S DIMENSION DRAWINGS

UNIVERSAL 'JEEP' CJ-2A

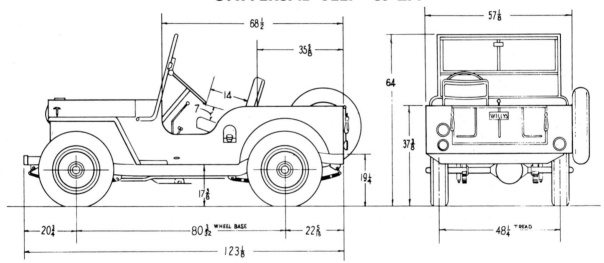

UNIVERSAL 'JEEP' CJ-3A

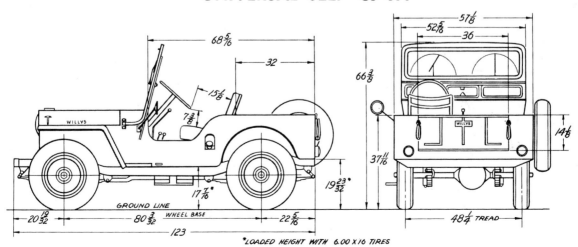

*LOADED HEIGHT WITH 6.00 X 16 TIRES

49

On 28 January, 1953 the F-head engine introduced earlier for the Jeep wagon and trucks was made available for the CJ Jeep. For a time the CJ-3A was continued but it was the CJ-3B that attracted the most interest.

Since the F-head engine was taller than the old L-head 4-cylinder, the hood of the new CJ was much higher than the CJ-3A's. At the front the extra space resulting from this revision was occupied by large "WILLYS" lettering. A one-piece windshield was carried over from the CJ-3A but the newest Jeep did not have the high-mounted air ventilator of the CJ-3A.

Tom McCahill, who always seemed to have a soft spot in his heart for the Jeep, liked his CJ-3B test vehicle so much that he ended up buying one for his own use. By the early fifties used Jeeps in prime condition were hard to find. McCahill, who spent several months looking for a used Jeep reported that "most of the Jeeps seen on the used car lots had more miles on them than the Pennsylvania Railroad and looked like they had been stored under water for several years."

As far as the new CJ-3B was concerned, McCahil reported that it was "undoubtedly one of the greatest vehicles ever conceived by man." Willys had no objection to McCahill expressing his opinion but, it was just a bit more modest in extolling the virtues of the CJ-3B. It was merely, said Willys, "one of the world's most useful vehicles."

Chapter 3

America's
first all-steel station
wagon

Obviously, Willys-Overland recognized the unique nature of the Jeep and its unchallenged status in the marketplace. But it also was aware of the difficulty and perils in basing its survival solely on the success of a single model whose sales had to total 54,000 units a year just to meet expenses.

In December, 1942, when Joseph Frazer and Barney Roos were groping towards a viable postwar strategy, an article, written by Brooks Stevens, appeared in *Popular Mechanics* magazine that was to impact heavily upon Willy's future. The article, titled "Your Victory Car" was just one of several written presentations by Stevens that ran counter to predictions by many journalists of outlandish-appearing and powered postwar cars.

In 1942 Stevens' industrial design firm was only seven years old. Yet, it had already established an impressive reputation for innovative and original solutions to existing design problems. Among his clients were Cutler-Hammer, Montgomery Ward and Allis-Chalmers. The latter firm's 1939 models B, RC and WC tractors had been given what Stevens described as "A new and striking design" that was "functionally correct and enduring". The new Allis-Chalmers had a streamlined engine cover, tear drop-shaped gas tank and fender guards that were both graceful in form and functional in operation. A year earlier, Stevens had designed delivery trucks with custom bodies for the Wisconsin Ice and Coal Company, Oscar Mayer, Miller Beer and the Western Printing and Lithographing Company that reflected a common design theme – the combination of a distinctive exterior body with minimum dimensions, maximum load capacity and a standard production chassis. The molded "streamlined" look common to these vehicles had been used by Stevens in 1937 when he designed a $25,000 "Land Yacht" for William W. Plankinton, Jr.

Stevens, whose company was also involved in redesigning such mundane items as steam irons, electric fence controls,and packages for meat products was keenly interested in participating in the postwar car industry. In June, 1942 his views on that subject were given national exposure when they were featured in an advertisement for Durez Plastics and Chemicals. The ad was titled "Will Your *Next* Car Look Like This?" Stevens answered this question with a rendering of a modernistic-looking automobile and a short statement expounding upon the advantages of using plastics in postwar automobiles. Looking back to that proposal, Stevens later wrote that one of its purposes had been "to condition [the] public to expect a car that was [a] modification of a prewar model, rather than [an] atom beetle-car that was feasible and economically sound from a production standpoint."

Stevens expounded upon his vision of the postwar car in a paper presented to the Society of Automotive Engineers that was the basis of the article appearing in the December, 1942 issue of *Popular Mechanics*. Although the end of the war was still years away Stevens told readers that it was not premature to discuss the automobile's future form. Backing off just a bit from the implications of his illustration for the Durez ad, he rejected the notion that: "the postwar car will be a radically styled, all plastic, rear-engine vehicle with a completely transparent top." He was quick to explain that radically styled cars with increased vision, rear-engines, plastic body panels

and extensive comfort and convenience features were definite possibilties, but not at the war's end. Instead, he advised the public to expect to find revised versions of the 1942 models in dealer's showrooms when the war was over.

But the main thrust of this essay was remarkably similar to the views held by Willys-Overland president James Mooney. "With the ever-rising cost of the war and the possible taxation measures brought on by it", Stevens concluded, "We may find the average American forced to accept an undersized car in comparison to prewar models. It is entirely possible that a civilian version of the army jeep [sic] might be a most acceptable and desirable piece of transportation equipment."

Although it had absolutely no relationship to the Jeep, the automobile shown by Powell Crosley in January, 1946 indicated that he also held the view that America might be ready for an undersized car. Crosley had built a small prewar model but this new car was a much more ambitious effort to secure a larger share of the new market. His car was only 145 inches long, 57 inches high and 49 inches wide. With a weight of about 1,000 pounds and a 26 horsepower engine it was the antithesis of the atomic-powered fantasy postwar car.

The car Stevens envisioned was not as diminutive as Crosley's. Furthermore, Stevens had, like so many others, been impressed with the impact of the Jeep upon military operation and had concluded that Willys could not afford to ignore the Jeep after the war. Instead of retooling for a new version of its prewar Americar model, he argued it would be far better if Willys started out with a vehicle, even if just a workhorse-utility model, based upon the Jeep.

At the same time, Stevens wanted to avoid reminding people of the agony of war and thus, he suggested conservative but pleasantly-styled open and closed models that could be produced with simple tooling and minimal expense. Ironically this vehicle was suggestive of an updated American Bantam. Whereas Bantam had first attempted to convert its civilian car into a general purpose military, Stevens was proposing to convert the Willys Jeep into a simple and inexpensive civilian runabout.

It should be noted, however, that Stevens was not copying the Bantam design. If anything, it was his avid interest in sports cars that lead to the open model of his proposal with its dropped door line, storage bin behind the seats and room for just two passengers. Looking back at that design, Stevens depicted it as "an American version of the MG TC." An intriguing aspect of Stevens' SAE paper had been the envisioning of these sedans and roadsters as available with optional 4-wheel drive trains to expand their sales appeal.

At this time Stevens did not have extensive knowledge beyond what he had read in automotive journals about the operation of Willys-Overland. Yet, his desire for active involvement in automotive design and Willys' unique status in the industry convinced him the Willys was "the place to start". He didn't have long to wait for a phone call from Barney Roos, Willys-Overland vice-president-engineering, telling him to "get on the train and come over here and see us."

Barney Roos was not merely the man who had made the original Willys Jeep possible – he was one of the ages' truly great talents. He had been Willys' top engineer since 1938, having come to Toledo from the Rootes Group in England. Previously he had worked at

Studebaker, Marmon, Locomobile and General Electric.

To say the least, Roos was not an easy person to deal with. Stevens recalled him as an intimidating individual who "could reduce you to nothing … [he was] probably the most difficult and sarcastic human being in the world. He ruled his efforts with an iron hand. He possessed so much ambition, zeal and aggression that anyone who appeared weak, stupid or not as bright as he was just went down for the count."

None of this was known to Stevens in 1943 when he departed from Chicago on the sleeper train bound for Toledo. Although Stevens arrived early at Willys-Overland Administration building for a 11 am appointment with Roos he spent three hours reading back issues of *Fortune* magazines. At the time Stevens wondered how anyone could be so involved with their work to fall so hopelessly behind schedule. Later he learned that was just Roos' standard operating procedure intended to soften up the person before he finishes him off in his office. "He had almost a Hitlerian complex", Stevens recalled in 1979. "He would reduce you to nothing and by the time he got to you, you were so weak you did whatever he said."

When noontime came Stevens saw Roos leave with another person, apparently on their way to lunch. Fearing he would lose out on his chance to see Roos, Stevens remained in the building's marble-lined lobby, like, he explained "a dummy". But finally he received a go-ahead from the receptionist to go up to Roos' office on the fourth floor. Even after being subjected to a grueling wait Stevens was not prepared for what was to come. Roos' office was fully fifty feet deep and as Stevens entered this room he saw Roos standing at its end watching some inconsequential event happening outside. Roos' reaction to Stevens was an icy stare followed by a brusque "Now what do you want?" After Stevens reminded Roos that he had come to Toledo at his request, Roos settled down a bit. But the environment was far from relaxed. As Stevens reviewed his proposal Roos acted as if a matter of grave concern would call him out of the office at any moment. But this was far from what was really taking place. Roos had a vital interest in Willy's future and he was keenly involved in what Stevens had to say. When Stevens finished his presentation Roos leaned back in his chair and said "Well, to tell you the truth, you have guessed exactly what we are going to do. Now let's get down to business. Can you work for us? What kind of arrangement do you want?" Roos said, "That's all right with me. Let's go."

Stevens was formally retained by Willys on 1 October, 1943 to "design and style the company's line of postwar automobiles." His efforts resulted in the 6-70 prototype (subsequently identified as the 6/66, 6/70 and 6-71) which used the Jeep engine but with totally different body and chassis. Three operational models were built, one of which was destroyed in a collision with a train at a railroad crossing in 1943.

On October, 1946, at the Willys-Overland "Institutional Day" activities held at Toledo to excite the financial markets about W-O prospects, a mock-up of the new Willys, was displayed. At that time Willys president, James Mooney, told reporters that it was scheduled to get into production in sedan form in May, 1947. A coupe was to follow in August, 1947. A year later when no sedans or coupes had been built, W-O said it was "pointing to" production in late 1948.

Actually, this project had been essentially terminated in June, 1944 when Charles Sorensen succeeded Frazer as W-O president. To that point Roos had made a tremendous effort to keep the passenger car's production costs low. Concurrently Stevens had completed a full-scale model which was displayed in the Willys experimental lab located on the Administration building's second floor when Sorensen arrived for

a tour of the company's facilities.

The sequence of events leading to Sorensen's arrival at Willys-Overland concerned conditions both at Willys and the Ford Motor Company where Charles Sorensen had worked for nearly forty years. Sorensen's power at Ford began to erode in the early forties when his skills and contributions to the success of the Ford Motor Company increasingly became publicized. This went against the grain of Henry Ford who resented their obvious implications. After the death of Edsel Ford in 1943, Sorensen's days at Ford were numbered as Harry Bennett, the notorious chief of Ford's "Service Department" moved to gain total control of the company.

While the human tragedy at Ford was moving towards its climax, events at Willys-Overland were also in turmoil. Joseph Frazer, its president, and Ward Canaday, its board chairman and principal stockholder, increasingly were at odds over fundamental corporate policy. In 1943 this conflict reached the point of no return. Frazer, in partnership with a syndicate of investors made an unsuccessful attempt to gain control of the company. Subsequently he submitted his resignation to Canaday. At least one aspect of the affair pleased Frazer – by exercising options on 75,000 shares of Willys he netted approximately $200,000.

To say the least, these developments made Sorensen's arrival at Toledo somewhat traumatic for many officials at Willys-Overland. Stevens recalls for example, a call from Roos telling him to "get on the train and get the hell over here tomorrow. We're both going to get fired."

For good reason, Stevens remembered Sorensen's entry into the lab and his comment that "We have a very tight schedule. Can you see me in my office at 2 pm?" Stevens had hoped to show Sorensen the Willys' virtues at that point and regarded his remarks as paving the way towards his dismissal.

Instead, when the two men later met, Sorensen told him: "There's only one thing wrong with our arrangement here – we don't pay you enough. Consider your retainer doubled … Can you stay awhile?" After listening to Stevens' response that "he could stay 'til spring … six months … whatever …", Sorensen then outlined his plans for Willys-Overland. "This Goddamn passenger car is a joke" was how Sorensen viewed the 6/66. Stevens recalled how Sorensen summed up his feeling about Willys' future: "We've got to do something with the fact that the only image this company's got, at the moment, is the Jeep. We can't just pass that over, because it's known the world over. It would be silly to ignore that and come out with the 6/66. It won't compete with anything!"

Those words of Sorensen were prophetic. In July, 1987, when Chrysler Corporation was about to complete its take-over of American Motors, Lee Iacocca outlined the reasons why Chrysler was acquiring AMC in the Summer, 1987 issue of *Dodge Adventurer*. "First, of course, we get 'Jeep', which just happens to be the best known automotive name in the world, and the leader in four-wheel drive technology. It says 'America' better than anything else I can think of."

Sorensen's harsh assessment of the sedan was due, at least in part, to his view (which was correct) that Willys lacked the resources to produce a car requiring heavy-press passenger-car body stampings.

Furthermore, Willys was in the view of the major body builders, such as Briggs and Murray, not blessed with a bright future. With plenty of work available from what were regarded as much stronger companies they weren't inclined to seek any business from Willys. "Willys-Overland has no chance and no rapport in the body building business" said Sorensen. Thus, it was out of the question for Willys to even consider producing a car with deep draw fenders and side panels. Eventually Sorensen contracted with a company in Connersville, Indiana that usually produced refrigerator shells that was willing to manufacture bodies for Willys. This relationship with the American Central Division of the Avco Manufacturing Corporation continued until October, 1948 when Willys-Overland announced that it would begin building all its bodies in the Toledo plant. This development resulted in the creation of approximately 700 new jobs at Willys. However, Willys did not complete this operation until late 1949.

Sorensen's objections aside, it should be noted that the Stevens' design did receive its share of favorable reactions. For example, after a display of the prototype in October, 1946, Stevens received a telegram from E.C. DeSmet, Willys top body engineer, that read: "Presentation of new Willys-Overland passenger car designed by you brought unlimited admiration and praise. Congratulations and thanks to yourself and associates and to your entire staff." It's also worth noting that the 6/70 had an independent suspension with half-axles, ball joints and semi-elliptical leaf springs attached to each half axle. Although it had the same wheelbase as the station wagon the sedan's overall length was 182 inches as compared to the 175 inch length of the wagon.

But the message from Sorensen was "forget about the conventional car. We have to do something like your first idea. Sit down and give me something and I'll see you tomorrow." Having convinced the Willys-Overland board that Willys' best chance was for a series of utility vehicles along with production of the civilian Jeep, Sorensen emerges as one of its key postwar officials.

Within three days after getting his marching orders from Sorensen, Stevens had completed the basic plan for the world's first mass-produced all-steel station wagon which debuted in July 1946 as the Model 463 Jeep Station Wagon. Production began on 11 July, 1946 and a total of 6534 were built in 1946. An early rumor about these vehicles; that they were made from old Jeeps purchased by Willys from the military was totally false. The two vehicles had different frames and the 463 was a 2-wheel drive vehicle. As can be seen from the following chart, they also differed in all critical dimensions:

Model	463	CJ–2A
Wheelbase	104.0 in.	80.09 in.
Overall length	175.0 in.	123.125 in.
Overall height	71.0 in.	64.0 in.
Overall width	68.0 in.	57.125 in.
Front track	55.25 in.	48.25 in.
Rear track	57 in	48.25 in.
Tires	6.00 × 15	6.00 × 16

An early 1946 Model 463 Station Wagon. (Courtesy of author's collection)

The 463 used a conventional ladder-type frame with four straight and one K-shaped cross-member. The front suspension design was well known to owners of earlier Willys products since it was the Barney Roos-designed "Planadyne" independent-type suspension

which used a seven-leaf, 45.5 in. × 2.5 in. transverse semi-elliptic spring (with a spring rate of 220 lb./in.) as the axle and lower suspension mount. Nine-leaf semi-elliptical springs measuring 1.75 in. × 50 in. were used for the Hotchkiss drive rear suspension. Their deflection rate was 150 lb./in. The semi-floating rear axle had a 5.38:1 ratio. A three-speed Warner Model TY–96 transmission was used with synchromesh on the top two gears. Its ratios were 2.605 (first), 1.63 (second) and 1.0:1 (third). It was linked to an Auburn single dry plate clutch with an 8.5 inch diameter and 72 sq.in. of engagement area. Standard on the 463 (except on some of the earliest models where it was listed as a $100 option) was a Borg-Warner overdrive unit with a 0.70:1 ratio with an in-or-out switch mounted on the instrument panel. When the overdrive was engaged the transmission shifted into overdrive at speeds above 30 mph when the driver momentarily lifted his foot off the accelerator. To return to direct drive required a quick pressing of the accelerator to the floor. In the view of Willys' "It's modern … it's thrilling … it's thrifty".

A Bendix 4-wheel hydraulic brake system was used with 9.9 inch drum diameters and a total area of 133.7 sq.in. Steering was by a Ross cam-and-lever system with a 14:1 ratio and 3 turns lock-to-lock. The Willys' turning radius was a tight 17.5 feet. A 15 gallon fuel tank was located under the body just behind the rear axle's center line. The filler cap was positioned in a cove on the right rear fender. The spare tire was mounted in the Jeep's interior on the right-side of the rear load area.

Performance of the 463 was acceptable if you accepted it for what it was. Its curb weight was 2935 pounds – quite a bit for its 4-cylinder engine to propel at exceptional speeds. As a result its top speed was estimated by the factory as being approximately 65 mph. But lest anyone misinterpreted this to suggest the 463 was a weakling, Willys reminded buyers that 'The Power-Heart of the 'Jeep' Station Wagon is the war-tested Willys-Overland 'Jeep' engine, used in 500,000 fighting Jeeps – world famous for stamina, performance and economy. This mighty engine has been further improved in many ways and refined for even more brilliant performance and longer gas and oil mileage."

The Station Wagon's utilitarian appearance remains attractive today. (Courtesy of author's collection)

As used in the Station Wagon the 134.2 cubic inch engine, with a 1.25 inch Carter single barrel downdraft carburetor developed 63 horsepower at 4000 rpm. This output was the rationale for the Willys' 463 designation: 4 cylinders, 63 horsepower. Peak torque was 150 lb.ft. at 2000 rpm. A 6.48:1 compression ratio was standard but, a "High Altitude" cylinder head was offered at no extra cost which raised this to 7.0:1.

Willys used this engine for its two- and four-wheel drive trucks that were introduced in 1947 as well as for the 463 wagon. Some engines had their four counterweights forged as an integral part of the shaft while others employed four separately forged counterweights attached to the shaft by a dowel and cap screw. All used unusually long, 9.18 inch, drop forged connecting rods and T-slotted, tin-plated aluminum pistons. Starting with engine number 50705, the piston head thickness was increased from 0.1875 inches to 0.25 inches to provide greater strength and heat conductivity. Commencing with engine 3J–1000 a new, 4.5 inch starter and new bell housing, rear engine plate and a flywheel with 129 instead of 97 teeth were used.

The serial number for the L-head engine, which was the same as the vehicle's, was found on the top of the water pump boss at the front of the engine block. It was often followed by any one of a number of letter suffixes. Those engines with 0.010 inch undersize main and

connecting rods had the letter "A". If a 0.010 inch oversize cylinder bore was used the letter "B" was found. When both conditions existed the letters "AB" were found. Other letters and their significance were: "C": 0.002 inch oversize piston pins; "D": 0.010 inch undersize main bearings and "E": 0.010 inch undersize connecting rod bearing journals. The same nomenclature was used on other Jeep engines.

Brooks Stevens' initial renderings for the 463 used a front grille and fender format highlighted by the curved and flowing lines that characterized cars of the late thirties. The headlights were set inward from the fenders next to an attractive grille of simple vertical bars. This was a pleasing design but more importantly it was linked to a main body section with the ribbed, brown and cream color scheme that was adopted for production. This was intended to emulate the mahogony and birch colors of wooden station wagon bodies and the result was extremely effective. The only body color offered was a dark burgundy.

In creating this format Stevens was demonstrating his ability to combine functional forms with attractive appearances. The need to use thin side panels limited his options but by using indentations and waffle lines he not only provided the necessary body stiffness (without them Stevens said the wagon "rattled like a tin box") but gave the Jeep a trim and pleasing appearance.

All that was needed to complete the Willys Station Wagon's design process was to adopt a front end that was a close facsimile of the Jeep's. Once that was done, it's not unreasonable to conclude that Stevens had created one of the most distinctive, attractive and long-lived designs ever to appear on an American utility-type vehicle.

The arrangement of angular front fenders, a grille with narrow vertical openings enclosing seven-inch sealed beamed headlights and circular parking/directional lights plus a simple squared-off passenger-load area were key elements of the 463's functional look.

This was not, of course a mere impression. Throughout the Willys design (*The Autocar*, 15 January, 1947, depicted the station wagon as "robust-looking") there were countless examples of functional forms and features. The two-piece windshield provided plenty of glass area. Yet, its 2-piece, flat-glass design made it inexpensive to replace. Similarly, access to the rear was an example of straight-forward design combined with clever thinking. The upper portion of the rear section, housing a 2-section glass panel, was controlled by a simple T-handle. When opened it was supported by two hinges. The tailgate lowered to form a flat surface with the interior floor. Both the taillight and license plate holder swivelled 90 degrees so that they were visible when the tailgate was dropped.

Since the Willys body was full-width without old-style, space-robbing rear fenders, it had an immense carrying capacity for a vehicle with such a short wheelbase and overall length. With all seats except the driver's removed useable cargo volume was 98 cu. ft. (from time to time Willys cited different figures for the wagon's capacity. Some literature reports it as only 56 cu.ft. Later, in 1949 it cited a figure of 120 cu.ft.). In this form the cargo area measured 60.5 inches wide, 57 inches long and 49 inches high. If even more space was required the front passenger seat could be folded forward against the dash panel. Regardless of how it was measured, the Willys had a prodigious capacity. The classic standard for station wagons was the ability to carry a load of 4 × 8 feet sheets of plywood. The Willys, like many other wagons, could carry them loaded flat. But no wagon could match its ability to carry them in a vertical position! And it was nice, after using that 8½ feet long (with tailgate open and rear seat removed) cargo area to carry some untidy load to simply flush it out with a hose.

Both the front and rear seats were of the 60/40 design. In other words, the driver's seat panel accompanied two passengers while the third passenger sat on a separate, foldable seat. The rear seat had its 60/40 division in the reverse fashion. There wasn't room for a third forward-facing seat but, as an option, a single seat, facing to the vehicle's right-side was available. The seats were simple affairs with their springs covered by hair felt and cotton padding. Their upholstery was a durable simulated leather. They were mounted on a tubular steel frame. The headliner was finished in a patterned red washable plastic-coated fabric which contrasted with the body and door panel's aspen-grain finish. The arm rests were upholstered to match the seats.

An extremely simple dash panel was used with a painted metal surface surrounding a centrally-positioned square-shaped instrument cluster. The speedometer, which read up to a maximum of 80 miles per hour, was bracketed by smaller, also square, gauges for the fuel

Willys hoped the 463 would be popular with younger car buyers. (Courtesy of author's collection)

level, oil pressure, ammeter and engine coolant temperature. A glove box was located to the right of these items with the ignition key receptacle, choke and starter controls directly below them. If the optional radio was installed it was found directly in front of the steering column. A standard "Deluxe" steering wheel with a horn button rim was fitted as were front and rear dome lights. Other items included in the Willys' base price were a neat storage compartment under the front seat complete with a door, three ashtrays; one dash-mounted, the others located on the rear side panels, dual sun visors, front and rear arm rests and dual horns.

Even with its 2-wheel drive the 463 had excellent traction on snow covered roads. (Courtesy of author's collection)

With considerable justification Willys was immensely proud of this product. "The 'Jeep' Station Wagon", it said, "is the modern expression of Willys-Overland's years of experience in pioneering with automobiles that in utility, size, value and economy of operation truly meet the need of the times. The functional design of the 'Jeep' Station Wagon is a clean break with the traditional limitations of the conventional vehicles of this type ... the full realization of the inherent possibilities of the station wagon. Its broad usefulness – with comfort for passengers and large load space – meets the pattern of today's living."

In this context it's worthwhile to compare the Willys Station Wagon with station wagon models offered by other American producers in 1947 (this is a more representative year to compare American cars since many did not offer a full range of models in 1946):

Model	Price	Weight	Production total
Willys 463	$1608	2845 lbs.	32,214†
Buick Super	$2940	4170 lbs.	786
Buick Roadmaster	$3249	4445 lbs.	300
Chevrolet Fleetline	$1893	3440 lbs.	4912
Ford Super Deluxe V-8	$1972*	3520 lbs.*	16,104
Mercury	$2207	3571 lbs.	3558
Oldsmobile Series 66-6	$2456	3785 lbs.	1460
Pontiac Steamliner-6	$2312	3715 lbs.	NA

† Production for 1946 was 6533
* The Ford 6-cylinder wagon listed for $1893; its weight was 3487 lbs.

Unlike these models, which were available in four-door form, the Willys was produced with only two doors. Years earlier Stevens' sister-in-law had experienced a mishap in which the occupants of a 4-door wagon she was driving were tossed out onto the pavement when the rear door flew open when the car rounded a curve – thus he was partial to 2-door wagons. Then there was the matter of economics, Willys had to save money where ever possible and tooling costs for a 2-door wagon were substantially less than for a 4-door version.

When the station wagon was first announced its factory list price was $1337, or $1437 with overdrive. Later, when overdrive became standard, its price advanced to $1608.

61

All of the domestic station wagons for 1947 used the old style wood construction. In contrast the Willys' all-steel body was free of the squeaks, peeling and weathering as well as the annual refinishing required if a wooden station wagon body was to be kept in top condition. Not until Plymouth introduced its first postwar models in March, 1949 was there anything resembling a domestic counterpart to the Willys wagon. Following after the Plymouth all-steel Suburban wagon was Ford's 1952 Ranch Wagon models. Chevrolet's first all-steel wagon arrived in 1953.

Willys regarded the 463 as just the first example of a bold new corporate philosophy that it said was "based upon realism and not upon expediency." In a 1946 brochure titled "A New Concept of Automotive Production and Distribution", Willys-Overland elaborated on this perception. "It is not an exaggeration", said Willys, "to say that the war years marked the end of an era in the automobile industry. Although cars have grown steadily into their role of a vital necessity in modern living, there remained a strong tendency among manufacturers to treat them as luxuries and evidence of social and financial

position by means of style and decoration."

Willys indirectly admitted that this trend had worked against its efforts to market its small car in the thirties by noting that "the small car buyer wanted his new model to look as much as possible like a medium-priced car ... The result was wasteful. This constant urge for the latest and biggest in automobiles was encouraged by the industry through yearly model changes and the creation of false obsolescence. It turned into a race for sheer size, an excess of power and elaboration of styling that added weight and cost at the expense of real economic value."

Willys wasn't so naive as to believe that attitude would disappear, but it did believe, as did Brooks Stevens who had written several years earlier, that "the needs of our time also call for a different type of personal car – built for economical transportation ..." In that context the 463 was, said Willys, "a vehicle that in utility, value and economy, meets the needs of the time. Designed with a steel body and top, and seats that are removable, the styling is a clean break with the traditional limitations of the conventional station wagon. It provides a smart, comfortable family car as well as a practical utility vehicle with large cargo space for business use. The body design grew out of

A 1948 model Station Wagon. (Courtesy of author's collection)

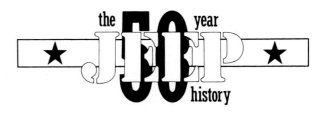

functional purpose, rather than from pointless streamlining, a full realization of the inherent dual-purpose possibilities of the station wagon adapted to the modern way of living. It will live up to its essential function of carrying people and goods. We believe it is the kind of car more and more people need and more people will buy."

Consumer Reports, which evaluated a Willys station wagon in its October, 1950 issue, agreed with Willys' view of the automobile's development. Whereas it regarded the contemporary American car as a myriad of conflicting concepts such as power, speed, comfort, beauty and space, *Consumer Reports* acknowledged the obvious; this had been a prescription for economic success. But it also gave Willys-Overland high marks for building specialized cars that weren't "all things to all men and women. On their home grounds they are hard to beat." There were, in the view of *Consumer Reports*, plenty of shortcomings in the Willys. For example, it didn't accept the notion that it was suitable for high-speed, long distance-driving. But at least it did so with humor – A 1950 Willys ad depicted a couple leaving their Willys wagon after what was obviously a long journey. Turning to her male companion the woman remarks, "It didn't seem like 400 miles". The caption supplied by *Consumer Reports* read: "CU's expert reply, 'It seemed like 800 miles'."

Many drivers, disgusted with the vague steering and what seemed to be endless turns of the wheel to go from lock-to-lock common to American cars regarded the Willys' quick steering as a refreshing improvement. But this feature along with the tendency to be affected by cross-winds, in the view of *Consumer Reports* reduced its usefulness for long-distance runs.

An advertisement dated 11 October, 1947 for the 463 Station Wagon. (Courtesy of author's collection)

But despite this criticism and grumblings about the shaking about of the Willys' hood and the lack of modern seats that folded to become part of the floor, *Consumer Reports* found plenty to praise about the Willys. Time after time it referred to its practical design as the basis for its ease of entry and exit; its excellent traction and interior space. Overall, *Consumer Reports* concluded that "The Willys Station Wagon, used as it is intended to be used, has no equal in its field ... It is a working car and it does its work well."

The assessment of the Willys Station Wagon as a true, dual-purpose vehicle was a key element of its promotion until the end of its production in 1965. For example, in 1947 the Station Wagon was advertised as "a roomy, comfortable passenger car and a practical utility vehicle for family and business errands." The following year it was "the great new combination of economy, utility and value." In 1951 it was promoted as the car that "goes a long, long way on a gallon ... carries the lowest price of any full-size station wagon."

By 1954, after having been in production longer than any other contemporary American automobile (and still having nearly a decade ahead of it!) the Station Wagon was rightfully touted as the "pioneer in production of the steel-body station wagon". It was "the common-sense car that leads a double life". Like the original Volkswagen Beetle, the Jeep Station Wagon was a vehicle built on a solid foundation of good engineering and design. Its long and useful production life reflected Willys' promise that it would "build its line of utility vehicles and passenger cars to fit needs rather than fancies. It will not be becessary to outmode each year's models by changes made largely for their own sake. There will be continuing refinements and improvements in Willys-Overland products, but expensive retooling and shutdowns for new models each year can be largely avoided – to the greater benefit of Willys-Overland customers."

This obviously worked to Willys-Overland's advantage as well; a point made abundantly clear on 6 January, 1948 when Willys announced that its production for 1947 was the highest for a peacetime year since 1929. President and board chairman, James D. Mooney, reported that the 119,733 vehicles turned out included 77,400 Jeeps, 78,118 trucks, and 33,285 Station Wagons and 899 Panel Delivery models. The Panel Delivery was introduced on 18 May, 1947. (Beginning in 1950 this model was listed as the Sedan Delivery.) In essence the Panel Delivery was a Station Wagon with the rear side windows replaced with sheet metal. At the rear double doors swinging on vertically-mounted hinges opened to provide an entry way measuring 41 inches high and 44 inches wide to what Willys said was up to 112 cubic feet of cargo space. Seating, in the form of a single seat measuring 32 inches wide was provided.

Compared to the 1946 total of 77,988 vehicles Willys production in 1947 of almost 120,000 vehicles represented an increase of over 53 percent. But Mooney nevertheless set as a goal for 1948 the output of 238,000 vehicles. One of the means by which Mooney hoped to reach this level was with an up-market version of the 463 Station Wagon, the 663 Station Sedan, of which only a few (53) had been completed in 1947. The Station Sedan was previewed at Willys-Overland's second annual "Institutional Day" by 450 business leaders, bankers, publishers and distributors.

The centerfold of a 1947 Jeep Station Wagon sales brochure. (Courtesy of author's collection)

Formal introduction of the 663 by Willys-Overland vice-president in charge of distribution, Arthur J. Wieland, took place on 17 January, 1948. At that time Wieland noted that the 663 was the first 6-cylinder model produced by Willys-Overland since 1932.

In appearance, the 663 was obviously a derivative of the 463. But its base price, (initially $1985 – later $1866) compared to the 463's price for 1948 of $1732), was justified by a number of refinements. The simulated wood paneling of the 463 was replaced by a solid color finish which was set off by a 2-piece, cane-weave panel extending around the body. The grille, while still retaining the same form as the Station Wagon, had a chrome vertical center section identical to that used on the Jeepster. Initially, the 663 was available in either Tunisan Red or Pine Green Metallic. As production progressed two new colors, Midnight Cloud Metallic and Autumn Brown Metallic were offered. Wheels were painted to match the body color as well as being striped in a contrasting Wake Ivory. The side hood lettering read "Jeep Station Sedan".

The Station Sedan interior was upholstered in gray "vinylite" and mohair. The floor was carpeted from the front seat back to the luggage compartment. Polished chrome trim was added to the dash board. Like the Station Wagon the new Willys had a divided front seat. Its rear seat, however, was of a solid, full-width design.

THE "JEEP" STATION WAGON...available in smart color combinations. Delivered with 5 wheels, 4 tires. Specifications and prices are subject to change.

The "Jeep" Station Wagon
of Willys-Overland's years
with automobiles that in uti
my of operation truly meet
functional design of the "
clean break with the trad
conventional vehicle of this
of the inherent possibiliti
broad usefulness—with co
large load space—meets th

Easily the most interesting feature of the Station Sedan was its engine. With a 3 inch bore and 3.5 inch stroke resulting in a displacement of 148.44 cubic inches, it was America's smallest 6-cylinder engine. Originally it had been intended for use in the 6/70 sedan and as such had been introduced in January, 1948. Its L-head format was strictly conventional but its thin wall casting and siamesed cylinder bores reflected the up-to-date outlook of its designer, Barney Roos. Peak horsepower was 70 at 4000 rpm and maximum torque was 118 lb.ft. at 1600 rpm (some sources cite its maximum torque as 117 lb.ft. at 1600 rpm). A four main bearing crankshaft was used along with aluminum alloy, tin plated pistons. The intake valve head diameter was 1.375 inches with the exhaust valves measuring 1.28 inches. Solid valve lifters were used with maximum lift being 0.30 inches. The compression ratio was 6.42:1. A Carter Model WA1 645–5 single-barrel carburetor was installed.

An interesting advertisement of July, 1948 illustrating the 463's "world-wide success". (Courtesy of author's collection)

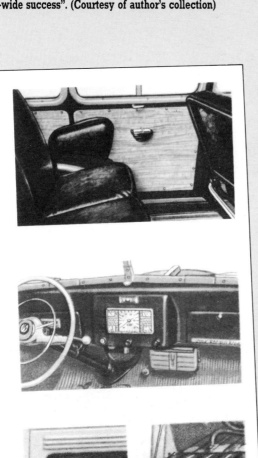

The Jeep Station Wagon interior featured aspen-grain body and door panels with simulated leather seat upholstery. (Courtesy of author's collection)

The 1947 Jeep Station Wagon instrument panel. (Courtesy of author's collection)

Details of the Station Wagon's swiveling taillight and license plate holder. (Courtesy of author's collection)

All-Steel Body and Top.

THE 'Jeep' Station Wagon WITH ALL-STEEL BODY AND TOP

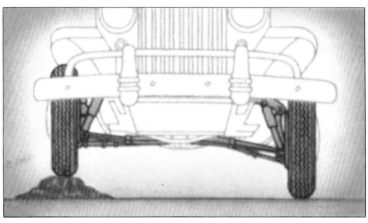

Touring in a 1948 Jeep Station Wagon. (Courtesy of author's collection)

Top Right: This illustration from a 1948 sales brochure shows the position of the Station Wagon's optional rear seat which enabled it to carry seven passengers. (Courtesy of author's collection)

Right: Details of the Willy's independent front suspension (Courtesy of author's collection)

Below: The Station Sedan debuted in 1948. (Courtesy of Ed Shultis)

Below Right: This November, 1949 advertisement is of particular interest since it featured the 4-wheel drive Station Wagon. (Courtesy of author's collection)

A January, 1951 advertisement of classic simplicity. (Courtesy of author's collection)

This June, 1951 advertisement emphasized the practicality of the Station Wagon's design. (Courtesy of author's collection)

67

In 1950 this engine, in a larger, 161 cubic inch form, along with the 134.2 cubic inch Willys engine were used by Kaiser-Frazer for their new Henry J economy car. Beginning in December, 1948 the Station Wagon was alo offered with this engine. The model and price schedules for 1948 and 1949 were as follows:

1948

Series	Model	Price
463–4	Station Wagon	$1732
	Panel Delivery	$1477
663–6	Station Sedan	$1985

1949

Series	Model	Price
463–4	Station Wagon	$1708
	Panel Delivery	$1375
4 × 463–4	Station Wagon	$2008*
663–6	Station Sedan	$1866
663–6	Station Wagon	$1814

* This new model is discussed shortly.

During 1949 Willys-Overland experienced a major management change that saw James Mooney submit his resignation as board chairman and president as well as his membership on the Willys' board on 20 May, 1949. Before he left Mooney offered his views on the state of the industry on two occasions. In January, 1949 while speaking in Cincinnati, Ohio, he predicted that within six months it would be possible for customers to walk into any automobile agency and buy any model car they wanted. "We've switched to a buyer's market", Mooney told reporters, "High prices are shrinking the use of motor cars." Describing the automobile industry as unhealthy, Mooney added, "A lot of rocks have been thrown at management and labor because of the high prices of motor cars." Mooney singled out two causes for these prices: "lower purchasing power of the dollar for all manufacturers because of our devaluation of the dollar" and the fact that "The present cost of motor cars is heavily loaded with direct and indirect taxes amounting to several hundred dollars per vehicle".

Later, at the annual metropolitan council luncheon of the Automotive Old Timers held at the Roosevelt Hotel in New York on 28 April, 1949, Mooney suggested abolishing the 40 hour work week, extending the work day and decreasing taxes to make possible the production of a true low-priced car. "The only way we can build the thousand dollar car", he said, "is with an honest day's work at an honest day's wage."

Although selection of a new president was deferred, Ward Canaday was appointed as chairman of the board. Canaday, who had previously served as board chairman, had a disappointing year ahead of him as indicated by a decline in production during 1949 to 83,250 units (of this total 29,928 were Station Wagon and Sedan Wagon models) as compared to 136,648 in calendar year 1948. The reasons for this decline included a fall in exports (total U.S. auto exports dropped almost 20 percent) and a steel strike that disrupted the company's supply of key components. In October, for example, the company suspended operation for a week. This was followed by another shutdown in mid-November idling 7000 workers. Not until early December was production resumed and even then only 4000 workers were called back. This was followed by a longer down time from mid-December until early January when tooling was installed for Willys to

Another example of Willys 1951 "Willys Makes Sense" advertisement campaign. (Courtesy of author's collection)

build its own station wagon bodies. Although this gave Willys a modern $5,000,000 body press shop in addition to a foundry turning out forged parts for its use as well as for outside customers, its implementation was costly.

Furthermore, soft sales had forced adoption of a 4-day week work schedule. Adding to Willys' frustrations had been a shortage of brake parts. Unable to obtain brakes from strike-bound Bendix Aviation Corporation, Willys had to seek out an alternative source which was not available in time to avoid a shutdown idling about 5000 workers in late May.

Willys-Overland's Annual Report, which covered a fiscal year ending 30 September, 1949, was issued on 28 December, 1949. It reflected both the impact of the poor economic environment of the past months as well as some fundamentally sound policy changes. One of these was a price reduction taking place in March, 1949 which lowered prices on every Jeep model. The second was a change in policy relating to inventories which were reduced by over 36 percent. Net sales fell to $142,362,944 (of this amount $26,647,614 or 18.7 percent was from overseas sales) from $175,346,360 in 1948. Net income after taxes and all charges was $3,423,711. In 1948 it had been $7,077,401.

But there was plenty of evidence indicating that Willys-Overland was positioned for a much better year in 1950. Its postwar expansion was essentially complete and during 1949 demands by the government for Jeeps, trucks, station wagons and replacement parts had increased to the point where at year's end Willys had approximately $15,000,000 in unfilled government orders.

In his concluding remarks, Canaday, while expressing concern over the current state of international and domestic economic conditions was mildly optimistic about Willys' future. "It is reasonable", he said, "to believe that Willys-Overland, with no debt, low inventory and a good product will continue to meet conditions aggressively and successfully."

In fact, Willys-Overland had already demonstrated that it still possessed plenty of innovative gumption in 1949 by its introduction of a new model, the 463 4-wheel drive station wagon. Its price of $2008 made it the most expensive Willys model. Based purely on price it competed with such cars as the $2095 Buick Super Sedanet, $2020 Chrysler Windsor Sedan and $2031 Mercury Sport Sedan.

In reality the new Willys had no domestic competition whatsoever. It used a Spicer full-floating front axle and a semi-floating Spicer rear axle and a Spicer Model 18 transfer case with a 2.42:1 Low and 1.0:1 High Range. The shift lever was floor-mounted. Front and rear suspension was by semi-elliptical leaf springs. Unlike the 2-wheel drive 463, which used 6.70 × 15 tires, the 4-wheel drive version had 6.50 × 15 tires. Except for "4-Wheel Drive" identification instead of "Jeep Station Wagon" (very early 463 wagons built in 1946 lacked this latter trim piece) on the hood sides, the new model had the same body appearance as the original model. Whereas the 1949 463 and 663 continued to be fitted with overdrive as standard, the 4-wheel drive 463 was available only with a 3-speed transmission. Use of the 4-wheel drivetrain resulted in a few changes in the Willys' dimensions. The wheelbase of the 4-wheel drive model was 104.5 inches and its height was about three inches greater than the 2-wheel drive model's.

Willys promoted the new model together with its 4-wheel drive truck and CJ–2A models as an ideal farm vehicle. "Four-Wheel-Drive Traction is the difference between being pulling through and being pulled out", it proclaimed. "That is why Willys-Overland farm vehicles with all-wheel traction outperform ordinary cars and trucks. In all kinds of weather and road conditions, be it deep-rutted mud, loose sand, snow or ice – or even rough roadless country – you can be assured of going through with Willys 4-wheel-drive vehicles …'

As far as the new 4-wheel drive wagon was concerned, Willys

promised that "Four-wheel-drive and greater adaptability makes this full-sized, 104 inch wheelbase car ideal for farm and ranch needs. Six adults ride in roomy comfort … with extra large parcel space. Removing all but the driver's seat provides up to 120 cu.ft. of load space. You get a safer, longer lasting all-steel body with washable interior … flat dent-resisting fenders … high clearance for brush and gullies."

Tom McCahill's test of the 4-wheel drive 463 appeared in the January, 1950 issue of *Mechanix Illustrated* and not surprisingly, he was enthusiastic about its attributes. "I drove this four-wheel-drive wagon up and down 40 percent grades that would have stopped any other American-made vehicle in its tracks. I got the impression that this wagon could almost climb the side of a building", wrote McCahill.

Out on the highway, McCahill, who probably had more first-hand experience with automobiles than any other American automotive journalist of the time, wasn't quite as thrilled with the Jeep's performance. Top speed was just about 60 mph and an acceleration run from zero to 60 mph took approximately 35 seconds. Yet, McCahill noted that "This car was designed for field work, so perhaps it wasn't fair to put it through any performance tests … in its own elements – over the fields and through the woods, where all the acceleration records are held by four-footed instead of four-wheeled travellers – this is the greatest car in the world, bar none."

Two series of 1950 models were produced. The first were unchanged from 1949 and were available through the spring of 1950. The second series was shown to the press on 30 March, 1950 and went on sale on 16 April, 1950. To kick off a major publicity campaign, Willys staged a large dealer meeting in Toledo on 3 March, 1950. If the exterior body changes were mild by Detroit's standards, they were quite startling for a product from Toledo. The grille now was slightly 'V'eed and had five chrome horizontal bars dividing the vertical units which continued to be painted the body's color. The front edge of the hood was now rolled under for added strength and rigidity. Added to the hood's leading edge was an ornament highlighted by a circular red Willys emblem. A new front fender form was very apparent. The

Willys often applied a dual purpose theme to its promotion of the Station Wagon. This advertisement appeared in August, 1951. (Courtesy of author's collection)

A 1952 685 Station Wagon. (Courtesy of Old Cars Weekly)

lower valance used on older models was removed and the fender's front section now had a slight V'shape which was emphasized by a modest crease line which faded back into the fender's top surface.

These changes were probably enough to keep Willys-Overland fans content for a couple of years but it was just the start of a series of improvements that collectively made 1950 a record year for Willys-Overland. The real bombshell came from Barney Roos who designed a new first F-head engine which replaced the old L-head engine in the Willys station wagon line. Working as Roos' assistant was A.C.

THE NEW WILLYS STATION

TWO GREAT NEW WILLYS ENGINES

POWER-SURGE PERFORMANCE   *FUEL SQUEEZING* ECONOMY

HURRICANE 4   LIGHTNING 6

Engine choices for 1952.
(Courtesy of author's collection)

The 1952 Willys Station Wagon. (Courtesy of author's collection)

A 1953 Willys DeLuxe Station Wagon.
(Courtesy of author's collection)

4-WHEEL DRIVE TAKES THIS CAR THROUGH WHEN OTHERS CAN'T!

If you live in a part of the country where bad roads or weather interfere with driving—the 4-Wheel-Drive Willys Station Wagon is the car you need. Its 4-wheel-drive traction pulls through mud and snow... takes you over ice with more safety—and gets you there when conditions are too tough for ordinary cars. With all the dual-purpose advantages of the Willys De Luxe Station Wagon *plus* 4-wheel-drive traction, and powered by the high-compression *Hurricane* 4 Engine, the 4-Wheel-Drive Willys Station Wagon assures you of useful, dependable transportation the year around.

4-WHEEL DRIVE WILLYS STATION WAGON

"All-weather" Companion of the New Willys De Luxe Station Wagon

A 1953 4-wheel drive Station Wagon.
(Courtesy of author's collection)

Details of the new taillights used
on the 1953 DeLuxe Station Wagon.
(Courtesy of author's collection)

71

Sampietro, who later played a key role in the development of the overhead cam 6-cylinder engine which went into production in 1962. At one time F-head engines had been fairly common in American cars. For example, Essex, from 1919 to 1923 had an F-head as did earlier Locomobile models. The last American car to use an F-head was the 1929 Hudson Super Six. By 1950 only Rover and Rolls-Royce/ Bentley were using F-head engines.

The Willys engine was not an all-new design. This would have involved expensive retooling costs that Willys wanted to avoid. Thus the new engine had the same bore and stroke as the old L-head, which, it will be recalled, originated as the 1926 Whippet engine. Actually, only a relatively few new parts such as a new cylinder head, valve train and cam were used. But the net result was startling as this chart shows:

At the same time, Willys said the new engine was as much as 25 percent more economical than the old L-head as well as having a horsepower per cubic inch of displacement output of 0.536 which was exceeded only by one American engine, the Crosley.

A review of the design attributes of the Hurricane F-head engine explains why Roos said that "When we started with this engine we had no idea of how good it was going to be." In proportion to engine displacement the Willys engine had the industry's largest intake valves. Even when not measured by this scale their 2 inch diameter was impressive since it allowed them to draw in an exceptional amount of air-gas mixture. Inside the engine the F-head format positioned the sparkplug virtually at the center of the cylinder's volumetric center as well as at the highest point of the combustion chamber. This had many benefits including no-knock operation on

	L-head 4-cylinder	"Hurricane" F-head 4-cylinder
Horsepower	63 @ 4000 rpm	72 @ 4000 rpm
Torque	105 lb.ft. @ 2000 rpm	114 lb.ft. @ 2000 rpm
Compression ratio	6.48:1*	7.6:1**
* 7.0:1 optional, ** 8.0:1 optional		

An attractive 1954 DeLuxe Station Wagon. (Courtesy of author's collection)

Ready for Family or Business

America's GREATEST ALL-PURPOSE CAR!

CARRIES GUESTS OR PERSONNEL
OVER TRAILS...CROSS COUNTRY
WHERE OTHER VEHICLES
DARE NOT GO!

regular fuel plus a very complete and efficient fuel burn. Also, the F-head design reduced the distance between the carburetor and the intake manifold. With the carburetor located on top of the manifold, which was cast in the head, the gas flow was exceptionally smooth and short. Roos saw to it that the manifold was kept at a constant temperature which assured good gas vaporization, by jacketing it with water passages.

Accompanying the debut of the Hurricane engine was a larger version of the L-head 6-cylinder identified as the Lightning Six. With a larger 3.125 inch bore and the same 3.5 inch stroke as before its displacement was increased to 161 cubic inches. Along with a higher 7.40:1 compression, horsepower increased to 75 at 4000 rpm. Torque remained unchanged at 117 lb.ft. at 1600 rpm.

These changes resulted in a revised Willys station wagon line-up (the Station Sedan was not carried into the 1950 model line-up) that replaced the 463 models with the 473 models powered by the Hurricane F-head. Similarly, the 663 line was superseded by the 673 line. Compared to the first series models of 1950 the new lines and designations were as follows:

First Series		Second Series	
Model	**Price**	**Model**	**Price**
463–4 St. Wag.	$1709	473–SW–4	$1605
463 P.D. Pnl. Del.	$1374	473 S.D. Sed. Dely	$1374*
4 × 463 St. Wag.	$2010	4 × 473–SW–4	$1990
663–6 St. Wag	$1814	673–SW–6	1690

* The Sedan Delivery was also available with 4-wheel drive on special order.

Note the added chrome trim installed on the 1954 4-wheel drive model. (Courtesy of author's collection)

It didn't take long for the new Willys models and their lower prices which were from $20 to as much as $104 less than those of the older models, to impact favorably upon Willys-Overland's sales. On 15 July, 1950, W.E. Paris, vice-president in charge of manufacturing, reported that factory shipments of Jeeps, trucks and passenger cars by Willys was the highest in the past 17 months. This pattern had actually been taking place since March but factory shipments to dealers in June represented a gain of 62 percent over the monthly average for the past 12 months. Paris credited June's record shipments to a strong public reaction to the new Willys models. In addition, Willys had also made substantial shipments of both four- and six-cylinder engines to Kaiser-Frazer during May and June. From this point the news from Willys for 1950 was all good. In late May it reported that company employment had increased by 37 percent since March. On 19 June, 1950 the 100,000th Willys Station Wagon left the Toledo assembly line. The production of these wagons represented in excess of $160,000,000 in factory sales volume since the line had been introduced in mid-1946.

The next day Willys announced that demand from Kaiser-Frazer for engines as well as the increased number required for its own use had necessitated the start of a third engine assembly line shift at Toledo. Also welcomed was the largest order placed by the United States Ordnance Department for five years for 8350 M38 Jeeps. This came on the heels of an order filed in June for 4000 Jeeps and parts valued at $12,139,500.

Obviously, Willys workers wanted a share of the company's good fortunes and on 21 September, 1950 an agreement was reached on a new contract with Willys' 7100 employees. Among its key features was a 26.9 percent increase that included a blanket hourly wage hike of

FROM THE MAKERS OF THE BELOVED 'JEEP' KNOWN AND RESPECTED AROUND THE W

The Common-sense Car that Leads a Double Life

WIDER OPENING TOP DOOR GIVES WIDEST OPENING OF ANY STATION WAGON IN ITS FIELD

AS A FAMILY CAR, the Willys DeLuxe Station Wagon is amazingly compatible with the needs of most American families. With easily cleaned seats, sides and floors it is a good companion to children and pets. Carries "problem" items (such as bicycles and lawnmowers) without removing seats. Comfort for 6 adults, with huge luggage space behind rear seats. And its powerful *Hurricane* engine is *so* economical to run. Why not let your Willys dealer fit one of these into *your* life today?

AS A BUSINESS OR WORK CAR, more than 100 cubic feet of usable space is available for tools or bulky packages. Seats lift out easily. Interior can be cleaned almost as easily as a kitchen sink!

Why not start this motoring season with the car that gives you *double utility; low first cost; low operating costs; high trade-in value?* At your Willys dealer now. *Kaiser-Willys Sales Division*—Willys Motors, Inc., Toledo, O.

Willys
STATION WAGON

- With 6-Cylinder *HURRICANE* Engine, 2-Wheel Drive
- With 4-Cylinder *HURRICANE* Engine, 4-Wheel Drive

10 cents per hour, an extra 5 cents per hour for skilled workers, a night shift differential, increased vacation pay, a company-financed health insurance program and a fully funded pension plan. Under the agreement Willys also extended to its employees the same increases granted to workers at the other auto manufacturers.

Note the stylized "Willys" of this 1954 advertisement produced by the Kaiser-Willys Sales Division. (Courtesy of author's collection)

Willys also followed the industry's lead by raising list prices between 2 and 8 percent on 27 September, 1950. It thus became the third auto maker to raise prices in a three-week time span. At the same time it announced another impressive jump in output. September shipments, it said, would exceed those for the same period in 1949 by 25 percent. Actually Willys was being conservative since an actual output of 8,141 units was shipped to dealers which represented an increase of 27 percent over the 6430 shipped in 1949. On 10 October, 1950 L. W. Slack, vice-president in charge of distribution, reported that since 30 March, when the new models were introduced, factory shipments totalled 51,198 units, a rise of 24 percent as compared to the 41,338 shipped in the same 1949 period.

Less than three weeks later, Canaday announced the receipt of more orders from the Army for 20,700 Jeep engines worth $5,665,700. Canaday also took the opportunity to say that Willys' current order backlog exceeded $125,000,000, of which the civilian portion was the largest for any October in the company's history.

In 1954 with sales of the Aero Willys declining the Willys Station Wagon once again assumed a prominent position in Willys advertising. (Courtesy of author's collection)

The good news from Toledo continued in November and December. On 7 December, 1950 Slack said the number of unfilled orders for Willys' station wagons and trucks had more than tripled since June. As a result the company turned out 8934 vehicles or 77 percent more than were produced in the same month of 1949.

In the company's Annual Report Ward Canaday reviewed the year's activities for Willys stockholders: "Operations for the first half of the year", he explained, "were adversely affected by the necessity of making changes in the production program involving expenses incident to retooling for new models and realignment of factory facilities for more economical operations, as well as by strikes of national scope affecting supplier's plants. As a consequence, shipment for the period were abnormally low and a loss of $908,307 was sustained."

But with the bad news behind him, Canaday turned to the good news: "In the second half following introduction on 30 March of new models which met with immediate and widespread consumer acceptance, sales were raised 97 percent over the first half, 23 percent over the comparable 1949 period and established an earning pattern that resulted in a net profit for the six months to 30 September of $2,513,824."

This outstanding sales performance resulted in net income for the year totalling $1,605,577, which was down considerably from the 1949 level of $3,423,716. Net sales of $107,886,249 were also lower than those of 1949 which were $142,362,944.

These figures for the entire year tended to distort the momentum of Willys' sales on the eve of 1951. Of almost equal importance was the limited dependency Willys had upon government orders for its economic well-being. Of its total net sales only five percent rep-

FROM THE MAKERS OF THE BELOVED 'JEEP' KNOWN AND RESPECTED AROUND THE WORLD

Suburban *Comfort* with a Capital "SEE"

Illustrated: Willys Deluxe Station Wagon   Pioneer in production of the steel-body station wagon, the Willys continues its popularity because of its double life, its economy, its all-around common-sense design. Carries 6 adults in comfort or, carries 1,000 pounds of cargo or tools with more than 100 cubic feet of useful space.

SEE the practical long-wearing interior
SEE the softer, sensible seats for relaxed ride
SEE the big, roomy space for passengers or cargo
SEE the big visibility for safer driving, easier parking
SEE how easily seats, sides and floor can be cleaned
SEE how upper tailgate opens for maximum ventilation
SEE how the *Hurricane* engine delivers brute power at low cost
SEE how much your whole family enjoys the Willys Station Wagon

Car of the Hour – *27%* More Power

WILLYS

When the Aero Willys hit the market two years ago with its combination of auto and aero engineering, lots of people sat up and took notice. With its hereditary stamina and economy, cockpit visibility all 'round, 61-inch seating front and rear, the Aero Willys makes conventional car-buying obsolete. *You owe it to yourself* to see and drive it before you decide. *Kaiser-Willys Sales Division*—Willys Motors, Inc.

resented deliveries to the government. Looking towards 1951 Canaday noted, "A high level of production may reasonably be anticipated in the coming year."

No significant changes were made in the station wagon line for 1951. Overdrive, which had previously been standard on the 663-6 was now optional, at $80, for all wagons except the 4-wheel drive models. At the same time prices were also increased:

1951 Price Schedule

Model	Price
Series 473-SW-4 Station Wagon	$1783
Model 473SD Sedan Delivery	$1390
Series 4 × 473-SW Station Wagon	$2204
Series 673-SW-6 Station Wagon	$1866

For its 1951 fiscal year Willys-Overland had the largest dollar sales volume in its history. The total of $219,861,553 was up 104 percent from the $107,886,248 recorded in 1950. It was also three percent higher than the previous record year of 1944. Earnings before taxes were $14,267,566 or nearly six times the $3,005,517 level of 1950. Net profit of $4,585,566 was also substantially higher than the 1950 level of $1,605,517.

The major news from Willys-Overland in 1952 was its return to passenger car production with its Aero Willys line of sedans. Willys had showed off various versions of the original Brooks Stevens sedan as late as October, 1947 and it had been Ward Canaday's intention to re-enter the small car market at an opportune time.

He was not alone in having an interest in producing a small American-made automobile. Both Ford and Chevrolet, as well as Chrysler Corporation, for example, had active small car projects. In the case of Chevrolet and Ford variations were eventually produced by their foreign affiliates. In 1948 Canaday was approached by Clyde R. Paton, an independent designer who, while working at the Ford Motor Company, had proposed a modern version of the Model A Ford. Although this idea was rejected by Ford, Paton remained a believer and formed his own firm with the intent of selling this concept to another producer. What he discovered was that the independents also had small car ideas of their own. For example, Nash-Kelvinator introduced the Nash Rambler in 1950, Kaiser-Fraser's Henry J arrived in 1951 and the Hudson Jet came along in 1953. But at Willys Paton found a sympathetic listener in Ward Canaday and the result was the 1952 Aero Willys.

The addition of the new sedan with its very attractive lines did not by any means result in Willys turning away from the old station wagon models. Instead, the occasion was taken to announce a new DeLuxe Station Wagon model. Styling changes were minor but easy to detect. At the front a wider hood ornament was used and a new side trim piece was installed that ran from the hood into the cowl region. The weaved side panel inserts seen on the old Station Sedan were revived for the DeLuxe wagon. At the rear new flush-mounted, vertically-positioned tail lights were installed midway up on the body's side corners. The license plate bracket and light assembly was given a more decorative chromed style as well as a new center location on the tailgate. As before, it was adjustable to the position of the tailgate. With the tailgate open or closed the license plate could be brought into full view.

The Willys DeLuxe Station Wagon achieved a degree of historical significance by becoming the first American car to have as standard

equipment an all-vinyl plastic upholstery. The arrangement was attractive, consisting of vertically pleated seatback and seating areas with contrasting solid bolsters and facing. The seats were also of a new design that provided, said Willys, "proper posture for complete relaxation [and] contribute to the greater riding comfort of the new Willys DeLuxe Station Wagon". The headliner was also covered with the same vinyl as the seats. Other changes incorporated into the new wagon included ignition starting, called "Startakey" by Willys, a revised braking system requiring less pedal pressure and improved "live-rubber" engine mounts that were calibrated and positioned to absorb more vibrations.

Joining the 4-cylinder F-head engine was a new 6-cylinder, 161 cubic inch "Hurricane 6" also of F-head design. This engine like the smaller F-head was based on an existing model, in this case the L-head Lightning engine. The relative specifications of these two engines indicates the impact of the new design:

	Lightning Six	Hurricane Six
Displacement	161 cu.in.	161 cu.in.
Bore × Stroke	3.125 × 3.5 ins.	3.125 × 3.5 ins.
Compression ratio	6.9:1	7.6:1 (8.0:1 opt.)
Horsepower	75 @ 4000 rpm	90 @ 4400 rpm
Torque	117 lb.ft. @ 1700 rpm	135 lb.ft. @ 2000 rpm

Even though it was not offered for the 4-wheel drive wagons, the Hurricane 6-cylinder was one of the most overlooked engines built in America during the 1950s. Overshadowed by the huge overhead valve V-8s that soon dominated the industry, it deserves recognition as one of the most efficient, small displacement engines of the day.

For example, the following chart comparing its horsepower per cubic inch of displacement with other engines used in cars and trucks from other manufacturers is extremely enlightening:

Horsepower per cubic inch of displacement

Hurricane 6	0.559
Pontiac 6	0.402
Nash Statesman	0.462
Chevrolet 6	0.425
Ford V-8	0.418
Ford 6	0.420
Plymouth	0.445
Studebaker Champion	0.501
Oldsmobile V-8	0.528
Cadillac V-8	0.574
Chrysler V-8	0.543

Promotion of the Station Wagon in the early fifties emphasized its versatility as a family-type car suitable for utility use and its low price and modest upkeep expenses. One ad noted that "Willys works on weekdays ... and helps you have fun at weekends". Willys also promoted the new wagon in association with the Aero Willys in numerous nation-wide advertisements. For example, one that appeared in several publications in August, 1952 displayed the sedan and the wagon and was headlined: "Willys Scores a Double Hit". Continued from 1951 was the depiction of the wagon as a "dual-purpose car" during the 1951 model year the Willys had been promoted as having the lowest price tag of any full-size station wagon. This was indeed true as a comparison of 1951 prices for the least expensive 6-cylinder station wagon offered by American companies indicates:

Make – Model	
Willys 673–SW–6	$1866
Chevrolet Styleline	$2119
Ford Custom Squire	$2253
Plymouth Suburban	$2064

It should be noted, however, that Chevrolet's Suburban, based on a truck chassis, was available for $1818.

Predating by over 20 years Studebaker's portrayal of itself as the producer of "common sense" cars was the 1951 "Willys makes sense – in economy – in ease of driving – in comfort" ad campaign. Readers were advised that the Willys offered "lower running costs" thanks to the Hurricane engine which required just four quarts of oil to fill the crankcase; only three quarts of antifreeze to protect to 10°.

As far as maintenance was concerned the Willys was "Trouble-free as a car can be … costs less to keep tuned to top efficiency – lower weight means long tire life".

Willys wasn't the only American manufacturer to still be using a flat, 2-piece windshield in 1951 (Ford retained this style until its 1952 models arrived. Chrysler held on until 1953. But after that Willys was the only holdout). None of this bothered Willys at all. In 1951 one ad showed a station wagon with a cracked windshield section. The caption proclaimed: "Repairs cost less! Extra visibility and easier handling help avoid accidents … and repairs cost less if your Willys is damaged."

At times these Willys ads came close to being works of art. An example was of a green wagon making its way along a lonely stretch of two-lane road somewhere in the American Southwest. The caption simply read: "Goes a long, long way on a gallon."

Sales of station wagons began to drop off significantly after the arrival of the Aero Willys. In 1952 their sales totalled 12,890 units as compared to the sale of 48,016 Aero models. The next year this dropped to 5417 wagons and 35,417 Aero sedans. This can easily be misinterpreted since Willys truck registrations and total output of commercial vehicles remained constant during this difficult time period. In 1953 Jeep vehicle production was a respectable 94,071. The next year the total was 92,165, of which 1597 were station wagons.

In 1954 The wagon received a revised grille arrangement that remained unchanged until production ended after the 1965 model year. This wasn't a significant change – the number of horizontal bars was reduced from five to three.

Popularity of Jeep vehicles remained strong in spite of the loss in public confidence about the viability of Kaiser's automotive operations. Kaiser-Frazer had reported profits in only two years (1947 and 1948). The financial situation at Kaiser-Frazer was dismal in 1953 when the merger with Willys took place. *Business Week*, 9 March, 1953 noted, "Even the friendliest critics admitted that Kaiser-Frazer was in trouble. About all it had to show since it was set up in 1945 were accumulated deficits of some $18,000,000 and a $48,000,000 debt to the Reconstruction Finance Corp." In this perspective not everyone at Toledo viewed the merger with Kaiser as boding well for Willys' future. But there were some positive aspects that could not be ignored – not the least being the huge tax write-offs the Kaiser-Frazer losses represented. In 1952, for example, Willys had earned $6,083,599 while Kaiser-Frazer's loss amounted to $4,711,876.

But through all this turmoil the old Station Wagon soldiered on,

filling a niche in the marketplace that seemed to revive in 1955 as indicated by an increase in production to 12,265 units. Identifying the latest version was a new two-tone paint combination in which the color of the roof and the lower body section contrasted with that of the wagon's mid-section.

Added to the engine choices for the Willys Station Wagon was a 226 cubic inch L-head 6-cylinder that had been used by Kaiser since it began production in 1946. It had also been available for the Willys sedans beginning in March, 1954. Like the Willys F-head 4-cylinder, which continued to be available, this engine went back a long way. As the Red Seal engine it had powered the pre-war Graham automobile. In 1954, a futile attempt to give the Kaiser a bit of a performance image involved the use of a supercharged version that developed 140 horsepower. But with 300+ cubic inch V-8s the norm an L-head, 226 cubic inch 6-cylinder engine needed more than a McCulloch supercharger to be an effective competitor.

As installed in the Station Wagon, identified as the Model 6-226, this engine developed 115 horsepower at 3650 rpm and 190 lb.ft. of torque at 1800 rpm. Its bore and stroke were 3.312 in. and 4.375 in. respectively.

Beginning in 1955 Willys offered a less expensive, Utility Wagon, model as an alternative to the Station Wagon. Its place in the Willys line was as this chart shows:

Series	Price
Model 685 (6-cyl. F-head, 2WD)	
Sedan Delivery	$1545
Station Wagon	$1997
Model 6-226 (6-cyl. L-head. 4WD)	
Sedan Delivery	$2036
Station Wagon	$2420
Model 6-226 (6-cyl. L-head, 2WD)	
Sedan Delivery	$1584
Utility Wagon	$1837
Model 465 (4-cyl. F-head, 2WD)	
Sedan Delivery	$1494
Utility Wagon	$1748

With the demise of the Willys passenger car line in 1955 production of the F-head 161 cubic inch engine also ceased. This brought about a revised wagon line-up that consisted of these models:

Series	Price
Model 6-226 (6-cyl.)	
Sedan Delivery (2WD)	$1683
Sedan Delivery (4WD)	$2190
Utility Wagon (2WD	$NA
Station Wagon (4WD)	$NA
Model 475 (4-cyl.)	
Sedan Delivery (2WD)	$1583
Sedan Delivery (4WD)	$1949
Utility Wagon (2WD)	$NA
Station Wagon (4WD)	$NA

From 1955 until mid-1959 the wagons were available with a 2-tone body paint scheme that featured the mid-body region finished in a color contrasting with that of the roof and lower body. Beginning on 12 May, 1959, with the introduction of a new 2-wheel drive model, the Maverick, Jeep wagons were available with another paint scheme in which the side trim's forward edge paralleled the curve of the front fender.

Having been in production for so many years made the Willys wagon a topic seldom examined by the media. But in August, 1959 *Car Life* magazine published a major test of a L6–226 Utility Wagon. Even in the sybaritic era of automatic transmissions, power steering, tail fins and 300+ horsepower V-8 engines, the old Willys was still capable of endearing itself to the *Car Life* test team. After admitting that he expected a "rough-riding, noisy and brutally uncomfortable vehicle", author Jim Whipple reported that "The Jeep wagon is a thoroughly civilized passenger vehicle." Sometimes, it seemed, old was better than new. It really mattered little that the basic Jeep body had remained unchanged since its introduction. In 1959 it offered more front seat headroom than any other American car. In an age of panoramic wraparound windshields the Willys' two-piece windshield (Willys adopted a one-piece windshield later in 1959) seemed hopelessly outdated. Yet, visibility was excellent. Power steering wasn't offered but power brakes were now optional and with just three turns lock-to-lock the Willys' steering was precise and responsive.

Of course the Willys remained a utility vehicle that had not lost any of the functional, no-nonsense approach to transportation of its predecessors. Thus its interior was still finished in a durable plastic that could be easily cleaned. Its cargo floor still had steel paneling with hardwood rub rails. But all of this was a refreshing alternative to the conventional transportation fare then provided by Detroit. Driving the Willys with its nearly-vertical steering wheel position and floor-mounted shift lever was both enjoyable and easy. Somehow there was more satisfaction on a hot summer day to open the Willys' screened cowl ventilator and feel the cool air enter the interior than there was in pushing the buttons on the family car's air conditioner.

Willys labelled the 105 horsepower (the horsepower rating of this engine was changed in 1958 to 105 at 3600 rpm from the previous level of 115 at 3650 rpm) L-head 6-cylinder the "Super Hurricane", but Whipple advised his readers; "let these strong words deceive no one. The wagon's top speed is just about 75 mph with 60 to 65 being the effective cruising speed." But with the optional, at $67, free-wheeling front hubs the wagon remained a versatile and endearing vehicle. Whipple summed up his impressions by noting; "the Willys Jeep Utility Wagon is a roomy, comfortable family wagon ideal for short trips, practical for long-distance driving at average speeds and amazingly stable and powerful in deep snow, mud or crossfield motoring. For a country family with a regular need for off-the-road or heavy duty operation and a desire for a neat, comfortable road car as well, yet limited to a one car budget, the Willys is literally THE car."

A beautifully maintained 1961 4-wheel drive Station Wagon (Courtesy of Old Cars Weekly)

On 12 June, 1960 Willys Motors introduced the Maverick Special which with a $1995 list price was the lowest-priced American station wagon available. Its close competitor was the 2-door Rambler American station wagon which was priced at $2020. In the Willys line the model priced closest to the Maverick Special was the four-cylinder Utility Wagon which listed for $2258 in 2-wheel drive form.

Willys used the Maverick Special title only for one year. In 1961, however, the same model was again offered identified as the Willys Station Wagon. Unlike the earlier model which used the same two-tone paint style of the earlier Maverick, the new version had new side body trim very similar to that seen earlier on a Jeep show vehicle, the Harlequin. The production version carried two wide chrome pieces which ran parallel until they reached the cowl region then they angled towards each other before joining at a point just behind the grille. *Motor Trend* tested a 1961 model and published the results in its March, 1961 issue. Even with its standard 75 horsepower F-head 4-cylinder engine and 2-wheel drive the Willys impressed *Motor Trend* with its ability to operate in a no-nonsense way on sub-standard country roads. Furthermore, even though *Motor Trend* noted that its suspension with its solid I-beam front axle and semi-elliptical leaf

springs at all four wheels was cast in the mold of the thirties, it applauded its ability to carry nearly three quarters of a ton of cargo – far more than most other conventional American station wagons.

The Willys had a standard rear axle of 4.89:1 which, even when overdrive was engaged remained fairly numerically high at 3.42:1. But *Motor Trend* found the little F-head only slightly noisier at highway speeds than other small American wagons. The Willys also scored well in terms of its overall riding characteristics. *Motor Trend* depicted the ride as "firm but precise". It wasn't very happy with the Jeep's very slow steering which required six turns lock-to-lock. "What will impress most persons", said *Motor Trend*, "is the room available inside the passenger compartment." Noting that the station wagon had 100 cubic feet of total interior space, *Motor Trend* observed that "when usable space is considered, the Jeep station wagon will double many other wagons, for practically every inch is useable when the front seats are removed."

With just 75 horsepower and a test weight of 2993 pounds the Willys wasn't a strong accelerator. Zero to 30 mph required 7.2 seconds; from zero to 45 mph, 14 seconds and zero to 60 mph, 26.6 seconds. But like earlier Jeep wagons this low-priced version had attributes that more than compensated for its limited straight-line performance.

Willys, even as late as 1961, was eager for buyers to compare its Utility Wagon against other supposedly more modern competitors from other manufacturers. To facilitate this process Willys Motors

published a fairly comprehensive brochure in 1961 comparing the Willys with four competitors: the Chevrolet Carryall, Dodge Town Wagon, GMC Suburban and International Travelall. Instead of downplaying the Utility Wagon's almost vintage status, Willys regarded it as a virtue, explaining; "The 'Jeep' 4 × 4 Utility Wagon ... the only vehicle in this comparison that is clearly the result of *continuing improvement of a basic design*. The others appear to be examples of the 'new model' concept of design, and new model 'bugs' are often part of the package the customer buys under this plan".

Jeep went on to compare the Utility Wagon and its alternatives in seven basic areas: "First Cost". "Maneuverability", "Performance", "Capacity and Convenience", "Standard Equipment", "Comfort and Appearance" and "Economy". In the first category Jeep offered the following chart as evidence:

Willys then turned to maneuverability where, it said "A vehicle that is engineered for off-road use must be trim and maneuverable ... The 'Jeep' Utility Wagon is nearly two feet shorter than its nearest sprawling competitor and has several inches less width ... [It] will cut a circle up to seven feet less in diameter than the competition, allowing turns which are impossible for those vehicles bred for broad highways ... On slopes, where the angle is sudden and sharp, the 'Jeep' Utility wagon with its shorter front and rear overhang has no trouble. But competitive wagons jut so far over the wheels, front and rear, that bottoming is a constant threat."

Supporting Willys' claims was this chart:

Brooks Stevens redesigned the Station Wagon for production in Brazil. This is a 2-wheel drive model. (Courtesy of Brooks Stevens)

Wagon	Max. G.V.W	Delivered Price	More than Willys
Jeep Utility Wagon	4500 lbs.	$3010.29	—
Dodge W 100 Town Wagon	6000 lbs.	$3410.00	$33.31
IHC C-120 Travelall	7000 lbs.	$3759.54	$62.43
Chevrolet K1416 Carryall	5600 lbs.	$3379.00	$30.72
GMC K1001 Suburban	5600 lbs.	$3504.00	$41.14

	Jeep Wagon	Dodge	IHC	Chevrolet	GMC
Overall length	176.25 in.	197.1 in.	202 in.	201 in.	200 in.
Overall width	71.8 in.	75.1 in.	75.5 in.	79.25 in.	79.37 in.
Wheelbase	104.5 in.	114 in.	119 in.	115 in.	115 in.
Turning dia.	43.8 ft.	46.8 ft.	50.5 ft.	50.7 ft.	47.7 ft.
Front overhang	25.75 in.	31.75 in.	N.A.	31.75 in.	32 in.
Rear overhang	46 in.	51.75 in.	N.A.	54.25 in.	53 in.

Willys next turned to performance where, on the surface, it appeared the Utility Wagon was at a disadvantage due to having the least powerful engine. But as this chart indicates, when measured on the basis of weight-to-torque ratios the Willys was very competitive. Similarly its braking system also scored well:

	Jeep Wagon	Dodge	IHC	Chevrolet	GMC
Engine type	In-line 6	In-line 6	In-line 6	In-line 6	V-6
Torque (lb.ft.)	190 @ 1400 rpm	215 @ 1600 rpm	233.5 @ 2000 rpm	217 @ 2000 rpm	260 @ 1600 rpm
Horsepower	105 @ 3600 rpm	140 @ 3900 rpm	140 @ 3800 rpm	135 @ 4000 rpm	150 @ 3600 rpm
Lbs./torque	23.6	27.9	35.7	25.8	21.5
Brake lining (sq.in.)	176.2	199.8	172.9	167.0	174.0
Lbs./ lining sq.in.	25.5	30	40.4	33.5	32.1

In the area of cargo capacity the Willys' short wheelbase appeared to also place it at a disadvantage to larger 4-wheel drive vehicles:

	Jeep Wagon	Dodge	IHC	Chevrolet	GMC
Max. cargo platform length (in.)	68.5	94.7	82.1	99.6	99.7
Max. platform width (in.)	58.25	65.25	62	57.7	57.7
Rear opening width (in.)	58.2	50.2	49.5	57.7	57.7
Rear opening height	39.5	45.8	35.1	44.7	44.0
Platform to ground (loaded in.)	25.0	33.1	26.3	31.7	31.7
Actual payload (lbs.)	1155	1305*	2255[a]	1000[b]	735

*: required optional springs and tires

[a]: Willys explained that "The International C–120 Travelall has been included in this comparison even though it is not really in the 'Jeep' Utility Wagon's G.V.W. class ... because it is the only 4 WD utility wagon this manufacturer offers that is close to the 'Jeep' Utility Wagon's class, and second, to prove that the Travelall offers no real advantage over the 'Jeep' vehicle even though the Travelall costs hundreds of dollars more."

[b]: Optional extra cost tires required.

The Brazilian Rural Willys had 4-doors. This example is a 4-wheel drive model. (Courtesy of Brooks Stevens)

After noting that 'The 'Jeep' Utility Wagon has more payload capacity than both Chevrolet and GMC Suburban, and only slightly less than the Dodge, even after the customer has paid extra to have these vehicles beefed up!", Willys explained that "The competition creates a false impression – that their wide platforms will allow the loading of wide objects. Dodge has a load space more than five feet wide, but it won't carry objects that wide because they won't go through the narrow rear opening! The only wagon with a rear opening width comparable to that of the Utility Wagon is the GMC, however,

GMC's platform is narrower than the 'Jeep' platform. So the 'Jeep' Utility Wagon will not only carry a *heavier* load than two of the others, it will also carry a *wider* one than all of them."

In the area of standard equipment and the cost of commonly ordered optional items the Jeep also scored well against the competition:

Ease of entry was just one of the virtues of the 4-door Rural Willys. (Courtesy of Brooks Stevens)

	Jeep Wagon	Dodge	IHC	Chevrolet	GMC
Right Sun Visor	Std.	Std.	$3.75	$11.85	$8.65
Left Armrest	Std.	Std.	$3.75	$11.85	$9.15
Right Armrest	Std.	Std.	$3.75	$11.85	$9.15
Rear Seat	Std.	Opt.	Opt.	Std.	Std.
Chrome Bumpers	std.	$36.10	$22.50	$22.55	$64.60*

*: Part of the GMC chrome trim package

Rear view of a 4-wheel drive Rural Willys. (Courtesy of Brooks Stevens)

In the final category, "Economy", Willys noted that "Not only does the 'Jeep' Utility Wagon cost less to buy, [but] upkeep is less expensive too." The reason was again "the competitive practice of 'change for change's sake'" which caused "frequent *price* changes as well."

The introduction of the new Wagoneer line in 1962 signaled the end of the "classic" Willys wagon. Yet, they remained in production through 1965 available with either the L-head 226 or the new overhead cam 6-cylinder engines. Even then they still had a future. When Willys began operations in Brazil, one model offered was the Rural Willys station wagon which was an updated version of the old wagon with a new front end. One interesting variation had four doors.

In 1967 the Ford Motor Company purchased Willys-Overland of Brazil but the Rural models remained in production until 1976.

Chapter 4

The first
generation post-war
pick-ups

James Mooney made the worst of a good situation at Willys-Overland's Annual Institution Day activities held in Toledo on 15 October, 1947. He bemoaned rising prices which he said would remove hundreds of thousands of buyers from the market, monetary restrictions that were causing a decrease in foreign sales and what he labelled as "the sacred five-day week" which in his view was an obstacle to "sorely needed manufacture".

After asserting that "people cannot and will not pay premium prices for automobiles", he cautioned that "when a certain level is reached the business will begin to fade rapidly although no one can predict just when this will occur, I believe that the showdown will come much sooner than expected now."

Mooney's pessimism was strangely out of synch with the performance of his company and its future prospects. In the first nine months of 1947 Willys-Overland had earned a tidy profit of $415,721 for the corresponding 1946 period. It was also winding up the year some six months behind in filling orders in spite of a steadily increasing production level that enabled Willys-Overland to produce 26,733 vehicles in the first quarter of its fiscal year; 28,933 in the second and 31,089 in the third. Equally important had been the expansion of the Willys-Overland dealership from 2200 to 2500 during 1947.

One of Willys' major modernization efforts, the rehabilitation of its steel forging shop was over 80 percent complete. In addition to its own work schedule, Willys had over $2,500,000 in orders from outside sources.

Reflecting upon Willys' achievements, Mooney noted that "at the same time as our voloume increased, we have managed to iron out some of our cost problems, with a result that is reflected in our earnings. Our expansion and plant improvement program has progressed to the point where we are achieving more efficient production through our own machine shops, forges and press shops."

As evidence that Willys wasn't sitting on its laurels and letting up on its aggressive postwar expansion program, Willys-Overland showed off Jeepster and Station Sedan prototypes along with a plaster mock-up of its phantom-like 6–71 sedan. But of at least equal importance in expanding Willys' presence in the marketplace had been the May, 1947 introduction of a new line of two and four-wheel drive trucks.

Prior to World War Two Willys had, from 1937 through 1942 marketed a pick-up truck with a front end virtually identical to its passenger car's and with either a stake-platform or pick-up bed. This philosophy was resurrected for the 2T (2-wheel drive) and 4T (4-wheel drive) postwar trucks. Use of these model designations was short-lived as customers tended to interpret them as indicating truck tonnage. In their place Willys announced the adoption of 2WD and 4WD model labels on 5 March, 1948. The first 4WD truck, serial number 15251 was built on 10 February, 1948 with the initial 2WD truck, serial number 15200, leaving the assembly line on 19 February, 1948.

Regardless of their labelling, these trucks were vigorously promoted. "The new 'Jeep' Trucks are the biggest news in the medium-duty field", proclaimed an early ad. It also noted that "Willys-Overland engineers cut off every ounce of gas-eating dead-weight, producing trucks that whack operating costs but still have the strength and stamina that spell low maintenance and long service."

External identification of the earliest models as Willys-Overland products was limited to a W-O logo on the tailgate. This was soon supplanted by a "Jeep Truck" plate mounted on the hood which was found on trucks produced up to serial number 25414–2WD and 42135–4WD. Beyond that point the 4-wheel drive models carried a "4 Wheel Drive" plate with 2-wheel drive models reverting to a plain hood. The serial number was located on a plate found on the outside of the left frame side rail at the front and also on the left of the driver's seat on the floor riser. The engine number was stamped on top of the cylinder block water pump boss.

A rendering of a pre-production 2-wheel drive Jeep truck. (Courtesy of author's collection)

In most dimensions the Jeep truck was considerably larger than the 463 wagon. Its wheelbase was 118 inches and overall length measured 182.5 inches. Pick-up models had a maximum width of 66.625 inches with the stake platform version stretching out to 73.156 inches. The pick-up box measured 80 inches in length with a 48.5 inch width. The platform body was 1.5 inches longer and had a 73 inch width. Height of all models was 74.5 inches. Ground clearance was 8.125 inches.

The 2-wheel drive trucks were rated as 3/4 ton models with a gross vehicle weight range of 4700 to 5300 pounds. The respective shipping weights of the pick-up and platform versions were 3071 and 3299 pounds.

The 4-wheel drive models, with a one-ton rating, had shipping weights of 3205 pounds (pick-up) and 3431 pounds (platform). Willys also offered both models in 12 other body and chassis forms including canopy tops and demountable steel van versions. Four-wheel drive trucks could be equipped with either front or rear power take-off kits.

The business-like lines of a very early 4-wheel drive Jeep stake truck. (Courtesy of author's collection)

Channel steel side rails were used for the truck chassis which was reinforced with six cross-members. The trucks did not use the 463's Planar-type independent front suspension. Two-wheel drive models were fitted with a Clark Model 155 reverse Elliot-type steel forged, heat-treated axle supported by 10-leaf semi-elliptic springs. A semi-floating Timken Model 51540 rear axle with ratios of either 5.38:1, 6.17:1 or 4.88:1 was used. The 4-wheel drive truck used the same rear axle/suspension system but was available only with a 5.38:1 axle ratio. Its front axle, also with a 5.38:1 ratio, was a Splicer Model 25 full-floating type. The Splicer Model 18 transfer case had a 1:1 high and 2.43:1 low range. Front and rear tread measurements were 56 and 63.5 inches. Both models had a 15 gallon fuel tank mounted at the rear of the chassis. The standard wheel size was 16 × 5.00.

The Jeep trucks used an Auburn single dry plate clutch with a 120 lb.ft. of torque capacity. When installed on a 4-wheel drive model the clutch had a slightly higher, 183–203 pounds, instead of 180–195 pounds, spring pressure range. Also found on all trucks was a Warner ASI-T909E 3-speed transmission with ratios of 3.44:1 1.85:1 and 1.1:1.

The close proximity of the Sedan Delivery to the Station Wagon is apparent. (Courtesy of author's collection)

As expected the Willys trucks were powered by the 134.2 cubic inch L-head 4-cylinder engine. The only change of consequence from the version used on the 463 was the installation of a different Carter carburetor, Model 626S. All 4-wheel drive models and 2-wheel drive models up to serial number 19307 used an oil bath air cleaner. Beyond that point the 2-wheel drives had a dry-type air cleaner. If desired, a high altitude cylinder head with a 7.0:1 instead of 6.47:1 compression ratio could be installed.

Willys' promise to avoid annual model changes merely for the sake of change while making continuing refinements and improvements was manifested both in the consistency of its truck's design and by the numerous changes made from 1947 through 1950 that did not require expensive retooling or assembly line shutdowns. The very early trucks (up to serial number 11197-2WD and 10342-4WD) were fitted with doors having stationary vent windows. Beyond that point they were movable. Found on vehicles produced up to serial number 22346-2WD and 34678-4WD was a divided front seat as used on the 463. Subsequently, a full-length seat cushion was adopted. Also found on trucks produced before serial number 22112-2WD and 33385-4WD was a "Jeep Truck" nameplate on the dash panel. On 4-wheel drive trucks produced thereafter a shift plate was installed in the same location.

One of the most significant revisions was a shift from a remote-control column shift mechanism to a floor-mounted shift lever. This took place after serial number 22536-2WD and 34787-4WD. It was accompanied by a major interior revision.

Both 2- and 4-wheel drive models used a centrally-located instrument cluster assembly dominated by a large square speedometer. It read from 0 to 80 mph, included an odometer and carried a "Willys-Overland" script. To its left were the fuel and ammeter gauges, balanced on the right by oil pressure and temperature gauges. Column shift models had an ash receptacle placed directly above the speedometer. The windshield wiper control knob was mounted just below the windshield division. Beneath the instrument cluster, from left to right, were the ignition, main light switch, receptacle for the optional cigarette lighter and the choke control. On either side of the main instrument panel cluster were recessed panels with the right-side serving as the glove box.

When the floor shift was adopted the windshield wiper control switched locations with the ashtray and a floor mat with provision for access to the transmission was installed. Regardless of the shift mechanism a 2-spoke steering wheel was used with a large "W-O" logo mounted on the center horn button.

Until serial numbers 20243-2WD and 26719-4WD the instrument cluster had an engine-turned aluminum finish which at that point was superseded by an aluminum painted mask with black decorative lines. Trucks built up to serial number 19428-2WD and 23710-4WD had Burnt Coffee-coloured wiper control, cowl ventilator knobs, window regulators and door lock knobs. Those built after that point had Ivory-colored controls. Until serial number 23434-2WD and 37627-4WD the ash tray cover was painted. Subsequently it was chrome plated.

A July, 1947 advertisement for the new Jeep Truck. (Courtesy of author's collection)

Willys used a small garnish molding for the center windshield divider up to serial numbers 2117-2WD and 30779-4WD when a garnish piece extending the full length of the divider bar entered production. This had been preceded by use of a revised door garnish

2-OR 4-WHEEL DRIVE MODELS

Gangway, America! Here come the New 'Jeep' Trucks

14 BODY AND CHASSIS STYLES—'Jeep' Truck bodies are functionally designed for long life and low maintenance costs. Top of page: steel-bed pickup. Above: platform stake, wood floor and gates. Below: (*left*) canopy top, (*center*) cab and chassis, (*right*) demountable steel van.

The new 'Jeep' Trucks are the biggest news in the medium-duty field. Here are tough, long-lived trucks with low gross vehicle weights in relation to pay-load capacity . . . 4700-5300 gross vehicle weights, ¾ to 1 ton nominal pay-load.

Willys-Overland engineers cut off every ounce of gas-eating dead-weight, producing trucks that whack operating costs but still have the strength and stamina

that spell low maintenance and long service. Their lower weight, teamed up with the world famous 'Jeep' engine, make 'Jeep' Trucks the ace buy for reliable performance and rock-bottom costs.

See them now, with their functional bodies that make sense to truck buyers . . . hard-to-damage fenders, well protected lights, full opening hoods, sturdy doors and comfortable cabs.

WILLYS-OVERLAND MOTORS, Toledo, Ohio
MAKERS OF AMERICA'S MOST USEFUL VEHICLES

THEY'RE ALL TRUCK, ALL OVER

A Type for Every Farm Job...Powered by the 'Jeep' Engine

TWO AND FOUR-WHEEL DRIVE

TWO GREAT NEW LINES OF 'JEEP' TRUCKS BUILT FOR LOW COSTS AND LONG SERVICE

You know the power, efficiency and economy of the war-proved 60-hp "Jeep" Engine. Around this world-famous power plant, Willys-Overland has built two models of rugged, full-size "Jeep" Trucks designed feature by feature to meet the needs of farmers.

Willys-Overland dealers from coast to coast invite you to see them now. Inspect the gas-thrifty, long-lived "Jeep" Engine, easy to service under the big, full-opening hood. Look at their functional *truck* bodies with common-sense fenders, comfortable cabs and sturdy bodies.

TWO MODELS IN STANDARD BODY STYLES

Model 2WD—2-Wheel-Drive, 4700-5300 lbs. GVW. A money-saving truck that will give you low-cost operation and maintenance. Pick-up, van, canopy and platform-stake bodies.

Model 4WD—4-Wheel-Drive, 5300 lbs. GVW. Sensational new all-weather farm truck with selective 2- and 4-wheel drive—6 speeds forward, 2 reverse. All-wheel traction for hauling in the field, through mud, on icy roads. Pick-up, platform-stake and other bodies.

THERE'S A 'JEEP' TRUCK to meet every farmer's requirements— the 2-wheel-drive "2WD" for ordinary service—the 4-wheel-drive "4WD" for hub-deep mud, icy roads and steep grades that call for the extra traction of all-wheel drive.

TRUCK WITH POWER TAKE-OFF! Model 4WD can be equipped with optional power take-off to deliver up to 30 hp for belt work, ample power for operating silo fillers, hammer mills, buzz saws and other farm equipment.

EXPECT LONG LIFE from "Jeep" Trucks, engineered for rugged-ness and stamina by the men who made the Universal "Jeep" world-famous for ability to stand up under hard use. See the "Jeep" line before you buy any truck.

New TWO AND FOUR-WHEEL DRIVE 'Jeep' Trucks

WILLYS-OVERLAND MOTORS, TOLEDO, OHIO—MAKERS OF AMERICA'S MOST USEFUL VEHICLES

molding after serial number 11197–2WD and 10342–4WD which fully encircled the window frame instead of just covering the lower portion.

Beginning with serial number 14144–2WD and 14399–4WD and continuing to serial numbers 22048–2WD and 34026–4WD an embossed leather grain insert was used for the interior door panel. It replaced a smooth unit and, in turn, was replaced by a Taupe-colored version.

The 1947 Jeep trucks were advertised as tailor-made for the modern farmer's needs. (Courtesy of author's collection)

Trucks with serial numbers up to 19428–2WD and 23710–4WD had Coral Gray-colored armrests. The armrests on those produced after that point were Ivory-colored. At various points Willys used either Brown or Black floor mats in conjunction with either a basket weave (up to serial numbers 22048–2WD and 34026–4WD) or a gray headliner.

Willys included a tool-kit containing an adjustable nine-inch wrench and handle, hammer, pliers, screwdriver and sparkplug wrench as standard truck equipment. Some items from the truck's lengthy optional equipment list were Zenith, Detroit and Philco radios with speakers mounted in the instrument panel or cowl trim pad, heater-defroster, cigarette lighter, sun visors, interior and exterior rear

A 1948 Model 4T truck with canopy top. (Courtesy of author's collection)

Willys-Overland Engineers Trucks to
CUT HAULING COSTS!

If low cost per mile and per year is your guide in truck buying, look to the company that specializes in economy—Willys-Overland.

Every part of these long-lived 'Jeep' Trucks was engineered to save you money on operation and maintenance. Functional bodies eliminate every pound of unnecessary weight. Their 'Jeep' Truck Engines are world-famous for long mileage and low-cost repairs.

At Willys-Overland dealers, see our two lines on 118-in. wheelbase—the 2-wheel-drive (4700-5300 lbs. GVW) and 4-wheel-drive (5300 lbs. GVW)—and the 104-in.-wheelbase 'Jeep' Panel Delivery (4000 lbs. GVW).

'Jeep' TRUCKS
Now at New Low Prices

FUNCTIONAL FENDERS, with no deep skirt to invite dents, make sense on trucks. High clearance of fenders makes it easy to change tires or put on chains.

CAB FEATURES—Wide-vision windshield and windows—wind wings—arm rests —easy-posture seats—extra head-room— stand-open doors—button latches.

ON THE ROAD or in the shop, the wide-opening hood and narrow fenders of 'Jeep' Trucks give easy accessibility to every part of the power plant.

WILLYS-OVERLAND MOTORS · TOLEDO 1, OHIO · MAKERS OF AMERICA'S MOST USEFUL VEHICLES

A 1949 advertisement illustrated by the 118 in. wheelbase truck and the Panel Delivery with a shorter, 103 in. wheelbase.
(Courtesy of author's collection)

The new F-head Hurricane engine was vigorously promoted in 1950. (Courtesy of author's collection)

An October, 1951 advertisement for the Willys pick-up. (Courtesy of author's collection)

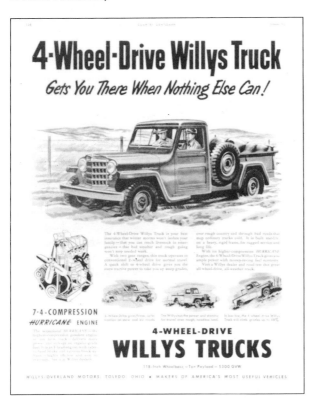

mirrors, license plate frame, dual horns, lockable gas cap, tire pump, spare tire lock, dual tail lights, foglights or combination fog-driving lights, gasoline filter, starter crank, spotlight, underhood light and a deluxe tool kit. The fully-equipped Jeep truck would also have a fire extinguisher, tire inflator, directional signals, a summer insect bug screen as well as a winter grille front.

Willys offered its trucks in any of a dozen color choices including Emerald Green, Harvard Red, Jungle Green, Luzon Red, Manila Blue, Michigan Yellow, Potomac Gray, Princeton Black, Tarawa Green, Tropical Silver, Universal Beige and Wake Ivory. Apparently someone in the Willys design office had a firm grip not only on color variations and geography but also an eagerness to blend some Jeep military history into the paint buckets at Toledo.

The line up of 1947 Jeep trucks was as follows:

Model 463 (½ ton, 2WD, 104 in. wb.)	Price
Panel	$1358

Model 2WD (¾ ton, 2WD, 118 in. wb.)	
Chassis	$ 914
Chassis and Cab	$1267
Pick-up	$1360
Stake	$1427

Model 4WD (1 ton, 4WD, 118 in. wb.)	
Chassis	$1175
Chassis and Cab	$1529
Pick-up	$1620
Stake	$1685

Production of 2-wheel drive trucks totalled 3734 units in 1947. Output of 4-wheel drive trucks was 4114. Production of both types was 41,462 in 1948 and 18,342 in 1949.

Initally, the 1949 models were carried over as 1950 models, from October, 1949 until March 30, 1950, when a second series of 1950 model trucks were introduced. These trucks received a major styling change in the form of the same new front end appearance as used on the latest station wagons. Removed was the full length hood ornament that on earlier models had been either painted body color or chromed. The result was a smoother hood line that blended into a new V-shaped front hood with a winged Willys-Overland emblem, five horizontal and nine vertical grille bars. The front edge of the hood was rolled under for added strength and rigidity. The front fenders had deeper, head-on cut-outs and crease lines matching the one found on the hood.

At the same time Willys introduced a ½ ton version of the 2-wheel drive truck with a New York City delivered price of $1400. It replaced the older ¾ ton model. Willys also announced that the New York City price of the 4-wheel drive version was being lowered to $1798 from $1896 as part of an across-the-board price cut.

This price reduction was made more appealing by the concurrent introduction of the new 4-cylinder F-head engine with its overhead intake and side exhaust valve arrangement. No changes were made in its bore and stroke but the new cylinder head provided for a compression ratio boost to 6.9:1. The high altitude head had a 7.4:1 compression ratio. When installed in a 2-wheel drive truck the 8.4:1 cylinder head was standard with a 7.8:1 version optional. The repositioned intake valves had a larger, 2 inch to 1.53 inch head diameter which, said Willys, "allow rapid, unobstructed flow of fuel and air to the combustion chamber through short, water-jacketed

93

Famous Willys F-h
The HURRICAN

This power plant is outstanding for efficiency—for higher horsepower output in relation to size and fuel economy. The 72-horsepower *Hurricane* Engine is of F-head design—only one of its kind in America—with valve-in-head intake and valve-in-block exhaust. Compression ratio is 7.4 to 1, yet premium fuel is not required. With its higher compression and even combustion, the *Hurricane* literally squeezes more energy from every drop of gasoline.

EXTRA LARGE INTAKE VALVES allow free passage of fuel mixture into the combustion chamber. Notice comparison between valves used in conventional engines and those in the F-head *Hurricane* Engine.

HEAVY-DUTY CRANKSHAFT is carbon steel, drop-forged and heat treated to assure long wear. Crankshaft is fully counterweighted and dynamically balanced for smooth engine performance.

F-HEAD DESIGN provides full downward flow of fuel mixture and controlled combustion for high efficiency and less susceptibility to carbon. This design for "better breathing" also assures quiet operation. *Intake Manifold*, cast in the head and completely water-jacketed, gives uniform thermal control of fuel mixture and delivers a full power charge through an extra large intake valve to each cylinder. It means *full-powered* operation—*at all speeds*. It is one of the most efficient engines made.

ad Economy Engine

!

7.4 COMPRESSION

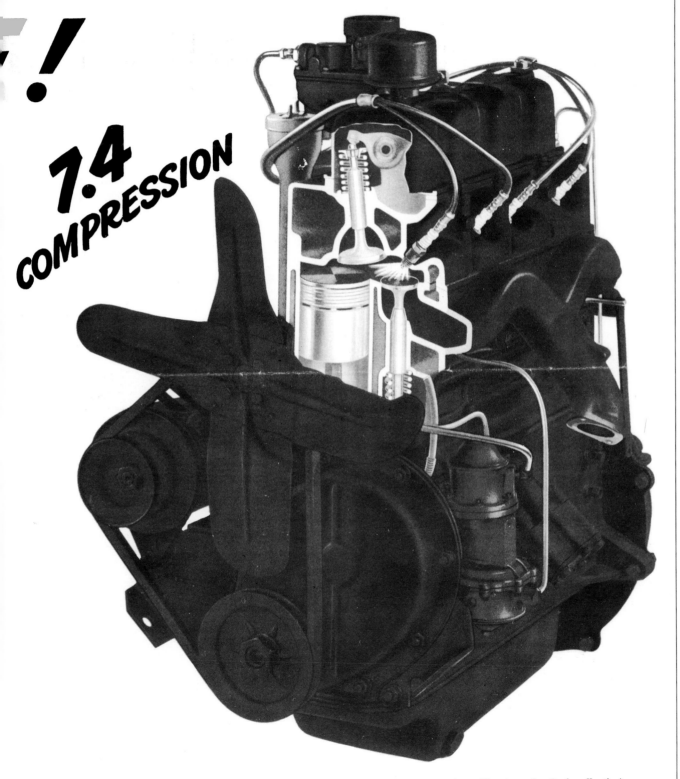

Pertinent features of the Willys F-head engine are displayed in this 1954 sales brochure. (Courtesy of author's collection)

intake passages." Peak horsepower was increased to 72 at 4000 rpm in 4-wheel drive models and 75 at 4000 rpm for 2-wheel drive models. Both types had an identical peak torque output of 114 lb.ft. at 2000 rpm.

Use of the new engine, known as the 473, brought with it new model identifications:

First Series 1950 Models

Model 463PD	Price
Panel Delivery (½ ton, 2WD, 104 inch wb.)	$1374

Model 2WD (¾ ton, 2WD, 118 in. wb.)	
Chassis and Cab	$1282
Pick-up	$1375
Stake	$1441

Model 4WD (1 ton, 4WD, 118 in. wb.)	
Chassis and Cab	$1700
Pick-up	$1792
Stake	$1856

Second Series 1950 Models

Model 473 SD (½ ton, 2WD, 104 in. wb.)	Price
Sedan Delivery	$1374

Model 473 HT (½ ton, 2WD, 118 in. wb.)	
Chassis and Cab	$1208
Pick-up	$1296
Stake	$1358

Model 473–4WD (1 ton, 4WD, 118 in. wb.)	
Chassis and Cab	$1604
Pick-up	$1690
Stake	$1750

WILLYS SEDAN DELIVERY

A 1954 2-wheel drive Sedan Delivery. (Courtesy of author's collection)

The 1954 4-wheel drive Sedan Delivery. (Courtesy of author's collection)

Key physical dimensions of the Willys Sedan Delivery. (Courtesy of author's collection)

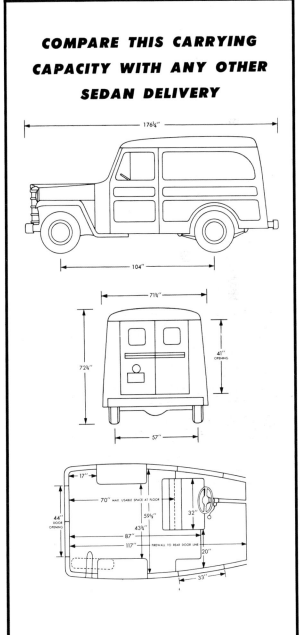

COMPARE THIS CARRYING CAPACITY WITH ANY OTHER SEDAN DELIVERY

The Brazilian truck retained its identity as a Jeep product. (Courtesy of Brooks Stevens)

Changes made in the F-head engine were not extensive during its years of production. For example, beginning in October, 1952 it was fitted with a larger 4.5 inch starter motor as well as a 129 tooth ring gear in place of the older 124 tooth unit. The changes required use of a different bellhousing, engine plate and flywheel ring gear. This version of the F-head was identified as the 475 engine.

Effective with engine number 13869 (engine number 16822 for station wagons) the piston head thickness was increased from 0.1875 inches to 0.25 inches to provide greater strength and heat conductivity.

In general, changes made to the Jeep truck's styling and engineering matched those introduced on the contemporary station wagons Beginning with the 1952 model year the 2-wheel drive models, except for the Sedan Delivery were dropped. The following year the Sedan

Brooks Stevens' updated pick-up for sale in Brazil. (Courtesy of Brooks Stevens)

Delivery became available in 4-wheel drive form.

For 1954 the grille had three instead of five horizontal bars and two new engines were offered. The 2-wheel drive Sedan Delivery used the 161 cubic inch 6-cylinder F-head engine introduced in 1952 for the Aero Willys sedan. It developed 90 horsepower at 4200 rpm and 135 lb.ft. of torque at 2000 rpm. The 4-wheel drive series could be ordered with the "Super Hurricane" L-head 6-cylinder engine.

The trucks received a one-piece windshield and the side trim introduced on the Maverick for the 1960 model year. Like the wagons their production, which continued into 1965, overlapped that of the new models introduced in 1962.

Chapter 5

The Jeep
goes to college

The introduction of the Jeepster on 15 October, 1947 coincided with the debut of the Station Sedan and, in plaster model form, the Willys 6/71 sedan. All three were part of Willys' Second Annual Institutional Day which attracted 400 bankers, writers and industrialists to Toledo. Willys-Overland president, James Mooney, was at his best as he showed off the results of a $21 million modernization project along with the three new Willys products.

But in the weeks prior to Institutional Day the situation at Willys had been anything but tranquil. Indicative of the times was a memo written by Delmar Roos, dated 8 September, 1947, to key members of the Willys engineering staff. Referring to the 6/71 Roos wrote: "Every effort should be made to complete this plaster model in time for the bid day – October 15th. If necessary, overtime should be used."

In late August, 1947, W.D. Appel, who headed Willys operations divisions, noted that "the last revision of our engineering progress chart on the Jeepster models shows that the vehicle would not be completed until about November 3. This of course means that it would be too late to be on exhibit on Institutional Day, 14 October, 1947. Mr. Mooney is very desirous of having this model on display at that time."

Mooney was, after all, president and that meant that the Jeepster was, as earlier indicated, ready for Institutional Day. It was not, in the strictest sense, a true prototype of the production model VJ–2. Since many parts for the Jeepster were not on hand Appel told Roos: "It will be necessary for you to make by hand or procure in any manner possible those items which you feel would not be available by Institutional Day in order that a completed vehicle can be presented at that time. It is not necessary that these emergency parts be necessarily made from drawings … They will serve only to present a picture for exhibition purposes to a non-technical crowd and will be removed immediately after Institutional Day."

The Jeepster, which Willys referred to as "the college boy's delight" was a manifestation of Brooks Stevens' original idea broached back in the early forties to Willys-Overland management. That proposal, it will be recalled, was re-directed by Sorenson to become the Jeep station wagon. But with both that project and development of the spin-off truck models completed, Stevens once again raised the idea of a sporty phaeton-type car. A rendering of the Jeepster in what would become one of its most popular color combinations; yellow and black, won Sorensen, albeit reluctantly, over to Stevens' side. "I don't think there's a market for this thing", he told Stevens, "but if you can keep tooling costs down you can have it." Stevens held both tooling and production costs very low. The front end and A-pillars were from the station wagon and much of the Jeepster's running gear came straight out of the Willys' parts inventory.

By 2 August, 1946 the specifications for the Jeepster, then referred to internally as the V–J Phaeton, were fairly well defined. For the most part they followed closely those of the 463 Station Wagon. The wheelbase was 104 inches, overall length was 178 inches and overall width measured 68.5 inches. With the top lowered the Jeepster's height over its windshield was 60 inches. Front and rear track measured 55.25 and 57 inches respectively.

The Jeepster suspension was identical to the Station Wagon's with a single seven leaf transverse front spring rated at 110 lbs./in. Nine semi-elliptic leaf springs were used at the rear. They had a 100 lb./in. rating. The Ross steering system was identical to the Station Wagon's with a variable ratio of 14- 12- 14:1. Willys specified "Goodyear or equivalent" 5.50 × 15 4-ply tires mounted on 4K drop center 15 inch wheels. These were the same as those used on the Station Wagon.

The close design proximity of the Jeepster to the 463 model can be seen by excerpts from a listing of V-J Phaeton Body Specifications released by Willys on 2 August, 1946:

"1. All steel open body type two-door body with stationary Vee windshield and folding one-man top.
2. Location of all body mounting points to be the same as on the Station Wagon (S.W.).
3. Cowl ventilator, same as S.W. revised.
4. Front floor pan, same as S.W., revised-provided with special rib pattern and shielded holes for draining below rubber floor mats.
5. Instrument panel, same as S.W., revised. Instrument cluster, controls, glove boxes and doors, same as S.W. except new name plate on glove box door.
6. Accessories such as heater, defrosters and radio, same as S.W. Windshield frame to be made of stainless steel stampings.
7. Rear fenders, same as 2T and 4T trucks.
8. All underbody braces and brackets to be the same as S.W. whenever possible.
9. Foot rests for rear seat passengers (same as S.W.).
10. All seats to be of the Station Wagon type, with the same kind of tubular frames, seat pans, seat springs, pads and imitation leather coverings.
11. Entire front sheet metal assembly, including hood assembly, grille and air deflector assembly, front fender and side splasher assembly stone guard, headlights and parking lights, to be the same as Station Wagon, except that the rearward portion of the front fenders will be trimmed off and flanged and will be made to match with new valance panels running on each side, full length up to the rear fenders, along the lower side of the body.
12. Tail-and-license lamp and auxiliary tail-lamp to be the same as S.W. but provided with suitable mounting brackets.
13. Front and rear bumpers, and bumper guards to be the same as Station Wagon."

Nonetheless, the final VJ–2 production model differed in many ways from the original VJ–1 experimental prototype. An early revision, undertaken in July, 1947 was promoted by W.D. Appel who explained in a 26 July, 1947 memo to Roos: "I have a suggestion to make in regard to the Jeepster model which I feel would be a considerable improvement as far as appearance is concerned. This has to do with the bead at the front edge of the cowl where the bonnet ends. As you will note by looking at the same the highlights on this bead always accentuate the same by means of a vertical line which tends to cut the distance from the front of the grille to the windshield into two parts, thereby giving the optical effect of shortening the same and preventing a rather long, unbroken surface which would do much towards

enhancing its appearance." The cowl was a new stamping and thus this sort of change did not involve any alteration of existing dies or assembly equipment.

In early March, 1947, Willys adopted a final set of revisions in the Jeepster design. To provide additional body stiffness a "flat-shaped section replaced the prototype's ribbed section. The rear bumper stone guard was widened and its ends were lowered in order to cover the tail pipe. The tail light embossments were now separate stampings, not drawn into the rear panel as on the original model. In order to facilitate manufacturing the instrument panel was changed to a two-piece affair and the glove boxes were moved further towards the outside of the car. At the same time the heater was lowered some four inches which allowed the glove boxes to be increased in size. Two results of this revision were that the main instrument board stamping was the same for either right- or left-hand drive cars and that the entire glove box and radio installations were the same as on the standard station wagon. Replacing the chromed steering column and gear shaft of the prototype were painted units. Also apparent to anyone who had examined the original model closely was the production model's lower, by 2.5 inches (on angle), windshield. In addition, the windshield was to be made of two main stampings instead of being built-up from several pieces as on the first Jeepster.

The 1948 Jeepster and a gathering of postwar collegians. (Courtesy of author's collection)

The original style of the 1948
Jeepster was carried over into 1949.
(Courtesy of Brooks Stevens)

D 36 4111
1949 - OHIO

The restyled Jeepster of 1950. (Courtesy of author's collection)

In spite of its 1949 license plate this is an example of a 1950 Jeepster. (Courtesy of author's collection)

Both the front and rear seats were lowered and the seat cushions were moved ahead relative to the backs to provide more rack. In order for the left-hand corner of the passenger seat to clear the instrument panel when folded, the front seat was shifted laterally to the right.

The first Jeepster had a five bow top. This was changed on production models to a four bow unit with an altered top contour. The top bows were constructed from the same tubing as used for the station wagon seats.

In order to simplify production and reduce costs a new side curtain design was adopted for the production model. These were larger than the original version but had only one instead of two openings per curtain. Each front side curtain had a zippered triangular opening for signaling in traffic.

The Jeepster, unlike the CJ-2A, was promoted as a vehicle suitable for woman drivers. This is a 1950 model. (Courtesy of author's collection)

Making a major change both in the Jeepster's appearance and weather protection was the decision to include hinged ventilating wings mounted to the windshield posts. Originally, Stevens planned for the Jeepster to have a folding windshield like the CJ-2A. Also adopted at this time were the small hub caps from the station wagon.

By 22 September, 1947 numerous changes had been finalized. These included use of rear seat cushions that were two inches longer and had more tilt than those on the first model and the placement of step-on pads on the rear fenders. Roos' comment in regard to this latter revision, that "the step-on pads ... add distinctly to the appearance of the car and also will appeal to the user, particularly youth", is another indication that Willys had a good grip on the market that it hoped would respond favorably to the Jeepster.

Inset: **No doubt the suburban owners of this 1950 Jeepster used it as a second "sunshine" car. (Courtesy of author's collection)**

Yet, one problem that adversely affected the Jeepster's popularity was the public's problem in determining precisely what type of car the Jeepster was. Recalling the early days of the Jeepster's development, Brook Stevens noted that "we originally intended it to have been a low-priced American sports car. But because of management politics and internal problems we had to price it at around $1900, which was at the time fabulously expensive. The MGTC was more expensive (the Jeepster's base price was $1896, the MG listed for $2228. A Chevrolet convertible could be had for as little as $1750). But you couldn't really call one the equivalent of the other because the Jeepster was never meant to be a road racer or a sporting English countryside hot-dog car. But it was to hopefully give the next segment of drivers a shot at the open car market."

Tom McCahill's road test of a Jeepster which appeared in the January, 1950 issue of *Mechanix Illustrated* fell well short of the mark as an enthusiastic evaluation of the Jeepster's virtues. McCahill complained of the Jeepster's relatively high price, lack of power and styling. He admitted that the Jeepster's appearance tended to "grow on people" but nonetheless McCahill noted, "As it is there isn't a production-line car made in America today and costing more than $1000, that can't top it in performance ... It's not a sports car and it's not roomy enough for a general utility car – so what is it?"

McCahill did feel that the Jeepster had "excellent potential" – if Willys used a more powerful engine and made what he described as "a few other minor alterations." The original specifications for the Jeepster called for it to have a "W.O. Special" engine with an aluminum

cylinder head ("for increased power and torque") in place of the cast iron head used on the 463. This raised horsepower to 66 at 4000 rpm. Maximum torque was 111 lb.ft. at 2000 rpm.

A quarter-scale model of Brooks Stevens proposed Brazilian Jeepster. (Courtesy of Brooks Stevens)

In this form and with a 3-speed transmission, rear axle ratio of 4.1 and a road weight of 2650 pounds Willys-Overland obtained a top speed of 77 mph for the Jeepster. As released to the public the Jeepster reverted to the cast iron cylinder head with a 6.48:1 compression ratio. Its power ratings were 63 horsepower at 4000 rpm and 106 lb.ft. of torque at 2000 rpm.

It was exactly the type of comparison McCahill made between the Jeepster and other American cars that Barney Roos had wanted to avoid. In September, 1947 the question of what type of floor covering should be installed in the production Jeepster led to a detailed

discussion by Roos revolving around the Jeepster's nature. "This vehicle is *not* a convertible", he wrote in a 9 September, 1947 memo to James Mooney. "It is not equipped with a top which can be put up by pressing a button and lowered in a few seconds by similarly pushing a button. Likewise it does not have side windows which rise quickly and constitute substitutes for side curtains.

"This job is a sports roadster with two seats. If you choose to call it a convertible, then we could say a semi-convertible, but I believe if we ever indicate that this job is a convertible that odious comparisons will be made between it and the modern full-type convertible, and the whole concept of the vehicle was as far away from a modern convertible as we could possibly make it.

Stevens retained much of the flavor of the original Jeepster in his new design. As with the first Jeepster, Stevens made extensive use of inexpensive stampings for the South American version. (Courtesy of Brooks Stevens)

The operational prototype differed in only minor details from the quarter-scale model. (Courtesy of Brooks Stevens)

The rear view of the updated Jeepster was very similar to that of the original. Note also the ⅔–⅓ front seat division. (Courtesy of Brooks Stevens)

109

"How does this affect the use of a carpet as against a rubber mat? In this way: In many cases the car will be driven on the open road and may be left outside and a rainstorm comes up and the inside of the job will get wet. We will have to provide adequate drainage on the floor for any water that is caught in the job, and a rubber mat will not absorb and retain water. There will be many times when the people driving the car will put the top up and let the curtains go, especially if they are in the front seat, because we have provided glass wings which will give them some protection, and if they are driving in a light rainstorm they may not bother to put the side curtains on. This means that the rear seat will get wet and the carpet too.

"We have chosen the type of upholstery for the seats which will not be hurt by water, just as we did in the Station Wagon, with the idea that rain wouldn't hurt. On the other hand again, there will be many times when the owner of this job will not bother to protect it from the rain, and here a rubber mat is the proper thing." In December, 1947 the Jeepster's specifications were frozen and they included standard floor mats.

The body dies for the Jeepster were purchased on the basis of producing a minimum of 50,000 Jeepsters. It soon was apparent that this was wildly optimistic. First year production of the Jeepster totalled only 10,326 units.

The next year output fell to just 2960 cars. This was in spite of the mid-year availability of the 148 cubic inch, 70 horsepower 6-cylinder engine as an option. The VJ–3 (as the 1949 model was identified) was carried over into 1950 without any change. In March, 1950 new Jeepsters powered by either the new 72 horsepower "Hurricane" F-head 4-cylinder engine or the 75 horsepower "Lightning" L-head engine which displaced 161 cubic inches were introduced. Their model designations were 473VJ and 673VJ respectively. Both models shared the new front grille design used on the second series Station Wagon and truck models. Public interest in the Jeepster perked up in 1950 as indicated by the production of 4066 473VJ models and 1779 673VJs. But this wasn't sufficient to warrant further development of the Jeepster. By that time the Aero Willys sedan was in its final stages of development and there was little logic, in the view of the Willys' board of directors to funnel more money into the Jeepster.

As a result, production of the Jeepster was not carried over into 1951 although 1597 4-cylinder and 1703 6-cylinder Jeepster left over from 1950 were available. The Jeepster's less than spectacular sales, as have been suggested, were due to several factors, not the least being its limited weather protection. The effect of the Jeepster's price upon its sales is less clear. In 1948, when it was priced higher than subsequent models the bulk of the 19,131 Jeepsters built were sold. Future price reductions positioned the Jeepster fairly competitively against other American convertibles:

Model	Price
1949 Jeepster (4-cyl.)	$1603
1949 Ford Convertible	$1948
1949 Chevrolet Convertible	$2134
1949 Plymouth Convertible	$1982
1949 Dodge Wayfarer Roadster	$1727

It's possible that the Jeepster's somewhat lethargic performance hindered sales. Even with the 6-cylinder engine the Jeepster could do no better than a 25 second time from zero to 60 mph. As early as 3 December, 1947 Barney Roos was expressing concern about the Jeepster's weight. "The weight of the VJ as it comes out is very disappointing. I appreciate that we have had very little time and, therefore, very little chance to do much studying as regards weight.

"The biggest penalty seems to be in the frame itself, but there are doubtless other places in the vehicle where lighter gauge material could be specified, particularly as we are not depending very much on the body for stiffness."

Regardless of the Jeepster's limited life span both its name and to a certain degree its design philosophy was destined to be reborn 16 years later in 1967. This time the Jeepster was pure Jeep since it came only in 4-wheel drive form. At the least the Jeepster was an interesting and rather adventurous endeavour by Willys-Overland. In the larger perspective of Jeep history it was a premature thrust into the recreational vehicle market that in the late forties barely existed.

As displayed in 1961 the Jeepster was known as the Saci. (Courtesy of Brooks Stevens)

110

Chapter 6

The
Kaiser-Frazer/Willys
merger

Like other manufacturers, Willys-Overland had to accept the harsh reality that the postwar seller's market would eventually dry up. But its president, James M. Mooney, did not take the position that this would be caused by satisfaction of existing demand. Speaking in Cincinnati, Ohio on 12 January, 1949, Mooney predicted that within six months it would be possible for a customer to walk into any automobile showroom and purchase any vehicle he or she desired. "We've switched to a buyer's market", he remarked, "High prices are shrinking the use of motor cars." This had been one of Mooney's favorite themes and although he depicted the automobile industry as healthy, he noted, "A lot of rocks have been thrown at management and labor because of the high prices of motor cars. The fact is that the principal causes for the present high price level are the lower purchasing power of the dollar for all manufactured goods because of our devaluation of the dollar [and that] the present cost of motor cars is heavily loaded with direct and indirect taxes amounting to several hundred dollars per vehicle."

But regardless of Mooney's views, there was a lessening of demand for Willys-Overland products in spite of some mid-year price reductions ranging from $25 on the Jeep to $270 on the Jeepster. Early in February, 1949 the Willys plant was shut down due to Midwest blizzards that put a chill on Jeep sales in that part of the country. The Jeep plant opened in mid-March just a week before the price reductions were announced. At that time Mooney predicted that sales would return to peak levels within a few months. He also cited four reasons why Willys was able to reduce prices. These included an increased availability of lower-priced steel, fewer production disruptions because of a smoother flow of supplies, Willys' policy of avoiding costly model changeovers and its fundamental design which kept costs low.

Nonetheless, Mooney, on 7 April, 1949, had to announce that Willys was adopting a 4-day work week for production employees at least through April. Mooney attempted to put the best possible spin on this bad news, explaining that "it provided maximum efficiency at lowest cost based on our present volume".

A few weeks later, on 20 April, 1949, Mooney announced he had submitted his resignation as president to the Willys-Overland Board of Directors. All had not been tranquil between Mooney and power brokers on the board as George W. Ritter and Ward Canaday over the sales slump and other matters for a number of months prior to Mooney's resignation.

Just over a week later, on 29 April, 1949, Mooney, speaking at the Annual Luncheon of the Automotive Old Timers at the Roosevelt Hotel in New York City, seemed to still be pursuing the dream of a postwar car selling for $1000. He suggested abolishing the forty-hour week, lengthening the work day and reducing taxes to make possible the production of a low-priced car. "Costs of goods and services cannot be brought down with a forty-hour week and a short measure of work for high hourly wages", he said. "The only way we can build the thousand dollar car", he added, "is with an honest day's work at an honest day's wage. We must demand lower tax rates."

Back in Toledo there were more pragmatic and less philosophical problems to deal with that were adversely affecting Willys-Overland

production. In May a strike at Bendix Aviation, which supplied brakes to Willys, forced the plant to shut down until deliveries could be arranged from another supplier. This affected 5000 of the 7000 workers who had been on a four-day work week. Later, in October, Willys felt the sting of the nation-wide steel strike which resulted in numerous work stoppages including the lay-off of about 4000 workers because of part shortages. All of these developments took their toll upon the production of Willys-Overland vehicles which in 1949 took a sharp downward turn from their 1948 levels:

	1948	1949
Station Wagons	22,309	29,290
Trucks	41,462	18,342
Jeeps	63,170	18,342

The impact of this decline upon Willys-Overland was apparent in its Annual Report issued on 28 December, 1949 and which applied to its fiscal year ending on September 30, 1949. Net sales fell to $142,362,944 from $175,346,360 in 1948. Net income after all taxes and charges was $3,423,711 compared to $7,077,401 in 1948. Willys told its stockholders that these earnings reflected lower prices of its vehicles, the readjustment of product line in the last half of the year and a change in policy regarding dealer's new car stocks which were drastically reduced during the year.

What was soon to loom very important as a catalyst upon Willys-Overland fortunes was the report that the year had been marked by an accelerated demand by the Federal Government for Jeeps, trucks, station wagons and spare parts that left Willys-Overland with approximately $15,000,000 in unfilled government orders at the end of the fiscal year. In his concluding remarks at the Annual Stockholder's Meeting Canaday noted that "It is reasonable to believe that Willys-Overland, with no debt, low inventory and a good product will continue to meet conditions aggressively and successfully."

Much of this optimism was justified by a June, 1950 order for 4000 military Jeeps which totalled $12,139,500. Both of these amounts paled in light in the announcement by Willys-Overland on 5 July, 1950 of an order for $22,291,300 from the U.S. Ordnance Department. This was the largest order placed with Willys-Overland in the past five years and was for 8350 Jeeps.

A 1962 portrait of Henry J. Kaiser. (Courtesy of Kaiser Aluminum)

Both the June and July orders called for the production of a new Jeep model, the MC, M38. Later, in October Army Ordnance placed an order for 20,700 Jeep engines amounting to $5,665,700. From 1950 through 1952 Willys built 60,345 M38s which provided a substantial increase in its revenues at a time when expenses for development of the F-head Hurricane and 6-cylinder Lightning engines, introduced in March, 1950, as well as the costs involved in development of the CJ–3A along with those of the new Aero Willys cut deeply into Willys-Overland profits.

At the end of its 1950 fiscal year Willys-Overland's working capital and earned surplus were at record levels. Its unfulfilled orders amounted to approximately $93,000,000. By November they had reached $110,000,000 and were still rising.

Reviewing the year, Board Chairman Ward Canaday said, "Operations for the first half of the year were adversely affected by the necessity of making changes in the production program involving expenses incident to retooling for new models and realignment of factory facilities for more economical operation, as well as by strikes of national scope affecting supplier's plants. As a consequence, shipments for the period were abnormally low and a loss of $908,307 was sustained." But in the year's second half, with the new models in production the company returned to profitable operations and earned $2,513,824 in the fiscal year's first half. Overall, Willys-Overland earned $1,605,517 for the fiscal year.

Willys-Overland had, ever since the end of World War Two, been developing experimental models of the military Jeep. This put it in a strong position in June 1949, when the government, according to *Business Week*, 13 January, 1951, told it to "stop experimenting and get ready to produce the military model as it stood." The new MC, M38 Jeep differed in a number of respects from the old MB model. The latest Jeep was fitted with a 24 volt waterproofed electrical system and a one-piece windshield. Also making indentification of the MC, M38 easy were its headlights which bulged outward in bug-eye fashion from their mountings and the lower windshield base mountings for the wipers.

Following on the heels of this development in 1951 was a more drastically revised military Jeep the MD–M38A1, which was produced until 1971. This model was five inches lower and two inches wider than the MC, M38. For a Jeep its appearance was almost revolutionary, with rounded front fenders, a much higher and curved hoodline, a two-piece windshield and headlights recessed in the grille structure. Also

setting the MD–MB38A1 apart from its predecessor were its more deeply cut front entrance passageway. Powering the MD–MB38A1 was Willys new F-head engine.

The swift movement of Willys-Overland back into large-scale production of military Jeeps while illustrating its facility to rapidly adapt to changing market conditions, also revealed some of the fragile aspects of its existence. Certainly not the least important of the latter was the frequent change in its leadership. In the years since 1936 when Ward Canaday and George Ritter had gained control of Willys-Overland there had been three key men who had served either as Willys-Overland chairman or president: Joseph Frazer, Charles Sorensen and James Mooney. The lack of an orderly format for managerial change both adversely affected morale and hampered long-term product planning that was necessary for Willys-Overland to expand beyond the limits of the Jeep field. While the general consensus at Willys in 1951 was that the decision not to produce the 6/71 was correct, it's also a historical reality that the lack of a strong presence in the passenger car field was a major impediment to every Jeep producer up to the acquisition of American Motors by Chrysler in 1987.

Also lurking in the background as a source of potential problems for Willys was its very slim profit margin which, according to *Business Week*, 26 March, 1951, was smaller than that of most other automotive producers. *Business Week* placed Willys' profit on each vehicle it built in 1948 as only $54.

Then there was the nature of the market for Jeeps and models based on their design. In 1949 fully one-third of Willys' civilian output was purchased by farmers. And when that segment of the American population experienced a drop in income during 1949 the impact upon Willys-Overland was predictable. From October, 1949 through March, 1950 it lost $900,000 and in June, 1950 Canaday was back as its president.

On the opposite side of the ledger were some impressive entries as well. Since 1946 Willys had invested some $35 million in plant improvements that enabled it to meet the growing demand for military Jeeps. When the government awarded it an additional $63 million contract in 1951 its backlog of both military and civilian orders exceeded $200,000,000. On top of this came an order for production of major components for the General Electric J–47 jet engine. This order, which exceeded $63,000,000, led to the purchase of an old Chevrolet plant in Anderson, Indiana and the commitment of $7,000,000 for tooling to build the J–47 parts.

Also strengthening Willys-Overland's position was the winning of a contract to supply Kaiser-Frazer with engines for its forthcoming Henry J economy car. These were both four- and six-cylinder engines of 134.2 and 161 cubic inches respectively and they were built on the same tooling used by Willys for its engines. This work necessiated the start-up of a third shift on the engine assembly line.

These developments added to a strong level of business at Willys-Overland that, by June, 1950, was the highest in nearly eighteen months. In addition to substantial deliveries of engines to Kaiser-Frazer, shipments of all models was 62 percent higher than the average for the previous twelve months.

Willys' expertise in designing and producing the Jeep resulted in an unexpected call from Canada in 1951 for it to provide the Ford Motor Company of Canada with the necessary information to build a modified version of the Jeep as part of Canada's $5,000,000,000 military build-up. Initially, Willys was less than enthused about providing a company as large as Ford with the means to produce a vehicle that could eventually become a civilian competitor to its own products. But

114

on 29 September, 1951, Willys-Overland, the Canadian government and the Ford Motor Company of Canada Ltd. agreed on the production of Jeeps in Canada for the exclusive use of the Canadian military forces.

When Willys-Overland reported the results of its 1951 fiscal year the news was, not surprisingly, all good. Its sales of $219,861,553 were not only up 104 percent from the level of 1950, but were also the highest in its history. They exceeded the level of the previous peak year of 1944 by three percent. The following year the impact of large military orders upon Willys-Overland was equally dramatic. For its 1952 fiscal year Willys had record sales of $301,695,020, up 37 percent from 1951, and a net income of $6,083,599 as compared to $4,585,566 in 1951. Of the 148,216 vehicles produced in the 1952 fiscal year, military Jeeps accounted for slightly more than 32 percent. In the 1951 fiscal year Willys-Overland had built 119,216 vehicles of which slightly more than 21 percent had been military Jeeps.

Edgar F. Kaiser. (Courtesy of Kaiser Aluminum)

On 28 January, 1953 Willys-Overland introduced the new CJ-3B. Just a month later, on 28 February, 1953 public disclosure was made concerning negotiations between Willys and Kaiser-Frazer involving a possible merger. Ward Canaday's office released a statement in which he disclosed that "various individuals and groups, including Kaiser-Frazer, have approached us in the past few years for discussion of merger possibilities. At this time there is no proposal before us and no action has been taken." But this was at best a thin smokescreen for the intense negotiations (in fact, discussions between the two companies dated back to 1951) needed to merge two corporations with very distinct backgrounds.

Kaiser-Frazer had entered the postwar automobile market with grandiose plans that, if successful, would have been nothing short of revolutionary. Amidst the dreams and schemes of its namesakes, Henry J. Kaiser and Joseph W. Frazer were cars with front-wheel drive, aluminum-bodied vehicles and, the Holy Grail of many automobile executives, production of a one thousand dollar car.

Of the two men, Kaiser was better known to the American public, having been involved in construction of the monumental Hoover Dam during the thirties in conjunction with such firms as W.A. Bechtel. This was really just the start for Kaiser as he went on from strength to strength. In 1938 there was the Bonneville Dam project; scarcely a year later, the Grand Coulee Dam. During World War Two vessels left the Kaiser shipyards by the hundreds. No wonder the specter of challenging the most entrenched industry in the world hardly phased Henry Kaiser.

Joseph Frazer was a man who knew that industry from the inside out. After gaining sales experience with Packard and Saxon automobiles Frazer joined General Motors where he held various financial positions before leaving to become a key figure in Walter Chrysler's plans to build a company capable of competing with Ford and General Motors. In 1939, as earlier noted, Frazer left Chrysler to become president and general manager of Willys-Overland.

After locking horns with Ward Canaday over the path into the future that Willys should follow, Frazer became the head of Graham-Paige which by that time was at best a ragged remnant of the Depression. Graham-Paige was alive in 1944 only because of the profits it made from government defense work. Its last automotive effort before the war had been the Graham Hollywood which used Cord 812 body dies.

Thus the match-up of Kaiser and Frazer brought together two remarkable men with a common dream – to do what so many others

before them had failed to do; challenge Detroit on its own turf on their terms.

Although Kaiser-Frazer had a profit of $344,064 in the three month period ending on 30 September, 1953, it had lost over $5 million in the first nine months of 1952. This was not an abberation. Since 1945 Kaiser-Frazer had earned profits in only two years and its most recent earnings had come from defense work. For example, in the first nine months of 1952 its sales from automobiles totalled $35,001,908; sales to the government amounted to $22,263,429. But while losing $175,158 on its automobile operations Kaiser had earned $519,158 on defense contracts.

The pride of Kaiser-Frazer had been its Willow Run plant which it had acquired from the government in 1948 for $15,100,000. But although Willow Run had the capacity to turn out over 1500 cars daily, it was currently producing only 350 per day.

The under-utilization of Willow Run was suggested as one reason why Kaiser-Frazer was interested in Willys-Overland since it could then make beter use of that plant. This premise ignored the substantial amount of Willow Run space that was then being used to construct Fairchild C–119 military cargo planes. Certainly more plausible as an explanation for Kaiser's desire to link up with Willys was Willys-Overlands' numerous assets, not the least of which was its stature as the third largest exporter of commercial vehicles from the United States.

After several more weeks of negotiation, and the creation of the Kaiser Manufacturing Corporation as a subsidiary of Kaiser-Frazer to serve as the purchasing agent, an announcement was made on 24 March, 1953 that Kaiser-Frazer was acquiring Willys-Overland for $62,300,000.

The president of Kaiser-Frazer, Edgar F. Kaiser, reported that the combined companies would, with assets of over $200,000,000 and a consolidated net capital in excess of $60,000,000, be the world's fourth largest automobile manufacturer, exceeded in size only by General Motors, Ford and Chrysler. At the time this was also ranked as the largest merger in automotive history.

As expected, this combination aroused considerable discussion and debate. As far as Willys-Overland was concerned once its stockholders accepted the plan at a special stockholder's meeting on 24 April· (of the 2,795,713 outstanding shares, 2,110,823 were voted in favor of the sale), it would exist only as an investment company. The Kaiser Manufacturing Company would become the Willys Corporation.

Ward Canaday lead the fight to gain approval of the proposal by Willys shareholders. He expressed the view that the price offered by Kaiser-Frazer amounted to about $17 a share which was higher than Willys-Overland stock had traded in the past six years. On the day the merger talks were disclosed Willys-Overland stock was the second most active stock on the New York Stock Exchange, closing up ⅜ at 14⅛.

Canaday also declared that Willys-Overland, in spite of its good earnings was hard pressed to undertake needed plant expansion and tooling. Later, at the stockholder's meeting held to vote on the merger, Canaday was more blunt about the future prospects of Willys-

Overland remaining an independent manufacturer. "Companies of larger size, of greater capital, integrated facilities and organizational depth have certain profit advantages over smaller companies of more limited facilities", he said.

Indicating a meeting of the minds was the announcement by Edgar Kaiser that Canaday had been invited to become chairman of Willys Motors.

When news of the impending union was first reported Harry A. McDonald, the head of the Reconstruction Finance Corporation, to which Kaiser-Frazer owed $48,417,000 said that the merger "looked improbable at this point". But late, on 25 March, 1953, he had switched to a supportive mode. "I don't want to give Kaiser-Frazer any bad publicity", he said, "but they were staring into a liquidation picture before this purchase of Willys-Overland development. The Government, as a creditor of the Kaiser interests, also was happy. Now both Kaiser-Frazer and the Government have a earning asset." Helping to cheer Mr. McDonald was the plan for the R.F.C. to receive a payment of $15,000,000 as part of the merger agreement.

Less enthusiastic about this affair were at least two senators, John J, Williams, Republican of Delaware and John W. Bricker, Republican of Ohio. Williams claimed that the R.F.C. had failed to protect the Government's interests and the result would be a loss of several million dollars to the Government. Williams was also critical of the roles played in the purchase of Willys-Overland by Kaiser-Frazer of both McDonald and John W. Snyder, the former Secretary of the Treasury who became a vice president of Willys Motors Corporation.

Also critical of the sale was a group calling itself the "Kaiser-Frazer Stockholders Protective Committee". Its leader charged that "directors and officers of Kaiser-Frazer are trying to complete the transaction without informing the stockholders of Kaiser-Frazer of the details and without giving us a chance to voice our opinion."

But none of this bombastic activity derailed the merger and on 28 April, 1953 the closing documents were signed in Toledo, Ohio at the Willys headquarters. A week later Edgar F. Kaiser was named president of Willys Motors with Raymond R. Rausch his executive vice president. Since 1950 Rausch had served as a vice president and executive assistant to the Willys-Overland president. Ward Canaday did not choose to serve as an officer in the new firm, citing his obligation to the stockholders of Willys-Overland until all details of the merger were completed.

It was soon very apparent that the creation of Willys Motors did not solve one fundamental weakness of Kaiser-Frazer; the poor sales of its automobiles. Production at the huge Willow Run plant was gradually shifted to Toledo and on 10 November, 1953 the sale of Willow Run to General Motors for $26 million was announced.

After this, it was just a matter of time before production of both Kaiser and Willys passenger cars in America would come to an end. The 1954 Kaiser was attractively styled and was unique among American cars by having a supercharged engine. But it also carried the stigma of being perceived as a car about to become an orphan which put a damper upon its sales. Furthermore, in an age when modern overhead valve V-8 engines were considered to be *de rigueur* for any successful American manufacturer, the Kaiser's old and relatively small (226 cubic inches) side-valve 6-cylinder engine was clearly out of step with current buyer atitudes. The graceful Aero Willys, which had been warmly received by most critics, found itself pitted against the Henry J, not exactly a strong position in light of who was running Willys Motors.

The result was predictable: sales of the Kaiser, Henry J and Aero Willys all plunged in 1954 while sales of Jeep CJ, station wagon and truck models held fairly steady. A half-hearted facelift of the Willys plus some significant price reductions failed to stimulate its sales in 1955. Total Aero Willys output in 1955 was only 6,564. The Kaisers were virtually unchanged for 1955 and their output was a mere 1,291. The end of production both of both the Kaiser and Willys passenger cars in 1955 came as no surprise. But if this episode ended one short era in Willys history, it also pointed the way towards another one – a major presence by Willys in foreign countries as a manufacturer. When Willys-Overland was acquired by Kaiser-Frazer it had foreign assembly facilities in Belgium, the Netherlands, Denmark, India, Ireland, Mexico, Australia and Brazil. These outposts were just the start of a major effort by Willys to expand far afield from Toledo.

Chapter 7

The CJ-5, CJ-6, CJ-7:
The Jeeps that wrote the
book on four-wheel-drive

Just as the old MB military Jeep had served as the basis for the first civilian Jeep, the CJ–2A; the MD–MB38A1 was the starting point for the CJ–5 which was announced on 11 October, 1954. Compared to the CJ–3B, which continued in production, the CJ–5 had a one inch longer wheelbase of 81 inches. Its 135.5 inch overall length was 5.75 inches greater than that of the CJ–3B which remained at 129.75 inches. Overall width of the new Jeep and the older model was 71.75 and 68.75 inches respectively. The CJ–5's cargo bed measured 36 in. × 39 in. with the tailgate closed and 36 in. × 49 in. with it closed. Whereas the older model carried "Willys" lettering on its hood sides, the CJ–5's primary marque identification consisted of "Jeep" lettering just ahead of the door cutout. Respective shipping weights for the CJ–5 and CJ–3B were 2164 and 2134 pounds. Pricewise, the CJ–5 was, as $1476, positioned just $65 above the base price of the CJ–3B.

Since the arrival of a new Jeep was quite unlike the introduction of the typical American passenger car, it attracted a considerable amount of attention which Willys welcomed. "Take a good look at the new Jeep" it told prospective buyers. "Although it seemed impossible", Willys added, "to build a more rugged Jeep … Willys has done it … and the new Jeep proves it with increased stamina reflected in every detail. Scores of advanced features … tested in exacting military and civilian use … all yours in the magnificent new Universal 'Jeep'."

Physically, the CJ–5 was similar, but not identical to the MD–MB38A1. One of the more apparent differences was the positioning of the headlights which extended forward slightly from their openings on the CJ–5. They also had chrome dress-up rings. Whereas the military model had blacked-out parking lights, those on the CJ–5 were of conventional design. As expected, the civilian Jeep's electrical system was of 6 volt design rather than the military's 24 volt format.

Military models used both windshield base and cowl-mounted driver side mirrors. All CJ–5s had mirrors located on the windshield support base. A two-piece windshield was incorporated into the MB38A1. CJ–5 Jeeps for the domestic market had a one-piece windshield standard with a divided opening type optional. All export models had the divided opening windshield standard. Incidentally, the old Willys-Overland name lived on after the Kaiser merger in the form of the Willys-Overland Export Corporation.

The CJ–5's reshaped body easily set it apart from the "classic" form of the CJ–3B. Perhaps because it felt an explanation was needed for the CJ–5's new appearance, Willys noted that "body sheet metal is flanged and overlapped for greater strength … center mounted to relieve road strain and for even greater durability." In similar fashion Willys reported that the use of a "fully boxed front cross-member adds to carrying strength, rigidity and endurance of the new Jeep's frame." At the same time the Jeep's suspension was revised by the use of slower-rate springs which in conjunction with the longer wheelbase was claimed to give the CJ–5 a "vastly improved ride". But just in case this created the impression that the Jeep was getting soft, Willys explained that this change also resulted in "greater stability, comfort and longer life".

There were also many other features unique to the CJ–5. Compared to that used on the CJ–3B, the CJ–5 windshield had almost 100 more

square inches of glass area and folded flat on stronger hinges. While the front seat occupant probably welcomed the availability of the extra-cost "passenger safety rail", the driver was treated to a new dash panel with a back-lighted instrument cluster. Also debuting on the CJ–5 was a passenger-car type handbrake, a glove compartment that could be equipped with a cover and improved seating. The front seats were now softer due to their new coil springs. The driver's seat had three fore and aft adjustments. At the rear a new optional seat allowed four passengers to be carried.

The CJ–5 was derived from the military M38A1 Jeep. This is a 1955 model (Courtesy of author's collection)

Welcomed by Jeep operators who used their vehicles in adverse weather was an improved "All Weather" top. Obviously, this didn't give the Jeep a water-tight interior but, it was much easier to put up and its fittings were far more flush with the body than before.

Just a year after the introduction of the CJ–5 Willys introduced the DJ–3A dispatcher which it called "America's lowest priced four-wheel delivery vehicle". With a starting price of $1284 it was also the most inexpensive automobile built in the United States. But a low price wasn't the dispatcher's only claim to fame since it was the first Willys vehicle with a Jeep body to be available in 2-wheel drive.

The Dispatcher was offered in three basic forms, each with a particular appeal and function. The basic model was provided with either a half or full top constructed of canvas duck. Both tops had removable doors and rear panels. As an alternative to this type of weather protection, Willys offered the dispatcher in a hardtop model whose basic form forecast that of the Postal Service model. This DJ–3A had a fixed cab with steel sides and a fiberglass top that was rippled for added rigidity. One of its more unusual features was the design of its doors. At first glance they appeared to be of the old-fashioned "suicide-type" that were rear hinged and opened into the wind. Actually they slid backward on a top runner which allowed the Dispatcher to operate in close quarters without harming adjacent vehicles. Each of these Dispatchers were equipped with a tailgate that lowered to provide access to 40 cubic feet of cargo space. The Hardtop Dispatcher also had a top-hinged rear door.

A 1954 CJ–5 at work. (Courtesy of author's collection)

The final member of the Dispatcher trio was in many ways a reincarnation of the late and lamented Jeepster. Like the other DJ–3A models it was a two-seater but the profile of its convertible top (which when lowered rested on the rear body edge) gave it a sporty appearance that appealed to younger drivers. Willys, obviously hoping this would be the cause suggested that "the sporty, continental lines of the Soft-Top Dispatcher appeal to the fun-loving Prep School and College Set."

All Dispatchers had body-color wheel rims with chrome hubcaps bearing the stylized Willys "W". The Soft-Top was alone in having a spare tire which was vertically-mounted on its rear deck. Whereas the bumper of the Hardtop and open model had rear bumpers that mounted flush with the lower body edge, the Convertible's was divided into two units on either side of the spare tire.

Down on the farm the CJ-5 found plenty to do. (Courtesy of author's collection)

Another point of difference between these cars was the design of their windshields. None of them had the traditional Jeep fold down feature. The open-bodied Dispatchers had a lower silhouette than that of the Convertible's. But while the former had a small vent mounted just below the windshield base, the Convertible's occupants received their fresh air directly through the windshield which was hinged to open upward. Yet another windshield-air vent arrangement was used on the Hardtop model. Its windshield was the same as the open models' but was mounted in a wider and higher frame. In addition, the front vent panel was smooth rather than having three raised sections as found on the open body.

Due to its body type the Hardtop Dispatcher was dimensionally larger than the other Dispatchers. All were mounted on the 80 inch Jeep wheelbase. The open and soft top models measured 57.125 inches in width with the Hardtop bodies extending to 72.75 inches. The open body was the shortest of the Dispatchers measuring 126.5 inches. The Hardtop had an overall length of 129 inches with the Convertible just an inch longer. The various distinctions between the three Dispatchers also accounted for their weight variations. The open model was the lightest with a shipping

weight of 1709 pounds followed by the Convertible at 1769 pounds. The Hardtop, as expected, was the heaviest at 2004 pounds.

The Dispatcher's interior was austere but, like that of other Jeep's, extremely functional. A column-mounted shift lever was used and did not look out of place keeping company with the classic black three-spoke Jeep steering wheel. All instrumentation was enclosed within a single circular dial with the manual choke and main light switch on each side. Mounted in the dash center was an old friend of veteran Jeep drivers, the L-shaped emergency brake handle. The ignition and starter switch were incorporated into a single unit.

Since the Dispatcher was a 2-wheel drive vehicle, intended for less vigorous use than the Universal Jeep, its undercarriage differed in numerous ways. At the front a Clark Model 130097, Reverse Elliot axle was used providing 6.9375 inches of road clearance. Hydraulic double action shock absorbers that measured 11.4375 inches and thus were slightly longer than those used on 4-wheel drive models were installed. The 36.25 × 1.75 inches dimensions of the DJ-3A springs

120

were identical to those of the CJ. However, they consisted of three instead of ten leaves and were rated at 95 lb./in. instead of 269 lb./in. as were the CJ's. A similar situation existed at the rear where 42 × 1.75 inches springs with three leaves were used. Their load capacity was 450 pounds. The DJ rear shocks measured 12.9375 inches as compared to the 10.75 inch units found on the CJ. The DJ used a Spicer Model 23 rear axle with a ratio of 4.56:1. Ground clearance was 6.9375 inches and the Powr-Lok differential was optional. The Dispatcher frame was essentially that of other Jeep models but the K-member was replaced by a straight cross-member.

The Dispatcher's brakes measured nine inches in diameter as did those of the CJ. But with slightly larger shoes the DJ had 132.1 sq.in. of area as compared to the CJ's 117.8 sq.in. Kelsey-Hayes steel disc 15 × 4.00J wheels were used along with 4.60 × 15 tires for which Willys specified a 27 pound inflation level. The parking brake operated on the rear service brake rather than on the rear propeller shaft as on the 4-wheel drive Jeep.

For any experienced Jeep owner a look under the Dispatcher hood was a peek at an old friend since it used the ever-faithful 4-cylinder 134.2 cubic inch L-head. There were a few items unique to the DJ. It used a different model AC fuel pump (number 1539716) as well as a different Carter carburetor, a Model YF-2392S, and an AC wire gauge air cleaner rather than the oil bath type found on the CJ.

The DJ used the same Auburn or Rockford single dry plate clutch as the CJ-3A and 3B models with a larger 9.5 inch Auburn model optional. Engine power was transmitted through a Warner T96

transmission with ratios of 2.605:1, 1.630:1 and 1.0:1. The reverse ratio was 3.536:1.

Another point of interest found on the DJ was the location of the fuel tank which was moved from its time-honored position under the seat to the right-side of the rear body panel.

Willys touted the DJ as a vehicle whose low initial cost was matched by its low cost of upkeep. It offered, said Willys, "ruggedness and dependability characteristic of the built-in stamina for which the Willys 'Jeep' Family of vehicles are noted the world over ... It fills the need for a 2-wheel drive vehicle that will really take punishment.

Production of the Dispatcher continued until 1973. By any account this was a respectable achievement that expanded the Jeep's appeal to a new class of customers who didn't need the CJ's go-anywhere ability, but who appreciated its virtues of simple design and reliability.

One Dispatcher user, the Package Delivery Service of Toledo, Ohio reported in 1956 that their Dispatcher had an operating cost per mile of 1.47 cents. This compared to an average of 4.09 cents per mile for

The long wheelbase CJ-6 model. (Courtesy of author's collection)

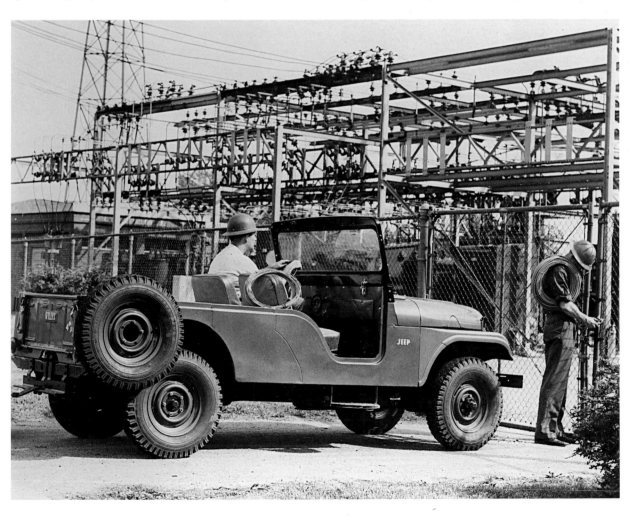

the one ton delivery models that were replaced by the Dispatcher. The company's president reported that "This comparison in operating expense was made during the three toughest months of the year in our work, December, January, and February. During this period we had no mechanical failures of any kind with the Dispatcher. It keeps traction well in deep snow and on ice. Its ease of handling in traffic is wonderful.

"So in referring to the 'Jeep' Dispatcher as an answer to a problem in light delivery work, we have to term it a 'Rugged Little Individual', and tops in economy."

dropped from four to five percent, to under one percent. Strong dealers with high volume operation were able to survive. But the low volume independents couldn't hold on. That's when we decided to leave the passenger car market to the high volume companies."

The Camper feature added to the Jeep's versatility. (Courtesy of author's collection)

The Jeep Universal Camper option. (Courtesy of author's collection)

The popularity of the CJ–5, a policy of avoiding costly annual model changes in favor of incorporatng improvements into the current model on a regular basis plus the successful introduction of the Forward Control models in late 1956 were key factors in Willys' ability to have profitable operations after the end of automotive production in 1955. As reported in *The Iron Age* magazine for 12 June, 1958, Kaiser and Willys passenger car operations lost $27 million in 1953 and $35.5 million in 1954. In 1955 profits from the sale of Jeep models was $4.6 million. The next year they moved up to just over $5 million. In 1958, a bad year for the automotive industry overall, Jeep sales volume was down only some 6 percent which compared favorably with a drop of approximately 40 percent for the entire commercial vehicle field. Reviewing the situation back in 1954 that lead directly to the decision to get out of the passenger car field, Mr. Cruse Moss, Willys Sales Corporation vice president, told *The Iron Age* that late in the fall of 1954 "Ford introduced 'giveaway sales techniques and dealer profits

Interior appointments of the Camper. (Courtesy of author's collection)

The CJ–5 had no difficulty in carrying the Camper to off-road sites. (Courtesy of author's collection)

The Camper was relatively easy to separate from the CJ–5. (Courtesy of author's collection)

122

Introducing:

America's Lowest Priced

DELIVERY VEHICLE

MODEL DJ 3A
HARDTOP

**THE
2-WHEEL DRIVE** `Jeep` *Dispatcher*→
™

MODEL DJ 3A
CONVERTIBLE TOP

WILLYS . . . MAKERS OF THE WORLD'S MOST USEFUL VEHICLES

The DJ-3A Hardtop Dispatcher. (Courtesy of author's collection)   The DJ-3A Convertible. (Courtesy of author's collection)

This philosophy had numerous ramifications. One was the development of specialty-type Jeeps such as the Dispatcher and the Forward Control Trucks. Another result was the offering of limited-production versions of the CJ-5 and DJ-3A that in retrospect appear as important steps in the evolution of the Jeep from strictly a workhorse to a recreational vehicle.

During 1959 Willys produced a small batch of 2-wheel drive DJs, known as the Jeep Gala, with a fancy pink and white striped top, matching upholstery and white sidewall tires for use by the Las Brisas resort hotel in Acapulco. This wasn't the largest special order ever processed by Willys but it suggested that another niche existed for the Jeep that was large enough to pursue. Reflecting on Willys' success in responding to this type of opportunity, Willys Motors president Steve A. Girard explained, "We're pretty much of a specialized builder. We don't make just one standard Jeep or truck or station wagon. We'll build just about any kind of body to suit the customer."

In 1960 this attitude was manifested by the introduction of the Jeep

Surrey. By this time most Americans were familiar with Jeeps in colors other than olive-drab. But the Surry took this liberated view a good deal further since it was available in three exterior finishes: Delicate Pink, Pastel Blue and Pastel Green. The front wheel wells were painted white as were the grille, windshield frame and the Willys lettering on the side of the engine hood.

Whitewall, 6.40 × 15, four-ply tubeless tires were standard as were

The Convertible DJ-3A had a sporty profile. (Courtesy of author's collection)

A rear view of a DJ-3A Hardtop with the optional exterior step pad installed. (Courtesy of author's collection)

The jaunty Jeep Gala. (Courtesy of author's collection)

125

- EXCITINGLY ORIGINAL, DIFFERENT, PRACTICAL
- THE 'SURREY' WITH THE FRINGE ON TOP
- CREATED FOR CAREFREE BUSINESS-PLEASURE TRANSPORTATION
- PERFECT FOR ECONOMICAL DELIVERY SERVICE
- LOWEST INITIAL COST, LOWEST OPERATING COST

Jeep 'SURREY'
MODEL DJ3A

The DJ-3A Surrey was derived from the Gala model. (Courtesy of author's collection)

full size chrome hubcaps with two concentric rings and a circular center section finished in the body color. The rims were also body colored and a prominent "W" was positioned in the hub center. Large chrome bumpers identical to those used on other Jeep models were also installed on the Surrey.

The real attention-getter of the Surrey was its candy striped top and seats which had white stripes alternating with body colored stripes. These styling features blended surprisingly well with the timeless lines of the DJ body as did the Surrey's continental tire mount with its candy striped cover. In a jesture to the origins of its name, the Surrey was equipped with a pair of leather hood straps angled downward from the top windshield corners to the front fenders. In time-honored Jeep tradition, the Surrey had roll-down side curtains in the same color scheme as the top.

With a price of $1650 the Surrey was, with the exception of the $1367 Dispatcher, the lowest priced Jeep model available. "We don't regard the Surrey as a big mass production vehicle", said Girard. "But it does represent part of the continual updating of our overall Jeep line. And the world-wide market, we feel, will make it quite an item."

In addition to resort hotels which either included use of a Surrey in their basic charges to clients or offered them for an additional fee,

Tropical Motors on the island of St. Thomas rented them to tourists for $8.80 a day.

Beyond sales to these customers Willys envisioned the market for the Surrey to include architects, specialty shops, country clubs, candy stores, dress shops and liquor stores. It also hoped that it would be regarded as a low-cost sporty car for recreational use.

With its 2-wheel drive and 60 horsepower engine the Surrey, said Willys, would "save money every mile". Furthermore, added Willys, the Surrey "costs less than any competitive American-built vehicle. Easy on gas, it needs only a minimum of maintenance, costs little to operate. Famous Jeep construction means more service miles, higher resale value."

A 4-wheel drive counterpart of the Surrey was the Tuxedo Park model of 1961. It was essentially the CJ-5 with dress-up items such as chromed hood hinges, exterior mirror supports and bumpers, turbine wheels, whitewall tires, spare tire cover and new color combinations. Willys offered a "Parade Blue Convertible Top and Accessory Kit" for the Tuxedo Park Mark II in March, 1962. Parade blue was a new color for the Jeep and it was used for the kit's convertible top, hood and spare tire cover. All of these items were also treated with a "Scotchguard" process for color fastness and stain resistance. This kit, which retailed for $130.20, was also available for other CJ-5 Jeeps.

The Tuxedo Park remained available through the 1966 model year. In its final form it had variable rate springs for a smoother ride and was available in five new exterior colors. Along with the Universal CJ–5 the Tuxedo Park had new foam padded seats in 1966.

By the mid-sixties Jeep no longer had the American market for 4-wheel drive vehicles to itself. One of its earliest foreign rivals was the British Land-Rover which had entered production in 1948. The 100,000th Land-Rover was built in late 1954 and in April, 1954 Land-Rover production passed the 500,000 mark. In contrast, the 500,000th postwar Jeep had been built on 23 February, 1954.

It was no secret that the Jeep had been the inspiration for the Land-Rover. In his excellent volume, *The Land-Rover: Workhorse of The World*, (published by David and Charles, 1976) Graham Robson wrote, in regard to the work done on the first Land-Rover, "The designers are adamant that nothing in a production Land-Rover was exactly copied from the Jeep, but they all admit to looking very carefully at every detail, and being encouraged to do so."

Like many other British vehicles of the time the Land-Rover was intended for export and well over 70 percent of its production, by the mid-seventies, had been sold in foreign markets. Surprisingly, the Land-Rover had only modest success in America where its peak year was 1965 when 1840 were imported.

But gaining a strong following in the United States were 4-wheel drive models such as the Toyota Land Cruiser and the Nissan Patrol from Japan. The basic specifications of these two models was as follows:

	Nissan Patrol	Toyota Land Cruiser
Wheelbase	86.6 in.	90.0 in.
Width	66.5 in.	65.6 in.
Length	148.5 in	152.4 in.
Height	78 in.	76 in.
Engine	6 cyl./ohv	6 cyl./ohv
Displacement	242 cubic inches	237 cubic inches
Horsepower	135 @ 3400 rpm	138 @ 4000 rpm

Meanwhile, several American companies were also becoming aware that the market for off-road, 4-wheel drive was growing far beyond its original bounds. In 1961 International Harvester entered the recreational/utility vehicle field with its Scout. Four years later the first Ford Bronco was announced.

Initially the Scout was available with just one engine, a 152 cubic inch 4-cylinder with 94.3 horsepower. Beginning in 1965 the Scout was offered with an optional turbocharger that raised output to 113 horsepower. The following year a 155 horsepower, 267 cubic inch V-8 as well as a 195 cubic inch 4-cylinder with 110 horsepower were available.

Ford's 1966 Bronco had a standard 170 cubic inch 6-cylinder with 105 horsepower. A 200 horsepower, 289 cubic inch V-8 was optional.

That these developments placed the standard CJ–5 with its 75 horsepower F-head at a disadvantage in acceleration was evident by the results attained by varous publications testing the Jeep and its competitors. For example, Tom McCahill's test of a Bronco in *Mechanix Illustrated*, September, 1965, resulted in a zero to 60 mph time of 15.8 seconds. *Popular Science*, August, 1965 reported that its Nissan Patrol test vehicle needed only 11 seconds for the same acceleration run. A turbocharged Scout that was part of a *Popular Science* four vehicle test also did well with a 13.2 second time. Indeed, the only participant in this evaluation that was slower than the CJ–5 was the Land-Rover which needed 28.4 seconds. The CJ–5's time was 24.0 seconds.

Many long-time Jeep drivers were quick to correctly point out that

off-road driving seldom called for a zero to 60 mph run and that under those conditions the CJ–5 did just fine with 75 horsepower. But this sentiment ignored both the change occurring in the utility vehicle field where many buyers were using their cars for every-day driving where good acceleration did matter as well as the numerous Jeep owners who had installed more powerful engines in their CJs.

To be sure, Jeep was still doing very well in both the domestic and international markets. In 1964 Kaiser Jeep and its affiliates built approximately 257,000 vehicles which was 42 percent more than the 181,000 cars built in Kaiser-Frazer's best year in 1948. In the U.S. 1964 output was 120,830, as compared to 110,457 vehicles built in 1963. Jeep registrations had also held up fairly well. In 1964 they totalled 44,385 which was virtually unchanged from the 44,339 level of 1963.

But the rising tide of the utility market clearly wasn't lifting Jeep sales at an equivalent rate. As a means of strengthening Jeep sales, a V-6 engine option was offered beginning in 1966.

The origin of this engine, at least in terms of being regarded as an offspring of an aluminum 215 cubic inch V-8, dated back to two General Motors show cars of 1951; the XP–300 and the LeSabre. Both cars had the desired effect of demonstrating General Motors' styling and engineering prowess. Powering the XP–300 and LeSabre was a 215 cubic inch V-8 of very compact size with numerous aluminum components including the cylinder block, crankcase and heads; a Rootes-type supercharger and a 10.0:1 compression ratio. Total weight was just 350 pounds and a maximum horsepower output of 335 was achieved.

In the meantime, another aluminum V-8, originally developed by GM Engineering (the LeSabre/XP–300 engine was a Buick project from start to finish) progressed to the point where, in 1958, it was transferred to Buick. At that time it was approved for use in the Oldsmobile and Buick compact cars scheduled for introduction in 1961.

In that form the aluminum engine had a checkered career. It was compact and at only 324 pounds, lightweight. Its peak horsepower rating in 1961 was a respectable 185 at 4800 rpm. But the high cost of building this engine, which was standard for the Buick Special and optional for the Oldsmobile F–85, as well as corrosion and reliability problems forced Buick to consider a less expensive alternative engine design.

The eventual solution was a V-6, that while based on the aluminum V-8, was of cast iron construction. In time this V-6 evolved into another V-8 which would still be in production in the 1970s. By 1965 the V-6, with a 3.75 inch bore and 3.40 inch stroke, displaced 225 inches and had ratings of 155 horsepower at 4400 rpm and 225 lb.ft. of torque at 2400 rpm. Buick was planning to drop this engine at the end of the 1967 model year and was more than happy to supply them to Kaiser Jeep beginning in 1965. In fact, it was eager to sell the entire manufacturing line to Kaiser after production of its 1967 models ended.

This proved to be an extremely wise acquisition by Kaiser. By 1968 over 75 percent of all Jeeps were being ordered with the "Dauntless" V-6 and the total cost in both plant and equipment for Kaiser Jeep Corporation to produce the V-6 totalled less than $6 million which was just a fraction of the cost to General Motors for its development. Perhaps of even greater importance was the savings in time acquisition of this engine represented for Kaiser. Joseph Geschell, the Detroit editor of *Automotive Industries* reported in that journal's 1 August, 1968 issue that "the availability of this equipment has allowed Kaiser Jeep Corporation to begin building its own V-6s about two years earlier than could be expected."

To assure a steady supply of V-6 engines Kaiser constructed a

100,000 sq.ft. building adjacent to the Jeep Universal assembly plant at its 230 acre facility in Toledo. A production rate of 30 engines a day provided sufficient volume both for Kaiser Jeep's needs and to fill orders from original equipment manufacturers for the boating industry.

Years later, when American Motors owned Jeep and the V-6 had been dropped from the Jeep line-up, Buick repurchased the V-6 engine line from AMC. During the later seventies it was produced in both 196 and 231 cubic inch form and installed in Buicks as well as in other General Motors cars.

Beginning in 1978 when a turbocharged version was offered for the Buick Century this engine emerged as one of the premier American performance engines of the post-fuel crisis era. In 1987 it reached its pinnacle in the Buick Grand National and the even more powerful Buick GNX.

Kaiser Jeep identified the V-6 version of the CJ–5 as Model 8305–A as compared to the 4-cylinder 8305 designation. In several areas besides their engines the two CJ–5 models had different specifications as the following indicates:

	8305	8305–A
Cooling System	11 gal.	9 gal.
Clutch Diameter	9.25 in.	10.4 in.
Front Spring Rate	240 lb./in.	176 lb./in.
Rear Spring Rate	200 lb./in.	230 lb./in.
Curb Weight	2274 lbs.	2336 lbs.

The changes in the spring rates for the 4-cylinder and V-6 models was accomplished by using 5-leaf front springs on the 4-cylinder and 10-leaf units on the V-6. Both versions used 5-leaf rear springs of a 2-stage design. No change was made in the Jeep's cam and lever steering but the V-6 powered CJ–5 had an overall ratio of 19.0:1 instead of the 17.9:1 ratio used on the 4-cylinder models. As in earlier years, the CJ–5, regardless of its engine, was available with optional heavy-duty springs and shock absorbers.

Kaiser Jeep also used the introduction of the V-6 option to make a few alterations in the Jeep's specifications. The most significant was the use of the single lever, dual range transfer case already installed on Jeep station wagons and trucks in place of the older unit with its front driving control lever. No changes were made in its ratios and provision was retained for a power take-off. In its full forward position the lever was in 2-wheel drive high range. Moving back one position engaged 4-wheel drive high, which was followed by neutral and 4-wheel drive low. It was not necessary to stop or slow down when shifting from 2-wheel drive high to 4-wheel drive high. Also enhancing the Jeep's overall driving performance were new brakes with a total effective area of 174 sq.in.

The CJs with V-6 engines had small identification shields placed below the JEEP lettering located on the lower body panel. All had new bucket seats made by the Bostrom Corporation of Milwaukee, Wisconsin which used a new process to incorporate the frame, springs and foam cushions into a single unit. This was accomplished by pouring polyurethane foam into a mold containing the steel frame and springs. After being baked in a high-temperature oven the elements formed a one-piece molded seat. With the addition of vinyl outer surface the thin-wall seats were ready for the installation into a waiting CJ. Rounding out the features of the latest CJ were several new chromed appearance options and an expanded list of available body colors.

The added power of the V-6 engine resulted in the offering of a new

Jeep camper option in 1969. Although the camper would fit any CJ-5 Jeep manufactured since 1955, Kaiser Jeep strongly recommended that it be used only with Universal Jeeps powered by the V-6 engine and having a 4.88:1 axle ratio instead of the standard 3.73:1 ratio.

A 1970 Jeep Renegade I. (Courtesy of author's collection)

The camper attached to the Jeep via a hook-up that slipped into the CJ's rear body section. The camper's two-tone exterior was contemporary in appearance and accommodation was provided for four occupants. Among the standard convenience features was a kitchen with running water, built-in cabinets, stove and oven. Options included a 10,000 BTU heater, toilet, gas/electric refrigerator and another roof vent in addition to the single standard unit.

The CJ-5 was the first Jeep vehicle to reflect the influence of American Motors after Kaiser Jeep was acquired by AMC in 1970. This was manifested in the form of the Jeep Renegade II which AMC described as a "limited-edition model based on the famed 4-wheel drive Jeep Universal CJ-5." Jeffrey C. Williams, Jeep's sales manager, explained that the Renegade II was "designed to meet the most exacting tastes of the 4-wheel drive enthusiast. It incorporates custom touches that permit Jeep owners to express their individuality in off-road events." The Renegade II was offered only in a "Big Bad Orange" body color (originally introduced during 1969 on the Javelin and AMX models) with charcoal striping. Its standard equipment included a roll bar and a tachometer.

Although no changes were made in the CJ-5 Jeep for 1971, it participated in a general price reduction that lowered the price of some Jeeps as much as $110. The CJ-5's price change, and that of the CJ-6 was as follows:

	1970 Price	1971 Price
CJ-5	$2930	$2886
CJ-6	$3026	$2979

It was apparent, in spite of AMC's heavy losses in 1971, that it planned major revisions in the CJ design for 1972. Overall, the company lost considerable money ($56.2 million for the fiscal year) in 1971 due to a five week strike at the start of the model year, a decline in the economy which affected the demand for domestic automobiles and rapid increases in the costs of labor and raw materials.

Also causing a drag upon AMC's financial performance were the costs involved in assimilating Jeep into American Motors' corporate structure. But by the fourth quarter Jeep operations were profitable and AMC told its stockholders that "Jeep can and will be a major profit contributor to American Motors."

"There are a number of reasons why Jeep has considerable potential", continued AMC, "Its commercial vehicle lines are well engineered and well known. What has been lacking is the kind of complete program combined companies are now in a position to carry out – research to gain specific market information, then product development and aggressive merchandising and sales programs based on reasonable assessments of what buyers of 4-wheel drive vehicles require."

The changes made in the entire Jeep line for 1972 dramatically demonstrated that AMC intended to carry through on that strategy. Many long-time Jeep enthusiasts, since they regarded the CJ-5 as the living link with the Jeep's origins, were prone to regard any change with suspicion.

One source of their concern had been the X001 experimental Jeep 129

built in 1970 by AMC's Jeep stylists. It rode on an unchanged CJ-5 chassis but its plastic body was a radical departure from traditional Jeep lines.

Any fear on the part of the Jeep faithful that AMC was about to tamper with the basic CJ-5 design was allayed when they viewed the 1972 CJ-5. Yet, that familiar form contained some of the most sweeping changes made in the CJ-5 since the original model debuted in 1955. The most dramatic of these was the elimination not only of the V-6 engine but the F-head 4-cylinder from the CJ's engine line-up. The F-head was still available for export but now standard for the U.S. market was American Motors' 232 cubic inch 6-cylinder engine developing 100 horsepower at 3600 rpm (beginning in 1972 all AMC horsepower and torque ratings were net figures) and 185 lb.ft. of torque at 188 rpm. This was not an unexpected development since AMC engines had been carried as options for the Wagoneer and Gladiator models since early 1971.

Inset: **The Renegade II was first displayed at the 1971 Detroit Auto Show. (Courtesy of author's collection)**

What was a bit startling was not just the offering of AMC's larger 258 cubic inch 6-cylinder engine with 110 horsepower at 3500 rpm and 195 lb.ft. of torque at 2000 rpm as a CJ option but the availability as well of the AMC 304 cubic inch V-8. This was the first V-8 engine ever installed at the factory in a CJ and the impact of its 150 horsepower at 4200 pm and 245 lb.ft. of torque upon the CJ-5's performance was profound. *Motor Trend*, after conducting a major test of the latest CJ-5 and its various power combinations, reported in its August, 1972 issue that "The 304 V-8 is naturally the best of the lot. It gives the Jeep new speed over rough land and makes climbing hills an enjoyable experience rather than a heart-rendering disappointment."

A V-8 powered 1972 Jeep Renegade. (Courtesy of author's collection)

All CJ-5 Jeeps, regardless of their engine had as standard equipment a new all-synchromesh 3-speed Warner T-14A transmission and a larger (10.5 inch diameter instead of 9.25 inch diameter) clutch. Both 6-cylinder engines could also be joined to a Warner T-18 4-speed gearbox with a non-synchromesh first gear. Its low gear ratio of 4.02:1 was reassuring to Jeep fans that AMC had no intention of reducing the CH-5's ability to traverse the most difficult of off-road terrain. It should be noted though, that the transfer case used for 1972, a Dana Model 20, had a 2.03:1 low range in place of the 2.46:1 ratio found on the earlier models. The standard axle ratio remained 3.73:1 with 4.27:1 optional.

The use of these new components necessiated a lengthening of the CJ-5 chassis. Wheelbase was increased three inches to 84 inches while overall length moved up to 142 inches from 135.6 inches. All of this additional length was located behind the engine hood. The front and rear track were also increased outward by 3.1 and 1.5 inches respectively. They now measured 51.5 inches (front) and 50.0 inches (rear). At the same time the CJ-5's turning circle was reduced to 32.9 feet from 35 feet. Credit for this improvement was due to the new Dana 30 front axle which replaced the open-end ball joint Dana 20 unit

The CJ-5 was extensively redesigned in 1973. (Courtesy of author's collection)

A pair of 1972 Renegades exercising.
(Courtesy of author's collection)

A 1973 CJ-5 with the optional
304 cid V-8. (Courtesy of author's collection)

133

previously installed on the CJ-5. No change was made in the design of the CJ-5's semi-floating rear axle but a new version was used with a 3000 pound capacity instead of the older model's 2500 pound capacity.

Replacing the cam and lever steering which had been used on the CJ-5 since its introduction in 1955 was a recirculating ball system with a slower, 24.1:1, ratio that increased turns lock-to-lock while reducing steering effort. Even more significant as an example of American Motors' influence upon the design of the CJ-5 was the availability of Saginaw power steering with a ratio of 17.5:1 as an option.

Both 6-cylinder and V-8 engined CJ-5s had larger brakes measuring 11 × 2 inches for 1972 as compared to the 10 × 2 inch linings used in 1971. These provided 180.8 sq.in. of effective lining area. At least receiving an equal amount of applause from veteran Jeep owners was the CJ-5's 16.5 gallon capacity fuel tank which gave the CJ a much longer cruising range than did the old 10.5 gallon tank.

Although it was difficult to detect the greater length of the new CJ, it wasn't difficult to discover many of the interior revisions for 1972. While it was an option, a new fixed tailgate alternative to the standard drop-down version allowed the spare tire to be mounted on the Jeep's rear. This was popular with owners who found the side-mounted spare a bother in close-quarter, off-road conditions. Also new for 1972 were optional gauges for the oil pressure and ammeter. When installed they were located on the left-side of the dash-board. Although it didn't exactly suggest that the Jeep was becoming a genteel-type of vehicle, the availability of an ashtray on a CJ must have elicited a smile or two from drivers who had ground out thousands of cigarettes on their Jeep's floorboards. Cast in the same mold were such new options as a cigarette lighter, wheel covers for 15 inch wheels, an improved Whitco vinyl top and a more efficient heater.

But on the other hand, who could have mourned the passing of the Jeep's floorboard-mounted clutch and brake pedals? Not many trips through puddles and the resulting stream of cold water hitting the driver on his legs were needed to have a Jeep owner fall in love with the 1972 CJ's cowl-suspended pedals.

Additional changes for 1972 included a longer handle for the transfer case and a foot-operated parking brake. Another change that was not apparent but was significant was the abandonment of the old "Universal" label for the Jeeps. They were now identified simply as CJ models.

Prices for the CJ-5, CJ-6 and DJ-5 and representative options for 1972 were as follows:

CJ-5	$2955
CJ-6	$3045
DJ-5	$2475
Free-wheeling hubs	$98
Power steering	$148
Power brakes	$46
Limited slip rear differential	$62
Oil and ammeter gauges	$17
Heavy duty frame	$20
Heavy duty springs and shock absorbers	$39
Front passenger bucket seat	$74
Split front bench seat	$89
Rear bench seat	$92
55 amp alternator	$28
70 amp battery	$12
Cigarette lighter	$7
Draw bar	$28
Padded instrument panel	$38

Fuel tank skid panel	$10
Sun visors	$14
258 cid engine	$56
304 cid engine	$130

After the many changes introduced into the CJ-5 design in 1972 and the development of Quadra-Trac for the 1973 Wagoneer and truck models, it wasn't surprising that the 1973 CJ-5 was basically a slightly more refined version of the 1972 model.

The question of just how much change the CJ owners, both of the present and future variety, wanted in their Jeeps was the basis of an interview of AMC board chairman Roy Chapin by Bill Sanders, editor of *Four Wheelin'* magazine which was published in its November, 1972 issue. Responding to that matter, Chapin said: "When American Motors took over Jeep, dealers pleaded with us not to make *any* changes in the CJ-5. We agreed to that request, and since the CJ-5 is built to over specifications now, I don't think we will be making any changes in the CJ-5 in the near future. We did widen the front tread and lengthen it in 1972 to allow the V-8 to fit in, but other than that, we don't foresee any major changes."

To be sure, some changes were to be found in the 1973 CJ-5 but they were definitely of the evolutionary type, intended to improve the Jeep's basic design rather than to alter its fundamental character. Seeking to reassure buyers that this was the situation, the sales brochure for the 1973 CJ-5 noted, after listing some of the new features for 1973, "But don't worry. The Jeep is, deep down, the same basic vehicle it has always been. We keep making it better – not different."

Now included in the CJ-5's standard equipment was the fuel skid plate. The U-joints for the front axle and drive shaft were strengthened for an extended service life. AMC also installed upgraded standard tires on the 1973 CJ5. Whereas in 1972 the base tire was a 7.35 × 15, four-ply, the latest model was fitted with F78 × 15, four-ply tires.

Additional technical changes included induction-hardened exhaust valves for the 6-cylinder engine (which for 1973 was designed to operate on regular, low-lead gasoline of 91 octane or higher), a mechanical linkage in place of the decades-old cable clutch linkage design and an all-new standard two-speed windshield wiper system with an integrated washer system.

All dash panel control knobs were of a "soft feel" design with international-code symbols. The gauges had improved green lighting as well as flame orange, instead of white colored, needles. The instrument cluster as well as the optional oil and ammeter gauges (which were located on each side of the primary instrument dial) were surrounded by bright ring moldings. Also easy to spot was the new position of the parking brake which was moved from behind the steering wheel to the left-side of the dashboard. The heater controls now had a separate fan toggle switch and black and white "Standout" knobs. For the first time a factory installed roll bar was offered.

The base price of the 1973 CJ-5, CJ-6 and DJ-5 as well as those for major options was as follows:

Product	Price
CJ-5	$3086
CJ-6;	$3176
DJ-5	$2606
Heavy duty cooling system	$25.60
Draw bar	$26.80
Power steering	$143.25
Semi-automatic hubs	$59.80

Heavy duty frame	$18.90
Heavy duty 51 amp alternator	$26.75
Track-loc 3.73:1 rear axle	$59.40
4-speed trans.	$107.30
H78–15 polyglas Suburban tires	$81.10
258 cid engine	$53.85
Heavy duty springs and shocks	$37.60
Oil and amp gauges	$16.65
Cigarette lighter	$8.65
Dual sun visors	$13.55
Front passenger seat	$72.10
Rear bucket seats	$89.35
Front passenger safety bar	$6.85
Padded instrument panel	$31.90
Roll bar	$54.65

Beginning in January, 1973 the Jeep Renegade became a regular Jeep model. Included in its long list of standard features was the 304 cubic inch V-8, roll bar, specially styled wheels, H78–15 Whitewall tires, blackout hood, side body racing stripe with Renegade lettering, fender extensions, transmission skid plate, oil and ammeter gauges, dual exterior mirrors, dual visors, custom vinyl interior and rear-mounted spare.

Later in the model year another limited-production model CJ-5, the Super Jeep, was offered. It was easily identified by its wildly curving red, white and blue striping which swept off the hood, down the lower body and then up and over the rear wheels to circle the rear deck. Along the way it also became star-studded. A similar, but abbreviated, rim theme was placed on the front fenders.

The Super Jeep's standard equipment included vertically striped front and rear seats, 258 cubic inch 6-cylinder engine, rubber lip extensions on the fenders, chrome front bumper and a passenger safety rail.

The attention grabber of the 1974 Jeep line was the all-new Cherokee. In contrast the CJ-5, since it looked exactly like it had in 1973, seemed to be the perfect example of the carry-over model. But this conclusion really was the result of a superficial examination of the latest CJ-5 since it was the recipient of numerous refinements and improvements.

Leading the list was the use of induction-hardened exhaust valve seats on the 304 cubic inch V-8. All CJ Jeeps had stronger body-to-chassis mounts, a higher output heater and optional bumpers that met the government's 5 mph standard. No engine changes were made except those needed to conform to evaporative and exhaust emission standards for utility vehicles that went into effect for the 1974 model year. Providing a higher degree of braking performance was a system with new linings, master cylinders and, for the first time on the CJs, proportioning valves.

For 1975 AMC told potential Jeep buyers that "The spirited Jeep CJ-5 is what the fun of 4-wheel driving is really all about. Bold, sporty styling ... and under that paint job – 30 years of tough, brawny dependability to back it up. Jeep CJ-5 ... the fun machine that invented back road excitement." Descriptions such as that usually were verbal camouflage hiding a reality in which nothing of consequence had been changed from the previous year. But as far as the CJ-5 was concerned it was simply a statement of fact. There were many changes for 1975 and for the most part they made the CJ-5 more of a Jeep than ever while providing a few new niceties.

Certainly placed in the former category was the CJ-5's stronger frame with increased gauge steel in the side rails. Giving the Jeep a

good dose of fun tonic was the new Levi's seat trim option. This weather-resistant vinyl interior was installed on the 1975 Renegade as well as being available for the base CJ-5 model. With classic Levi's stitching it was offered in either blue or tan and covered the front and rear seats, instrument panel pad and padded sun visors. All CJ models had new Jeep lettering on the cowl side. On models so equipped, a Levi's decal was positioned above the Jeep name. In addition, the CJ-5 designation also found on the cowl side was moved to a point just below the passenger side front directional signal on CJ's with the Levi's package. A new black or white Whitco top was, for the first time, a factory option. It remained, as in previous years, a dealer-installed option. It was available in blue or tan when ordered with the Levi's package.

Another first for the CJ was the availability of a factory-installed AM, radio. It was mounted below the instrument panel and had a plastic weatherproof case and was connected to a fixed-length whip-type antenna. For the first time a passenger-side sun visor and bucket seat were standard for the CJ Jeep.

The CJ Renegade had a new broad two-color hood tape stripe as well as two new exterior colors, Renegade Blue and Orange. With the exception of Green Apple and Reef Green, all 1975 Jeep colors were also available for the Renegade.

No changes were made in the CJ engine line-up but they were the only Jeep engines in 1975 to be fitted with catalytic converters. As a result they were required to use unleaded gasoline. Warning labels to this effect were placed on the instrument panel and near the fuel filler. Like all 1975 Jeep engines, those used for the CJs had electronic ignition systems. The CJ electrical system also incorporated an all-new, more reliable wiring harness with a dash connect plug permitting easier diagnosis and servicing. Also used on the 1975 CJs was an improved exhaust system with more effective mufflers. Six-cylinder engines had a modified intake manifold which enabled operation with a leaner air/fuel mixture. This resulted in improved fuel economy and better throttle response. Both the six-cylinder and V-8 engines had improved insulation which reduced heat input from the engine to the carburetor.

Unlike 1974 when a gauge package was an option for the CJs it was standard for all models in 1975. Replacing the ammeter was a voltmeter which showed the battery's condition and indicated if the alternator was functioning correctly.

New options included a "cold climate group" consisting of an engine block heater, 70 amp battery and a 62 amp alternator; a column-mounted tachometer and HR78-15 Whitewall radial tires.

Due to the higher income level of 4-wheel drive vehicle buyers, the Jeep market was not affected by the 1975 recession. As a result, domestic wholesale sales of 69,3000 Jeeps was just below the 1974 record level of 69,300. Jeep sales in Canada increased 11 percent over those of 1974. In spite of a strike at the Brampton plant early in 1975, AMC and Jeep dealers had their third-best sales year in history.

In April, 1975 the 400,000th Jeep vehicle built since American Motors' acquisition of Jeep in 1970 came off the assembly line. This achievement symbolized the success AMC had experienced in tailoring the Jeep to the changing nature of the 4-wheel drive recreational vehicle market. For 1976 this expertise was manifested by the introduction of the CJ-7.

This expansion of the CJ series coincided with the elimination of the CJ-6 from the Jeep line. The CJ-6 was never a strong seller in either the United States or Canada but it remained available for export.

It was obvious from the start that AMC had high hopes for the CJ-7 which is described as the "most exciting vehicle to hit the 4-wheel drive market in years". In comparison to the latest CJ-5 which retailed for $4199, the CJ-7's base price was $4299. Size-wise, the CJ-7 compared to the CJ-5 and the CJ-6 as follows:

Model	Wheelbase	Overall Length	Turning Diameter
CJ-5	83.5 in.	138.4 in.	33.5 ft.
CJ-6	93.5 in.	147.9 in.	35.9 ft.
CJ-7	104.0 in.	158.9 in.	37.6 ft.

The two CJ models were virtually identical in weight. The curb weight of the CJ-7 was, at 2750 pounds, just forty pounds greater than the CJ-5's.

The added weight of the CJ-7 provided more front and rear leg room as well as a wider, 33.8 inch, door opening. But unlike the CJ-6 whose main claim to fame was its extended length, the CJ-7 made Jeep history by being the first CJ available with both Turbo Hydra-Matic and the full-time Quadra-Track 4-wheel drive system. Also distinguishing the CJ-7 from the CJ-5 was its standard tailgate which was flush-mounted with a double-wall, dual-latch construction. A rear-mounted swing-away spare-tire carrier was optional.

Available only for the CJ-7 was a one-piece injection-molded structural polycarbonate removable hardtop with metal doors, vinyl door trim panels and roll-down windows. Color selections for this top were limited to black or white.

Installation of the 246 pound hardtop on the CJ-7 brought with it both advantages and disadvantages. For security-minded owners its lockable doors were a big plus, although their operations were contrary to those on most American cars. For example, if a door was locked by a key it had to be unlocked the same way. Similarly, a door locked by a push knob could be unlocked only by the push knob.

In terms of interior comfort there was no contest between a hardtop and soft top CJ-7. Jeeps of the latter variety were notorious for rain leaks, high noise levels and an assortment of roof parts flapping in the

AMC introduced blue or tan "Levi's" seat trim in 1975. (Courtesy of American Motors)

The 1975 CJ-5 was available with a factory-installed radio. (Courtesy of American Motors)

absorbers and a front frame tie bar. These components increased gross vehicle weight from 3750 pounds to 4150 pounds on both open or softtop models. Relative spring weights for the standard and optional suspensions were as follows:

	Standard	Optional
Front springs	170 lb./in.	170/230 lb./in.
Rear springs	185 lb./in.	185/250 lb./in.

As in 1975 the standard CJ transmission was an all-synchromesh 3-speed gearbox. For 1976 it was of a new design with a higher torque capacity. Although easier and smoother in operation it was also more durable than the older model because of its heavier gears, shafts and synchronizers.

Change in the CJ engine line was limited to the use of an electric-assist choke and exhaust gas circulation system on both 6-cylinder engines. Improving hot-engine starting on all engines was a new fuel return line.

Viewed from the front the 1976 CJ Jeeps were identified by their new folding windshields with screw-type hold-downs and inside-mounted windshield wiper motor. At the rear were higher-mounted and larger tail lights with integral back-up lights. These lights were rectangular rather than circular as on the older model.

The list of interior changes began with a more attractive steering wheel with two instead of three spokes that was installed on an energy absorbing steering column with an anti-theft ignition and steering lock. The dash panel was completely rearranged to allow for location of the optional radio and speaker within the panel instead of the under the dash installation used in 1975. If the extra-cost tachometer and "Rally" clock were ordered they were placed on each side of the steering column. The gauges for the engine temperature and ammeter were moved from their old locations just below the speedometer to its right-side.

Increasing leg room on the CJ-5 were new floor dash panels. Improving interior air circulation were redesigned defroster outlets. Replacing the old "fold and tumble" seat was a four-bar arrangement for the front passenger seat allowing the entire seat to move forward for easier entry to the rear of the vehicle.

New options offered for the CJ-5 and CJ-7 included a convenience group package consisting of courtesy lights, passenger side mirror, passenger assist handle, cigarette lighter, ash tray and eight-inch day/night mirror; decor group (rocker panel protecting molding, instrument panel pad and overlay, and sports steering wheel), full-foam ⅔-⅓ seat, indoor/outdoor carpeting, sports or leather-wrapped steering wheel and a front stabilizer bar.

The popular Renegade package was available for both the CJ-5 and CJ-7. When installed on a CJ-7 it included a rear swing-away spare tire carrier. A rear-mounted spare with a solid back panel was used for the CJ-5 Renegade. For the first time the following items were included in the Renegade package: under dash courtesy lights, eight-inch day/night mirror, sports steering wheel, instrument panel overlay and bright rocker panel protection molding between the front and rear wells.

wind. For purists this was part and parcel of CJ ownership. But the new breed of Jeep buyers, towards which the CJ-7 was directed, expected higher levels of creature comfort.

By no means, however, could it be suggested that a hardtop CJ-7 pampered its occupants. Plenty of rain still found its way into the Jeep's interior and with the arrival of the catalytic converter the insulated top tended to trap an inordinate amount of heat within its confines. Furthermore, removal of the hardtop wasn't likely to take place every sunny weekend since it involved the release of numerous hold-down bolts.

The Whitco full softtop for both the CJ-5 and CJ-7 was of a new design with improved visibility and larger door openings.

Both the CJ-5 and CJ-7 had new frames and suspensions. The springs followed the path of tradition with four leaf front and rear units. CJ-7's with the hardtop had higher gross weight ratings of 4150 pounds instead of the standard CJ-7's 3750 pounds rating due to their five leaf front and rear springs. The rear springs on all CJs were wider spaced than in 1974 due to the new frame of splayed side rail design which widened from front to rear. These changes, along with new shock absorbers, said AMC, "affords excellent lateral vehicle stability". Being depicted as minimizing "vibration and noise" were new body hold-down mounts.

Ranked as one of the new frame's most important features was its greatly increased bending strength and significantly greater torsional rigidity. Contributing to these were side rails with increased depth and, from the front to the fuel tank cross-member, the frame's full box-section construction. Integral with the frame were stronger cross-members and a combination cross-member skid plate for the engine, transmission and transfer case extending the full length of the vehicle. The fuel tank skid plate was continued as standard CJ equipment.

Available on all CJs was a new extra-duty suspension consisting of seven leaf, two-stage front and rear springs plus heavy-duty shock

137

The new CJ-7 introduced for 1976. (Courtesy of American Motors)

As in 1975, two hood tape stripe combinations were offered with the Renegade package – blue with orange and white accents or gold with brown and white accents. The Levi's seat trim in blue or tan with matching instrument panel and sun visors was again included in the Renegade package. It remained available as a separate option on models without the Renegade package.

American Motors observed its 75th anniversary in 1977 and unfortunately, sales of its passenger cars fell from the 1976 level. This was due mainly to a major swing in the market away from the subcompact car segment where most of AMC's cars were positioned. As a result, AMC's retail sales fell to 292,087 from 328,181 in 1976. But this decline was taking place at the same time when Jeep sales reached a record 95,718 units, up from 67,771 in 1975.

American Motors wasted no time on placing its new CJ-7 in competition. This CJ-7 participated in the November, 1975 Press-On-Regardless Rally. (Courtesy of author's collection)

The impact this popularity had upon Jeep's status at AMC was dramatic. In the six years since AMC acquired Jeep from Kaiser, production had been increased ten times, from 175 units a day to 560 on a two-shift basis. But even this level was insufficient to meet consumer demand. During the first three months of 1977 Jeep dealers sold 25,754 vehicles as compared to 20,581 delivered in the same 1976 period. Moreover, few Jeeps were of the bare bones variety. After visiting the Toledo plant, Jack Walsh, truck editor for *Automotive*

The Press-On-Regardless CJ-7 in concours form. (Courtesy of author's collection)

News, noted in its 25 April, 1977 issue: "Watching Jeep vehicles roll down the assembly line in Toledo, an observer will quickly note that few people want stripped vehicles. More than half of all vehicles have a special paint treatment or special stripes and decals." Specifically, 25 percent of CJ-5 and CJ-7 Jeeps built in 1977 had the Renegade package. Also very popular was the new Golden Eagle package for both the CJ Jeep and the J-10 trucks. Production began in January, 1977. The Golden Eagle CJ was priced less than $200 more than a comparably equipped Jeep Renegade and was available for softtop CJ-5 and CJ-7 models. All regular production options were available for a Golden Eagle CJ. The Golden Eagle package consisted of the following items: a single unique exterior color – Thrush Brown, gold black and white eagle decal on hood, Golden Eagle name on hood side in black lettering edged in gold, "Limited Edition" decal on grille panel, gold stripe on grille panel and 15 × 8 styled wheels, painted gold with a black accent stripe.

In addition, regular options included in the Golden Eagle package consisted of 9–15 Tracker RWL tires, rear mounted spare tire, Levi's tan mounted vinyl softtop, Levi's tan interior, roll bar, Levi's tan instrument panel pad, wheel lip extensions, spare tire lock, Convenience Group, Decor Group, black anodized rocker molding, tachometer and clock, and full, brown colored carpeting. By late April 2000 had been built and a second batch of 2000 were nearly completed. Of the plant's 560 vehicle daily output, 300 were CJ Jeeps.

A 1976 CJ-7. (Courtesy of author's collection)

The longer wheelbase of the CJ-7 did not detract from its handsome lines. (Courtesy of author's collection)

A 1976 CJ-7 with hard top. (Courtesy of author's collection)

A view of the 1976 CJ-7 which details the form of its roll bar. (Courtesy of author's collection)

The Golden Eagle option for the CJ Jeep was announced on 5 October, 1976. (Courtesy of author's collection)

Of the total U.S. 4-wheel drive market Jeep controlled 16 percent. This was impressive, but even more imposing was Jeep's sales performance in the recreational-utility segment where the CJ, Cherokee and Wagoneer accounted for nearly 40 percent.

Nineteen seventy-seven was also a year of "firsts" for the CJ Jeeps. For the first time they were available with air conditioning and front disc brakes. Neither of these were inexpensive. The air conditioning listed for $499. The power assisted disc brakes retailed for $73. They were also available without power assistance. Incorporation of air conditioning to the CJ body and the inclusion of air ducts in the CJ dash required the relocation of the ashtray to the upper dash section.

The hefty prices asked for these two options were tip-offs that the cost of acquiring a new CJ was on the way up. The time hadn't yet arrived when a CJ Jeep would carry a five digit sticker price but, in 1977, the price spiral was headed upward.

Representative prices of popular CJ options for 1977 are listed below:

Year	Base CJ-5 Price
1966	$2284
1967	$2361
1968	$2683
1969	$2823
1970	$2930
1971	$2886
1972	$2955
1973	$3086
1974	$3574
1975	$4099
1976	$4199
1977	$4399

Option	Price
304 V-8 engine	$140
258 6-cylinder engine	$73
Free-wheeling front hubs	$95
Power steering	$166
Center console	$62
AM radio	$73
Tachometer and rally clock	$73
Indoor/outdoor carpeting	$63
Whitco top	$275
Front stabilizer bar	$27
Steering damper	$10
Renegade package	$839

Added to the Renegade package in 1977 were 9.00 × 15 raised white letter Tracker A-T tires mounted on white-painted, styled steel spoke wheels highlighted by narrow red striping. Their use plus the introduction of the front 12-inch disc brakes was accompanied by adoption of a stronger front axle and wheel spindles. Also upgraded was the chassis which now was full boxed from the front to rear. Also of greater strength were the rear body panels.

No change was made in the CJ's standard 3-speed transmission which, it will be recalled, was of a new design for 1976. The CJ's optional 4-speed (for the 258 cubic inch six only) had a new internal gearset which changed its low gear ratio from 4.02:1 to 6.32:1.

As so often was the case, 1977 was a year of contrast for American Motors. Its passenger cars experienced a sales decline dropping from 292,087 units in 1976 to 226,640 in 1977. But the story was quite different for Jeep sales which for the American and Canadian markets reached 117,077 units in 1977.

The reason for Jeep's success was succinctly summed up by AMC: "Jeep is successful because the company has developed a range of choices for customers – not just vehicle types, but a growing list of comfort, convenience and appearance items. Jeep buyers increasingly want style and individuality to go with toughness and durability."

Although no dramatic changes were made in the basic CJ design. AMC's response to those demands was even more emphatic in 1978. All CJ models used a completely redesigned heater providing improved heat distribution especially to the rear seat region, higher defroster temperature and air-flow rate and improved outside fresh air ventilation.

Items previously optional for the CJ that were now standard included manual, front disc brakes, ash tray and cigarette lighter, passenger-side exterior mirror and H78 Suburbanite XG fiberglass-

A 1977 CJ-7 with Renegade package. (Courtesy of author's collection)

belted tires. A new underhood light was added to the Convenience Group and the seat and door panels were now flax, rather than buff colored.

No changes were made in the CJ engines except for the use of a new ambient air intake system which improved overall engine efficiency.

Available for all Jeep vehicles were 14 body colors including three new colors – Sun Orange, Golden Ginger Metallic, and Captain Blue Metallic. Other colors included Alpine White, Loden Green Metallic, Mocha Brown Metallic, Autumn Red Metallic, Oakleaf Brown, Brilliant Blue, Classic Black, Firecracker Red, Pewter Grey Metallic, Sand Tan and Sunshine Yellow.

The Golden Eagle package, which had been introduced in mid-1977, was again offered for the CJ in 1978. It was priced at $1249 and was again highlighted by a huge white, gold and black eagle decal on the hood. On each side of the hood was larger "Golden Eagle" black lettering outlined in gold. The Golden Eagle package also included special grille and body striping, black fender flares, gold anodized 15 × 9 steel spoke wheels and 9.00-15 LT Goodyear Tracker tires with raised gold lettering. In addition to these features the Golden Eagle option included most of the items of the Renegade package.

The following body colors were available for Golden Eagle equipped CJs: Loden Green Metallic, Mocha Brown Metallic, Oakleaf Brown, Alpine White, Sand Tan, Classic Black and Golden Ginger Metallic.

During the year AMC raised the price of all Jeeps by $100 as well as

The 1977 CJ-5. (Courtesy of author's collection)

the prices of selected options by an average of $29 per vehicle Therefore, the following prices may vary slightly from those actually paid by customers during 1978:

Model	Base Price
CJ-5	$5095
CJ-7	$5195

Option	Price
Golden Eagle Package	$1248
Renegade Package	$799
Hardtop	$610
Tachometer and clock	$77
Rear bench seat	$106
258 cubic inch engine (std. in CA)	$77
304 cubic inch engine	$186
4-speed manual trans. (258 engine)	$153
3-speed Turbo Hydra-Matic with Quadra-Trac	$366
Low range for Quadra-Trac	$145
Free-wheeling front hubs	$101
Limited slip differential (N.A. with Quadra-Trac)	$82
Power steering	$176
Power brakes	$73
Extra-duty suspension	$85
Front stabilizer bar	$29

In early March, 1978, AMC announced plans to convert its Brampton, Ontario plant over to the production of CJ Jeeps. The reason for this move was the continued slump in American Motors' passenger car sales (production of the Concord compact, which had taken place just at the Brampton plant was switched to Kenosha) and the concurrent growth in Jeep sales. Although this operation, which cost $4.8 million, wasn't completed until September, 1978, it added another 50,000 units to AMC's CJ production capacity. At the same time AMC increased production of Jeep vehicles at Toledo through overtime work beginning in July. This stop-gap response to customer demand was followed by plans to expand capacity at Toledo.

AMC's description of demand for 4-wheel drive vehicles as "surging" was almost modest. On 27 June, 1978, the 150,000th Jeep assembled in the 1978 model year, a CJ-7 Renegade, was driven off the assembly line by Ohio Governor James A. Rhodes. It was for good reason that AMC stockholders were told: "Jeep vehicles are a vital part of American Motors' automotive plans."

For the calendar year production totalled 153,000 units while sales, which at year's end had risen above year-ago levels for 37 consecutive months, increased to 161,912. Worldwide, wholesale unit sales of Jeeps increased to 180,667 from 153,485 in 1977 and 125,879 in 1976. This represented year-to-year gains of 17.7 percent and 21.9 percent respectively. At the end of the year there were 1999 Jeep dealers in the U.S. and Canada along with 1517 dealers selling both passenger cars and Jeeps.

Noting that the growth of the market for Jeeps and other competing vehicles had "exceeded all industry projections", AMC reported that "The familiar desire of people for something new and completely different – something with multi-purpose uses – gives the 4-wheel

144

The 1978 CJ-5 in open form. (Courtesy of author's collection)

A 1978 CJ-5 with a Whitco top. (Courtesy of author's collection)

A Golden Eagle equipped 1978 CJ-7. (Courtesy of author's collection)

drive market its long-term potential. The company is prepared to capitalize on that potential."

Overall, the domestic market for 4-wheel drive vehicles was expected to exceed one million units in 1979. In 1978 it had totalled 964,000. Of that market's sports-utility segment, CJ, Cherokee and Wagoneer models captured 34 percent.

The decidedly upbeat outlook this situation nurtured was emphasized by AMC President W. Paul Tippett Jr. at a press conference held in conjunction with the February, 1979 Geneva, Switzerland Automobile Show. "We have a project going", he said, "that will add fifty percent to the output of our main Toledo plant in Ohio by 1981 ... Put it together, and our output of Jeep vehicles will have increased from about 170,000 units a year in 1978 to more than 350,000 – and in just three years."

Tippett viewed this development as a "big change ... a bold response to what's happening. The 4-wheel drive market in the U.S. and Canada will go over a million units in 1979. It was 200,000 a few

years ago. And this is only the beginning. Basic life-style changes are behind this phenomenon, so it isn't likely to stop."

Since he was speaking to press representatives from a major export market, Tippett took this occasion to predict that "The same changes are waiting to happen in many overseas markets. We must have the vehicles to take advantage of that potential. The Jeep product line is the best known in the world."

American Motors' first quarter report to its stockholders elaborated on Tippett's comments concerning Jeep sales and plans to expand output. For the first quarter of the 1979 fiscal year it noted, "Jeep vehicle sales were a record 54,070 units, up from 38,091 the previous year ... The company can now benefit from record demand for Jeep vehicles. The main Jeep assembly plant at Toledo has been running at capacity for many months. The Brampton, Ontario plant, converted to Jeep assembly only six months ago, is on an overtime schedule, with demand outrunning that output. So this year, we will add a third Jeep plant to North American production by converting a portion of the Kenosha, Wisconsin, facilities to production of Jeep vehicles."

In addition to these actions AMC also was constructing a new $30 million paint facility at Toledo as part of a two-year expansion

The 150,000 Jeep vehicle built in 1978, a red CJ-7 Renegade, was driven off the Toledo assembly line by Ohio Governor James A. Rhodes with AMC president Gerald Meyers his passenger. (Courtesy of American Motors)

program that would provide a fifty percent increase in production capacity by early 1981. When completed, AMC said this operation would incorporate "the world's most advanced automotive painting technology." For example, before the bodies would receive a protective primer they would be given a negative electrical charge. Since the rust-resistent primer had a positive charge, it was attracted to the body by reverse polarity. After the bodies left the dip tank filled with primer they moved through a cleaning rinse before receiving a second coat of special primer which was sprayed on prior to application of three coats of finish enamel.

AMC's euphoric outlook of the future indicated that the difficulties that would soon confront the 4-wheel drive market appeared almost without warning. Yet the outlook in early 1979 was not entirely sanguine. One strong challenge took the form of Federal Government fuel economy regulations, which for CJ Jeeps required them to meet a standard of 15.8 mpg in 1979.

Complicating the engineer's task in achieving this goal were more stringent Federal emissions standards. To meet this mandate all CJs, along with all 1979 Jeeps, had catalytic converters, thus requiring the use of no-lead fuel. Contributing to improved fuel economy was a

weight reduction of approximately eighty pounds through the use of several lighter body and chassis components.

The standard engine for the CJ now was the 258 cubic inch 6-cylinder fitted with a 2-barrel carburetor. It was, along with the 304 V-8 (also equipped with a 2-barrel carburetor), available with the optional 4-speed manual transmission which had an upgraded shift tower and new shift pattern. No change was made in the standard CJ axle ratio which remained at 3.54:1. This did not mean that overall performance was unaltered from 1978 levels since both CJ engines were less powerful than the year-earlier versions. The 304 cubic inch V-8, for example, was rated at 130 horsepower, down 20 horsepower in just one year.

Both the Renegade and Golden Eagle Packages were revised for 1979 to, said Jeep, "enable CJ buyers to add individuality to both the interior and exterior of their vehicles." The Renegade package included a new exterior stripe design with varying widths in three graduated shades of either blue or orange with gold borders. Other new or revised features included painted spoke steel wheels and L78–15 white letter tires.

The Golden Eagle package continued to include most of the items from the Renegade package in addition to a tan denim grain top (this top was available for other CJs in either black or white vinyl or tan and blue denim), clock, full carpeting plus its all-ready famous hood decal and special body, fender and grille striping.

Available only for the Golden Eagle was an optional tan injection-

The 1979 CJ-5 with Golden Eagle package. (Courtesy of American Motors)

Bottom Left: A 1979 CJ-7 Renegade. (Courtesy of American Motors)

A CJ-5 for 1979 in its Renegade form. (Courtesy of American Motors)

molded hardtop with bronze tone tinted glass in the rear quarter and tailgate windows. A sunroof was also available for the hardtop.

All CJs had a new vinyl convertible top with cotton-polyester fabric backing that, promised Jeep, "provides significant design improvements, including better fit, strength and leak resistence". It was offered in blue, black, white and tan.

Jeep sales for AMC's fiscal year were a record 207,642 units compared to 180,667 the previous year. This measurement, however, disguised the impact growing concerns about gasoline supplies and rising prices had upon the automobile market beginning at mid-year. At that point Jeep wholesale sales were at 63,436, up 41 percent from the 44,944 sold in the previous year. Three months later the situation was mixed with AMC reporting: "Even though Jeep vehicle sales were lower in the quarter, sales of our smaller Jeep CJ's have held up well,

and Jeep vehicle sales for the full model year will be well above 1978s record level." But for the 1979 calendar year Jeep sales totalled 140,431 as compared to 161,912 in 1978.

Even so, the popularity of the CJ had been nothing short of sensational as evident by the following:

Vehicle	1979 Calendar Year Sales
Jeep CJ	74,878
Dodge Ramcharger	18,863
Ford Bronco	69,724
Chevrolet Blazer/GMC Jimmy	62,185
International Harvester Scout/ Traveler	24,269

To commemorate the 25th anniversary of the Nash-Kelvinator Corporation and Hudson Motor Company merger which created American Motors on 1 May, 1954, a special version of AMC's Concord DL sedan was announced in May 1979. At the same time a limited edition Silver Anniversary CJ-5 recognizing the 25th birthday of the CJ-5 was also introduced. Among its features was a Quick Silver Metallic finish, silver-toned Renegade accent striping, black soft top, black bucket seats with silver accents and a commemorative dash plaque.

Nonetheless, the rapid destabilization of the American fuel supply made it imperative that significant efforts be made to foster the Jeep's image as a fuel-efficient vehicle. Strongly suggesting that the situation was well in hand was the comment made in AMC's 1979 Annual Report that "American Motors has demonstrated its ability to meet market disruptions and take advantage of changing opportunities and is prepared to meet the challenges ahead in 1980."

The most dramatic example that AMC was serious about that assertion was the announcement that the 1980 CJ's standard powerplant would be a 4-cylinder "Hurricane" engine. Actually, this had been a poorly kept secret. As early as May, 1978, *Motor Trend* told readers of its road test of the CJ-5 and CJ-7 that instead of downsizing the CJ models American Motors had decided to use Pontiac 4-cylinder engines beginning in 1980.

American Motors' experience with 4-cylinder engines had, to this point, been quite limited. From 1954 through 1962 it had sold the imported Metropolitan, which initially used a modified 42 horsepower Austin A40 4-cylinder engine. In 1962 it had been involved with the air-cooled aluminum V-4 Mighty Mite engine. And, of course, the Willys F-head Hurricane engine was still in production when AMC acquired Jeep in 1970.

For a time it had seemed probable that the 1980 CJ would be powered by an AMC-built 4-cylinder engine. After the first energy crisis of 1973–74, the Federal Government's mandate, that by the mid-eighties American cars would have to meet a corporate average of 27.5 mpg, posed a serious problem to AMC. Although its 6-cylinder engine had once been produced in 199 cubic inch form, it was not expected that it could, even then, pass the 27.5 mpg hurdle.

In the early seventies it appeared that the rotary engine was the solution to AMC's problem. In fact, its Pacer, on which so many hopes were pinned, was intended to be rotary-powered. But problems with emissions, not to mention difficulties with durability and fuel consumption closed the door on that plan.

AMC's dilemma at that point was depicted by Gerald Meyers, then an AMC executive vice president, in *Motor Trend*, February, 1977, "Anybody who builds a new engine from scratch", he said, "even if they can borrow from someone else, has to be looking at a minimum of five years. We didn't have five years. So we quickly abandoned the notion of designing our own powerplant."

Instead, AMC began a review of existing foreign engines that could serve its purpose. None of AMC's cars, not to mention the contemporary Jeep vehicles, were known for their lightweight construction. This didn't prevent AMC from seeking and getting approval from Volkswagen to build its Rabbit engine under license. This engine was used in some early Plymouth Horizon and Dodge Omni models but they weighed far less than such AMC cars as the Gremlin which was only some 200 pounds under the ton-and-a-half mark.

Eventually, a deal was struck with Audi, which had, by then, become a subsidiary of Volkswagen, to purchase the tooling for its 121 cubic inch single overhead cam engine. This engine not only was used by the Audi 100ls but also for the Porsche 924.

All-in-all this was a major undertaking for AMC calling for the investment of $60 million which included retooling its 500,000 sq.ft. plant in Richmond, Indiana for production of this engine beginning in late 1976. Although some Germlins were built with this engine, plans to manufacture it in the U.S. were cancelled during 1977. Instead, an agreement was reached with General Motors to purchase the 2.5 liter 4-cylinder engine produced by Pontiac for use in AMC cars and CJ Jeeps beginning with the 1980 model year. AMC reported that "The change saves millions of dollars necessary to purchase tooling and equipment, while providing a high-quality, fuel-efficient powerplant for future products."

The Pontiac "Iron Duke" engine originated in 1962 as a 90 horsepower Chevy II engine. Subsequently it was adapted for use in the Pontiac Sunbird in 1978 after the ill-fated Vega aluminum engine was withdrawn from production. As used in the CJ-5 and CJ-7 it displaced 151 cubic inches with a 4.00 inch bore and 3.0 inch stroke. With a Rochester staged 2-barrel carburetor, 8.2:1 compression ratio, single exhaust and a High Energy Ignition it developed 82 horsepower at 4000 rpm and 125 lb.ft. of torque at 2600 rpm. Its assembled weight was 319 pounds. On all CJs except those intended for sale in California, the engine was fitted with a PULSAIR Injection Reaction System instead of an air pump which remained part of the Fuel Feedback (FFB) system found on California CJs. The PULSAIR arrangement used the pulses of the engine's exhaust to draw air into the exhaust ports. CJs for California had a 3-way catalytic converter; all others had a 2-way unit.

In an interview with *Four Wheeler* magazine published in its January 1980 issue, Paul Tippett explained that "bringing back the 4-cylinder in the CJ was not only an economy move, but a move to fill a market niche. You can't buy a Blazer or a Bronco with an economical yet responsive engine like the 4-cylinder, so its introduction is an attempt to outflank the competition, thus giving the consumer something we feel is needed."

With its new 4-cylinder engine the CJ Jeep became the first conventional 4-wheel drive vehicle to break the 20 mpg barrier with an EPA estimated 21 mpg and 25 mpg in highway ratings. In the real world its fuel economy was equally sensational. *Pickup, Van & 4WD* magazine's road test of a CJ-5 in its April, 1980 issue noted that "our 1980 test vehicle was driven over PV4's 20 percent city/80 percent freeway mileage loop and at the end of 26 miles, our electronic fuel flow equipment had recorded a 23.1 mpg – an all-time high for a CJ. Compared to last year's CJ-5 (258 six, 3-speed and 3.54:1 axles) and its 16.4 mpg, our '80 model represents a 40 percent improvement in city/freeway mileage. What a switch. Overnight the CJ-5's fuel mileage has jumped from so-so to the best for an American 4×4 vehicle."

Contributing to this dramatic advance in fuel economy were manually operated free-wheeling front hubs, which were now standard on all CJ models and a new manual 4-speed SR-4 Borg-Warner transmission which was also standard on all CJ models. Among its key features was the use of lightweight aluminum for its case, top cover and adapter housing, and synchromesh on all forward gears. No longer offered was the previously optional 4-speed manual with its 6.32:1 non-synchromesh first gear.

The ratios of the new 4-speed were 4.07:1, 2.39:1, 1.49:1 and 1.0:1.

Since the 4-cylinder CJ's standard axle was still 3.54:1, some off-roaders feared that it had lost much of the rugged terrain virility that had always been a CJ trademark. This was essentially an unfounded fear for two reasons. The first was the concurrent use of a new transfer case, a Dana 300 model, in place of the Dana 20 of earlier years. Its low gear ratio was 2.62:1 which was significantly lower than the Dana 20's 2.03:1. Furthermore, the CJ was offered with an optional 4.09:1 axle ratio which resulted in a total reduction in first gear and low range of 43.59:1. This compared favorably with the optimum 1979 set-up of a 3.54:1 axle ratio and a 2.03:1 low range which yielded a 45.38:1 ratio. At the same time the new 4.07:1 first gear was also useable for normal every-day street driving.

For CJs with either the 258 cubic inch 6-cylinder engine or the 304 cubic inch V-8 another new 4-speed, all-synchromesh transmission, a Tremac model T-176, was used. Its ratios were 3.52:1, 2.27:1, 1.46:1 and 1.0:1.

Whereas the standard axle ratio for the 1979 CJ with either the 258 or 304 engines had been 3.54:1, it was, in 1980, 3.07:1 with 3.54:1 optional.

Now positioned as the top level CJ trim package was the new Laredo option priced at $1950. It was available for both the CJ-5 and CJ-7 in either soft or hardtop form. It consisted of 15 × 8 styled steel chrome plated wheels with a center hub cover, new Goodyear Wrangler 9R on-or-off road radial tires, chrome front and rear bumperettes, swing-away spare tire carrier with chrome latch and stop, chrome mirror heads and arms, black rocker moldings, hood insulation, body striping in either silver or blue tones, indoor/outdoor carpeting, leather-wrapped steering wheel and passenger assist bar, chrome grille panel with pin-striped instrument panel, covered console with special trim pad, special door trim panels and a Laredo nameplate on the instrument panel.

CJ-7s with the Laredo option had hardtops with tinted glass in the side quarter windows. Offered for the first time on a Jeep, and standard on the Laredo, were high back bucket seats available in black and silver or beige and brown. These were now joined by matching rear seats on the Laredo. The bucket seats were also included in the Renegade and Golden Eagle packages with respective prices of $899 and $1450.

The Renegade package was slightly revised for 1980 to include a soft feel sports steering wheel. The color scheme for its body striping was changed to either orange with gold or blue with gold.

Changes both of the technical and cosmetic variety set the latest CJ-7 apart from older models. Leading the list of the former was the replacement of the Turbo Hydra-Matic transmission by Chrysler's lighter weight TorqueFlite. This switch received mixed reviews since some critics regarded the GM transmission as superior to the Chrysler product. Aside from this debate, the major automatic transmission development was that automatic CJ-7s were available only with part-time 4-wheel drive.

With the exception of Classic Black, all Jeep exterior colors were new for 1980. The 13 new colors included Olympic White, Cameo Tan, Medium Teal Blue, Dark Green Metallic, Dark Brown Metallic, Bordeaux Metallic and Saxon Yellow. Not offered for the Laredo and

The new Laredo package for 1980 as installed on a CJ-7. (Courtesy of American Motors)

Golden Eagle were Medium Teal Blue, Smoke Grey Metallic and Cardinal Red. Available for the Golden Eagle but not the Laredo were Dark Green Metallic, Russet Metallic and Carmel. Not available for the Golden Eagle was Navy Blue.

For the first time the CJ–7 soft top was available with steel doors and roll up windows. Standard on all CJ–7s was a swing-away spare tire mount. Previously the standard spare tire location had been inside the vehicle with the new position available as an option.

Prices of the CJ models and selected options in 1980 were as follows:

Model	Price
CJ–5	$6195
CJ–7	$6445

Option	Price
Renegade package	$899
Golden Eagle package	$1450
Laredo package	$1950
Tachometer and rally clock	$84
Limited slip differential	$90
Power brakes	$73
Front anti-roll bar	$41
Steering damper	$21
Extra-duty suspension	$93
Heavy-duty shock absorbers	$28
258 cubic inch engine	$129
304 cubic inch engine	$383
Automatic transmission	$33
Hardtop (CJ–7)	$676

American Motors' two top executives, Gerald Meyers and W. Paul Tippett, didn't mince words in describing AMC's status in 1980. "The operating performance of American Motors Corporation", they explained in the 1980 Annual Report, "is to be viewed against the background of a most difficult period in the history of the U.S. automobile industry. Record high interest rates, a severe recession, rising fuel costs, excessive government regulations and the inroads of Japanese imports were factors that contributed to a massive decline in industry sales and the loss of more than $4 billion by the U.S. automobile industry."

Earlier, at the Annual Meeting, Gerald Meyers had been equally blunt: "Not since the Great Depression has the world economy been in the turmoil it is today. Not since the Cuban missile crisis has the truce between the superpowers been so threatened as it is today. The OPEC nations have created an international energy crisis that will not end quickly. Threats of cutoffs and rapidly rising oil prices have sent shock waves all over. So, as the decade begins, political and economic fears abound."

Caught up in this morass, it still seemed for a time that AMC might just escape its worst effects. But as the year progressed AMC's initially good start slowed to a crawl. Meyers and Tippett explained: "the negative external factors proved to be insurmountable ... The decline for us was further aggravated by a decline in the size of the 4-wheel drive market."

For the 1980 calendar year Jeep sales were 77,852, a drop of 62,579 units. CJ sales, while experiencing a significant decline, were not as hard hit as were those of other Jeep models, falling 27,574 units to 47,304.

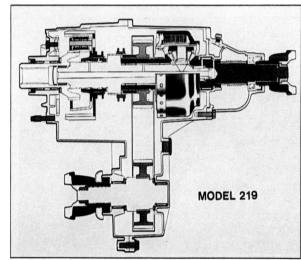

Front and rear views of the 1980 CJ-5 Renegade. (Courtesy of American Motors)

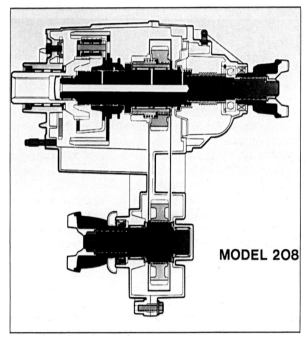

Jeep used two transfer cases in 1980, the Model 219 and 208. (Courtesy of American Motors)

The Jeep Hurricane 2.5 liter engine introduced in 1980. (Courtesy of American Motors)

In spite of these developments and American Motors' loss of $197.5 million (in 1979 AMC had enjoyed record profits of $95.2 million), there were a few points to cheer about. Beyond any doubt, the introduction of the 4-wheel drive Eagle in 1980 was a dramatic illustration of AMC's ability to secure a foothold in a market segment overlooked or ignored by its larger competitors.

Even though Jeep's sales had fallen sharply, its share of the 4-wheel drive market rose to 19.2 percent in 1980, indicating that its popularity had held up better than did that of many of its competitors. Furthermore, AMC was taking some highly visible steps to bolster the public's perception of Jeep quality. The most dramatic development was the establishment of a Final Inspection Acceptance (FIA) line at the Toledo plant. "The FIA line adds still more quality assurance checks to an already comprehensive program", said AMC. "Every Jeep vehicle", AMC continued, "is driven over a short road test course to the FIA line after being approved at the final inspection station on the assembly line. In addition to the road test, the vehicles are re-tested for water leaks and receive more than 150 additional checks before being released for shipment to dealers."

Perhaps the most important aspect of the FIA line was its large "Jeep Quality—Come See For Yourself" sign which was highly visible to drivers passing by on North Cove Avenue. Since that side of the Jeep building was lined with large plate glass windows, the sign meant

exactly what it said.

Also receiving considerable publcity was the report that AMC was in the process of designing a completely new generation of more fuel efficient Jeeps. AMC depicted this program as possessing an "overriding priority".

The 1981 CJ–5 Renegade. (Courtesy of American Motors)

Against this background of an industry in the midst of the most extensive retooling of its product line in history the 1981 Jeeps were introduced. In 1980 AMC had portrayed the CJ as "The Legend Continues". For 1981 a revised "The Legend Endures" motto was used. This wasn't entirely inappropriate since it had been forty years since the days of the MA Willys Jeep and 27 years since the first CJ–5 had been announced.

A 1981 CJ–7 Laredo. All 1981 CJ Jeeps had as standard equipment the 2.5 liter Hurricane engine. (Courtesy of American Motors)

Reminding the public that it had been the CJ that "almost singlehandedly launched the Recreational Vehicle Industry", AMC once again demonstrated that even though it was into its third decade, the old CJ design still was receptive to a fair amount of revision. This isn't to say, however, that even the most avid Jeep enthusiast wasn't getting just a little eager for something new. For example, in its test of a CJ–5, *Four*

A full Safari top was a popular 1981 option. (Courtesy of American Motors)

Electric winches were common options on CJ Jeeps. (Courtesy of American Motors)

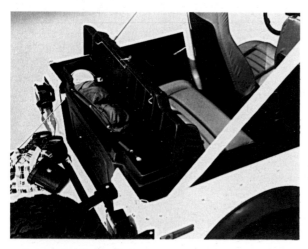

For added convenience the CJ could be fitted with a storage compartment. (Courtesy of American Motors)

Wheeler magazine for September 1981, noted, "Over the years, the Jeep CJ has built a reputation as a tough and rugged off roader and with its reputation has come much in the way of tradition. In 1981 the tradition has tarnished a bit, like an old pinstripe suit with a shine on the seat of the pants: still good but maybe time for a change."

With the Department of Transportation mandating a 16.5 mpg Corporate Average Fuel Economy (CAFE) for 4-wheel drive vehicles, it was almost a foregone conclusion that the CJ's gas mileage would be improved over 1980's already excellent level. A major contributor was the use of the new lighter weight 258 cubic inch 6-cylinder engine whose primary features are discussed in the Cherokee chapter.

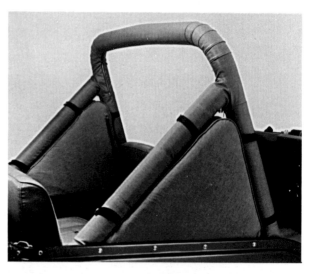

Roll-bar padding as well as "Saddle Bags" were offered as accessories in 1981. (Courtesy of American Motors)

Equally important was the incorporation of a locking torque converter in the Chrysler TorqueFlite transmission used in conjunction with the 6-cylinder engine. For the first time the 4-cylinder engine was available with a wide ratio automatic transmission.

Along with altered rear axle ratios there were changes made in the gearing of the 4-speed manual transmission. As expected, the primary reason for them was to enhance fuel economy without a major sacrifice in overall performance. There was, to be sure, a loss in pulling power in the top three gears but, fortunately for those Jeep owners concerned about off-road tractability, first gear performance remained unchanged.

CJs with the 6-cylinder engine now had a 2.73:1, instead of 3.07:1 axle ratio. A 3.73:1 was optional. The first gear ratio was 4.07:1 whereas it had been 3.5:1 in 1980. For CJs with the V-8 engine (which was not available in California), the first gear ratio was 3.82:1 rather than 3.52:1. Their standard axle, regardless of transmission, was 2.73:1. Previously it had been 3.07:1. The optional ratio was 3.31:1. While no changes were made in the gearing of the 4-cylinder CJs, their mpg ratings moved up to 27 highway and 22 EPA estimated mpg.

Beyond these changes minor revisions were made in a number of areas. For example, the optional sidestep was lengthened, the Renegade package had new body graphics and a vent window was added to the soft top/metal door option for the CJ-7.

The 1982 CJ-7 Laredo. (Courtesy of American Motors)

The 1981 color selection consisted of Cameo Tan, Vintage Red Metallic, Classic Black, Autumn Gold, Moonlight Blue, Steel Gray

Metallic, Dark Brown Metallic, Deep Maroon Metallic, Olympic White, Copper Brown Metallic, Oriental Red, Montana Blue, Sherwood Green Metallic and Chestnut Brown Metallic.

Prices for the 1981 CJs were increased substantially over their 1980 levels, The CJ-5 listed for $7240 or $1045 more than in 1980. The CJ-7's base price was increased the same amount to $7490. Similar increases were made in most Jeep options. For example, the Renegade package moved up to $945 from $899. The Laredo package was now $2049

Moving in the opposite direction were Jeep sales in general and those of the CJ in particular. Since these were the years of "sticker shock", it's likely that the sharply higher Jeep prices took their toll on sales. Only 30,564 CJs were sold in calendar year 1981. This represented a drop of 16,740 from the level of 1980. This situation might have been even worse if AMC had not decided in April to reduce Jeep prices by ten percent.

Commenting on this development at the 1981 Annual Meeting, AMC chairman Gerald Meyers told his audience that "Before I close, just a word about Jeep sales. American Motors is and has been the leader in 4-wheel drive vehicles. However, the recovery of this market segment has been very slow indeed. It was badly bruised by the fuel crunch and the price crunch. But we are fighting back here, too. Lately we decided to apply our ten percent reduction to Jeep vehicles and we are anticipating some improvement soon."

Overall, in spite of a sales decline to 63,275 from 77,852 in 1980, Jeep's share of its market for 1981 moved up to 21.2 percent. Equally important, although it was seen only in retrospect, was that 1981 was to

be the low point for Jeep sales. In the years to follow they would begin to climb out of this trough with increasing momentum. The greatest irony was that this tremendous success would eventually lead to the acquisition of AMC in 1987 by Chrysler.

Of considerable financial importance was the arrival of a new Jeep CJ option package, the Limited, in 1982. AMC had been following two concurrent, but quite different, marketing strategies with the CJ for many years in order to maximize its appeal. At one level was the traditional bare-bones CJ; a vehicle with only the basics, intended for use by no-nonsense types who weren't interested in what they regarded as non-essential features. This mentality had been buoyed by the energy crisis since it had returned the Jeep to its 4-cylinder roots.

But a much larger group clamored for every additional option or feature that AMC could implant into a CJ. They were 4-wheel drive enthusiasts who wanted their off-road action combined with the latest in creature comforts.

Pickup, Van & 4WD magazine for February, 1982, in a comparison test of a CJ-7 with the Limited package and a Dodge Ramcharger,

commented: "Let's face it, the CJ-7 in even its highest trim level is pretty bare-bones when compared to the lusher, plusher offerings of the competition. Even when fitted with the optional hardtop and solid doors, a dressy CJ-7 has a Spartan look to it."

The functional profile of a 1982 CJ-7 Renegade. (Courtesy of American Motors)

Nonetheless, Jeeps Sales promised that the Limited package would "set well with that special breed of drivers who want to blend an upgraded level of comfort and decor with their sports action on-road or off."

Left Bottom: **The new CJ-7 Limited for 1982. (American Motors)**

The list of features included in the Limited package was a lengthy one. Beginning with the basic CJ equipment it included power steering and brakes, AM/FM radio with two speakers, a monochromatic paint theme with color-keyed hardtop and wheel lip extensions, special dual-color body side striping, special grille panel strips, exterior "Limited" nameplates, chrome front bumpers and rear bumperettes, bodyside steps, black painted windshield and window frames, special

Below: **A 1982 CJ-5 Renegade with padded roll-bar and Saddle Bags. (Courtesy of American Motors)**

Bottom: **The same CJ-5 with its top in place. (Courtesy of American Motors)**

159

dual exterior mirrors, 15 × 7 steel spoke wheels with bright trim rings, Decor and Convenience Groups, high back front bucket seats with rear bench seat in Slate Blue or Nutmeg Western Weave (Nutmeg leather seats were optional), special sound/heat insulated carpeted floor, trim panels for the wheel housing, tailgate, innerbody and cowl sides, carpeted protective front floor mats, low gloss finish for the sports console, steering column and bezel and air conditioning housing, color-keyed padded roll bar, special door trim and headlining, door activated dome and courtesy lights, leather-wrapped steering wheel and passenger assist handle, and rear quarter beltline trim molding.

The Limited CJ-7 was available in five exterior/interior color combinations: Mist Silver Metallic, Slate Blue Metallic and Olympic White exteriors with a Slate Blue interior or Copper Brown Metallic or Olympic White exteriors with Nutmeg cloth or optional leather interior.

All 1982 CJ Jeeps benefited from revised front and rear tread measurements as indicated by the following data:

	1981 CJ-5	1981 CJ-7	1982 CJ-5	1982 CJ-7
Front tread	51.5 in.	51.5 in.	52.4 in.	55.8 in.
Rear tread	50.5 in	50.5 in	50.5 in.	5.1 in

In conjunction with new Arriva tires this wider stance resulted in better roadability. In the case of the Limited these changes were associated with what would have been considered sacrilegious just a few years earlier: an "improved ride package" which was an euphemism for softer front and rear springs and shock absorbers.

The 1983 CJ-7 Renegade.
(Courtesy of American Motors)

Since the price of the Limited package was now $2895, it was possible, as the following price schedule for the CJ jeeps and selected options indicates, to order a $12,000 Jeep.

Model	Price
CJ-5	$7515
CJ-7	$7765

Option	Price
258 cubic inch engine	$145
5-speed manual transmission	$199
3.31:1 axle ratio	$33

Extra duty suspension	$103
Power steering	$229
Power disc brakes	$499
Heavy duty battery	$45
Cold climate group	$115
Renegade package	$979
Laredo package	$2149
Limited package	$2895

Changes for 1983 were not extensive. The 258 cubic inch engine now had a higher, 9.2:1, instead of 8.6:1 compression ratio as well as a fuel feedback system and knock sensor. Unlike 1982 when the four-cylinder was standard in all CJ models, the 1983 CJ-5's base engine was the 258 cubic inch engine.

The CJs were offered with the same appearance/equipment packages as in 1982. The Renegade had revised graphics highlighted by added elements just behind the front fenders.

After losing money for 14 consecutive months American Motors reported a 1983 fourth quarter profit of $7.4 million. Although the major credit had to be given to the new Renault Alliance and Encore, as well as the introduction of the all-new Jeep Cherokee as a 1984 model, the CJs also contributed to this improvement as their sales moved up to 36,308 units.

Overall, Jeep sales were strong enough to warrant not only the recalling of all laid-off workers at Toledo but the hiring of more employees. This point was underscored by the encouraging report that Jeep production at Toledo was higher in 1983 than at any other time since it was acquired from Kaiser in 1970.

For 1984 AMC offered the CJ Jeeps with a new 2.5 liter engine. This is a CJ-7. (Courtesy of American Motors)

The arrival of the new Cherokee flamed rumors that the days of the CJ were numbered. This was a hard reality for long-time CJ fans to accept, but these signs, even if AMC had no official comment on this matter, meant that it was only a matter of time before the last CJ left Toledo. Furthermore, it was evident from the limited changes made in the 1984 CJ that AMC was placing its talent and resources elsewhere than in any major CJ project.

A 1985 CJ-7, which was available with a soft top, hard top or no top at all. (Courtesy of American Motors)

For the 1984 model year the CJ-5 was dropped, leaving only the CJ-7 to represent Jeep in the market category where it had once derived most of its sales. Also dropped from the CJ's optional equipment list was the Limited package. Still offered were the Renegade and Laredo trim packages. With AMC describing the CJ-7's styling as "legend-

163

A 1986 CJ-7 with Laredo trim and hard top. (Courtesy of American Motors)

ary", it was to be expected that no styling changes were made for 1984.

Also coming as no surprise was the use of AMC's newly designed 2.5 liter, 150 cubic inch 4-cylinder engine as the standard CJ-7 engine. The older 4.2 liter, 258 cubic inch 6-cylinder continued to be optional. Transmission choices included the standard 4-speed manual and an optional 5-speed manual. The 3-speed automatic was optionally available for the 6-cylinder engine only.

The 1985 CJ-7 was described by AMC as maintaining "Jeep

Corporation's long-standing reputation for providing one of the most durable and dependable 4-wheel drive vehicles, on or off the road." New for 1985 were the CJ's fold and tumble rear seats which replaced the fixed type of 1984. Up front were standard high back bucket seats. Both the Renegade and Laredo packages featured new interior and exterior decors. Common to both were revised tape stripe patterns, three new exterior colors and one new interior color, Honey, which replaced Nutmeg. The available exterior colors for the 1985 CJ consisted of four standard options: Olympic White, Classic Black, Almond Beige and Sebring Red. The extra cost metallic colors were Sterling, Ice Blue, Charcoal, Dark Honey, Dark Brown and Garnet. All extra cost colors had a clearcoat finish.

In its final form the CJ-7 for 1986 was one of the most recognizable forms in the world. (Courtesy of American Motors)

"Celebrating 40 years of Jeep heritage, the Jeep CJ-7 for 1986", said AMC, "will retain the overall design continuity and its long standing reputation for ruggedness and durability among 4-wheel drive vehicles." In other words, 1986 was another year of virtually no change for the CJ-7. No revisions were made in the CJ's color choices although all now had a clearcoat finish. Like all 1986 Jeeps the CJ-7 was covered by the same warranty as offered in 1985. The basic features of this plan included 12 month/12,000 mile coverage for the entire vehicle (except tires) plus three-year corrosion protection. In addition, major engine, transmission and powertrain components were covered for 24 months/24,000 miles.

Chapter 8

The
forward control
models

Just a year after introducing the CJ-6 and Dispatcher models Willys further expanded its sales potential by offering in rapid succession, two new trucks; the FC-150 on 27 November, 1956 and the FC-170 on 20 May, 1957. One look at these vehicles was all that was needed to understand why Willys referred to them as Forward Control models. Unlike the familiar Jeep truck which followed a traditional pick-up truck configuration, the Forward Control models used a cab-over-engine design. This gave them a very distinctive, almost futuristic appearance. Commenting on the lines of the FC in the February, 1957 issue of *Motor Trend*, Bob Scolly noted, "If Willys' designers were forced to refrain from jet aircraft styling in the FC-150 4-wheel drive Jeep, they can console themselves with the knowledge that they have introduced the 'helicopter look' in commercial vehicles."

Yet, the FC was both quite attractive and still identifiable as a Jeep product due to a grille arrangement that included seven vertical cutouts plus the head and parking lights within a perimeter shaped to suggest that of the CJ models.

Other aspects of the FC Jeep's styling was also simple, clean and functional. The Jeep grille design blended nicely with a cab which had an exceptional amount of glass area. The wrap-around windshield had a surface of nearly 1200 square inches while the rear window measured 628 square inches. This wide expanse of glass was in addition to large side door windows and, on Deluxe cab models, stationary windows in the rear side pillars. The result was more glass area (2747 square inches on the Deluxe cab) than any other truck in the Willys class. Willys described the FC cab as a "Safety View" design and claimed that forward visibility was nearly 200 percent greater than in conventional trucks. For example, the driver could see objects only six feet from the front bumper.

The rear fenders of the FC were angular, almost identical to those of the conventional Jeep trucks. Unlike most American trucks of those years which retained clearly defined front fenders, the FC carried only the slightest suggestion of a front fender shape in the form of a simple raised panel of rubber construction extending along the wheel wells.

Entrance into the FC's interior was through a wide door that when opened revealed a concealed "safety step" area. The cab interior was color-coded to the truck's exterior. A console-type instrument panel grouped the instruments and gauges in a cluster directly in front of the driver. Items such as the light switch, ignition key-operated starter and windshield wiper control were easily identified and operated. A useful feature was the placement of the brake fluid access tank cover on the dash panel. Both the clutch and brake pedals were of suspended design which provided more leg and foot room as well as easier pedal operation because of the greater lever mechanical advantage inherent in that type of arrangement.

Access to the engine was through an easily removed cover that completely exposed all major components. Use of heavy fiberglass insulation limited the amount of engine noise and heat that entered the cab.

Operation of the FC in 4-wheel drive was controlled by a single transfer case lever. As with other Jeep vehicles the FC could not be shifted into Low Range while in 2-wheel drive because of a built-in interlock. This was intended to prevent rear axle damage that could result from sudden shock loads. It could, however, be shifted into 4-wheel drive at normal road speeds without having to come to a complete stop.

With the standard 3-speed transmission, controlled by a floor-mounted cane shift, a total of nine forward speeds and three reverse combinations were available. If the optional 4-speed transmission was installed this increased to twelve forward power options.

An FC-150 with a special Medical Coach health care body. (Courtesy of Medical Coaches, Inc., Oneonta, NY)

The standard FC cab was, as expected, austere but not without the basic necessities such as dual windshield wipers, key locks on both doors, a dispatch box, ash tray, driver side visor, dome light, rear view mirror, adjustable driver's seat and "Plasti-Strand" upholstery.

The Deluxe cab had dual sun visors, rear quarter windows, acoustical trim on the doors and headliner, foam rubber seats, cigarette lighter, front kick pads and all items listed for the standard cab.

The optional equipment available for the FC models was primarily of the functional type but a few items were of the 'dress-up' variety. Specially designed for the FC was a new heating and ventilation system noted for rapid volume heating in cold weather. Also available for the FC was a radio, two-tone exterior paint, front bumper guards, directional lights, E-Z Eye tinted glass, windshield washer, front air vent (FC-170 only), electric windshield wipers, safety belts, double passenger seat (FC-150 only), power brakes (FC-150 only), oil bath air cleaner, oil filter, transmission brake (FC-170 only), Powr-Lok rear differential (vehicles with this option had a brass tag stamped with the letter "T" under one of the differential covers), heavy-duty rear axle, springs and shock absorbers, 4-speed transmission and a hot climate radiator.

Both FC models were also available with three power-take off points at the front, center and rear of the chassis. The unit at the rear delivered up to 40 horsepower to operate either belt or shaft-driven equipment as well as an optional draw bar. Rounding out the list of factory installed equipment were various tire sizes and types plus governors of both the constant and variable speed variety.

Willys dealers offered several "special equipment" items such as selective drive hubs, winches, snow plows and dozing blades plus a full complement of wrecker equipment. An example of the latter was the Watson Towboy manufactured by the H.S. Watson Company of Toledo, Ohio. It had the capability to tow a vehicle weighing up to two tons and could be removed from the FC in only five minutes.

Another FC-150 circa 1960 sent to Ceylon for field service work. (Courtesy of Medical Coaches, Inc., Oneonta, NY)

Both FC trucks were offered only on 4-wheel drive. Their exterior dimensions were extremely compact. One result was a turning radius for the FC-150 of just over 18 feet. The FC-170 would turn in a radius of 21 feet, 11 inches. The FC-150's wheelbase was just 81 inches with

167

overall length extending only 147.5 inches. But within those concise measurements was a pick-up box measuring 74.25 inches in length. This gave the FC–150 the greatest cargo area per inch of wheelbase of any truck in its class. Moreover, the cargo bed was only 24 inches from the ground which gave the FC–150 the lowest pick-up box of any 4-wheel drive truck then available. Perhaps the only shortcomings of the FC pick-up were its full-length wheel wells that limited the width of the bed bottom to just 36 inches.

The engine used for the FC–150 was the familiar F-head "Hurricane" 4-cylinder with a displacement of 134.2 cubic inches. Its power ratings were 75 horsepower at 4000 rpm and 115 lbft. of torque at 2000 rpm. A 6.9:1 compression was standard with a 7.4:1 ratio optional.

Powering the FC–170 was the larger 226 cubic inch L-head "High-Torque Hurricane" 6-cylinder engine with 105 horsepower at 3000 rpm and 190 lbft. of torque at 3600 rpm. Both trucks had single dry plate clutches but the unit used by the FC–170 had 100.5 sq.in. of surface area as compared to the 72 sq.in. area of the FC–150 clutch.

Aside from these items there were many other points of distinction between the two FC models as the following chart indicates:

Model	FC–150	FC–170
Wheelbase	81 in.	103.5 in.
Tread	48.375 in.	63.5 in.
Overall Length	147.4 in.	180.5 in.
Overall Width	71.375 in.	76.5 in.
Overall Height	77.375 in.	79.375 in.
Fuel Tank Capacity	16 gal.	22 gal.
Radiator Capacity	11 qt.	12 qt.†
Wheel Size	4.50 × 15 in.	5.00 × 16 in.
Tire Size	7.00 × 15, 4-ply	7.00 × 16, 6-ply
App. Curb Weight	2925 lbs.	3490 lbs.*
Frame Cross Members	6	7
Standard Axle Ratio	5.38:1	4.88:1

† With heater. Deduct one quart for models without heaters.
* Both models were offered in three body configurations; Pick-up,

Stake, Platform and Closed Cab and Chassis as well as stripped chassis, flat face cowl and open cab and chassis forms for installation of special bodies. In addition, the FC–170 was available in a dual-rear-wheel form. The actual curb weights measured in pounds with all fluids such as water, fuel and oil installed (in general, dry weight was about 160 pounds less) of these models was as follows:

Model	FC–150	FC–170	FC–170 (dual-rear-wheels)
Pick-up	3141	3490	—
Stake	3233	3724	4744
Platform	3121	3544	4434
Close Cab & Chassis	2885	3060	3720

Both models had full floating front and rear axles but the FC–170s had ratings of 3700 lbs. (front) and 4500 lbs. (rear) as compared to the FC–150's respective ratings of 2300 and 3000 lbs. Both trucks had identical brake systems consisting of Bendix hydraulic drums measuring 11 × 2 inches. Total area measured 178.5 sq.in.

Their suspension systems consisted of semi-elliptical leaf springs, front and rear, with full floating front and semi floating rear axles. A hypoid, Hotchkiss drive was used. The FC–170 had six springs measuring 46 × 2.5 inches at the front and 52 × 2.5 inches at the rear. The FC–150 was equipped with seven springs measuring 39.575 × 1.75 inches at the front and nine rear springs of 46 × 1.75 inch dimensions. Maximum load capacity of the FC–170 was 3700 lbs. (front) and 4500 lbs. (rear). The respective limits for the FC–150 were 2300 and 3000 lbs.

All FC models used the same 2-speed transfer case with ratios of 2.46:1 and 1.00:1. Their standard 3-speed transmission had ratios of 2.7988, (first), 1.441, (second) and 1.0:1, (high).

An FC–170 with a large health care body. (Courtesy of Medical Coaches, Inc., Oneonta, NY)

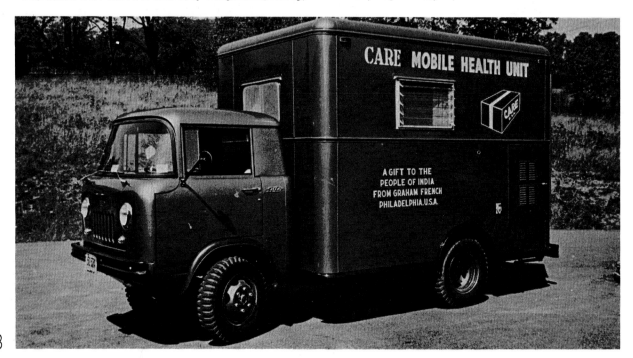

As evident by the following data, the FC models were priced similar to the L6–226 series of Willys trucks:

Body Type	L6–226	FC–150	FC–170
Ch. & Cab.	$2079	$2044	$2396
Pick-up	$2190	$2140	$2508
Stake	$2267	$2223	$2678

Although the FC models' appearance remained virtually unchanged during their production life, many modifications and revisions were incorporated into their design as running changes. Beginning with serial number 65548–18206 (produced late in the 1960 model year) the FC–150 had a wider, 57 inch tread. Prior to this point the last 48.43 inch tread models had a tie bar welded between the front spring hanger brackets to stabilize the frame and cure a problem with shimmy that

occured on some trucks. At the same time as the wider tread was introduced, the FC–150's height was increased to 78 inches and ground clearance moved up to 8.5 from 8.0 inches. In addition, curb weight of the FC–150 models moved up an average of 132 pounds.

An FC–150 "Medicoach Mobile" being unloaded in Istanbul, Turkey in the early 1960s. (Courtesy of Medical Coaches, Inc., Oneonta, NY)

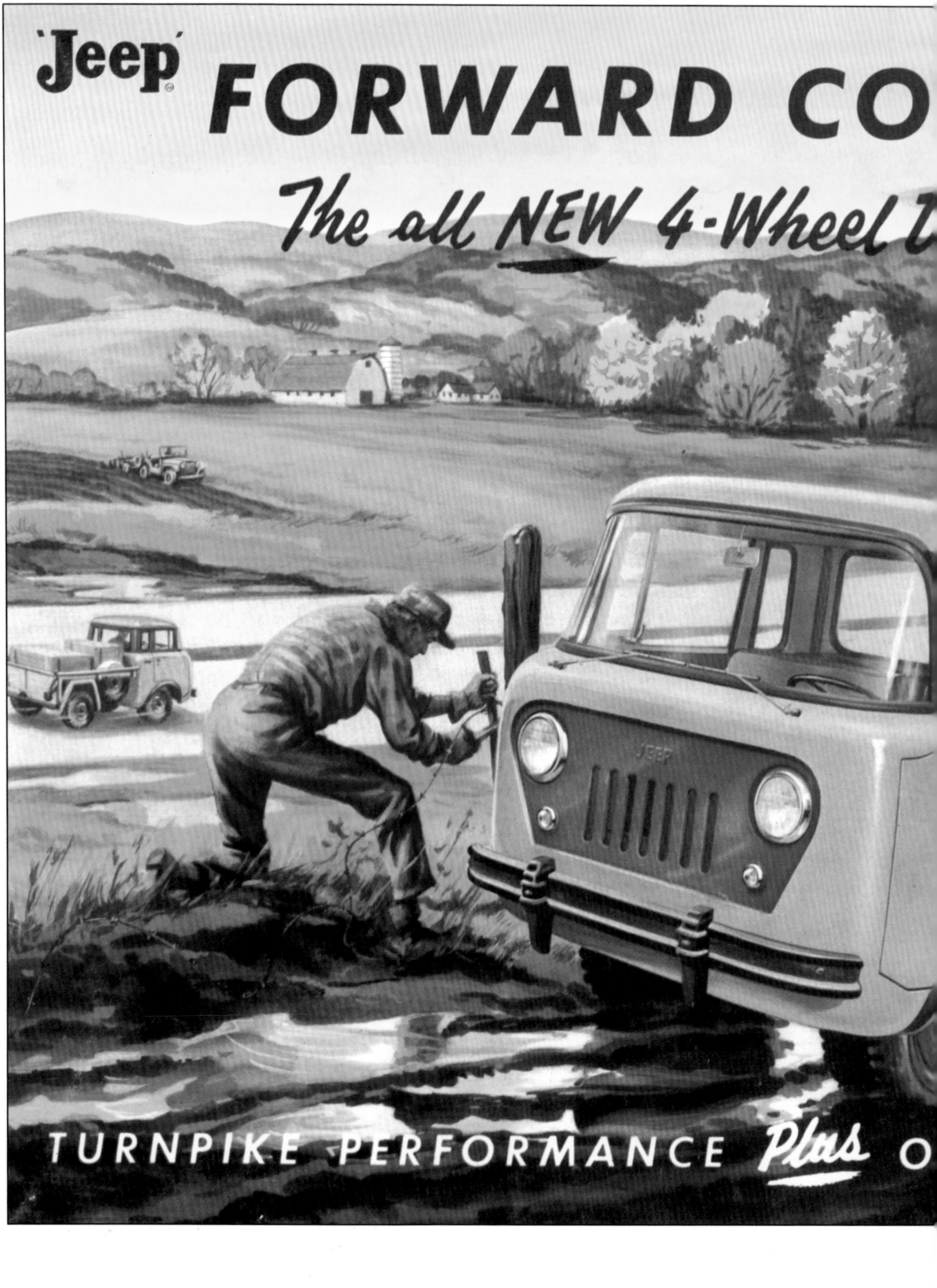

'Jeep' FORWARD CO

The all NEW 4-Wheel D

TURNPIKE PERFORMANCE *Plus* O

TROL FC-150

e Truck

ROAD TRACTION

NEW

SAFETY

COMFORT

and

CONVENIENCE

GREATER

CARGO AREA

per inch of

WHEELBASE

GREATER

"GO-ANYWHERE"

PERFORMANCE

The distinctive styling of the FC-150.
(Courtesy of author's collection)

The nearly vertical position of the FC steering wheel. (Courtesy of author's collection)

The FC's full-width rear window measured 628 sq. in. (Courtesy of author's collection)

The FC windshield contained nearly 1200 sq. in. of glass area. (Courtesy of author's collection)

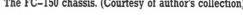

The FC–150 chassis. (Courtesy of author's collection)

The unique shape of the FC–150 cargo bed. (Courtesy of author's collection)

NEW

Jeep

FORWARD CONTROL

TRUCK FC-150

4-WHEEL DRIVE

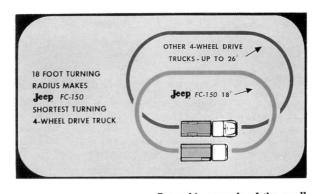

18 FOOT TURNING RADIUS MAKES **Jeep** FC-150 SHORTEST TURNING 4-WHEEL DRIVE TRUCK

OTHER 4-WHEEL DRIVE TRUCKS - UP TO 26'

Jeep FC-150 18'

A graphic example of the small turning radius of the FC-150. (Courtesy of author's collection)

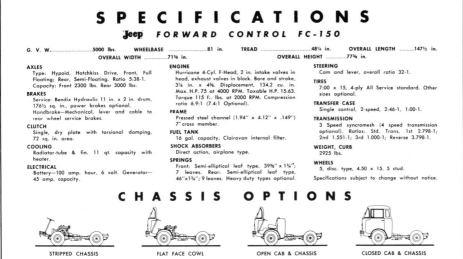

SPECIFICATIONS
Jeep FORWARD CONTROL FC-150

G. V. W. ....5000 lbs.　WHEELBASE ....81 in.　TREAD ....48¼ in.　OVERALL LENGTH ....147½ in.
OVERALL WIDTH ....71⅜ in.　OVERALL HEIGHT ....77⅜ in.

AXLES
Type: Hypoid, Hotchkiss Drive, Front, Full Floating; Rear, Semi-Floating. Ratio 5-38-1. Capacity: Front 2300 lbs. Rear 3000 lbs.

BRAKES
Service: Bendix Hydraulic 11 in. x 2 in. drum, 176½ sq. in., power brakes optional. Handbrake—Mechanical, lever and cable to rear wheel service brakes.

CLUTCH
Single, dry plate with torsional damping, 72 sq. in. area.

COOLING
Radiator-tube & fin. 11 qt. capacity with heater.

ELECTRICAL
Battery—100 amp. hour, 6 volt. Generator—45 amp. capacity.

ENGINE
Hurricane 4-Cyl. F-Head, 2 in. intake valves in head, exhaust valves in block. Bore and stroke, 3⅛ in. x 4⅜. Displacement, 134.2 cu. in. Max. H.P. 75 at 4000 RPM. Taxable H.P. 15.63. Torque 115 f. lbs. at 2000 RPM. Compression ratio 6.9:1 (7.4:1 Optional).

FRAME
Pressed steel channel (1.94" x 4.12" x .149") 7" cross member.

FUEL TANK
16 gal. capacity, Clairavan internal filter.

SHOCK ABSORBERS
Direct action, airplane type.

SPRINGS
Front: Semi-elliptical leaf type, 39⅝" x 1¾"; 7 leaves. Rear: Semi-elliptical leaf type, 46"x1¾"; 9 leaves. Heavy duty types optional.

STEERING
Cam and lever, overall ratio 32-1.

TIRES
7:00 x 15, 4-ply All Service standard. Other sizes optional.

TRANSFER CASE
Single control, 2-speed, 2:46-1, 1:00-1.

TRANSMISSION
3 Speed syncromesh (4 speed transmission optional). Ratios: Std. Trans, 1st 2.798-1; 2nd 1.551-1; 3rd 1.000-1; Reverse 3.798-1.

WEIGHT, CURB
2925 lbs.

WHEELS
5, disc. type, 4.50 x 15, 5 stud.

Specifications subject to change without notice.

CHASSIS OPTIONS

STRIPPED CHASSIS　　FLAT FACE COWL　　OPEN CAB & CHASSIS　　CLOSED CAB & CHASSIS

Chassis options offered for the FC-150. (Courtesy of author's collection)

The simple, but functional, FC instrument panel. (Courtesy of author's collection)

The FC offered its driver an excellent view of the road. (Courtesy of author's collection)

The 103.5 in. wheelbase FC–170.
(Courtesy of author's collection)

Two views of the FC–170 with major chassis
dimensions. (Courtesy of author's collection)

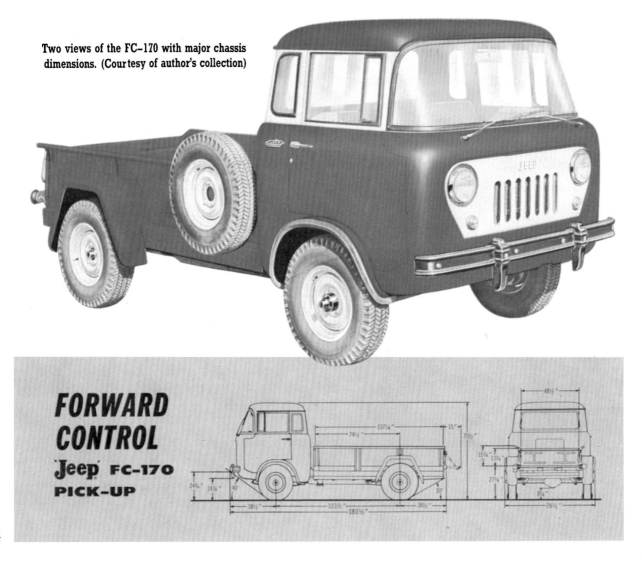

SPECIFICATIONS

FORWARD CONTROL Jeep FC-170

G. V. W.............**7000 lbs.**   WHEELBASE..........**103½ in.**   TREAD...............**63½ in.**   OVERALL LENGTH....**180½ in.**

OVERALL WIDTH......**76½ in.**   OVERALL HEIGHT....**79⅜ in.**

AXLES
Type: Hypoid, Hotchkiss Drive, Front, Full Floating; Rear, Semi-Floating. Ratio 4.88-1. Capacity: Front 3700 lbs. Rear 4500 lbs.

BRAKES
Service: Bendix Hydraulic 11 in. x 2 in. drum, 176½ sq. in.
Handbrake—Mechanical, lever and cable to rear wheel service brakes. (Drive shaft brake optional.)

CLUTCH
Single, dry plate with torsional damping, 100.5 sq. in. area.

COOLING
Radiator-Tube & fin. 11½ qt. capacity with heater.

ELECTRICAL
Battery—100 amp. hour, 6 volt. Generator 45 amp. capacity.

ENGINE
High-Torque Hurricane—6 cyl. L-head. Bore and stroke 3-5/16 in. x 4-3/8 in. Displacement 226.2 cu. in. Max. H.P., 105 at 3600 RPM. Taxable H.P., 26.33. Torque 190 ft. lbs. at 1400 RPM. Compression ratio, 6.86:1 (7.3:1 optional).

FRAME
Pressed steel channel. Section Modulus 2.581. 6 cross member.

FUEL TANK
22 gal. capacity. Clairavan internal filter.

SHOCK ABSORBERS
Direct action, airplane type.

SPRINGS
Front: Semi-elliptical leaf type, 46 x 2½''; 6 leaves. Rear: Semi-elliptical leaf type, 52'' x 2½''; 6 leaves.

STEERING
Cam and lever, overall ratio 32-1.

TIRES
7:00 x 16 6-ply All Service standard. Other sizes optional.

TRANSFER CASE
Single control, 2-speed, 2:46-1, 1:00-1.

TRANSMISSION
3 speed syncromesh (4 speed transmission optional). Ratios: Std. Trans. 1st 2.798-1; 2nd 1.551-1; 3rd 1.000-1; Reverse 3.798-1.

WEIGHT, CURB
3490 lbs.

WHEELS
5, disc. type, 5.00 x 16, 5 stud.

Specifications subject to change without notice.

CHASSIS OPTIONS

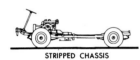

STRIPPED CHASSIS

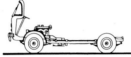

COWL AND WINDSHIELD

CLOSED CAB & CHASSIS

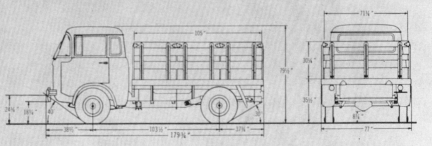

FORWARD CONTROL
Jeep FC-170
PLATFORM STAKE

Commencing with engine FW6L–226–141158, hardened exhaust valve seat inserts were installed in the 6-cylinder engine. Starting with engine FW6L–226–15478, the FC–170 engine used a new Morse timing chain and gear set in place of the older link belt type. Individual components were not interchangeable but the complete unit, consisting of crankshaft gear, camshaft gear and timing chain could be installed in older engines.

All FC–170 engines used a Carter model YF–2467–S carburetor but, several different units were used on the FC–150. Until early 1962 (up to vehicle serial number 65548–18842) a Carter model YF–938–SA was used. In the serial range from 65548–18842 to 65548–22077 a YF–938–SD was fitted. From that point until production ended a YF–938–1SO was used. These carburetors were all of the same basic design but the two earlier versions had a tendency to stumble at low speed and experience acceleration flat spots.

Initially, FC–170 models had a 4-blade fan. This was later replaced by a 6-blade unit in conjunction with use of a modified cooling system air intake.

During the 1958 calendar year Willys made a conversion to a standard 12 volt electrical system for all its vehicles. The 6 volt system remained available for export as well as an option for models destined for the domestic market.

Both the front and rear springs of the FC–150 were equipped with U-type shackles and threaded core bushings. After serial number 14961 conventional shackles and steel-backed rubber type bushings were used.

The final year for Forward Control production was 1966. Years earlier, in 1958, just shortly after the FC line had been introduced, the designer of the FC Willys, Brooks Stevens, had the German Reutter firm build three prototypes of a commuter-type vehicle based on the FC–150 chassis to his specifications. In retrospect, Stevens admitted that "We were probably too early with this, but we might have started the van fad with the youth of the nation at that time."

The FC van had six doors and room for nine occupants. To keep tooling costs low Stevens used interchangeable doors for both sides.

Chapter 9

The Jeep
Jeepster/Commando:
1967–1973

Sixteen years after the original Jeepster was discontinued, Kaiser Jeep Corporation decided the time was right for another go at turning out a vehicle with a close family resemblance to the Jeep, but directed towards a slightly different market. Although the new car brought the Jeepster name back to the world of the living, there were only limited similarities in concept between the original Jeepster and the new model.

In 1948 Jeep was offering a phaeton that with a 2-wheel drive system had no business travelling off the paved path. Willys had been correct in perceiving that there was some sort of link to be made between the Jeep's virtues as a strictly utilitarian vehicle and those cars appealing to individuals who used them mainly for pleasure. But if sales success was the criteria that really mattered, the first Jeepster didn't have the right formula.

Willys shouldn't be faulted for failing with the first Jeepster. A look at the contemporary MG sports car seemed to indicate that the Jeepster should have appealed to a fairly large market. Both cars had styling that was well known, giving them instant identification and, if the Willys was something less than a streak of lightning, neither was the MG TC. Of course the MG was low slung and cornered well. But the Willys, in its own way, was also fun to drive. The fact that the MG was in most respects a dated design didn't hurt its popularity in America. The Jeepster, with its "classic" styling, was in a good company. Even General Motors' styling boss, Harley Earl, was attracted to the Jeepster's concept which he used as the starting point for what eventually became the Corvette.

By 1967 the situation was much more in focus. The civilian Jeep had bounded far beyond its original role as a farm/utility vehicle to become America's premier recreation vehicle, and its popularity suggested that market was much larger than anyone had earlier believed. It was clearly an opportune time for Willys to revive the Jeepster concept.

The new generation Jeepster debuted in January, 1967 and its similarity to the original model was sufficient to cause some first-time viewers to confuse it with a well-restored original. But this was at best a superficial resemblance. The Jeepster was unmistakably a Jeep product but its designers had given it enough product identity to set it off from other Jeep vehicles. Up front was the CJ "face" with its seven vertical openings and close-set headlights that intruded into the outer grille bars. Its front fenders, like those that had been attached to every Jeep since the days of the MA model were simple, squared-off affairs.

Yet, there was something about the Jeepster that didn't quite fit into the Jeep mold and all it took was a second look to bring its appearance into clearer focus. For example, its front parking lights were set higher and further apart than on the CJ. Also apparent was the Jeepster's much wider hood.

Colors available for the Jeepster included Spruce Green, President Red, Empire Blue, Gold Beige, Glacier White and Prairie Gold. Any of these colors showed off the Jeepster's trim profile at its best. Its wheelbase measured 101 inches, width was 65.2 inches, height measured 64.2 inches and overall length extended 168.4 inches.

The sixties were the age when the long hood/short deck format dominated American automobile styling and the Jeepster was de-signed with that point in mind. Its rear deck was very abbreviated and ended abruptly in a sharply angled panel with vertically-mounted, rectangular-shaped taillights embracing a recessed center section. Definitely not a contemporary feature was the Jeepster's "continental" tire mount whose impact upon the Jeepster's length was accentuated by the rear bumper which angled outward to protect the spare tire and wheel from minor collision damage.

This antiquated feature was just one example of what happened when classic sports car design features intermingled with themes derived from the rough and ready character of the CJ Jeep. In some ways the result was amusing. For example, the Jeepster bristled with external hinges that would be tolerated by customers only on a Jeep product. Those installed on the hood looked as if they would be equally at home down on the cow barn doors. Then, there were the Jeepster's optional wheel discs that combined the look of knock-off hubs, bolt-on wheels and mag-type spokes; all in one package. "Like right off of a dragster" was Willys' comment on these wheel covers.

The standard Jeepster's price of $3195 placed it at a disadvantage when compared to automobiles such as the Camaro or Mustang which in 6-cylinder convertible form began at $2704 and $2698 respectively. It's true that this came close to comparing apples and oranges since the Jeepster wasn't in direct competition with those cars. But this didn't deter Jeep dealers from viewing the Jeepster as a vehicle that might enable them to take a few sales away from competing Ford dealers. A midwest Jeep dealer told *Sales Management* magazine, 15 January, 1967, that "We think that we will sell these to the guy who wants a Mustang but goes hunting or fishing and wants to take his car off the road." An eastern Jeep dealer noted, "For the first time we have something styled for youth and it's in the same price class as the Mustang. I won't be surprised if we sell a lot to college kids." No doubt this was the reason why Kaiser Jeep used a two-page color ad of the Jeepster to mark its debut as an advertiser in *Playboy*.

Yet, the combination of a steep price and limited practicability served as a brake upon Jeepster sales. For example, a fully optioned model's price could easily exceed $4000. Many people paying this amount of money in 1967 was less than enthralled to discover that with the top down the Jeepster had absolutely no cargo space to accomodate the needs of its four passengers. With the top erected the space behind the rear bench seat was available but only the front passenger bucket seat hinged forward to provide access to the rear.

This shortcoming was even more regrettable since the Jeepster's 4-wheel drive system made it ideal to carry four passengers to areas off-limits to conventional 2-wheel drive pony cars. With either the standard 3-speed all-synchromesh transmission or the optional Model 1400 Turbo Hydra-Matic (priced at $208), a transfer case with a low gear of 2.03:1 was used. Both transmissions had floor-mounted shift levers. With a torque converter ratio of 2.30:1, the automatic provided an overall ratio of 38.32:1.

A rigid ladder-type frame with five cross-members and front reinforcements supported a front suspension with longitudinal multi-leaf front springs, double action, 1.19 inch diameter telescopic shock absorbers and a stabilizer bar. The rear arrangement was not as familiar to veteran Jeep owners since it used single leaf, semi-elliptic springs mounted asymmetrically with the rear axle mounted five inches ahead of the spring centers to limit rear axle squat under acceleration.

This suspension gave the Jeepster a capability similar to that of the AMC Eagle of the 1980s. It was a car with excellent 4-wheel drive performance but definitely not intended for rugged off-road operations. A cam and roller gear steering system with an overall ratio of 24.01:1 plus 4.5 turns lock-to-lock gave the Jeepster a 43.5 feet turning circle. Low profile 7.35 × 16 black sidewall tires mounted on 15–5.5K wheels were standard. Either 8.45 × 15 Power Cushion whitewalls or Suburbanite mud and snow tires were available as $60 options. With standard equipment the Jeepster's curb weight was 2835 pounds. Maximum gross weight was 3550 pounds. It was possible to increase this to 4200 pounds by use of the optional heavy-duty suspension or

cylinder models could not be ordered with the automatic transmission. They were delivered with a standard 4.27:1 ratio unless a 5.38:1 was specified. No extra cost was involved for any optional ratio to be installed.

The Jeepster Sports Convertible was available in both standard and

A 1967 Jeepster prototype. (Courtesy of Old Cars Weekly)

overload springs-air bag combination. At both the front and rear were 10 × 2 inch hydraulic brakes with cast iron drums and a lining area of .174 sq. in. A dual master cylinder was used along with a double hydraulic circuit.

The base engine for the Jeepster was the F-head, 4-cylinder Hurricane with 75 horsepower at 4000 rpm and 114 lb.ft. of torque at 2000 rpm. For an additional $194 the Dauntless 225 cubic inch V-6 with a single 2-barrel carburetor and automatic choke (the 4-cylinder still had a manual choke) was offered. It develped 160 horsepower at 4200 rpm and 235 lb.ft. of torque at 2400 rpm. This engine made the Jeepster a quick accelerator With Hydra-Matic, a V-6 Jeepster reached 60 mph from rest in just over 12.5 seconds. It completed the standing-start ¼ mile in approximately 19 seconds at a speed of 72 mph. The Jeepster's gearing and poor aerodynamics limited top speed to the 85–90 mph range. The standard axle ratio for a V-6 Jeepster with Hydra-Matic was 3.31:1 with 3.73:1 available. The 3-speed version used a standard 3.73:1 with 4.88:1 optional. Four-

Custom versions. The basic equipment-feature list for the standard model included foam-molded seats, front arm rests, front and rear floor mats and door-side panels color-coordinated to the exterior finish, chrome bumpers, hood latches and hinges; hub caps, manual convertible top with a glass rear window, and an exterior-mounted rear-view mirror. The Custom model was equipped with vinyl-pleated seats, rear arm rests, front and rear thick-pile carpeting, rear seat rise cover, courtesy lights, wheel trim rings and a convertible top boot.

Kaiser Jeep praised the Jeepster's 4-wheel drive's ability to provide "twice the traction of ordinary cars on slick, rain-wet roads … twice the 'grip' on snowy and icy roads." But at the same time it could also point with pride to the Jeepster's standard passive safety features which included a padded instrument panel and sun visors, recessed instruments and gauges, 2-speed electric wipers with non-glare arms, high-impact windshield, seat belts and safety door hatches and hinges.

Of course Kaiser Jeep was equally eager to equip a customer's

179

Jeepster with such convenience options as a power top (the Jeepster was the only 4-wheel drive vehicle available with this feature), power brakes, a console (standard with Hydra-Matic), air conditioning, heater-defroster and E-Z Eye tinted glass. A transmission brake was available for Hydra-Matic as was a heavy-duty cooling system for the V-6.

A 1967 Jeepster Convertible, available with either manual or power top. (Courtesy of author's collection)

Dealer options included the mag-type wheel covers, transistor radio, selective drive, free-wheeling front hubs; locks for the gas filler and spare tire, electric clock (available only with the console shifter), overload springs and air bags; convertible top boot (standard models), snow plow, front-mounted winch, and for 4-cylinder models a ceramic fuel filter and oil pan magnetic drain plug.

The Jeepster's main dash panel was similar to that used on the Gladiator trucks and Wagoneer models with fuel and temperature gauges plus warning lights for oil pressure and alternator. Directly to the driver's left were recessed switches for the lights, windshield wipers and washers, fan, defrosters and heater. If a radio was installed it was mounted in the dash center section adjacent to the glove box.

A single transfer case control was mounted to the right of the transmission tunnel. Most drivers complained it was located too far forward for easy operation. When moved to the rear it placed the Jeepster in 4-wheel drive mode. To activate the low range the lever was moved forward in a U pattern which many operators found difficult to master.

As less plush alternatives to the Jeepster, Kaiser Jeep offered four spin-off models; the Jeepster Commando Station Wagon, Convertible, Pick-up Truck and Roadster. All shared the Jeepster Sports Convertible's basic structure but each also had its own unique functions and appeal. For example, their bodies lacked the Sport Convertible's upper body chrome trim but they carried a Commando identification plate on their hood panels. A similar arrangement was found on their deck. Unlike the Sports Convertible, the Commandos had fold-down rear tailgates that made access to their interiors very easy. All exterior dimensions except overall length, which was 168.40 inches, were identical to those of the Sport Convertible.

The Station Wagon was outfitted with a steel top, a top-hinged rear window casing and a standard rear seat. Available only on the station wagon were roof racks for either luggage or skis. Another Station Wagon exclusive was what Kaiser Jeep called "Deluxe Trim Group B". This included deluxe seats, headliner and door trim, front and rear carpeting and arm rests, cigarette lighter, courtesy lights, rear quarter side-open windows, chrome outside mirror and bumpers, hubcaps and wheel trim rings. All models were also available with the "Deluxe Trim Group A" option which consisted of the cigarette lighter, front arm rests, door scuff plates, front and rear floor mats, chrome bumpers, hubcaps and trim rings.

Both the Commando Station Wagon and Convertible had their spare tires installed flat on the cargo door behind the rear seat. The Convertible's top was reminiscent of the old CJ–3A's with a zippered rear window insert and roadster-type installation.

The Commando Pick-up, which Kaiser Jeep described as combining "great riding smoothness, fine fashion and real truck function in a 4-wheel drive rig" was well ahead of its time as a mini pick-up truck. By positioning the spare tire horizontally in a well directly behind the cab, its designers were able to provide a cargo bed 63.5 inches long. When the tailgate was lowered this was extended an additional 18.7 inches. Maximum width was 59 inches and the distance between

the wheel wells was 36 inches. Like all Commando models the Pickup's overall length was 168.4 inches or nearly seven inches less than the Sport Convertible's.

The last Commando model, the Roadster, was offered with either a soft full or half top, or with no top at all. Like the Pick-up it was strictly a two-seater but with the full station wagon top (which had non-yellowing vinyl rear and tailgate windows) a rear seat was available.

Since the Commandos were intended for more energetic lifestyles than the Sports Convertible, they were offered with such traditional Jeep options as a spindle hook, draw bar, push plate and power take off. All Jeepster models could have their standard 15 gallon fuel tank supplemented by an auxiliary unit with a 9.5 gallon capacity.

A wide choice of exterior colors were listed for the Jeepsters. The top for both the Roadster and Sports Convertible was offered in Glacier White, Empire Blue or Charcoal. The top for the Station Wagon and Pick-up was available only in Glacier White. Body color selections for the Sports Convertible consisted of Prairie White, President Red, Glacier White and Empire Blue. These colors plus Spruce Tip Green and Gold Beige were available for the remaining Jeepster models.

Changes made in the Jeepster design from 1968 through 1970 were limited to a new top design and a hinged tailgate for the Sports Convertible in 1969, and the availability of power steering for models with the V-6 engine in 1970.

During 1971 two special Commando models were introduced that are today the Jeepsters most sought after by collectors. The first, introduced as a 1971½ model was identified as the Commando SC–1. Based on the Station Wagon body, it featured a Butterscotch Gold body, a white top and black rally striping across its hood and body sides. Included in the latter was "SC–1" identification. Its standard equipment included the V-6 engine, luggage rack and radio.

A 1973 Commando Station Wagon. (Courtesy of author's collection)

Also based on the Commando wagon was the Hurst/Jeepster Special, a joint effort by American Motors and the Hurst Performance Company. In the late sixties Hurst and AMC had begun their association by collaborating on the S/C Rambler Scrambler, AMX SS and Rebel Machine. These were all high performance models intended to help AMC separate itself from its old conservative image.

Initial plans for the Hurst/Jeepster Special called for production of 500 units of which 300 were to have automatic transmissions controlled by a Hurst Dual Gate shifter. The remaining 200 units were to have three-speed manual transmissions with Hurst T-Handle shifters. Eventually, however, less than 100 were built. All were finished with a white exterior with blue and red rally striping running down the hood's center line and across the front cowl and rear tailgate.

Linking the Hurst/Jeepster to the Rebel Machine was its special ABS plastic hood scoop which contained a 0–8000 rpm tachometer easily visible from the driver's seat. A roof rack was installed along with Goodyear Polyglas F70 × 15 tires with raised white lettering. Unique to the Hurst/Jeepster's interior was a 15 inch foam steering wheel with brushed chrome spokes, and bucket seats offered in any of three colors-charcoal, blue or buckskin. Power brakes were standard.

For 1972 the Jeepster name was dropped along with the Sports Convertible model. The remaining versions were now known as Jeep Commandos. By this time AMC was ready to incorporate them more closely into its corporate structure. This resulted in many substantial changes for 1972. The most important technical development was the dropping of both the F-head (except for export models) and V-6 engines. Instead, the AMC 232 cubic inch 6-cylinder engine with

100 horsepower became its standard engine. Two engines were optional, the 110 horsepower 258 cubic inch 6-cylinder, priced at $56 and the $130, 150 horsepower, 304 cubic inch V-8. Along with these engines came a revamping of the Commando's transmission line-up. Whereas customers previously were limited to a choice of either a 3-speed manual or 3-speed automatic, the latest version added a heavy-duty 4-speed manual to this selection. However, it was available only with one of the 6-cylinder engines. The automatic was offered only in conjunction with the 258 or 304 cubic inch engines. The standard final drive line ratio supplied with all engines was 3.73:1 with 4.27:1 optional. In 1971 the standard ratio had been 3.31:1.

Use of the new engines necessitated a stretching out of the Commando chassis which now had a 104 inch wheelbase. Replacing the old single-leaf rear springs were multi-link units. A stronger, Dana 30, front axle was installed that, with an open-end ball joint design was easier to service. It also reduced the Commando's turning circle to 37.6 feet. The front tread was widened to 51.5 inches from 50 inches while the rear tread was unchanged at 50 inches. Also revised was the lower attachment point of the front shock absorbers. They were now anchored ahead of the axle rather than behind as had been the case on the 1967–71 models. Additional chassis/suspension revisions included a higher capacity rear axle with a rating of 3000 pounds (the older axle was rated at 2500 pounds) and stiffer front and rear springs. These changes increased the Commando's Gross Vehicle Weight rating to 3900 pounds from 3550 pounds. An extra cost heavy-duty package with a 4700 pound capacity was also available.

Also optional (with the V-8 engine only) were power brakes. The standard drum brakes had dimensions of 11×2 inches front and rear. Earlier models were fitted with smaller, 10×2 inch, units. Rounding out the design changes for 1972 were a 16.5 instead of 15 gallon fuel tank and a self-balancing hood in place of the older side hook-latch set-up.

Although the original Jeepster displayed a family relationship to other Jeep models via its CJ–5-type front end, its overall appearance wasn't universally applauded by critics. For example, *Off-Road Vehicles*, May/June, 1972 depicted the 1967–71 models as "squarish and ungainly looking". Reacting to the 1972 Commando's appearance *4WD Recreation Vehicles*, Spring, 1972 noted: "We lament the necessity for such changes as these but styling does sell cars and we think the Commando will be more appealing in the marketplace as a result."

The big change in the Commando's appearance took place at the front where virtually all the body's added length was found. The longer hood extended into a very broad grille with single headlights set at its ends and directional/parking lights inlaid in its broad mesh grille. Viewed from the rear, the new Commando was identified by its tailgate's extruded center section which provided room for the spare tire to be mounted flat behind the optional (at $10) rear seat or directly behind the bulkhead.

Substantial revisions were made in the Commando's interior beginning with the use of standard full-foam front bucket seats. A more comfortable riding/driving environment resulted from the positioning of the front seats 1.5 inches to the rear and the movement of the rear seat 4.8 inches further back. Rear seat passengers appreciated the smaller wheel housings. Additional interior revisions included use of an elliptically shaped rather than circular steering wheel and a white instead of black headliner. Both the standard interior and the "B" interior trim package included front arm rests.

The price of the 1972 Commando and its popular options was as follows:

Commando Model	Price
Roadster	$3334
Pick-up	$3431
Station Wagon	$3491

Option	Price
Hydra-Matic	$262
Air conditioning	$411
Power steering	$148
Power brakes	$46
Free running hubs	$98
Limited slip rear differential	$61
Decor Group	$121
Custom Decor Group	$225
Rear seat (Station Wagon)	$92
Split front bench seat	$89
AM radio	$74
Heavy duty springs and shock absorbers	$39
Heavy duty 4-speed manual trans.	$175
Heavy duty cooling system	$24
258 cubic inch engine	$56
304 cubic inch engine	$130
55 amp battery	$25
70 amp battery	$12
Cigarette lighter	$7
Luggage rack	$72

In 1973 changes were limited to improvements in the Commando's suspension including the use of new more durable extended-life front axle and propeller shaft joints and upgraded F78 × 15 4-ply tires in place of the 7.35 × 15 4-ply tires used in 1972. The Commando also used the new mechanical clutch linkage (in place of the older cable set-up) and improved front axle and driveshaft introduced on the 1973 CJ models. The Commando's 6-cylinder engines also had induction hardened exhaust valve seats. Added to the Commando's option list were sliding rear windows for the Station Wagon plus a new Decor Group trim package for all models and a new Custom Decor Group with wood trim for the Station Wagon. Green seat trim replaced the blue color previously used in wagons with the Custom Decor Group. The seats were also available in black or buff. The Base and Decor Group seat trim was all-vinyl in buff or black, as in 1972.

Rather than make changes in a design that was generally regarded as uncompetitive with the Chevrolet Blazer, American Motors decided to drop the Commando after the 1973 model year and replace it with the new Cherokee series.

Chapter 10

The Jeep Wagoneer:
1962–1988: From
Pioneer to Grand Dame

On 14 November, 1962, just a little more than ten years after the introduction of its short-lived passenger car, Willys returned to the mainstream automotive market with its Wagoneer model. To make certain the public was properly aroused, Willys sent the new model off in style with what was depicted as its "biggest ever" advertising theme. Willys purchased a 100 second Wagoneer television commercial at the beginning of the popular "Lloyd Bridges Show" on both 13 and 20 November as well as a one-minute commercial of the new Gladiator truck at the show's end. An even more ambitious effort was a media blitz in 18 major national publications including *Farm Journal*, *Life*, *The New Yorker* and *Time* magazine.

Development and design of the Wagoneer and its derivatives took place over a three year time span and cost $20 million. Much of this time and treasure was committed to the creation of a new engine that aroused a good deal of attention due to its overhead cam design. This interest wasn't limited to Jeep enthusiasts since the overhead cam format, (although last seen on the 1949 Crosley among American cars), was associated by American enthusiasts with such classics as the Duesenberg and Stutz. In recent years, the Crosley being the exception, overhead cam engines had been regarded as strictly a European product.

As a result, the ohc Willys engine was often compared (favorably) with the Jaguar overhead cam 6-cylinder engine. In addition, there was a fair amount of speculation that Willys might just be planning something else besides a new line of passenger cars and trucks, perhaps a modern update of the Jeepster, for example.

Of course, a new Jeepster wasn't far off, but it was not the overhead cam, true sportscar that some hoped for. But that dream had no negative impact upon the appeal of the new Willys. The only body style available was a station wagon with two or four doors in either two- or four-wheel drive. The two-door version was also offered as a panel delivery vehicle with its rear quarter panel windows replaced by sheet metal. In this form only a front seat was installed. This model also had two vertically hung rear doors instead of the conventional tailgate, upwardly hinged rear window arrangement found on other Wagoneers. Willys used a J–100 series identification for all two- or four-door station wagons and panel delivery models. Those with 2-wheel drive were designated 162 models while 4-wheel drive counterparts were the 164 models.

Willys used the following serial number prefixes for the J–100 body styles.

Serial number prefix	Body style	Drivetrain
1312	2-door Station Wagon	2-wheel drive
1312C	2-door Custom Station Wagon	2-wheel drive
1314	4-door Station Wagon	2-wheel drive
1314C	4-door Custom Station Wagon	2-wheel drive
1313	2-door Panel Delivery	2-wheel drive
1412	2-door Station Wagon	4-wheel drive
1412C	2-door Custom Station Wagon	4-wheel drive
1414	4-door Station Wagon	4-wheel drive
1414C	4-door Custom Station Wagon	4-wheel drive
1413	2-door Panel Delivery	4-wheel drive

The base 162 two-door station wagon weighed 3496 pounds with fuel, oil and water. The four-door wagon and panel delivery weights were respectively 3546 and 3326 pounds. As expected, the 4-wheel drive models were heavier. Following the 3701 pound 4-door station wagon were the 3498 pound panel delivery and the 3668 pound 2-door station wagon. The use of an automatic transmission added 87 pounds, with power brakes and steering adding 13 and 20 pounds respectively. The heater added another 34 pounds to the vehicle's curb weight.

The styling of the Wagoneer was assigned to Brooks Stevens Associates headed by Brooks Stevens. Years earlier Stevens had designed the original Jeepster. In addition, the Stevens organization had been responsible for the design of the reborn Willys sedan for the Brazilian market as well as the Rural Willys trucks and sedans produced by Willys to Brazil.

Since Willys wasn't in the habit of frequently changing body styles as was the policy in Detroit, the goal of the Stevens' designers was to create an appearance avoiding easily dated styling cliches. At the same time it was imperative to maintain a close product continuity with other past and present Willys models. What better way, thought Stevens, than to use the classic Willys Jeep "face" as a starting point. Thus the Wagoneer had a functional front end with a simple grille consisting of vertical dividers. This arrangement was incorporated into a slightly raised hood line that gave the familiar grille outline a bit of elegance by linking it to cars of the classic era. At the same time, its creators endowed the Wagoneer with a fresh look by extending the outer edge of the fenders and hood just far forward enough to encircle the grille and front lights. Mounted inboard of the single headlamps were air intakes for the interior. Rectangular parking/directional lights were positioned directly below the headlights. An attractive Jeep logo was mounted in the lower right side of the grille. It had a modern look with an outer ring of turbine vanes surrounding quadrants of alternating gold and red fields. In the center was the Jeep name spelled out in broad gold letters. Custom models were identified by the stainless steel trim around their windshield, rear backlight and side windows.

With a 110 inch wheelbase, overall length of 183.69 inches, width of 75.6 inches and a height of 64.2 inches the Wagoneer was the antithesis of the popular longer, lower and wider school of thought then dominating the styling of American cars. While these dimensions made the Wagoneer a tremendously practical vehicle, they didn't promise much in the form of a pleasing design. But Brooks Stevens had long been famous for a brand of creative thinking that his Big Three contemporaries, insulated by big budgets and almost limitless facilities, lacked. The result was a Wagoneer whose appearance and virtues enabled it to outlast all of its contemporaries from Detroit. On this point it's good to remember just how obsolete such cars as the 1963 GM, Ford and Chrysler models look today while the Wagoneer still remains an attractive, still very much accepted design in the mid-eighties.

Stevens achieved this design success by using horizontal lines as the main styling theme for the Willys' side body in conjunction with a high green house with lots of glass area. Jeep described the Wagoneer's windows as "pano-scopic". The combination of doors that opened 82 degrees (wider than those of any other station wagon) and a windshield that wasn't plagued by the "dog's leg" window post made it easy to enter or leave a Wagoneer.

At the same time there was just a touch of CJ heritage in the Wagoneer's angular wheelwell cutouts. At the rear simple uncomplicated square taillights and circular back-up lamps graced a rear deck devoid of unnecessary trim.

Car Life, April, 1963, liked the looks of the Wagoneer, noting that it "looks like what it is – an honest, extra-heavy-duty station wagon that has been designed to do a wagon's work ... it successfully follows the prior Jeep wagon theme (stylists call this 'product identity'). It looks truck-like enough to give the Wagoneer a sturdy feel, and yet the slim corner posts and large glass area help avoid bulkiness and impart a modern appearance."

Danny Collins, who tested a Wagoneer for Floyd Clymer's *Auto Topics*, March, 1965, noted that "the Wagoneer's rugged, good looks went down well with both the men and women who viewed the car in our presence."

With good reason Willys was immensely proud of the new Wagoneers, depicting them as "All new, all Jeep". Sales literature noted that "The Wagoneer is not a converted passenger car with a tailgate thrown in, nor a modified truck with windows ... The all new 'Jeep' was conceived and designed as a wagon from its wheels to its reinforced roof."

The Wagoneer was touted as a multi-use family car with "'Jeep' reliability and ruggedness'. These were, for many American new car buyers, refreshing concepts. Moreover, in combination with careful refinements to the Wagoneer's appearance they contributed to the evolution of the Wagoneer into a late 20th century status symbol. In 1987 a survey by American Motors showed that purchasers of the 1986 Grand Wagoneer had a higher medium income than did buyers of the 1986 Cadillac Seville.

But all of that was unimagined in 1962 when Jeep was emphasizing Wagoneer virtues such as its excellent road clearance due to frame protected control arms and lack of exposed axle shafts; and the use of galvanized steel for all lower body sills and underbody structural members as examples of its fidelity to traditional Jeep ruggedness.

Jeep enthusiasts would have flocked to their dealers for a closer look at this new offering from Toledo even if it had been powered by one of the seasoned Willys engines. But as mentioned earlier, it created a minor tremor in the industry because of its sensational ohc engine. Credit for this engine, which Willys identified as the Tornado OHC, went to its chief engineer since 1952, A.C. Sampietro, who had come to Willys at that time from Europe where he had worked for Donald Healey. Healey had been an important player in the scheme of things leading to the postwar renaissance in sports cars that swept across America in the decade after the Second World War ended.

The popularity of the Austin-Healey was just one example of Healey's influence. In addition to the creation of this car Healey also built his own Healey automobiles as well as the Nash-Healey in cooperation with the Nash-Kelvinator Corporation. In that context, Sampietro had attracted attention by developing a cylinder head for the Nash engine that increased its output from 140 horsepower to 189 horsepower. Furthermore, Sampietro, who had been involved in chassis design at Healey that contributed to the demise of the old, saw that it was not possible to combine a soft ride with good road holding capabilities.

Development of the new Willys engine was influenced both by existing trends in the industry and Willys' heritage which included considerable experience with L- and F-head engines, overhead valves and even sleeve-valve engines. In a paper presented to the Society of

Automotive Engineers in June, 1962, Sampietro noted that Willys had "learned to appreciate the good points of these different engines and to live with their shortcomings".

From the very beginning, development of the new Willys engine was heavily influenced by the hemispheric cylinder head design. Sampietro reported that "Our tests always confirm the opinion expressed in many papers presented to the S.A.E. that overall performance of the hemispheric combustion chamber without fail is superior to that of any other known shape of combustion chamber."

To substantiate this assertion Sampietro alluded to tests conducted on a "very good" 6-cylinder 250 cubic inch engine with both a standard overhead valve cylinder head and an experimental hemi-head. The result showed the conventional model developing approximately 140 horsepower at 4200 rpm. The modified version attained an output of nearly 190 horsepower at 4400 rpm.

This particular engine, with a 3.5 inch bore and 4.375 inch stroke, was quite the opposite of the modern over-square (bore larger than stroke) engine. In order to confirm his belief and silence critics who believed the advantages of a domed cylinder head were lost with an over-square engine, Sampietro had, several years earlier, conducted a test program with a V-4 air-cooled engine identified as the AO–4 with a 4 inch bore and 3.25 inch stroke. One of these 164 cubic inch engines was fitted with a wedge head, the other with a hemispheric head. The results, said Sampietro, "were conclusive. It was decided that the new engine should have a domed combustion chamber cylinder head". For the record, the wedge-head AO–4 had approximate power levels of 85 horsepower at 4000 rpm and 142 lb.ft. of torque at 2400 rpm. Its hemi-head counterpart's respective outputs were 105 horsepower at 4000 rpm and 158 lb.ft. of torque at 2600 rpm.

Development of the new Willys engine also included three experimental engines based on the 161 cubic inch 6-cylinder then being produced by Willys. Actually, two of them weren't very experimental at all since they used the familiar L-head and F-head formats. For comparison purposes their horsepower ratings were 72 at 4000 rpm and 87 at 4300 rpm, respectively. The third engine, revealing Sampietro's European background, was far more interesting. It used a hemispherical combustion chamber with inclined pushrods operated by a cam mounted in the crankcase side. The rods operated the exhaust rockers by way of short cross-over pushrods. This arrangement had been seen in earlier times on the BMW 328 engine and its derivative, the British Bristol engine. The latter engine was, in the early sixties, powering the AC Ace-Bristol to numerous Sports Car Club of America racing victories and championships.

The Willys version performed very well in its initial stages of testing, developing 112 horsepower at 4300 rpm and displaying the high volumetric efficiency desired by Willys. In addition to out-producing the L- and F-head versions this engine also demonstrated superior fuel economy. Sampietro wasn't, however, happy with its complex valve train.

He rejected its "somewhat complicated" cam drive and relatively heavy cylinder head. A conventional block-mounted camshaft could be used but, noted Sampietro, "this complicates the casting and interferes with good cooling passages". Also distasteful, from his

187

perspective, was the double pushrod set-up which, while he conceded worked satisfactory possessed an "inherently awkward" design. As a result a single overhead cam layout was adopted with hemispherical combustion chambers (that Willys preferred to call "spheroidal") that was designed around three basic percepts: There were to be as few components as possible between the valve and cam; the valve gear was to be light and rigid, and the lash adjustment was to be simple, accurate and sturdy.

Design of the new Willys engine started in February, 1960 and the first prototype was operational a year later. Guiding its development were the following objectives:

1. Its power output per cubic inch and fuel economy were to be superior to any other competitive engine.
2. It should possess simplicity of design; be capable of a long service life and be easy to maintain.
3. Tooling costs were to be kept to a minimum by adaptation of its design to existing plant facilities.
4. Maximum interchangeability of parts was to exist with both shorter stroke and four-cylinder versions that could be developed at a later date.
5. The engine was to be suitable for production with a die-aluminum cylinder head and crankcase at a later date if development warranted it.

As a result of the third stipulation the new engine could be regarded as a complete redesign of the old flathead 226 cubic inch engine Willys had inherited from the days of the Kaiser-Frazer/Willys-Overland merger. Even in 1953 this engine had been around for a long time. Originally produced by Continental for the prewar Graham, it had been the only engine used for the full-size Kaiser and Frazer from the start of production in 1946 through 1955. In both 1954 and 1955 it had been fitted with a McCulloch supercharger which had increased its output from 118 to 140 horsepower. Checker had also purchased this engine with either side or overhead valves for its taxi cabs. The ohv version developed 122 horsepower.

Although the Willys' overhead cam six had the same bore center, block height and length as the old 226 cubic inch six, the two engines shared very few interchangeable parts. Among these were their connecting rods and flywheel. The overhead cam engine had its own block, cylinder head, pistons and crankshaft as well as many other components that weren't applicable to the previous versions of the 226 engine. In addition, the new Willys engine had a slightly larger bore of 3.4375 inches rather than 3.31 inches which along with an unchanged stroke of 4.375 inches increased its displacement to 230 cubic inches. This long stroke was just a bit old-fashioned but it offered the advantage of excellent low speed torque output.

The most interesting feature of the Tornado engine was its overhead cam which was operated by a silent-type Morse chain. The design of the chain was unusual in a number of ways. Its contacting surfaces were covered with a special chilled cast iron, selected for long life and compatability with the cam lobes. Also of interest was the use of only six cam lobes which meant that each lobe operated one intake and one exhaust valve. The timing for both the intake and exhaust valves was 250 degrees with 30 degrees of overlap. The valves were inclined and respective intake and exhaust valve head measurements were 1.895 and 1.618 inches. Valve spring pressure was 130 pounds.

"The crankshaft", said Sampietro, "is the real basis of a heavy duty high performance engine." Therefore, it was not surprising that the Willys engine engineers paid a good deal of attention to the Tornado's crank design. Sampietro noted that the "first wish of an engine designer is to make as rigid a shaft as possible with as many main bearings as possible". Nonetheless, there were, in his view, sound reasons to favor a four, rather than seven main bearing arrangement. For example, while his goal of torsional rigidity and a high natural frequency of the crankshaft were achieved only by a seven main bearing engine with large diameter bearings, these, in turn, absorbed an unacceptably high amount of energy, particularly under part-load condition. But even so, the battle was, at this point, only half won since, explained Sampietro, "a satisfactory four-bearing crankshaft for *heavy duty* work is far from simple to design and develop".

Before Willys achieved its objectives extensive analytical and laboratory stress testing was conducted both on Willys' design and on crankshafts from competitor's engines. The Willys' engine crankshaft ran in four main bearings with a width of 1.375 inches. The journals measured 2.375 inches with 2.125 inch crankpins. The crank was constructed of SAE 1045 steel and was Tufftride treated. Tufftride was a liquid nitriding process developed by the Dequssna-Durferrit Company of Frank/Main, Germany and was introduced into the United States by the Kolene Corporation of Detroit, Michigan which was its sole licensee.

The Tufftride process involved soaking the crank in a special salt bath for two hours at 1025 degrees. This increased, said Willys, the engine's fatigue life by fifty percent and made the journal surfaces hard enough to be compatible with heavy duty tri-metal engine bearings. Obviously, this process was considered essential due to the high rpm capability of the new engine. In comparison, shot peening the crank improved its hardness by approximately 25 percent while the increase from using cold rolled SAE 1045 steel was some 35 percent. Furthermore, Sampietro pointed out that these two alternatives "have the disadvantage of not producing a sufficiently hard surface for the use of higher capacity bearings". His faith in the merits of Tufftriding was substantiated by the successful completion by the Willys engine of a rigorous testing program which consisted not only of thousands of miles of road operations but also hundreds of hours of running at both its rated 4000 rpm speed and at 4400 rpm which was 10 percent over speed.

The pistons selected for the Tornado engine were cam-ground, tin-plated aluminum-alloy "Autothermic" units with two compression and one oil control ring. The top compression ring was chrome plated while the lower one was taper-faced cast iron.

The ohc six weighed, with flywheel, 575 pounds. This didn't make it America's lightest engine by any means. By comparison, the Buick 198 cubic inch V-6 weighed 169 pounds less. Willys did, however, use aluminum where ever possible to keep weight down to an acceptable level. For example, the front engine and valve covers plus the oil pump body were constructed of cast aluminum. For ease of maintenance all engine accessories except the oil filter were mounted on the front cover.

Even though it was constructed of SAE grey iron, the Willys cylinder head, at 58 pounds, weighed just eight pounds more than the Jaguar's aluminum head. Its design enabled both relatively large valves to be used along with what we noted Willys called a spheroidal-shaped combustion chamber. This differed from the typical dome-shaped chamber by having a slight offset and partial pocketing of the exhaust valve. In effect this created a secondary spheroid combustion chamber which effectively controlled the swirling nature of the gas flow. The off-setting of the exhaust valve by 0.375 inches from the cylinder center line enabled the spark plugs to be positioned close to the combustion chamber's center. This, in turn, resulted in a short and uniform flame travel to all points of the chamber. In addition, both the port shapes and valve head contours were designed for maximum gas flow.

Among the other salient features of the Willys engine were its rocker arms which were steel stampings and were mounted on ball pivots, and its cast iron unlinered cylinder block which had a very low rate of heat distortion and subsequently excellent wear qualities. The cylinder head had a longitudinal intake manifold runner making possible use of a simple two-branch cast aluminum external manifold with six separate ports.

Willys was justifiably proud of its new engine and wasn't the least bashful in comparing it to the fifteen 6-cylinder engines produced by Chevrolet, Buick, International-Harvester, GMC, Ford, Chrysler, Continental, and American Motors. Of these engines the Willys had, with the exception of the intake valves of the 304.7 cubic inch V-6 produced by GMC, the largest valve head diameters. In terms of torque the Tornado engine was outproduced by a number of engines including the 235 cubic inch Chevrolet, 225 cubic inch Chrysler and the 240 cubic inch International-Harvester. None of these, however, matched the Willys' low rpm torque output and only one, the 198 cubic inch Buick V-6, was capable of producing significantly more torque output per cubic inch of displacement than the Jeep engine. But even then, reported Willys, "since this engine must run at 650 more rpms to deliver that torque it is a very questionable benefit in terms of economy-particularly with its loss of gas mileage and need for more frequent servicing".

Willys also pointed to the Tornado's spheroidal combustion chambers, large valves, overhead cam and carbo-nitrided crankshaft as prime contributors to its long life and low maintenance costs. It claimed that with a simple valve train there is at least 50 percent less likelihood of the need for valve train maintenance. Similarly, the Willys crankshaft was depicted as a fresh solution to the demand for more powerful engines. "To attain higher power levels or greater engine life," said Willys, "the size of the crankshaft must *ordinarily* be increased. This also necessiates an increase in the size of other components, and the result is simply a bigger heavier engine. But the new carbo-nitriding hardening and toughness process of the crankshaft used in the Tornado-230 allows much higher performance *without* an increase in crankshaft and engine size."

Willys also linked the new engine to the traditional simplicity and soundness of design associated with previous Jeep engines. It pointed out to prospective customers the accessible positioning of such items as the carburetor, fuel pump, distributor, generator, oil filter and filler, dipstick and spark plugs. In addition, the valve cover was quickly taken off by the removal of only four bolts.

The power curve of the Willys engine was impressive. Officially Willys rated it at 140 horsepower at 4000 rpm and 212 lb.ft. of torque at 2000 rpm. These were net figures at a time when gross ratings were almost exclusively used by American manufacturers to inflate advertised power ratings. On that basis the Willys' output was 155 horsepower at 4000 rpm and 230 lb.ft. of torque at 1750 rpm. Underscoring his obvious pleasure with the final product was Sampietrio's comment that "higher speed versions of the engine would obviously be capable of a substantially higher output."

Wagoneers with a manual transmission were fitted with a single-barrel Holley Model 1920 carburetor. Those with automatic transmission had a Holley Model 2415 2-barrel unit. The standard cooling system had an 11 quart capacity which was increased to 12 quarts if a heater was installed. On early models the exhaust and tail pipes were of a 2 inch diameter. Later models had this size increased by 0.25 inches. Several other changes also took place during the 1963 model run. These included use of a doweled front engine plate to assure correct alignment of the plate to the cylinder head. Also found on late production engines were special zinc plated head bolts installed in the number 12 and 14 cylinder heads bolts. Finally, the crankcase ventilating system was altered by the addition of a breather hose connecting the air cleaner with the breather pipe on the left-side of the crankcase.

The electrical system consisted of a 12 volt, 50 amp battery (mounted under the hood) and a 35 amp alternator. A larger, 40 amp unit was optional. Standard sparkplugs were 14 mm Champion L12Y models. A full-flow oil filter was standard.

For early production model 2-wheel drive Wagoneers a 9.25 inch dry plate clutch with a rated torque capacity of 240 lb.ft. was used. Later 2-wheel drives and all 4-wheel drives used a larger 10 inch clutch with a 250 lb.ft. rating. These clutches were supplied by Borg & Beck which also produced an optional 10.5 inch, 265 lb.ft. rated version. Yet another clutch, manufactured by Auburn with a 10.5 inch diameter and 290 lb.ft. capacity was available for the 4-wheel drive models.

Performance of the 4-wheel drive Wagoneer with automatic transmission was well within the realm of conventional automobiles. Zero to 30 mph required 4.6 seconds; zero to 45 mph, 8.8 seconds and zero to 60 mph, 16.1 seconds. The standing start quarter-mile was completed in 20.5 seconds at a speed of 68 mph. Top speed was 90 mph.

Attracting nearly as much attention as the overhead cam engine were the new front suspension systems Willys offered for the J-series wagons. In all, there were four different versions available: 2- and 4-wheel drive units with independent suspension plus two solid front axles for both 2- and 4-wheel drive heavy-duty use. Standard on 2-wheel drive J-162 models was an independent unit with torsion bars and a swing axle. The axle (a Dana model 27DFSO), which was articulated near its center, served as the lower suspension wishbones. A strut bar was used for lateral axle control and for caster adjustment. The upper suspension components consisted of short A-arms and ball joints linked to the 0.78 inch diameter torsion bars.

Sempietro commented that "this arrangement was arrived at after considerable work, and gives a good roll center condition without large tire scrubs, or introducing large gyroscopic reactions." This suspension was also offered as $160 option for the 4-wheel drive versions.

For heavier duty operation both the J-162 and J-164 models were available with the more familiar (at least to Jeep enthusiasts) solid front axle with longitudinal leaf springs. As applied to the J-series this arrangement used four leaf, semi-elliptical springs measuring 44 × 2.5 inches. A Rockwell standard reverse Elliott axle was used for the J-162 while a Dana model 27AF was installed on the 4-wheel drive J-164. Its standard ratio was 4.89:1 with 3.73 and 4.27:1 units optional.

Both the independent front suspension and solid axle models used hydraulic, double-action shock absorbers but those on the latter measured 12.75 inches in contrast to the 12.18 inch units found on the former.

As expected, the independent suspension system provided a much smoother ride. Its spring rate of 110 lb./in. was 27 percent softer than the 150 lb./in. leaf spring's rating. This gave the J-162 a ride firmer than the conventional American station wagon but well within the realm of acceptability for family-type vehicles.

The J-162 and J-164 had interchangeable rear suspensions and axle systems. Hydraulic, double-action 10.75 inch shocks were used along with 52 × 2.5 inch semi-elliptic, 4½ leaf springs. Standard on the panel delivery model and optional on station wagons were 6-leaf springs of the same dimensions. Two-stage rear springs were offered as an option for all wagon models. A Dana Model 44, semi-floating rear axle was used for all J-100s. Except for early models all J-series 4-wheel drives were equipped with a transmission cooler which was optional for the J-162. Willys offered this as a retro-fit for customers who had purchased their vehicles when it wasn't available. From its introduction the J-series' sales were strong and before long, Willys had a healthy backlog of orders. One of many reasons for this state of affairs was the combination of an automatic transmission and 4-wheel drive. The transmission used for this purpose was a 3-speed Borg-Warner Model AS-8F with ratios of 2.4:1 (first), 1.467:1 (second), 2.0:1 (third) and 2.01:1 (reverse). The transfer case for automatic J-100s with 4-wheel drive was a Spicer Model 21 that was a single range unit controlled by a 2-position, floor-mounted lever.

Three different manual transmissions were available for the J-series Jeep. Standard for the J-162 was a 3-speed Warner Gear T-86 with ratios of 2.57:1 (first), 1.55:1 (second), 1.00:1 (third) and 3.489:1 (reverse). The same gear box, but with overdrive, was identified as a T-86E Model. It was available as an option only for the J-162. The overdrive unit had a minimum in-and-out speed of 26 mph and provided a reduction ratio of 0.7:1.

Four-wheel drive J-models used a Warner Gear T-90 gearbox with ratios of 2.789:1 (first), 1.55:1 (second), 1.00:1 (third) and 3.789:1 (reverse). This transmission was used in conjunction with a 4-position, dual-range Spice Model 20 transfer case. In its forward-most position its floor-mounted control placed the vehicle in 4-wheel drive-high range. The next stop activated the Jeep's 2-wheel drive mode. This was followed by a neutral position which disengaged power to all wheels. It was intended for operation of optional power take-off equipment. The extreme rear location provided the combination of 4-wheel drive and low range.

All 4-wheel drive models were equipped with transfer case indicator lights mounted under the center of the dash panel. Those with automatic transmission had a single green light which operated when 4-wheel drive was engaged. A two light unit was used for manual transmission versions. Its green light glowed when 4-wheel drive was either the low or high range. An amber light indicated the transfer case was in neutral. Neither light operated when the transfer case was in the 2-wheel drive mode.

As a mid-year option a 4-light system providing individual light indicators for each lever position was offered with the following color-drive-relationship:

White: 2-wheel drive
Green: 4-wheel drive
Amber: neutral
Red: 4-wheel drive, low range

A toggle switch, located to the left-side of the lights turned them off if desired.

Cast iron, hydraulic drum brakes with identical front and rear dimensions of 11 × 2 inches were used with an effective lining area of 161.16 square inches. Late 1962 production models used a servo-type brake with a star wheel adjustment in contrast to the non-servo self-centering-type brake found on the very early production models. The parking brake operated on the rear wheels but J-series with 4-wheel drive and automatic transmission could be fitted with an optional parking brake that operated on the drive shaft at the end of the transfer case.

Also offered were two power brake options. On those vehicles

equipped with automatic transmission a Bendix system was used with a wide and low pedal position. For those Jeeps with manual transmission a Midland version with a higher and narrower pedal was installed.

Both two- and four-wheel drive models used 15 × 5.5K steel disc, full-drop center wheels produced by Kelsey-Hayes. These carried, as standard equipment, 6.70 × 15-4-ply tires with a 7.10 × 15 size optional.

The Ross cam and lever steering used for the J-series had 5.6 turns lock-to-lock with an overall ratio of 24:1. Turning circles for J-100s with independent front suspension measured 38.3 feet while the solid axle version required a 41.16 foot circle. A Thompson power steering system was optional that initially had a 20.0:1 ratio. Later models adopted the conventional system's 24:1 ratio.

Since Willys used the same basic frame for both the two- and four-wheel drive models, its height was a relatively high 11.6 inches. The side rails were constructed of heavy channel steel, 5.5 inches deep, with a modest up-kick at both ends. Five cross-members whose design differed, depending on whether they were intended for a Jeep with two- or four-wheel drive and either independent or solid front axles, were used.

A 20 gallon fuel tank was positioned between the rear driveshaft and the right-side frame rail. Although of adequate capacity, its long and narrow form, in conjunction with an extremely long, nearly horizontal filler pipe made full tank fills a long and frustrating experience.

The J-series interior was modern, functional and attractive. Base models had all vinyl plastic trim with serviceable rubberized floor mats. The Custom interior package included front and rear seat area carpeting, covered cargo area, fabric seat inserts, higher quality headliner and door trim panels, wheelhouse covers, front and rear chrome-trimmed armrests, chrome-trimmed rear view mirror, chrome molding for the instrument panel and radio speaker, chrome cigarette lighter, foam seat cushions and a horn ring. Custom Wagoneers also carried additional exterior body trim consisting of a chrome grille, stainless steel trim for the door frames and windshield, and wheel rings.

Ten exterior colors were offered for the Wagoneer: White Cap, Spruce Tip Green, Parkway Green, President Red, Nordic Blue, Sierra Blue, Parade Blue, Jet Line Gray, Tree Bark Brown and Amber Metallic.

Interior finishes were available in three low gross paints: Sylvan Green for cars with exterior green paint, Nordic Blue for those with exterior blues and Amber Metallic for all others.

The Wagoneer's list of optional equipment was extensive. Primary drivetrain/mechanical accessories consisted of a 40–60 amp alternator, independent front suspension (2-wheel drive only), overdrive (2-wheel drive only), power steering, power brakes, drive line brake, Powr-Lok differential (rear axle only), oil bath air cleaner, front-mounted winch (4-wheel drive only), power take-off (rear-mounted), Warn free-wheeling front hubs and governors.

Convenience and comfort options included a locking gas cap, magnetic drain plug, a speedometer reading in kilometers, electric-operated tailgate, dual-speed wipers, windshield washers, fresh air heater and defroster, electric clock, back-up lights, push button AM radio, parking light indicator, compass, transfer case indicator lights, chrome exterior mirror, padded dash panel, seat belts, E-Z Eye windshield glass and a glove box light.

The price schedule for the 1963 Wagoneers was as follows:

Series	Factory advertised delivered price
J–100/2-wheel drive	
4-door	$2579
2-door	$2546
4-door Custom	$2783
2-door Custom	$2738
J–100/4-wheel drive	
4-door	$3332
2-door	$3278
4-door Custom	$3526
2-door Custom	$3472

Most road tests of the new Jeep were, not surprisingly, extremely laudatory. *Car Life*, April, 1963 began its review by noting the long history of Willys-Overland as a firm that had fought a "courageous fight" over ten years against many adversities including bankruptcy, economic downturns and financial reverses. Through all this Willys (early in 1963 the name of Willys Motors, Inc. was changed to Kaiser Jeep Corporation, a wholly-owned subsidiary of Kaiser Industries Corporation) was depicted as a firm that had never lacked "engineering acumen". The author of the *Car Life* road test was John R. Bond the publisher of both *Car Life* and *Road & Track* who was probably the most engineer-oriented publisher/writer/editor then working in the automotive publishing field. Naturally, he focused much of his attention upon the Willys ohc engine which he depicted as "one of the most interesting being built today".

Although Bond was a bit concerned about the high price of his Custom 4-wheel drive test Wagoneer, he declared it to be "seemingly well planned for many functions". Being from the "old school" he noted that "if you're used to a Corvair Monza, for example, the seats would feel tremendously high, though actually the seating position isn't much different from that of a 1948 Ford or Mercury." Bond liked both the Wagoneer's engine and ride characteristics. Reminding his readers that the Tornado OHC was a truck engine, Bond wrote that "it is also not quite as smooth and quiet as the modern V-8 passenger car engine … Nevertheless, this Tornado 6 feels exceptionally strong and solid at all speeds and especially so at low speeds."

Similarly, Bond praised the Wagoneer's ride quality as "quite exceptional, definitely somewhat firmer than a typical passenger car wagon and all the better for it. Certainly there's no truck-like ride here and the Wagoneer feels stable and controllable over roads that make lesser vehicles wobble, wander and weave."

Interest in the Wagoneer was aroused in England by the importation of a number of them by the J.C. Bamford excavating company which had its first model flown to England in a Boeing 707 prior to the availability of Wagoneers with right-hand drive directly from the manufacturer. The Bamford Wagoneer was the subject of a road test published in *The Autocar* in its 19 June, 1964 issue. With few exceptions *The Autocar* found the Wagoneer a capable and entertaining vehicle. It noted that its ability to combine the capability to "make light work of mud and ruts and keep going where even a trails special would come to a wheel-spinning halt … with the comfort, spaciousness and the effortless high cruising speed of a big American estate car is exceptional."

Also singled out for praise was the Wagoneer's performance. Noted *The Autocar*. "For a vehicle of such size and uncompromising styling, the top speed performance is excellent, and up to 80 mph … there is excellent performance." In light of the many years of testing high performance automobiles behind the perspective *The Autocar* brought to the testing of the Wagoneer, its comments on its road manners were particularly interesting. "Despite its exceptional height off the ground and its utilitarian appearance, the Wagoneer has unexpectedly good handling qualities, and there is a commendable absence of roll when corners are taken fast."

No changes were made in the appearance or basic mechanical features of the Wagoneer for 1964. As a new option air conditioning was available. Offered both for the Wagoneer as well as the old-style 6–230 models was a low compression, 7.5:1, version of the overhead cam engine with ratings of 133 horsepower at 4000 rpm and 199 lb.ft. of torque at 2400 rpm.

The prices of the 1964 models follows:

Series	Factory advertised delivered price
J–100/2-wheel drive	
4-door	$2673
2-door	$2629
4-door Custom	$2871
2-door Custom	$2827
2-door Panel Delivery	$2511
J–100/4-wheel drive	
4-door	$3434
2-door	$3379
4-door Custom	$3633
2-door Custom	$3578
2-door Panel Delivery	$3082

In April, 1965 the Wagoneer became the first Jeep vehicle to be offered with a V-8 engine when the American Motors' 327 cubic inch V-8 became available as an option. This move was announced by James Beattie, Kaiser Jeep Corporation's vice-president-marketing who explained that rather than wait for the new model year to begin, Kaiser's policy was to announce product improvements as they became available. The overhead cam six was still the standard engine, but this "Vigilante" V-8 was, at $190.83, an attractive alternative. With a 2-barrel carburetor the V-8 developed 250 horsepower at 4700 rpm and 340 lb.ft. of torque at 2600 rpm.

This engine was originally introduced in 1956 for the Nash Ambassador Special line. At that time it displaced 250 cubic inches with a bore and stroke of 3.50 × 3.25 inches. Peak horsepower was 190 at 4900 rpm with a 8.0:1 compression ratio and single 2-barrel Carter carburetor. Most engine analysts regarded it as a straightforward design that, if lacking in exciting features, was reliable and up-to-date. Four main bearings were used and with all accessories, but minus its flywheel and clutch this V-8 weighed 601 pounds. Thinwall construction was used for all iron castings and with good-sized valves (1.79 inch intake and 1.41 inch exhaust) plus a 4.75 inch bore center-to-bore center measurement it was easily expanded to 327 cubic inches with a 4 inch bore and 3.25 inch stroke in 1957. At that point its maximum horsepower was 255 at 4700 rpm with a 4-barrel Carter carburetor and 9.0:1 compression ratio. In December, 1956 American Motors announced that this engine would power its entry in the then popular limited production high-performance field, the Rambler Rebel. The 255 horsepower version would be standard. The V-8 was available with an optional Bendix electronic fuel injection system. Due to production problems no Rebels were sold with fuel injection but the next year a more powerful V-8 with 270 horsepower at 4700 rpm and a higher 9.7:1 compression ratio was offered.

In conjunction with use of this V-8 Kaiser Jeep also made available General Motors' Turbo Hydra-Matic 3-speed torque converter automatic transmission for both 2- and 4-wheel drive models. This engine-transmission did not replace any of the J–series' existing standard or optional engine-transmission choices.

The 2-speed transfer case used in conjunction with Hydra-Matic was a Spicer 20 unit with a 2.03:1 ratio. Other Wagoneers with automatic transmissions did not have this extra low set of gears since a manual clutch was required to shift them. General Motors, through its Saginaw division, also supplied the Wagoneer's full-time power steering which was of a recirculating ball worm design.

Performance of a V-8 Wagoneer was, as expected, superior to that of the 6-cylinder version. *Motor Trend*, September, 1965, tested a Wagoneer with a complement of options including Turbo Hydra-Matic (a 3-speed manual transmission was standard with the V-8; overdrive was also available), air conditioning and power brakes and steering. With a curb weight of 4200 pounds and the standard 3.31:1 rear axle supplied with the automatic transmission, the Wagoneer accelerated from zero to 60 mph in 14.5 seconds. A V-8 Wagoneer tested by *Popular Mechanics*, October, 1965, with a zero to 60 mph time of 13.1 seconds, was slightly quicker. The *Motor Trend* Wagoneer completed the standing start ¼ mile in 19.6 seconds at 68 mph. Top speed was 89 mph.

Compared to other American cars the Wagoneer was quite expensive. As tested by *Motor Trend* the Wagoneer's price was $5330.80. Its base price of $3633 compared to those of other 1965 American station wagons as follows:

Marque/model	Factory advertised delivered price
Chevrolet Impala 4-door, (9-pass.)	$3181
Buick Skylark 4-door, (9-pass.)	$3285
Dodge Custom 880 4-door, (3-seat model)	$3407
Ford Country Squire, (9-pass.)	$3283
Mercury Colony Park, (9-pass.)	$3511
Oldsmobile F–85 Custom, (8-pass.)	$3865
Plymouth Fury III, (9-pass.)	$3193
Pontiac Catalina Safari, (9-pass.)	$3202

The full range of Wagoneer models were priced as follows:

Series	Factory advertised delivered price
J–100/2-wheel drive	
4-door	$2701
2-door	$2658
4-door Custom	$2896
2-door Custom	$2853
2-door Panel Delivery	$2511
J–100/4-wheel drive	
4-door	$3449
2-door	$3395
4-door Custom	$3644
2-door Custom	$3590
2-door Panel Delivery	$3396

All Wagoneer models for 1965 had a new standard safety package consisting of front and rear seat belts, padded sun visors, high-impact windshield glass, chrome outside mirror, dual brake system, 4-way warning flashers, back-up lights, and dual-speed wipers and windshield wipers.

'Jeep'

The family-recreational nature of the 1963 Wagoneer was displayed to good advantage in this cover sheet from a 1963 brochure. (Courtesy of author's collection)

The weather Wagoneer owners loved. (Courtesy of author's collection)

The interior of the 1963 DeLuxe Wagoneer interior. (Courtesy of author's collection)

The handsome lines of the 1963 Wagoneer. (Courtesy of author's collection)

Wagoneer

ALL NEW ALL 'JEEP'

'Jeep' Wagoneers

A functional interior was a key feature of the 1963 Wagoneer.
(Courtesy of author's collection)

A standard 2-door 1963 Wagoneer. (Courtesy of author's collection)

The Wagoneer's cavernous interior
(Courtesy of author's collection)

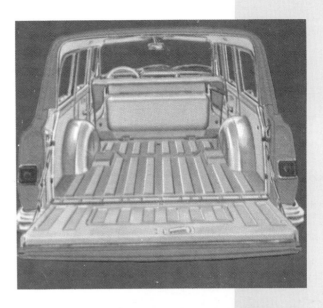

The Tornado OHC engine. (Courtesy of author's collection)

A phantom view of the Wagoneer
front suspension (Courtesy of
author's collection)

The positioning of the
optional Selector Drive Lights of the 1963
Wagoneer. (Courtesy of author's collection)

Gleaming chrome skid strips brighten the plush appearance of the Super Wagoneer's carpeted cargo area and provide additional ease in loading and unloading. The Super Wagoneer has a larger tailgate opening and a bigger cargo area than any wagon in its wheelbase class—an example of the superb craftsmanship displayed throughout this lavish wagon.

The electrically-operated rear window is activated by a slight touch of the power-control switch located conveniently to the driver, or by insertion of the ignition key into the tailgate lock. Unless this window is lowered, the tailgate can't be opened accidentally.

Even the roof of the Super Wagoneer is elegant. The smartly textured, padded vinyl covering is hand fitted, and especially treated for durability. Further enhancing the attractiveness of the 'Jeep' Super Wagoneer is a chromium luggage carrier that easily supports anything from safari equipment to resort luggage.

The careful attention paid to each design detail becomes apparent upon close examination of any of the carefully fitted components of the Super Wagoneer. The door panels keynote this design coordination. Each panel is carefully trimmed in supple pleated vinyl with simulated walnut wood-grain and chromium accents. And a carpeted scuff panel helps soften door closing noise.

The Super Wagoneer's 270 horsepower Vigilante V-8. (Courtesy of author's collection)

197

The 1966 Super Wagoneer. (Courtesy of author's collection)

More important in strengthening the Wagoneer's position in the marketplace was the introduction of the Super Wagoneer in 1966. This was the most dramatic example to date of the growing sophistication of the 4-wheel drive market. Kaiser Jeep spared no rhetoric in making certain the Super Wagoneer was viewed in the proper perspective by its intended clientele. Beyond depicting the Super Wagoneer as "A new dimension in motoring", Kaiser Jeep noted that: "No matter the number of automobiles possessed in a lifetime, there is little else of a material nature as exciting as the first hours and days of ownership of a truly fine car."

Two decades later with the Grand Wagoneer this status would be more evident, but in 1966 the introduction of the Super Wagoneer represented an important step in the evolution of the Wagoneer into a prestige vehicle.

The Super Wagoneer's exterior had, with the possible exception of the Gala and Surrey models, the most dramatic styling of any Jeep vehicle to date. Two side trim panels, widening from front to rear, were, if somewhat dated in concept, effective in setting the Super Wagoneer apart from lesser models. The top panel contained an "antiqued gold" insert while the lower and narrower panel was painted black to match the color of the standard padded roof. The Super Wagoneer's rear deck had similar detailing consisting of a wide upper panel with a vertically-ribbed gold insert and a much narrower black panel. Added to the Wagoneer script on the rear fender panel was a gold "Super" trim plate. Installed on the front fender tops were bull's-eye-shaped ornaments. Somewhat more contemporary were the Super Wagoneer's mag-styled wheel covers with simulated knock-off hubs. The Super Wagoneer was available in any of the following colors: Empire Blue, Indian Ceramic, Glacier White or Prairie Gold.

Kaiser Jeep depicted the Super Wagoneer as "the most elegant 4-wheeler auto ever crafted" and its interior appointments supported that claim. Courtesy lights were mounted in the ceiling and near the floor, and an adjustable steering wheel tilting to any of seven positions was installed. The seats (front buckets and rear bench) had foam cushions and were finished in pleated knit back British calf grain and Cranstone. Door panels were trimmed in soft vinyl with simulated walnut wood-grain and chrome accents. The scuff panel was covered in a color-coordinated carpet. Unlike those on many American cars

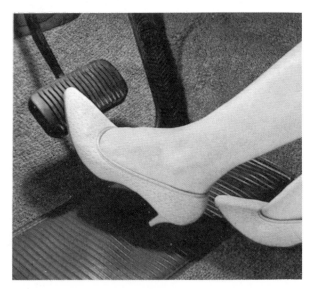

Subtle suggestion that the Super Wagoneer was a suitable vehicle for female drivers. (Courtesy of author's collection)

that had an embossed stitch pattern, the Super Wagoneer's seats were machine stitched. Both the dashboard and sun visors were padded and a vanity mirror was fastened to the back of the passenger's sun visor. The rearview mirror was equipped with a prismatic lenses with day and night positions. When not in use the front seat belts automatically retraced into belt retainers. Rear seat belts were also standard.

In addition to the items already noted the Super Wagoneer was fitted with a multitude of standard features including air conditioning, Turbo Hydra-Matic, power steering and brakes, power tailgate window, tinted safety glass in all windows, white sidewall 8.45 × 15 Power Cushion tires with a 4-ply rating, luggage carrier chrome outside rear view mirror, and a push-button transistor radio. An interesting feature of this radio was an automatic volume control which kept the audio amplitude constant.

Powering the Super Wagoneer was the 4-barrel version of the 327 cubic inch Vigilante V-8 with a 9.7:1 compression ratio. Its ratings were 270 horsepower at 4700 rpm and 360 lb.ft. of torque at 2600 rpm.

With the introduction of the Super Wagoneer the Wagoneer model-price line-up for 1966 was as follows:

Series	Factory advertised delivered price
J–100/2-wheel drive	
4-door	$2838
2-door	$2794
4-door Custom	$3033
2-door Custom	$2989
2-door Panel Delivery	$2650
J–100/4-wheel drive	
4-door	$3585
2-door	$3531
4-door Custom	$3780
2-door Custom	$3726
2-door Panel Delivery	$3223
4-door Super Wagoneer	$5943

The Super Wagoneer, like the other Wagoneers, had a new grille style with vertical bars extending nearly the full width of the front end that set them apart from the Gladiator trucks and the Panel Delivery model. All Wagoneer models were also equipped with the standard "safety package" that was also installed on the Gladiator models. Finally, all models were fitted with a wider selection of interior color selections.

No styling changes were made in the Wagoneer models in 1967 which left the reborn Jeepster model to attract most of the media's attention. But this didn't mean there weren't important changes to be found in the latest Wagoneers. Beyond doubt the most important of these was the replacement of the overhead cam engine by a 232 cubic inch 6-cylinder supplied by American Motors.

The dropping of the Willys engine after such a short production life was a disappointment to many Willys fans but the use of an engine that was far less expensive to purchase made economic sense. Its successor had been introduced in mid-1964 as the powerplant for a new deluxe model Rambler, the Typhoon 2-door hardtop. At that time its 3.75 inch bore and 3.50 inch stroke made it the largest 6-cylinder engine built in the U.S. Although it was of a very conventional design this engine which still remains in production as a 258 cubic inch engine in 1988, had many attractive features. First of all, it was, at 414 pounds, very light. Its casted crankshaft was carried in seven main bearings and its intake and exhaust valves measured 1.787 inches and 1.406 inches respectively. The valves were angled at a 10 degree angle to wedge-shaped combustion chambers. Peak power ratings were 145 horsepower at 4300 rpm and 215 lb.ft. of torque at 1600 rpm.

Although Kaiser Jeep significantly reduced the scope of the Gladiator truck line for 1967, it left the Wagoneer line intact:

Series	Factory advertised delivered price
J–100/2-wheel drive	
4-door	$2953
2-door	$2909
4-door Custom	$3150
2-door Custom	$3106
2-door Panel Delivery	$2783
J–100/4-wheel drive	
4-door	$3702
2-door	$3648
4-door Custom	$3898
2-door Custom	$3844
Super Wagoneer	$6048
2-door Panel Delivery	$3357

For 1968 the Wagoneer was available only in 4-wheel drive form. This move was accompanied with the establishment of the Super Wagoneer and a new model, the Custom V-8 as members of a new sub-series. As a result the Wagoneer line-up now appeared as follows:

Series	Factory advertised delivered price
J–100/4-wheel drive	
4-door	$3869
2-door	$3815
4-door Custom	$4065
2-door Custom	$4011
2-door Panel Delivery	$3457
J–100 V-8/4-wheel drive	
Super Wagoneer	$6163
4-door Custom	$5671

A 1968 Wagoneer. Observe that the right front fender reads "V-8 Jeep". On the left side it reads "Jeep V-8". (Courtesy of author's collection)

The 1968 Wagoneer was available with either a 145 hp six or 230 hp V-8 engine. (Courtesy of author's collection)

Although 1969 was the final year for Kaiser Jeep, it was also a year when many important changes were made in both the Wagoneer as well as its model choice. In the latter category all but four models were dropped. No longer offered were the 2-door models and the Super Wagoneer. The survivors and their prices were as follows:

Series	Factory advertised delivered price
J–100/4-wheel drive	
4-door	$4145
4-door Custom	$4342
J–100 V-8/4-wheel drive	
4-door	$5671
4-door Custom	$6163

These models were offered in a choice of seven colors: Empire Blue, Bronze Mist, Prairie Gold, Spruce Tip, Gold Beige Glacier White and President Red. All painted surfaces were first treated with a zinc-phosphate coating and primer. After painting was completed and inspected each Wagoneer was undercoated and sprayed with a wax coating for protection during shipping.

The base model Wagoneer's vinyl grain interior was offered in Rawhide, Charcoal or Marlin Blue. Color-keyed appointments included the headliner, instrument panel, sun visors, floor mats and seat belts.

The same color selection was available for the Custom interior which was upholstered in a combination of rayon-nylon fabric and a

soft expanded vinyl. An optional pleated vinyl was available in either President Red or Charcoal for the Custom Wagoneer.

The 145 horsepower "Hi-Torque" 6-cylinder engine remained the Wagoneer's standard engine but replacing the AMC 327 cubic inch V-8 was a 350 cubic inch "Dauntless" V-8 supplied by Buick. This "Buick Connection" came at a time when Kaiser Jeep had already acquired the tooling for Buick's V-6 engine for use in the CJ models.

Buick's entry in the compact car field, the Special, first used this V-8 (as an option to the standard V-6) in 1964 when it had become an intermediate-sized car. At that time the V-8 displaced 300 cubic inches and was rated at 210 horsepower at 4600 rpm and 310 lb.ft. of torque at 2400 rpm. In terms of design heritage the V-8 was related both to Buick's V-6 engine and the older aluminum V-8. Initially it used aluminum cylinder heads but these were replaced in 1965 by cast iron units. The following year a longer stroke of 3.85 inches instead of 3.40 inches along with an unchanged 3.75 inch bore boosted displacement to 340 cubic inches. For the 1968 model year Buick increased displacement of this "small block" V-8 to 350 cubic inches by using a larger 3.80 inch bore. In this form with a 2-barrel carburetor and a 9.0:1 compression ratio it was supplied to Kaiser Jeep. Its maximum horsepower was 230 at 4400 rpm. Peak torque was 350 lb.ft. at 2400 rpm. Wagoneers with this engine carried front fender trim reading "350 V-8 Jeep".

The 1970 Wagoneers, the last produced under the auspices of Kaiser Jeep, were identified by their new front grille design, revised rear deck trim, altered trim and new interior and exterior color selection. With the old Wagoneer grille transferred to the Gladiator trucks the Wagoneer retained its identification among Jeep models thanks to its new egg crate grille and front fender mounted side lights. The old grille-mounted circular Jeep logo was replaced by more contemporary-looking JEEP block lettering mounted in the grille's right portion. New side body trim consisted of Jeep lettering positioned somewhat lower on the front fender than was similar identification on 1969 models and revised 4-wheel drive/model identification located just in front of the back wheel cutout. The Wagoneer script previously located on the rear panel was no longer used. At the rear a checkered patterned insert bracketing the license plate panel was used on Custom models.

A total of nine body colors, two more than offered 1970, were available for the 1970 Wagoneer. They included: Island Blue, Candle-light Yellow, Burnished Bronze, Sprucetip Green, President Red, Candlelight Yellow, Burnished Bronze, Sprucetip Green, President Red, Champagne White, Vintage Gold, Avocado Mist and Spring Green.

In June, 1970, six months after American Motors acquired the Kaiser Jeep assets in January, 1970, it announced a new sun roof option for the Wagoneer priced at $490.50. Included in this price was a vinyl-covered roof and side body trim similar to that of the discontinued Super Wagoneer offered in a choice of four colors.

The pricing schedule for the 1970 Wagoneers was as follows:

Series	Factory advertised delivered price
J–100/6-cyl.	
4-door	$4284
4-door Custom	$4526
J–100/V-8	$5876

No changes were made in the 1971 Wagoneers until American Motors, on 4 January, 1971 began producing Wagoneers with a standard 258 cubic inch 6-cylinder engine. This was a derivative of the 232 cubic inch 6-cylinder and had a 3.75 inch bore and a 3.90 inch stroke. Peak horsepower was 150. As options, American Motors now offered its V-8 engines in either 304 or 360 cubic inch displacements. Their respective horsepower ratings were 210 at 4400 rpm and 245 at 4400 rpm. Maximum torque for the 360 cubic inch V-8 was 365 lb.ft. at 2600 rpm.

As indicated by the following, prices for 1971 were once again increased.

Series	Factory advertised delivered price
J–100/6-cylinder	
4-door	$4447
4-door Custom	$4697
J–100/V-8	
4-door Special	$6114

Although the Wagoneer was the least-changed model in the Jeep line-up for 1972, there were a few examples of AMC's influence to be found besides the all-AMC engine line-up which was carried over from 1971. For example, the standard interior now had an embossed vinyl seat trim while buyers of the Custom model could choose from either houndstooth fabric or perforated-pleated vinyl seats. A new door trim scheme was also used on the Custom Wagoneers. A large, 9 inch day/night rear view mirror was now used as was a quieter Saginaw power steering pump. Front bucket seats were now listed as a Wagoneer option. The Custom Special model was dropped for 1972 although all its features were still available as individual options.

In 1972 the Wagoneer's prices were almost unchanged. The standard wagon listed for $4398 or $49 less than in 1971. The Custom version's price was $4640 which represented a reduction of $57. Prices

of popular Wagoneer options were as follows:

Option	Price
360 cubic inch V-8	$218
Turbo Hydra-Matic	$275
Air conditioning	$455
Power steering	$148
Power brakes	$46
Warn hubs	$102
Limited slip rear differential	$61
Heavy duty shock absorbers	$15
Heavy duty springs	$23
AM radio	$72

For 1973 the big news from Jeep was the availability of the Quadra-Trac 4-wheel drive system supplied by Borg-Warner. Supporting the comment made by Marvin Stucky, American Motors vice-president in charge of Jeep product development, that "The Quadra-trac system, which has been under development for more than four years, represents an advance which is as significant to the four wheel drive vehicle as the first automatic transmission was to the automobile" was American Motors' observation that "the revolution in 4-wheel drive begins…" The basic philosophy of Quadra-Trac was simple; regardless of the driving conditions the front and rear differentials automatically adjusted the power and speed of the wheels they controlled, thus, each wheel received the correct proportion of driving power required.

In a similar fashion, a unique limited slip third differential (which received power from the rear of the transmission via a duplex chain) mounted mid-way on the drivetrain had a cone clutch set-up with a torque biasing ability which enabled it to transmit power to the front and rear differentials in the proportion required by road conditions. As a result, Stucky noted that the new system gives "maximum handling response on and off the road at all times and under all driving conditions."

Aside from the improved control and handling that resulted Quadra-Trac also was quieter in operation than competing systems, reduced tire wear and, of course, eliminated the need for selective drive hubs. Included with Quadra-Trac was Turbo Hydra-Matic and the 360 cubic inch engine with a single 2-barrel carburetor and an 8.5:1 compression ratio. Its net ratings for 1973 were 175 horsepower at 4000 rpm and 285 lb.ft. of torque at 2400 rpm. A 4-barrel carburetor version with 195 horsepower at 4400 rpm and 295 lb.ft. of torque at 2900 rpm was also available. Since Quadra-Trac had a capacity of 250 horsepower and 325 lb.ft. of torque, either engine was suitable for use.

As either a dealer-installed or factory option, a separate, self-contained Low Range was available for Quadra-Trac that provided a 2.57:1 ratio in addition to the standard 1.0:1 ratio. It mounted directly to the transfer case at the end of the transmission main shaft. Low Range was operated by a control knob located on the dash board to the right of the steering column. The Wagoneer could be either stopped or be moving no faster than five miles per hour when Low Range was to be engaged. To accomplish this the transmission was placed in neutral

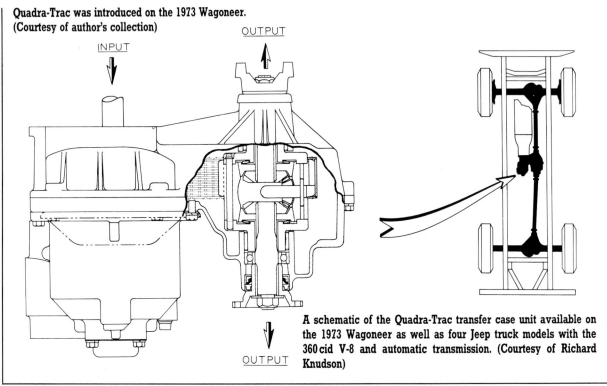

Quadra-Trac was introduced on the 1973 Wagoneer.
(Courtesy of author's collection)

INPUT

OUTPUT

OUTPUT

A schematic of the Quadra-Trac transfer case unit available on the 1973 Wagoneer as well as four Jeep truck models with the 360 cid V-8 and automatic transmission. (Courtesy of Richard Knudson)

and the handle pulled out. To cope with extreme or unusual conditions the third differential could be deactivated by a control knob located in the glove box. When this was turned counterclockwise the lockout was engaged and a light on the dash indicated this condition. When the knob was turned in the opposite direction the light did not function.

William G. Morgan, American Motors general sales manager explained that the Quadra-Trac system would be fed into Wagoneer production gradually to enable AMC to determine the extent of demand. Thus, Quadra-Trac Wagoneers were initially in limited supply.

Aside from this historic development there were many other changes made in the Wagoneer for 1973. Immediately obvious to anyone familiar with older models was the floor shift for the standard 3-speed, all-synchromesh manual transmission. The optional 4-speed manual continued to have a floor-mounted shift lever while Turbo Hydra-Matic once again used a column-mounted control lever. Also apparent was a new instrument panel with a three-section cluster housing the speedometer/odometer in the center with the fuel and temperature gauges along with warning lights for the parking brake and brake failure to their left. The third unit, with new oil and ammeter gauges, (in place of the almost universally despised "idiot lights") was positioned to the right of the center pod. Standard parking brake and brake-failure warning lights were located in the upper left cluster pod. All control knobs were of a "soft-feel" construction and were marked with international code symbols in white lettering. Also distinguishng the new dash was a much wider brow and an ashtray mounted on ball-bearings. All models also had a new energy absorbing steering column, a restyled steering wheel, new armrests, new optional clock, locking column ignition switch and a hazard warning light control.

The Wagoneer continued to be offered in both a standard and Custom version. The latter model had woodgrain trim for the instrument cluster and a color-keyed instrument panel, steering column and steering wheel as well as "double needle" switching for the seat inserts. A "Rio Grande" embossed vinyl upholstery was standard on the Wagoneer. Custom models had a "Leo" pleated fabric interior with "Uganda" perforated vinyl optional. The 1973 color selection consisted of nine colors: Champagne White, Fawn Beige, Jetset Blue Metallic, Fairway Green Metallic, Avocado Mist Metallic, Copper Tan Metallic, Butterscotch Gold, Daisy Yellow and Trans-Am Red.

The introduction of the new Cherokee in 1974 positioned Jeep in a very important and growing section of the 4-wheel drive field. It was accompanied by an equally dramatic elevation of the Wagoneer into a fully equipped, prestige vehicle without equal among domestic 4-wheel drive vehicles. Giving the Wagoneer a fresh face was a new grille featuring a gridwork with wider subdivisions and housing the parking/directional lights in rectangular pods. Also reshaped and repositioned were the front fender side markers. A roof rack continued to be offered but for 1974 it had adjustable cross bars and side rails with woodgrain trim. New options included a set of aluminum alloy wheels, 5-mph bumpers and a tilt steering wheel.

Although there were still two trim levels for the Wagoneer, standard and Custom, they now had a list of standard equipment that was startling, especially to anyone who still might be associating the term "Jeep" with "Spartan". Now powering all Wagoneers was the 360 cubic inch V-8 with a 2-barrel carburetor and a rating of 175 horsepower. Joining the 4-barrel 360 cubic inch V-8 with 195 horsepower at 4400 rpm and 295 lb.ft. of torque at 2900 rpm as an option was AMC's 401 cubic inch V-8 fitted with a single 4-barrel carburetor and

235 horsepower. The Wagoneer exhaust system now had 2.5 inch instead of 2.0 inch pipes as well as a new muffler. In total these changes were claimed to be more efficient than the older system. There were no transmission options. Instead, the Turbo Hydra-Matic was the Wagoneer's one and only gearbox. And, of course, it was joined to Quadra-Trac. Also included in the basic Wagoneer were power brakes (the front units were now 12 inch disc units while 11 inch rear drums were carried over from 1973) and a new Saginaw variable-ratio power steering system in place of the older version that had often been criticized for its lack of road feel. The Wagoneer was also equipped with a new windshield wiper set-up with articulated arms that cleaned a larger glass area than did the older system. If so desired the Wagoneer could be fitted with optional 5 mph front and rear bumpers, a tilt steering wheel and aluminum alloy wheels.

What was regarded as a far more important development by most Jeep enthusiasts was the use of a Dana Model 44 open-end front axle which reduced the Wagoneer's turning circle from 44.5 feet to 38.4 feet. Since the axle was now snubbed at the differential instead of at the springs the amount of spring travel was also increased. Also having the same consequence was the replacement of the old multi-leaf front springs with low-friction tapered units that were 1.5 inches longer. Due to the new axle the Wagoneer's wheelbase was reduced from 110.0 inches to 109.0 inches. Completing the list of technical revisions for 1974 was the use of 6 instead of 5-stud wheels and a change of final drive ratio from 3.31:1 to 3.07:1. A 3.54:1 ratio was optional.

In its road test of a Custom Wagoneer with the optional 360 V-8 with 4-barrel carburetor, *Pickup, Van & 4WD*, May 1974 was enthusiastic about many of its virtues and characteristics. Not the least of these was its performance. The Wagoneer, with the standard 3.07:1 axle ratio, accelerated from zero to 60 mph in just 12.5 seconds. Its standing start, 1/4 mile time and speed were 18.6 seconds and 75 mph. "In our brake tests", *PV4* reported that "we discovered that this Wagoneer is among the best stopping vehicle we have ever tested." The basis for this judgment was a 60 mph to zero mph stopping distance of 157 feet.

As far as off-road performance was concerned, *PV4* told its readers "don't let the appearance fool you; it's still a Jeep and off pavement is no problem. The Wagoneer is exemplary in ride and handling characteristics off road and the Quadra-Trac full-time 4-wheel drive is without equal." All in all there was no doubt where *PV4* stood on the issue of the Wagoneer's virtues compared to its competitors. Repeating what was found in its April, 1973 issue, *PV4* concluded that "the Quadra-Trac Wagoneer is the best 4-wheel drive vehicle in the world."

The 1975 Wagoneer engines, like those for other Jeep lines, featured a new electronic ignition system, new insulation intended to reduce heat transfer from the engine to carburetor, and on V-8s new carburetors with smaller primary and larger secondary metering valves. Shared with the Cherokee and J-trucks were new front and rear multi-leaf springs (a progressive type was used at the rear), longer shock absorbers mounted in a staggered position at the rear, heat shields for the muffler and exhaust pipes, a new power steering gear for improved road feel, a 3-belt accessory drive system on V-8 engines and a new stainless steel whip-type radio antenna. Like the Cherokee, the Wagoneer could now be ordered with optional HR-78 × 15 white sidewall radial tires.

The top-of-the-line Wagoneer Custom was available with a new optional woodgrain trim panel that was much wider than the older version. Added to the Custom's standard equipment was a new light group consisting of cargo, courtesy, glove box and ash tray lights. This latter feature was just one of several new or revised Wagoneer options that also included a stereo AM/FM radio with four speakers, electrically-heated rear-window defogger, Cruise Command speed control system, leather-wrapped, 15 inch sports steering wheel, cargo area carpeting and insulation pad, engine block heater, 70 amp alternator and a new convenience group consisting of remote outside mirror, visor vanity mirror and electric clock.

Both the standard and Custom Wagoneer interiors were available in four colors; blue, green, black and buff. The standard model had Laramie vinyl bench seats with the Custom equipped with Derby Check fabric bench seats with matching woodgrain trim installed on the door panels. Bucket seats continued to be an option for the Custom Wagoneer. For increased heat and insulation in the cargo area new color-keyed carpeting with a rubber insulation pad and protective skid strips were optional on all Wagoneers.

American Motors identified two vehicles as the prime domestic competitors of the Wagoneer, the Chevrolet/GMC Suburban Model K-10 and the International-Harvester Model 150 Travelall. The specifications of these vehicles makes possible some interesting comparisons.

rates for the 1975 and 1976 springs were as follows:

	1975		1976	
	Front	Rear	Front	Rear
Standard rate (lb./in.)	200	160/260	215	165
Optional rate (lb./in.)	260	230	260	165/265

Also introduced was a new optional heavy-duty suspension as well as an optional front stabilizer bar.

The 1975 Wagoneer was available with a new woodgrain side trim panel. Design changes included electronic ignition, power steering gear, shock absorbers and springs. (Courtesy of American Motors)

A welcomed change was the use of a new floor-mounted lever for the Quadra-Trac Low-Range control in place of the older cable-operated instrument panel-mounted control. The 1976 Wagoneer also had a more efficient dual-nozzle windshield washer system and a new standard seat-belt warning system with a three-point lap and shoulder

	Jeep Wagoneer	**Chevrolet/GMC Suburban K-10**	**International-Harvester Travelall Model 150**
Retail Price	$6013[A]	$5620	$5836
Base Engine	360 V-8	350 V-8	304 V-8
Transmission	3-speed auto	3-speed man.	3-speed man.
Front brakes	power disc	power disc	power drum
Steering	power	manual	manual
Wheelbase	109.0 ins.	129.5 ins.	120.0 ins.
Overall length	183.7 ins.	218.8 ins.	204.8 ins.
Overall height	65.0 ins.	73.5 ins.	71.3 ins.
Overall width	75.6 ins.	79.5 ins.	79.7 ins.
Turning circle	38.4 ft.	45 ft. (K-20)	42.7 ft.
Curb weight	4240 lbs.	4885 lbs.	4125 lbs.
Std. GVW	6025 lbs.	6200 lbs.	6600 lbs.
Std. Payload	1749 lbs.	1081 lbs.	1596 lbs.
Fuel tank size	22 gals.	25 gals.	21 gals.

A: Base price for the Custom model was $6246

Optional/Standard Equipment Prices

	Wagoneer	**Suburban**	**Travelall**
2-speed 4wd	$105	$286	$58*
Power steering	Std.	$170	$287
Rear seat	Std.	$184	Std.
Gauge pkg.	Std.	$17	Std.
Chrome bumpers	Std.	$36	$37

*Price for a 2-speed Part-Time system. International did not offer a full-time 4-wheel drive system.

As it had in 1975, AMC depicted the newest Wagoneer as "The ultimate 4-wheel drive experience". Similarly, the Wagoneer shared several key engineering advances with the Cherokee. For example, both had an all-new frame with a good deal of box section side rail construction for more ruggedness and durability that also allowed use of direct steering gear mounting. Similarly, the Wagoneer had the same specification front springs with increased clearance and new asymmetrical rear springs as the latest Cherokee. The relative spring

harness assembly. No change was made in the basic arrangement of the Wagoneer's dash board but the graphics for the instrument cluster, radio, clock, heater and other controls were more readable.

Although both the standard and Custom Wagoneer interiors were revamped they remained available in the same selection of blue, green, black and buff colors seats as were offered in 1975. The standard version used Fairway vinyl covered front and rear bench seats. Custom models now had a "Potomac Stripe" fabric with pleated patterned inserts. The Custom's standard and optional bucket seats were offered in a new "Soft Touch" vinyl.

1976 Wagoneer. (Courtesy of American Motors)

The woodgrain side body trim available only for the Custom reverted to its more conservative pre-1975 form. Also revised were the 15 inch wheel covers that were standard on the $6572 Custom and optional for the $6339 base model. For 1976 the center cap carrying Jeep identification was more rounded while the surrounding vaned portion was enlarged.

Only one model of the Wagoneer was available in 1977. Priced at $6966, it was the equivalent of the 1976 Custom model but did not carry

the Custom designation. Changes from 1976 were extremely limited consisting of a new vertical-mount interior spare tire carrier (also offered for the Cherokee) as an alternative to the standard under-the-rear tire mount and a new interior trim scheme. Now standard for the Wagoneers with bench seats was a Rallye perforated vinyl. An option for Wagoneers with either bucket and bench seats was a Brampton Plaid fabric. Both seat trims were available in tan, blue, black or a new berry color.

1977 Wagoneer. (Courtesy of American Motors)

The Wagoneer, along with other Jeep series was available in twelve body colors, including four that were new – Autumn Red Metallic, Loden Green Metallic, Mocha Brown Metallic and Tawny Orange. The carry-over colors were Alpine White, Brilliant Blue, Classic Black, Firecracker Red, Pewter Gray Metallic, Sand Tan and Sunshine Yellow.

Describing the Wagoneer as "well established as the industry's most luxurious four-wheel drive station wagon, American Motors had no qualms about noting that for 1978 "appearance changes [were] held to a minimum". Indeed, they were not only minimal but also quite hard to find. Leading the list were color-keyed seat belts and shoulder harnesses, a new horn bar pad for the standard steering wheel, a "soft feel" pleated vinyl seat trim, chrome-plated armrest bases and a relocated fuel filler cap. Joining the forged aluminum-styled wheels as an alternative to the standard wheels were 7 inch chrome-plated spoked steel wheels. Shared with the Cherokee was the addition of 2.5 inches for driver legroom due to an extended toe board and relocated accelerator as well as a new ambient air intake system that resulted in a lower engine operating temperature.

1978 Wagoneer. (Courtesy of American Motors)

No changes were made in the Wagoneer's engine line-up but unlike 1977 when the standard engine for California-bound Wagoneers was the 360 cubic inch V-8 with a 4-barrel carburetor, all 1978's had the 2-barrel version standard with the 4-barrel carburetor 360 V-8 as well as the 401 cubic inch V-8 fitted with a 4-barrel carburetor available in all states except California as options.

The price of the Wagoneer, at $7695, was given an extra boost upward mid-way during 1978 when AMC introduced the Limited model whose sticker price moved up an additional $3120 to $10715. Jeep depicted the Limited as "a cut above excellence ... built for the man who demands the ultimate in 4-wheel drive performance without compromising on luxury." Beyond the already high content of the standard Wagoneer was added a long list of features to create the Limited model. These items included air conditioning, tinted glass, power tailgate window, cruise control, tilt steering wheel, AM/FM/CB radio (or AM/FM 8-track), front sway bar, stabilizer bar, front bumper guards, extra quiet insulation package, headlights-on warning buzzer, intermittent windshield wipers, remote control driver's side mirror, leather seats, leather-wrapped steering wheel, extra thick carpeting in the seating and cargo area, special interior and exterior nameplates wide woodgrain side and rear trim, roof rack, special forged alunimum styled wheels and American Eagle Flexten white sidewall tires.

The extra-quiet insulation package became a new option for the regular Wagoneer model in 1979. Additional new options included a smooth ride suspension, lighted visor vanity mirror and dome/reading lamp as part of the convenience group, Caberfae corduroy fabric trim, all-vinyl seats, bodyside scuff molding with woodgrain insert and a new two-tone paint scheme (including three special two-tone exteriors for the Wagoneer Limited).

The latest Wagoneers were easy to spot with their new single piece grille of vertical bars and single rectangular headlights. Also appearing for the first time were one-piece aluminum bumpers. The only engine available for the Wagoneer was the 2-barrel 360 cubic inch V-8.

The following chart illustrated the sales of the Wagoneers relative to other 1979 Jeep models:

Model	Sales
CJ	74,878
Cherokee	27,568
Wagoneer	22,566
J–trucks	15,419

Respective prices of the standard and Limited Wagoneers were $9065 and $12,485 in 1979.

For the first time in seven years, the Wagoneer was, in 1980, offered with either a full- or part-time 4-wheel drive system. Both the new Quadra-Trac, which remained standard for the Wagoneer and its accompanying automatic transmission are described in the Cherokee chapter. Also returning to the Wagoneer specifications was the 258 cubic inch 6-cylinder which was available as a delete option with either 4-speed transmission, automatic transmission, part-time 4-wheel drive or Quadra-Trac. The last time a 6-cylinder Wagoneer had been available was 1973.

1980 Wagoneer Limited. (Courtesy of American Motors)

Beyond these significant developments the 1980 Wagoneers were offered with several new options including a pop-up sun roof and a cassette tape/AM/FM radio combination. The Wagoneer Limited had a new quartz electronic digital clock and new style aluminum wheels. All Wagoneers now were fitted with the previously optional front stabilizer bar as standard equipment.

Wagoneer prices once again moved upward. The base model listed for $9732 with the Limited retailing for $13,653.

Along with those of other Jeep models the Wagoneer's sales experienced a sharp decline in 1980 amounting to only 10,402 units.

Although the sales of all other carry-over models declined in 1981 from their 1980 levels those of the Wagoneer moved up 2152 units to 12,554. This wasn't a startling development, but it was at least a turnaround destined to gain momentum in the years that followed. Two reasons for this welcomed development was the expansion of the Wagoneer line to include three levels: Custom, Brougham and Limited; and Jeep's continued efforts to make all its products more fuel efficient.

In common with the Cherokee and J–trucks the Wagoneer now had a front air dam beneath the front bumper to funnel air downward, thus reducing wind resistance. The use of redesigned front and rear springs resulted in a lower profile for the Wagoneer as well as the Cherokee and J–10 truck. In the case of the Wagoneer its height was reduced from 66.9 to 66.7 inches. Also shared with the Cherokee and

Jeep trucks was the Wagoneer's new front brake system with drag-free calipers. The system also had many lighter weight parts, including a quick-take-up master cylinder with aluminum body and glass-filled nylon reservoir, new power booster and proportioning valve.

Unlike 1980 when the 360 cubic inch V-8 was the Wagoneer's standard engine, it became a $345 option for 1981. Replacing it was the 258 cubic inch 6-cylinder engine which was available in combination with either a 4-speed manual or 3-speed automatic transmission. This engine was the product of a long term AMC engineering effort that

resulted in it having not only substantially better fuel economy than its predecessor but also improved reliability and lower levels of maintenance and noise.

This engine's significant weight reduction of 90 pounds was achieved through the redesign of its primary componentry and the use of alternate materials – mainly aluminum. Details of this weight reduction, which are briefly reviewed in the Cherokee chapter, included use of an engine block 30 pounds lighter than its 1980 model counterpart. This was accomplished by reducing the wall thickness, web reduction and miscellaneous flange reductions. The cylinder head was redesigned for a weight reduction of 12 pounds. The rocker cover flange was straightened, and reshaped. This resulted in both the elimination of excess cast iron and a simpler geometric shape for the application of RTV sealer to the rocker arm. Contributing a net weight reduction of two pounds was a redesigned rocker arm cover fabricated of glass-filled nylon which replaced a stamped steel cover. Both the oil pump and water pump now used aluminum housings instead of cast iron. The exhaust manifold was simplified by its total separation from the intake manifold and the elimination of the heat valve. In turn, the intake manifold was also completely redesigned and

manufactured from aluminum rather than cast iron. It now incorporated an electrically heated warm-up device and a water heated circuit to replace the exhaust heat valve. Use of a new cam with an altered profile resulted in a lower idle speed plus more low speed torque output. Also contributing to a reduction in idle speed without compromise to idle quality was an idle speed control system.

The Wagoneer's TorqueFlite automatic transmission's new lock-up converter improved fuel economy, reduced engine wear and lowered engine temperature. This was accomplished by a lessening of the friction that occurred in a conventional torque converter. With the new

lock-up torque converter, a clutch within the transmission engaged automatically when the output shaft reached approximately 1100 rpm. When this took place the engine speed and transmission output shaft speed were the same, enabling smoother, more efficient transfer of engine power to the drivetrain.

Like the Cherokee, the Wagoneer for 1981 had lower numerical axle ratios and, for the manual transmission, higher first gear ratios. The only difference between those listed in the Cherokee chapter and the Wagoneer's was the availability of an optional 3.31:1 ratio for the Wagoneer with automatic transmission and the 258 cubic inch engine. On the other hand, the Cherokee's optional 3.31:1 ratio offered for the manual transmission model with the 360 cubic inch V-8, was not available for a similarly equipped Wagoneer.

The new Wagoneer line was given a proper send-off by Jeep which said: "The standard Wagoneer is the Custom … but it's hardly what you would call 'standard'." Among its standard features were a 4-speed, fully synchromesh transmission, free-wheeling front hubs, power steering and power front disc brakes. The passenger area was fully carpeted and the seats were trimmed in a Cara grain vinyl in black, blue or beige. Like all 1981 Wagoneers, the Custom had a new inside hood release.

The new Brougham model had all the appointments and equipment of the Custom plus a Coventry Check fabric upholstery for the standard bench or optional bucket seats. Also available was a Deluxe grain vinyl trim. Both were offered in black, blue, beige or nutmeg. Other aspects of the Brougham's appointments included premium door trim panels, a soft headliner and woodgrain trim for the instrument cluster and horn cover. Exterior identification included bright door and quarter window frames, lower tailgate moldings, and a thin bodyside scuff molding with a narrow woodgrain insert. The Custom, in contrast, used a wider bodyside trim similar to that used by the 1966 Super Wagoneer. All 1981 Wagoneers had standard P225/75R 15 Goodyear Viva radial tires. The Brougham's were installed on 15 × 7 inch chrome styled wheels.

Included in the Brougham's base price of $11,434, which was $970 above that of the $10,464 Custom, was extra quiet insulation, Convenience Group (consisting of underhood light, lights-on buzzer and digital clock), Light Group (consisting of interior cargo light and tailgate switch, lighted visor vanity mirror, courtesy, map/dome, glove box and ash tray lights), a roof rack, floor mats and a power tailgate window.

The Wagoneer Limited, priced at $15,164, which was $1511 above its 1980 price, was described by Jeep as "the most completely equipped, elegantly appointed full size American wagon you can own". Its list of features, beginning with those of the Brougham, consisted of bucket seats with leather/cord trim, center armrest, unique door panels in either nutmeg or beige, leather wrapped steering wheel, extra thick 22 oz. carpeting in the seating area (20 oz. carpeting was used in the cargo area with insulation), retractable cargo cover and woodgrain trim on the lower instrument panel.

Viewed from the outside the Limited's wide woodgrain side and rear trim was set off with wide moldings. The roof rack had woodgrain inserts, bright drip rails were used as were 15 × 7 inch forged aluminum wheels and Limited nameplates.

Additional technical and convenience features included Quadra-Trac, automatic transmission, air conditioning, tinted glass, power windows/door locks, power tailgate window, cruise control, AM/FM stereo radio, premium audio system, Convenience Group, Visibility Group, bumper guard and nerf strips, floor mats, Extra Quiet Insulation and power six-way driver and passenger seats.

Except for use of halogen headlights, the availability of an electronically tuned AM/FM cassette radio and the offering of a tilt steering wheel with the manual transmission (previously it was available only with automatic transmission), the Wagoneer line was unchanged for 1982. This did not impact negatively upon Wagoneer sales which moved up nicely from their 1981 level of 12,554 to 15,547. Commenting on this improvement, Joseph E. Cappy, then American Motors' vice-president-marketing group, noted, "Wagoneer sales increased 24 per cent in 1982 over 1981 and we expect them to continue strong for a long time to come". This was even more impressive in light of the Wagoneer's higher prices. The Custom listed for $11,114, the Brougham for 12,084 and the Limited for $15,964.

Popular options for the 1982 Wagoneers were priced as follows:

Option	Price
AM/FM stereo*	$249
AM/FM stereo/tape	$359
AM/FM stereo CB	$456
Cruise control*	$159
Rear window defroster	$125
Luggage rack*	$118
Sunroof	$377
Power sunroof	$1585
Power seats*	$169
360 V-8	$351

*Standard for Wagoneer Limited.

1982 Wagoneer Limited. (Courtesy of American Motors)

The 1983 Wagoneer had, as standard equipment, the new Selec-Trac 2/4-wheel drive system whose features are discussed in the Cherokee chapter. Aside from this major development and the reduction of the Wagoneer line to just the Brougham and Limited models, there were no significant changes found in the latest Wagoneers.

In 1984 with the arrival of the new down-sized Cherokee and Wagoneer models there was speculation that AMC might bring the curtain down on Wagoneer production just as it did with its Cherokee derivative. This did not take place, instead the Wagoneer returned as the Grand Wagoneer. AMC unashamedly described the Grand Wagoneer as the "Grand Daddy in 4WD".

But its advanced age and the strong sales of the new Wagoneer didn't seem to affect the popularity of the Grand Wagoneer whose sales of 19,081 were virtually unchanged from the 1983 level of 19,155. Overall, Jeep sales in 1983 amounted to 82,140, up 29 percent from 63,761 in 1982 and the best since 1979 when sales totalled 140,431.

The Grand Wagoneer's price, $19,306, provided, as standard equipment, virtually every option, including a clearcoat metallic paint, that AMC offered. Among the few options available were the 360 cubic inch V-8, a power-operated sunroof (by the early eighties this feature was increasingly depicted as a moonroof) and a 5000 pound towing package.

In introducing the 1985 Wagoneer Jeep posed several questions to prospective buyers: "Why do you suppose", it asked, "that year after year, the Jeep Grand Wagoneer is the solitary entry in the full-size 4-wheel drive luxury wagon class? Could it be [Jeep replied rhetorically] that those who build luxury vehicles know precious little about 4-wheel drive? And that those who provide 4-wheel drive vehicles show but a passing interest in luxury?"

Placed in that perspective, Jeep was far and away the industry's leader. In 45 years it had built over 4 million 4-wheel drive vehicles and ever since the time of the Super Wagoneer in 1966 it had been refining the concept represented by the Grand Wagoneer. The major

developments relating to the Grand Wagoneer in 1985 involved the use of a special "Handling Package" suspension that resulted in a smoother, quieter ride on all road surfaces. New components included new front and rear track bars and a longer front sway bar that Jeep said were "carefully balanced to improve directional stability". Gas-filled shock absorbers were also used as were improved suspension bushings and lower friction rear springs.

Through 1984 the main difference between Quadra-Trac and Selec-Trac had been the availability of the Selec-Trac 2-wheel drive mode for operating with greater fuel efficiency on paved dry surfaces. In 1985 Selec-Trac was revised to include a shift-on-the-fly capability from 2-wheel drive to 4-wheel drive under virtually every road and speed condition.

The operation of the new system was extremely simple through operation of a dash-mounted handle with settings for either 2WD or 4WD. The driver could shift in and out of either mode while driving or when the vehicle was at rest simply by moving the lever to the desired position. Since the controlled slip differential automatically and continuously fed torque to the axle with the most traction, it was possible to stay in the 4-wheel drive mode as long as desired without excessive drag or wear on front wheel drive components or tires. In addition, a 4-wheel drive Low Range could be selected for extreme driving conditions. This was, however, a part-time system. To select Low Range the Wagoneer had to be stopped with the Selec-Trac lever in the 4WD mode. At that point the 2-speed transfer case selector was moved to its Low position.

Following Main Picture: **For 1984 the Wagoneer was renamed the Grand Wagoneer. (Courtesy of American Motors)**

1983 Wagoneer Limited. Standard Wagoneer equipment for 1983 included the new Selec-Trac drivetrain. (Courtesy of American Motors)

Exterior colors offered for the 1985 Wagoneer included Olympic White, Classic Black, Deep Night Blue, and a new color; Almond Beige. There were also six clearcoat colors offered: Medium Green Metallic, Sterling Metallic, Champagne Metallic, Dark Honey Metallic, Dark Brown Metallic and Garnet Metallic. Added to the front seat was a fold-down armrest permitting center seating of a third adult.

These additions to the Grand Wagoneer had an effect upon its price

which had no difficulty in smashing through the $20,000 barrier in 1985 to settle at $20,462.

No wonder that Jeep, in describing the 1986 Grand Wagoneer, felt extremely comfortable in depicting it as being "synonymous with family travel at the highest plateau of elegance and practicality." Even more assertive was the claim that the Grand Wagoneer was "endowed with the amenities expected in a world class luxury vehicle."

Accordingly, the 1986 Wagoneer's non-performance/suspension options were limited to either a power sunroof and a padded full vinyl roof, available in white black, beige, dark blue or garnet. The only options of a technical nature available were the 360 cubic inch V-8, a California emission system (required in California), a high altitude emission system required for vehicles operating regularly at or above 4000 feet, an engine block heater, an auxiliary oil cooler, heavy duty shock absorbers and two trailer packages.

Unchallenged as the most luxurious full-size 4-door station wagon in the 4-wheel drive industry, the Wagoneer further strengthened its position in 1986 due to numerous design refinements as well as some fairly obvious styling changes. None of these, of course, were to be regarded as radical changes. "These are evolutionary improvements", said American Motors' vice president of product planning and design, John W. Mowrey, "to a vehicle that already has been the measure of distinction in its class for several years... We believe the steps we've taken for 1986 can only add to the Grand Wagoneer's reputation among discerning four-wheel drive buyers."

Most apparent of these was a revised front end with two prominent horizontal chrome bars dividing a field of narrow rectangular bars into

redesigned dash panel with both functional and stylistic changes. The controls for the heater, defroster and air conditioning (all of which were also more efficient for 1986) now were consolidated into a single unit. Joining this improved climate control arrangement was a redesigned dash with full gauge instrumentation and a woodgrain overlay. The radio was now of a "full-face" design employing a premium stereo sound system ("Accusound by Jensen") with four speakers. The steering column was also changed to include column-mounted controls for the light dimmer switch and the windshield wipers and washers. The Wagoneer's seats continued to be leather-trimmed, but a new Cumberland Cord fabric seat insert was added to both the front and rear seats.

Augmenting the Grand Wagoneer's Selec-Trac drive train was a new feature – a Trac-Loc limited slip rear differential which shifted engine power to the wheel with the most traction. This was especially useful when the vehicle was driven on slippery surfaces or when one or more wheels was hung up in an off-road situation.

The retail price of the 1986 Grand Wagoneer, whose sales totalled 17,254 was $21,350. Prices of selected options were as follows:

Option	Price
360 cubic inch V-8	$673
California emission system	$252
Auxiliary auto. trans. cooler	$63
Cold climate group	$34
Heavy-duty shock absorbers	$40
Power sunroof	$1295
Power sunroof with vinyl top	$1816
Trailer towing "A" package	$107
Trailer towing "B" package	$205

1986 Grand Wagoneer. (Courtesy of American Motors)

After these evolutionary changes, the Grand Wagoneer marked its 25th model year in 1987 with a few more changes to its credit. The most important was the use of the 360 cubic inch V-8 as its standard engine. In addition, the Grand Wagoneer became the world's first production vehicle to use new Michelin "Tru Seal" P235/75R 15 tires as

three equal sections. The headlights now were located in chrome receptacles while the grille's bright molding extended slightly into the fender region.

These changes, plus a stand-up Jeep hood ornament were, said AMC, "designed to enhance the Grand Wagoneer's already classic exterior, but it is on the inside of the vehicle where the most dramatic product improvements will be found." Leading the way was a

standard equipment. These tires had the capability to seal themselves from punctures.

The Grand Wagoneer exterior now had a new English Walnut woodgrain color as well as a new Grand Wagoneer nameplate and "V-8" identification. Two additions were made to the exterior color selection for the Wagoneer; Grenadine Metallic and Briarwood Metallic. Both had clearcoat finishes. Joining the list of interior color selections were Tan and Cordovan.

With Jeep now under the Penastar for the 1988 model year, Chrysler

After a quarter of a century the Grand Wagoneer was still popular in 1988.

felt it was appropriate to provide its newest customers with a short history lesson about the Grand Wagoneer. "Luxury is often taken for granted in today's four-wheel-drive market", it noted, "yet the vehicle that started it all a quarter century ago – the Jeep Grand Wagoneer – remains one of the most popular choices among discerning buyers... Perhaps the most significant aspect of the Grand Wagoneer when it was introduced by Jeep Corporation as a 1963 model was its automatic transmission – the first ever offered on a 4WD vehicle.

"This feature opened the 4WD market, previously restricted by technological innovation to a broader, more appreciative audience that demanded more amenities that earlier products could deliver. Evolutionary changes – such as the industry's first full-time 4WD

system in 1973, as well as name changes from Wagoneer in 1984 – have kept the Grand Wagoneer in the forefront of the luxury 4WD market ever since."

The latest Grand Wagoneer was fitted with a new standard sound system, an AM/FM MPX electronically-tuned stereo cassette with Dolby and four premium "Accusound by Jensen" speakers. A new option was an electric sunroof with an integral air deflector and venting capacity.

Chapter 11

The J–Series trucks

Although Kaiser Jeep kept the Forward Control, L6–226 and 6–230 trucks in production during 1963, the introduction of the all-new J-series was a clear signal that this would be the last year they would be available. Like the first postwar Jeep trucks, the newest models were very similar in appearance to their station wagon running mates. Two basic series were offered; the J–200 series based on a 120 inch wheelbase and the J–300 series which used a 126 inch wheelbase chassis.

Both versions were available in four basic body types: cab and chassis, Townside or Thriftside pick-ups and stake platform bodies. The latter type had either single or dual wheels in its J–300 form. The Townside models provided a wider rear bed and a smooth rear body appearance. The Thriftsides retained the separate rear fender/body assembly which, in spite of its reduced load area remained popular with pick-up truck buyers.

All J–200 and J–300 models had a full-width seat and were available in either standard or deluxe interior trim. The base model had a rear header trim panel with a vinyl welt covering the exposed edges of the roof header. The deluxe equipment package added such features as roof trim, front header panels and arm rests.

As it did with the L6–226 and 6–230 trucks, Kaiser Jeep offered many variations of these two J–series. The J–200 models, in addition to being available in two- or four-wheel drive with 6.70 × 15 tires were offered in the same form as the J–210 models with larger 7.60 × 15 tires. Both were rated as ½ ton models.

If a customer wanted a 120 inch wheelbase J–series truck with a ¾ ton rating he could select from the J–220 line which was also available either with two- or four-wheel drive. Similarly, the J–310 trucks had a 126 inch wheelbase and a ¾ ton rating and either two- or four-wheel drive.

Rounding up this diverse offering were three more versions, the J–320 with a ¾ ton rating, 126 inch wheelbase and 7.50 × 16 tires; the J–230, a 1 ton rated line with a 126 inch wheelbase and 7.00 × 16 tires, and the J–100, a panel delivery model on a 110 inch wheelbase. Both the J–320 and J–230 were available only in chassis and cab or stake platform versions.

The pricing schedule of the 1963 J-series trucks was as follows

Model	Price
J-100 2-WD Panel Delivery	$2438
J-100 4-WD Panel Delivery	$2996
J-200 2-WD Chassis/Cab	$1913
J-200 2-WD Pick-up Thriftside	$2014
J-200 2-WD Pick-up Townside	$2722
J-200 4-WD Chassis/Cab	$2596
J-200 4-WD Pick-up Thriftside	$2696
J-200 4-WD Pick-up Townside	$2722
J-210 2-WD Chassis/Cab	$1977
J-210 2-WD Pick-up Thriftside	$2078
J-210 4-WD Chassis/Cab	$2653
J-210 4-WD Pick-up Thriftside	$2734
J-210 4-WD Pick-up Thriftside	$2781
J-300 2-WD Chassis/Cab	$2017
J-300 2-WD Pick-up Thriftside	$2133
J-300 2-WD Pick-up Townside	$2160
J-300 4-WD Chassis/Cab	$2654
J-300 4-WD Pick-up Thriftside	$2769
J-300 4-WD Pick-up Townside	$2796
J-220 2-WD Chassis/Cab	$2062
J-220 2-WD Pick-up Thriftside	$2163
J-220 2-WD Pick-up Townside	$2189
J-220 4-WD Chassis/Cab	$2753
J-220 4-WD Pick-up Thriftside	$2854
J-220 4-WD Pick-up Townside	$2811
J-220 4-WD Stake Platform	$3060
J-310 2-WD Chassis/Cab	$2128
J-310 2-WD Pick-up Thriftside	$2243
J-310 2-WD Pick-up Townside	$2270
J-310 2-WD Stake Platform	$2468
J-310 4-WD Chassis/Cab	$2771
J-310 4-WD Pick-up Thriftside	$2886
J-310 4-WD Pick-up Townside	$2913
J-310 4-WD Stake Platform	$3111
J-320 2-WD Chassis/Cab	$2283
J-320 2-WD Pick-up Thriftside	$2398
J-320 2-WD Pick-up Townside	$2425
J-320 2-WD Stake Platform	$2623
J-230 4-WD Chassis/Cab	$3578
J-230 4-WD Stake Platform	$3870
J-330 4-WD Chassis/Cab	$3597
J-330 4-WD Stake Platform	$4011

As were the Wagoneers, all 4-wheel drive trucks were available with either independent front suspensions or solid front axles. Both the independent suspension system and solid axle used a full floating Dana model 44F axle with a standard 4.90:1 ratio. Customers could also select from optional ratios of 4.27:1 and 4.88:1. Both versions also used hydraulic double-acting shocks. Those installed with the solid axle were 13 inches long. For the independent suspension the shock length was 12.375 inches.

All 4-wheel drive trucks used semi-elliptical leaf springs whose size and number depended upon the vehicle's gross vehicle weight. The 2-wheel drive trucks had the torsion bar arrangement of the J–162 wagons but a semi-floating Dana rear axle was used on all trucks except on those with dual rear wheels. These were fitted with a Dana model 70 full-floating axle with either a standard 4.88:1 ratio or an optional 5.89:1 ratio. A Powr-Lok differential was optional on all models.

Two-wheel drive models were available with the Warner AS–8F 3-speed automatic transmission. All 4-wheel-drive models used a 4-position Spice model 20 transfer case with a 1:1 high and 2.03:1 low range. Manual transmission 2-wheel drive models used a Warner T–89 gearbox with ratios of 3.47:1, 1.92:1 and 1.00:1. Four-wheel drive models with GVWs between 4000 and 5600 pounds were equipped with a Warner T–90 transmission with ratios of 3.17:1, 1.75:1 and 1.0:1.

Trucks with higher weight ratings used a T–89 transmission with ratios of 3.17:1, 1.75:1 and 1.0:1. All J–200 and J–300 trucks could also be ordered with a 4-speed Warner T–98A which used a cane-type floor shift. Its ratios were 6.398:1, 3.092:1, 1.686:1 and 1.0:1. Trucks with this transmission used a 10.5 inch Auburn single dry plate clutch rated at 290 lb.ft. Installed on trucks with the standard 3-speed was a Borg & Beck 10 inch clutch with a 250 lb.ft. capacity. At extra cost a 10.5 inch unit supplied by either Borg & Beck or Auburn with a 265 lb.ft. capacity was available.

circle. Respective measurements for similarly equipped J–300 trucks were 49.67 and 57.67 feet.

Kaiser Jeep, in depicting the Gladiator truck as the "beautiful brute", was suggesting that it was a vehicle combining traditional Jeep ruggedness with a new level of appearance and comfort features. It was, said Kaiser Jeep, "the newest of the versatile, powerful, virtually indestructible 'Jeep' vehicles. On the highway it rides as smoothly as a passenger car. Off the road, it's as sure-footed as only a 'Jeep' vehicle can be."

The 1963 Gladiator pick-up. (Courtesy of Old Cars Weekly)

The Gladiator frame was similar to that of the J–100 line but was more robust and larger. Its overall length was 183.75 inches (J–200) or 195.75 inches (J–300). The J-series trucks also had wider front and rear treads of 63.5 and 63.75 inches respectively as compared to the J–100's 57 inch front and rear treads. At 71 inches the trucks were 7 inches higher than the J–100. In addition, the truck's 75.93 inch body width was slightly larger than the J–100's which measured 75.625 inches. The truck frame's 34.38 in. front and 44.50 inch rear width were identical to those of the J–100 frame. With its longer wheelbase, the J–330 measured 205.375 inches in overall length compared to the 193.375 inches of the J–200. Ground clearance of both trucks, at 8.75 inches, exceeded that of the J–100 by one inch.

All truck wheels were full drop center types supplied by Kelsey Hayes. Trucks with a GVW below 6600 pounds used 15 × 5.50 units, with 16 × 5.00Ks used on trucks with 660 pounds ratings. Wheels measuring 16 × 6.00L were specified for the 7600 pound GVW J–300. With dual rear wheels the J–300 used 16 × 5.50F wheels.

Although the trucks had the same steering system as the wagon models their greater size had a measurable impact upon their turning circles. J–200s with independent front suspension turned in a 44 foot

Since the Gladiator shared much of its features with the Wagoneer, it was, if measured by normal Jeep standards, a rather civilized vehicle. Its interior was spacious and optional equipment included automatic transmission, independent front suspension, power steering and power brakes. In 1963 no other American-made 4-wheel drive truck was available with all of these features. Furthermore, the Gladiator's overhead cam Tornado engine also made it unique among American trucks. Although the Gladiator had what was described as "traditional 'Jeep'" ground clearance, it was quite easy to enter or leave thanks to its doors that opened up 82 degrees.

True to previous Jeep policy appearance changes were slow in coming to the Gladiators. This really wasn't much of an impediment to their sales since most truck manufacturers made infrequent styling changes. Furthermore, the Gladiator's appearance, if angular and upright, had the great advantage of being straightforward and purposeful. These were attributes that would allow it to have a production run spanning three decades.

But for the keen of eye there were some changes made from year-

The cover of the 1966 Jeep Gladiator brochure. (Courtesy of author's collection)

4-WHEEL DRIVE 'JEEP' GLADIATORS

■ Rugged! Versatile! Powerful! Real work-horses. Here's a line of trucks that will take on practically any job. They'll handle all the everyday run-of-the-mill tasks you'd expect . . . plus, some of the roughest, toughest, pushing, pulling, or winching assignments you've ever imagined. The 4-wheel drive Gladiator tackles them all, and comes back asking for more. ■ In the city or on the farm . . . on turnpike or trail . . . anywhere you choose to go, famous 'Jeep' 4-wheel drive will get you through . . . safely and on schedule. **And it's standard equipment on every Gladiator model!** ■ Choose from two easy-to-service powerplants . . . the 'Jeep' Hi Torque 6 or optional Dauntless V-8 . . . with standard fully synchronized 3-speed manual transmission, or if you prefer, 4-speed manual or Turbo Hydra-Matic* automatic transmission. ■ Extra features inside the Gladiator's easy to get into cab include optional full-time power steering, power brakes and air conditioning.

Harmonizing interiors are designed to complement the stylish outside. ■ The big 'Jeep' Gladiator truck line includes models to fit nearly every need . . . from cab and chassis for specialized requirement installation to platform and p[?] form stake models. And there are two different styles of pick-up boxes . . . the stylish Townside or more conservative Thriftside. Basically, the 'Jeep' Gladia[tor] line is available with 120-inch or 126-inch wheelbase and in 5,000-lb., 6,000-lb., or 7,000-lb., gross vehicle weights. But, to determine which of the many availa[ble] models best meets your requirements, check the Basic Variations Section on the following page. ■ With normal use, 'Jeep' Gladiator trucks require an oil change only once every 4,000 miles and a major lubrication once in every 24,000 miles. ■ Visit your 'Jeep' dealer, slip into the cab, and take it fo[r] traction-action test drive. You've got to drive it to believe it!

A 1966 J-3000 Gladiator truck. (Courtesy of author's collection)

to-year. For example, a "Kaiser-Jeep" nameplate replaced the "Jeep" lettering on the 1965 Gladiator's front fenders. This change also applied to that year's Wagoneer models. In addition, a new range of 1965 model year Gladiator models joined the original models listed earlier. These Gladiators, which usually had higher GVW rating than the older models consisted of the following models: J–2500 (½ ton, 2- or 4-WD, 120 inch wheelbase, 5000 lbs. GVW), J–2600 (½ ton, 2- or 4-WD, 120 inch wheelbase, 6000 lbs. GVW), J–3500 (½ ton, 2- or 4-WD, ½ ton, 126 inch wheelbase, 5000 lbs. GVW), J–360 (½ ton, 126 inch wheelbase, 2- or 4-WD, 126 inch wheelbase, 6000 lbs. GVW), J–2700 (¾ ton, 2- or 4-WD, 120 inch wheelbase, 7000 lbs. GVW), J–3700 (¾ ton, 2- or 4-WD, 126 inch wheelbase, 7000 lbs. GVW), J–2800 (1 ton, 4-WD, 120 inch wheelbase, 8600 lbs. GVW), J–3800 (1 ton, 4-WD, 126 inch wheelbase).

Another important distinction of these new models was the availability of the American Motors 327 cubic inch "Vigilante" V-8 as an extra cost alternative to the standard 140 horsepower ohc six. This was the same engine used in the Wagoneer and its ratings were 250 horsepower at 4700 rpm and 340 lb.ft. of torque at 2600 rpm.

Beginning in 1966 Kaiser Jeep began to simplify the Gladiator model line up. The Jeep truck line that year consisted of nine series, ranging from the J–100 panel delivery to the 1 ton J–3800 line.

Beyond this development numerous other changes took place in 1967. Now standard on all Gladiators were seat belts, a high-impact windshield, outside rear view mirror, padded dash, dual-speed wipers, padded sun visor, 4-way warning flashers and windshield washer. Except for those models with a 8600 GVW rating all Gladiators also were factory fitted with a dual braking system and self-adjusting brakes.

Joining Turbo Hydra-Matic (which had been first offered in 1964) were improvements in the Gladiator's 4-wheel drive shift system, an improved power steering system and a number of new trim and paint options. Among the more popular options offered for the Gladiator were the following items: heavy-duty alternator, pintle hook, heavy-duty battery, step bumpers, front and rear chrome bumpers, full wheel covers, electric clock, E-Z Eye glass, selective drive hubs, power take-offs, push-button transistor radio, tonneau cover, deluxe rear window, rear axle Powr-Lok differential, mud flaps and, on trucks fitted with the Custom Cab option, bucket seats and console. Included in the Custom Cab option was such interior features as deluxe trim, color keyed instrument panel, cigar lighter, dual padded sun visors and harmonizing door panels. Three Custom Cab colors were offered: Rawhide, Charcoal and Marlin Blue. Exterior appointments consisted of stainless steel rear cab, windshield and door window frame molding, chrome front bumper and, on trucks with a 5000 lb. GVW, chrome hub caps. Seven body colors were available for the Gladiator: Prairie Gold, Bronze Mist, Spruce Tip Green, Gold Beige, Empire Blue, Glacier White and President Red.

Perhaps the most significant changes for 1967 was the end of production of the overhead cam engine and the dropping of 2-wheel drive Gladiator models. Replacing the ohc six as the standard Gladiator truck engine was a 232 cubic inch, overhead valve 6-cylinder supplied by American Motors and identified by Jeep as the "Hi-Torque Six". Its maximum horsepower was 145 at 4,300 rpm. Maximum torque was 215 lb.ft. at 1600 rpm. With a 8.5:1 compression ratio and single barrel carburetor its recommended fuel was regular grade gasoline. As an option the Gladiator was available with another out-sourced engine acquired from Buick. This 350 cubic inch V-8, labelled the "Dauntless V-8", developed 230 horsepower at 4400 rpm and 350 lb.ft. of torque at 2400 rpm. Although it had a higher, 9.0:1

compression ratio, than the standard engine, it also operated on regular fuel.

The Gladiators were given their first significant styling change in 1970 when they adopted the vertical grille style found on Wagoneer models since 1966. Also adding a dash of flash were new two-tone body color options available on all Gladiators with the Custom Cab option. This format consisted of an upper body section painted Champagne White, while the lower section could be finished in any of the other eight available color options.

Joining the Gladiator line were three new series, the J–3800, J–4500 and J–4700, all of which had a longer, 132 inch wheelbase. The standard engine for the J–3800 models was the 350 cid V-8 which was logical given their 8000 pound GVW rating. The J–3800 was offered only in a chassis and cab form which retailed for $4320. The other new models were offered in chassis and cab form and as Thriftside models.

Beginning in 1971 all Gladiators were either J–2000 models with 120 inch wheelbase or J–4000 models with the 132 inch wheelbase. The J–2000 was available in either Townside or Thriftside version with the J–4000 offered only with the Townside body. Their dimensions were as follows:

	J–2000	J–4000
GVW	5000 lbs.	5000 to 8000 lbs.
Wheelbase	120 in.	132 in.
Pick-up box length	7 ft.	8 ft.
Overall length	188.66 in.	205.64 in.

The J–4000 was described by Jeep as "the first 4-wheel drive truck specially built for Campers". As such it was an awesome pick-up with full floating front and rear axles and, in its 8000 lb. GVW form, possessing a payload capacity of 3633 pounds. Unlike many other 4-wheel drive pick-ups that had originated as 2-wheel drive versions the J–4000 did not have a jacked-up look. But its super-stiff rear springs gave it a purposeful forward rake. Furthermore, the J–4000's ride was extremely stiff. *Four Wheeler* magazine, February, 1972, noted in its test of a J–4000 that "without a load, to say that the ride is hard is an understatement". Yet, the Jeep was, if equipped with optional power steering, extremely easy to handle. But with a turning radius of 52 feet it was not intended for serious off-road trail exploration.

In 1971, when all Gladiators were fitted with AMC engines, the J–4000 in either 7000 or 8000 lb. GVW was equipped with a 360 cubic inch V-8 with 175 horsepower at 4000 rpm and 285 lb.ft. of torque at 2400 rpm as standard equipment. The 258 cubic inch six was standard in all other models with the 304 and 360 cubic inch V-8s optional. Whereas a three-speed manual, all-synchromesh transmission with a floor-mounted shifter was standard for all other models, the J–4000 had a standard four-speed heavy duty manual transmission.

The Gladiator name was dropped in 1972. Instead, AMC referred to these models simply as Jeep Trucks. Appearance and design changes were very minor. Shared with the Wagoneer was a wider day/night mirror in place of the older day-only unit, as well as a new Saginaw power steering pump. For the first time bucket seats were available as options. With a new 6000 lb. GVW model added to the J-2000 series the full Jeep truck line-up was as follows:

Series	Price
J-25700, 5,000 lb. GVW:	
Chassis and Cab	$3181
Thriftside Pick-up, 7-foot bed	$3328
Townside Pick-up 7-foot bed	$3328
J-2600, 6,000 lb. GVW:	
Chassis and Cab	$3302
Thriftside Pick-up, 7-foot bed	$3449
Townside Pick-up, 7-foot bed	$3449
J-4500, 5,000 GVW:	
Chassis and Cab	$3210
Townside Pick-up, 8-foot bed	$3365
J-4600, 6,000 GVW:	
Chassis and Cab	$3331
Townside Pick-up, 8-foot bed	$3486
J-4700, 7,000 GVW:	
Chassis and Cab	$3698
Townside Pick-up, 8-foot bed	$3853
J-4800, 8,000 GVW:	
Chassis and Cab	$4107
Townside Pick-up, 8-foot bed	$4262

Prices of popular options for 1972 were as follows:

Option	Price
304 cid V-8 (2-bbl. carb.)	$165
360 cid V-8 (2-bbl. carb.)	$223
Automatic transmission	$280 ($161.75: J-4000)
Air conditioning	$464.90
Power brakes	$47.45
Power steering	$150.80
Free-running hubs	$66
AM radio and antenna	$73.85
E-Z Eye glass	$26.20
Auxiliary fuel tank	$79.05
Brake warning light	$6.65
Custom trim package	$99.40
Bucket seats	$118.30
Two-tone exterior paint	$57.95

Along with the other Jeep products, the 1973 model trucks reflected the impact of American Motors' redesign efforts. Leading the list of changes was Quadra-Trac which was available in limited quantity for the trucks during the model year. As with the Wagoneer, the Quadra-Trac equipped Jeep Truck was powered by the 360 cubic inch V-8 and used the Turbo Hydra-Matic transmission.

1972 J-4000 pick-ups. (Courtesy of author's collection)

In addition, the trucks now used new double-wall side panels on their pick-up beds, a wider tailgate that opened with one hand and a completely new instrument panel. This last item was shared with the Wagoneer and featured easier to read circular gauges for all

220

instruments including oil pressure and ammeter, and increased padding. The dash, steering column and new floor mats were all color-cordinated to create what Jeep depicted as a "car-like interior".

Car and truck prices began to move upward with increasing rapidity in the early seventies, thus it is informative to list the prices of the 1973 Jeep Trucks as well as the costs of selected options.

Series	Price
J–2500:	
Chassis and Cab	$3206
Thriftside Pick-up	$3353
Townside Pick-up	$3353
J–2600:	
Chassis and Cab	$3327
Thriftside Pick-up	$3474
Townside Pick-up	$3474
J–4500:	
Chassis and Cab	$3235
Townside Pick-up	$3390
J–4600:	
Chassis and Cab	$3356
Townside Pick-up	$3511
J–4700:	
Chassis and Cab	$3723
Townside Pick-up	$3878
J–4800:	
Chassis and Cab	$4132
Townside Pick-up	$4287
Quadra-Trac (high and low range)	$149.50
Power brakes	$45.10
Power steering	$143.50
Air conditioning	$442.80
Heavy duty 70 amp battery	$11.30
Custom cab	$94.60
AM radio	$70.25
Front bumper guards	$16.10
E-Z Eye glass	$24.90
Fuel tank skid plate	$36.70
Dual horns	$7.00

With the Renegade version of the CJ Jeep gaining popularity, it wasn't surprising that AMC decided to spruce up the Jeep Truck with a similar treatment. The result was the Pioneer package for 1974 which consisted of woodgrain side body trim, bucket seats finished in "Tru-Knit" vinyl, "Adjust-O-Tilt" steering wheel, tinted glass, two-tone exterior paint and Pioneer lettering, air conditioning and full interior carpeting. For the first time the Truck was also offered with optional aluminum alloy wheels.

Although drum brakes were still standard, the trucks were now available with front disc brakes which were part of the optional power brake package retailing for $65. Use of a new front axle resulted in a much smaller turning circle for all models (the J-10's was now

Left: **1973 J-4000. All 1973 pick-ups had a new instrument panel and redesigned pick-up boxes. Quadra-Trac was available on four models.** (Courtesy of Richard Knudson)

Below Left: **A 1973 Jeep truck with an 8000 lb. GVW fitted with an 11 ft. slide-on camper unit.** (Courtesy of author's collection)

41.9 feet; the J-20's was 45.4 feet) and one inch reductions in the wheelbase of all models. This change also accompanied a revised and considerably scaled down model/series listing for 1974:

Series	Price
J-10:	
Model 25 Townside Pick-up (119 in. wb.)	$3776
Model 45 Townside Pick-up (131 in. wb.)	$3837
J-20:	
Model 46 Townside Pick-up (131 in. wb.)	$4375

Except for models fitted with Quadra-Trac, which continued to use the 360 cubic inch V-8, the J-10 Trucks had the 258 cubic inch 6-cylinder as their base engine. Its power ratings of 110 horsepower at 3500 rpm and 195 lb.ft. of torque at 2000 rpm were unchanged from 1973. Similarly, no changes were made in the ratings of the two and

four barrel carburetor equipped 360 cubic inch V-8s. For the first time the trucks were available with AMC's 401 cubic inch V-8 developing 235 horsepower and 320 lb.ft. of torque.

Prices of selected Jeep Truck options for 1974 were as follows:

Option	Price
360 cid V-8 (2-bbl. carb.)	$201
360 cid V-8 (4-bbl. carb.)	$245
401 cid V-8 (4-bbl. carb.)	$295 ($94 for J-20)
4-speed manual tran.	$102
Quadra-Trac (high range)	$38
Quadra-Trac (high and low range)	$142
3-speed automatic tran.	$254
Free-running front hubs	$60
Limited slip differential	$57
Power brakes (front discs)	$65
Power steering	$138
Heavy duty shocks	$14
Front stabilizer bar	$33
Bucket seats	$107
Tinted glass	$24
Air conditioning	$421

All Jeep pick-ups for 1975 featured numerous mechanical improvements and refinements as well as a broader choice of options, trim and body colors. Although no change was made in the models offered for the domestic market, there were, as the following chart notes, changes in both the GVW and payload capacities for the J-10 models.

	GVW (lbs.)				Approx. Payload Increase (lbs.)	
	Standard		Optional		Over 1974 (std.)	Over 1974 (Opt.)
Model	1974	1975	1974	1975		
25	5200	6025	5600	none	825	425
45	5200	6025	5600	none	825	425
46	6500	6500	7200	7200		
			8000	8000		

A 1975 J-20 Pioneer truck with its new woodgrain side body trim (Courtesy of author's collection)

Standard engine in the J-10 series remained the 258 cubic inch 6-cylinder. In the J-20 series the 360 cubic inch V-8 was continued. Both versions has a standard 3-speed manual transmission and Dana 20 manual-shift 4-wheel drive. The complete range of optional engines, axle ratios and transmissions offered for the 1975 Trucks was as follows:

	Engine	Axle Ratios		Dana 20 4-WD		Quadra-Trac 4-WD
		Std.	Opt.	3-speed.	4-spd.	
J-10	258/1 bbl.	4.09	N.A.	Std.	Opt.	Opt.
	360/2 bbl.	3.54	4.09	Std.	Opt.	Opt.
	350/4 bbl.	3.54	N.A.	N.A.	N.A.	Opt.
	401/4 bbl.	3.54	N.A.	N.A.	N.A.	Std.
J-20	360/2 bbl.	3.73	4.09	Std.	Opt.	Opt.
	360/4 bbl.	3.73	4.09	N.A.	Std.	Opt.
	401/4 bbl.	3.73	N.A.	N.A.	N.A.	Std.

For California, the 360 cubic inch V-8 with a 4-barrel carburetor and 4-speed transmission was standard. The only optional engine was the 401 cubic inch V-8 with the 4-barrel carburetor.

Numerous changes were made to improve the Jeep truck's fuel economy. These included new carburetors for the 4-barrel V-8 engines with smaller primary and larger secondary metering valves; new insulation to reduce heat input from engine to carburetor, new optional Cruise Control, and new optional HR-78 white sidewall tires for J-10 models. Mechanical and functional improvements for 1975 were lead by a new electronic ignition system totally eliminating the points and condenser that provided a stronger spark for better starting as well as longer sparkplug life.

Other mechanical improvements included new springs and shock absorbers for a somewhat smoother ride; heat shields for the muffler and exhaust pipe; stronger engine supports; a more efficient defroster; a new power steering gear for improved road "feel"; a new three-belt accessory drive system for V-8 engines that provided a more efficient power transfer to engine accessories and a new stainless steel whip-type radio antenna.

Jeep truck buyers also had a wider choice of options for 1975 including a new stereo AM/FM radio with two speakers; new two-tone paint treatment; new Pioneer woodgrain body trim; new sports steering wheel; new hub caps for the J-20 series; 70 amp. battery and 62 amp. alternator and a new convenience group with dual low profile mirrors, visor vanity mirror and electric clock, courtesy light, glove box light and ash tray light. All 131 inch wheelbase models could now be fitted with a 20 gallon auxiliary fuel tank (standard fuel tank capacity was 19 gallons).

The number of interior trim color combinations was increased from three to four. Two new colors, blue and green, joined two carry over colors, black and buff. Standard seat trim in the base model was vinyl Laramie. A new standard trim for the Custom and Pioneer packages, Derby Check fabric (similar to houndstooth), was introduced with the 1975 models. Optional for these two packages was a "Sport Knit" vinyl. The Pioneer package included woodgrain inserts for the instrument panel cluster, door trim panels that matched the exterior trim, deep pile carpeting, chrome front bumper, bright exterior window moldings, bright wheel covers (J-10) or bright hub caps (J-20), dual horns, locking glove box, cigarette lighter and bright armrest overlays. Bucket seats continued to be a Jeep truck option.

Prices of the 1975 Jeep truck models and of selected options were as follows:

Series	Price
J-10:	
Townside Pick-up	$3776
Townside Pick-up (131 in. wb.)	$3837
J-20:	
Townside Pick-up	$4975

Option	Price
360 cid V-8 (2-bbl.)	$201.25
360 cid V-8 (4-bbl.)	$245
401 cid V-8 (4-bbl.)	$295 ($94 for J-20)
4-speed manual trans.	$129
Turbo Hydra-Matic with Quadra-Trac	$291
Turbo Hydra-Matic with Quadra-Trac and low range	$395.80
Free-running front hubs	$85
Limited slip differential	$69
Heavy duty shock absorbers	$14.10
Heavy duty front springs	$35
Heavy duty rear springs (119 in. wb. only)	$30
Front stabilizer bar	$33
Power front disc brakes (J-10 only)	$65
Power steering	$138.10
Tinted glass	$23.65
Hub caps	$10.40
Fuel tank skid plate	$34.85
Air conditioning	$420.65
Pioneer package	$283.25

The overwhelming consensus of test drivers from the most respected 4-wheel drive oriented publications was that the 1975 Jeep trucks were vehicles deserving far more sales success than they enjoyed. *Four Wheeler* magazine, December, 1974, reported that "the ½ ton Jeep pick-up may be one of the best kept secrets in the four-wheel drive world ... it is amazing that American Motors doesn't sell more of them". Two reasons suggested by Bill Sanders of the *Four Wheeler* staff was that "the poor J–10 looks like any 2-wheel drive pick-up, and who wants a 4 × 4 if it doesn't *look* like one? Also, many people feel the Jeep pick-ups look dated. Perhaps that is true. While Ford Chevy pick-ups have been restyled in recent years, the Jeep pick-up still looks similar to the Gladiator truck that dates back to 1962."

But both *Four Wheeler* and *Pickup Van & 4WD* which tested a J–10 in its September, 1975 issue, found the Jeeps at least the equal of their domestic competition. *Four Wheeler* praised its ride noting that "of all 4 × 4 pick-ups this J–10 ½ ton was one of the smoothest riding ... The J–10 is nearly as comfortable as a passenger car and as comfortable as a 2-wheel-drive pick-up ... We think it is sad that more people aren't buying the ½ ton Jeep pick-up. It is a great all-around 4-wheel-drive truck with great performance and with excellent comfort and luxury."

Pickup Van & 4WD was even more enthusiastic in its praise of the J–10, declaring that "In terms of all-around 4WD performance this truck remains King of the Hill". In terms of sales PV4 spelled out some specific suggestions for AMC: "Whether the Jeep product, the J–10 Townside, again becomes King of the 4WD truck hill [in terms of sales] probably is a function of future revision in exterior styling, attention to detail in finish [PV4 complained about "completely careless application in a number of areas, not the least of which was the black painted 'Jeep' on the truck's tailgate], some quality control engineering, and just how many drivers are able to compare the features of New Process [used by GM and Chrysler] and Quadra-Trac 4WD systems."

There wasn't a major restyling in the Jeep truck's future, but, for 1976, there were many numerous mechanical improvements and refinements as well as new choices in options, trim and body colors offered.

All three models available in the domestic market had upgraded frames with splayed side rails, stronger cross-members and box section side rails. Besides allowing wider spaced springs to be used this frame design also made a direct steering mounting possible. Also introduced were new multi-leaf springs (on J–10 models) and new shock absorbers for a smoother ride.

The three-speed manual transmission previously teamed with the V-8 engine was now also used with the J–10's standard 258 cubic inch 6-cylinder engine. Its torque capacity was 325 lb.ft. compared to the 230 lb.ft. of the older transmission.

Other mechanical and functional improvements included a dual-nozzle windshield washer system; a new standard seat-belt warning system with a three-point lap and shoulder harness assembly; a new optional front stabilizer bar; more attractive 15 inch wheel covers for the J–10; and new graphics for the instrumental panel, radio, clock, heater and other controls.

All models had new seat and door trim designs available in a choice of color-keyed black, blue, green and buff. The base models were finished in a simulated knit "Fairway" vinyl. The Custom and Pioneer models had a "Potomac Stripe" pleated fabric upholstery. Both the bench seat and optional bucket seats were also offered in a "Soft-Touch" vinyl.

For the first time Jeep pick-ups were offered with a factory installed

"Snow Boss" plowing package consisting of a 90 inch Moldboard plow and complete mounting elements, hydraulic cylinders for power angling and lifting, electric control, switches and wiring, plow lights and body decals. This package joined the "Camper Special Package" which had made J–20 pick-ups popular with campers. For 1976 it included heavy duty shocks, large capacity radiator, 70 amp battery and 62 amp alternator, West Coast mirrors, sliding rear window and 9.50 × 16.5 Goodyear Cushion tires with a D load range.

In early 1976 Jeep introduced a sporty Honcho pick-up to compete with similar models from Ford and Chevrolet. The Honcho Package listed for $699 and required purchase of the $69 power front disc brakes and the $179 power steering option. This brought the price of a Honcho pick-up to $5680. A comparable "Short" Chevrolet listed for $5927.

The Honcho had a body side tape treatment of gold with accents of black and white. Its grille also had black accents. The fender lip strips were gold and white and tailgate striping was gold finished. A rear step bumper was installed along with a chrome front bumper. Stainless steel window molding were also included in the Honcho Package. Body color availability was White, Firecracker Red, Brilliant Blue, Black, Nautical Blue and Medium Blue. Just in case anyone missed the point, bold "Honcho" lettering was applied to the door panels. Goodyear Tracker AT 10 × 15 tubeless 4-ply polyester tires were mounted on slot-style 15 × 8 inch steel wheels.

The 1977 Jeep Honcho. (Courtesy of author's collection)

The Honcho interior consisted of a bench seat with blue "Levi's" fabric and door panels with a "Levi's" insert. A blue sports steering wheel was used along with an engine-turned instrument panel cluster overlay. Standard equipment included a cigarette lighter, floor carpeting in either blue or tan, glove box lock, bright armrest overlays. Also found on Honcho pick-ups were dual horns and hood insulation.

In both 1977 and 1978 mechanical and appearance changes for the Jeep trucks were held to a minimum. Mid-way through 1977 another new trim packages, the Golden Eagle, joined the Honcho package (which was priced at $749 for 1977) and now was offered in either gold with brown and orange accents or dark blue with gold and orange accents.

A 1977 J–20 truck. (Courtesy of author's collection)

Many items from the Honcho package such as its chrome front bumper, rear step bumper, 10–15 tracker OWL tires, bright window frames, bright armrest overlays and hood insulation were included in the $999 Golden Eagle package. In addition, it featured 8-inch spoked wheels painted gold with black accent stripes, pick-up box roll bar, steel grille guard, off-road driving lamps mounted on the roll bar, beige "Levi's" bucket seats and Custom interior and a "engine-turned" instrument panel cluster.

But the real standout element of the Golden Eagle package was its exterior body accents. Across the truck's hood was a huge eagle decal with double belt-lines stripes highlighting the door, cab and upper box sides. The gold, black and orange theme created by these graphics was carried over to the lower bodyside, tailgate and wheel-lip stripes. Golden Eagle lettering was placed on the lower door panel.

A third package, the 10–4, was introduced for 1978. Like the Honcho and Golden Eagle packages, it was limited to installation on the J–10 with the 119 inch wheelbase. It was offered in a choice of 10 body colors and was highlighted by bodyside striping in two-tone orange with black accent. A two-tone orange "10–4" decal was mounted on the body side panel. Also standard with the 10–4 were 10–15 Tracker OWL tires, 15 × 8 styled wheels (white with red in stripe), a truck bed-mounted roll bar and a rear step bumper.

Like the 1978 Cherokee and Wagoneer models, all Jeep trucks had increased driver legroom of 2.5 inches due to a modified toe board and relocated accelerator pedal. Also shared with those models was the truck's new ambient air intake system which lowered engine

temperature thus increasing engine efficiency. Gross vehicle weight rating of the J–10 series was increased from 6025 to 6200 pounds.

New options for 1978 included a factory-installed CB radio, offered in conjunction with AM/FM Stereo or with AM; a new AM/FM Multi-Plex 8-track tape system, 7 inch chrome-plated spoked steel wheels for the J–10 models; grille guard, and a pick-up bed-mounted roll bar.

Left: **The sporty J–10 Golden Eagle pick-up for 1977. (Courtesy of author's collection)**

With greater production capacity available for Jeep truck production due to the conversion of the Brampton, Ontario plant, American Motors made a special effort in 1979 to increase their share of the rapidly growing 4-wheel drive truck market. AMC, when it announced the 1979 models, noted that "Jeep J–10 and J–20 trucks are unmatched in their versatility. They measure up anywhere in terms of off-road performance, and in the many faceted utility market – farming, construction, snow plowing and a variety of work needs."

handle for the Honcho and 10–4 packages. The Honcho package had bolder multi-color, graduated body striping.

With both the 401 cubic inch V-8 and 4-barrel carburetor version of the 360 cubic inch V-8 no longer offered the Jeep truck engine line-up was limited to just the 258 cubic inch six (standard in the J–10) and the 360 cubic inch V-8 which was standard for the J–20 and optional for the J–10.

The 1980 Jeep trucks benefited from the monumental engineering changes taking place in the Jeep Wagoneer and Cherokee lines to make them more fuel efficient. As a result the list of revisions for the new model year were among the most extensive made in their design since they were originally introduced as 1963 models. Both the truck's part-time and Quadra-Trac 4-wheel drive systems were all-new and lighter in weight. The part-time system was available with the Chrysler TorqueFlite automatic that replaced Turbo Hydra-Matic in 1980 or with the new standard 4-speed manual transmission. This gearbox had lighter weight aluminum parts, close-spaced gear ratios and full forward gear synchronization. For the first time, Jeep pick-ups with

A 1978 J–20. (Courtesy of author's collection)

All 1979 model trucks had standard power brakes with front discs. Previously only the J–20 had them as standard equipment. For the first time since 1970 the Jeep truck had a new front end design. Identical to that used on the Cherokee Chief, it was an attractive one-piece item with single rectangular headlights and bright center bars. A new one-piece stamped aluminum front bumper was available with optional rubber bumper guards.

Left: **The 1978 Jeep Honcho. (Courtesy of author's collection)**

Interior trim of the 1979 base model was elevated to approximately the level of the 1978 Custom standard. Thus it had a Custom steering wheel and higher grade door panels. Its seats were covered in a Cara vinyl with accent striping.

New options included an extra quiet insulation package, intermittent windshield wipers as part of the Convenience Group, a "high style" pick-up box enclosure for both long and short wheelbase models, a

lighted visor vanity mirror in the light group and a passenger assist automatic transmission could be equipped with either the part-time or Quadra-Trac 4-wheel drive systems. The J–20 continued to use the same 4-speed manual transmission with a "creeper" first gear as in 1979. Manual free wheeling hubs were a standard part of the 4-wheel drive system on models with either of the 4-speed manual transmissions. Both the part-time and full-time 4-wheel drive units used by Jeep in the Pick-up, Cherokee and Wagoneer models were manufactured by New Process, a wholly owned subsidiary of Chrysler. However, their use was a Jeep exclusive. The full-time unit was derived from a system developed earlier in England by the Ferguson company which aroused considerable attention when the latter unveiled a 4-wheel drive grand prix racing car. The Quadra-Trac, or New Process 219, system was very similar to the New Process 119 model which was introduced in the 1980 Eagle. The main difference between them was that the 119 was a single-speed transfer case whereas the 219 had a high and low range.

AMC proclaimed the 1980 Jeep Trucks as the "most advanced on

Left: **A 1979 Jeep Honcho. (Courtesy of author's collection)**

Below Left: **A 1979 J-20. (Courtesy of author's collection)**

the market", and, to underscore the changes made in their drivetrain components, added numerous trim, standard or optional features for 1980. New options included power windows, power door locks, an electronic digital clock, dual remote controlled outside mirrors, a new cassette tape AM/FM radio combination, bodyside scuff moldings, a chrome step bumper and, for the J-10 only, chrome-plated styled wheels. The previously optional front stabilizer bar was now standard on all pick-ups. Also standard on models with V-8 or automatic transmission was power steering. All trucks had a new single loop seat belt system.

A rugged looking 1980 J-10 Honcho. (Courtesy of author's collection)

For the first time since 1973 Jeep offered a stepside body style for the J-10. Back in those days it had been called the Thriftside but in a world where the sport truck had made an audacious appearance, its reincarnated form was known as the Sportside. As before, this body style didn't have the capacity of the Townside version but that wasn't of prime importance to buyers who seldom used their trucks to the fullest capacity anyway. What mattered to them was appearance and the J-10 Sportside had plenty of good looks. Included in the Sportside model were all Custom features such as bright finish moldings on the door window frames, bodyside scuff moldings deluxe door trim panels, engine turned instrument cluster trim, armrest overlays with a brushed insert, hood insulation and a passenger assist handle. In addition, the Sportside was fitted with a flareside box with a metal floor (many models of this type from the competition had wooden floors), "balloon" fenders, 15 × 8 OWL Tracker A/T tires, rear step bumper, black and chrome grille (the Custom had a chrome plated grille with gray and black accent paint), vinyl bucket seats and floor carpeting.

When the Honcho package was installed on a Sportside truck it differed from its form on the Townside models due to its unique pick-up box fender decals, wood box side and front panel rails, contoured roll bar and denim bucket seats.

Adding even more luster to the Jeep Truck's image was the introduction of the top-of-the-line trim package, the Laredo, for 1980. Few observers disputed AMC's declaration that the Laredo "features unprecedented luxury in a Jeep pick-up". Included in its $1600 price was a long list of features including special painted hubcaps, 15 × 8 chrome styled wheels, 10R × 15 Wrangler radial tires, black and chrome grille, chrome rear step bumper, chrome exterior remote control mirrors, body striping in either silver or gold tones, full carpeting, high back bucket seats, door pull straps, leather wrapped steering wheel, center arm rest, instrument panel and glove box striping, extra quiet insulation, convenience group, light group, bumper guards, front and rear nerf bars and the visibility group.

Sales of the Jeep Trucks trailed off badly in 1980, falling from 15,419 in 1979 to just 8636. But as the following indicates, the entire standard 4-wheel drive pick-up truck market suffered a major setback in 1980:

Make	1979 Sales	1980 Sales
Jeep	15,419	8656
Dodge	43,419	21,191
Ford	196,104	93,191
Chevrolet/GMC	203,454	109,345

The 1981 Jeep Trucks shared many of the technical developments and styling revisions found in the Cherokee and Wagoneer models. Thus its 6-cylinder engine was 90 pounds lighter and all models reverted to the use of a vertically slotted grille. In addition, all models were fitted with low-drag front power disc brakes and power steering. Improving highway performance was the automatic transmission's lock-up torque converter. Also giving the 1981 trucks a look quite unlike that of earlier models was the elimination of the front roof lip and a new drag reducing front air dam. With fuel economy paramount in the public's view, every improvement in vehicle aerodynamics was of major importance. All models also had new upper windshield, and caps and drip moldings.

No changes were made in the gearing of the J-20 but the 4-speed manual transmission for the V-8 powered J-10 now had a 3.82:1 instead of 3.52:1 first gear ratio. This change was accompanied by a drop in standard axle ratio for the J-10 from 3.31: to 2.73:1.

All pick-up trim options except the 10-4 package were carried over from 1980. The Honcho received new bodyside tape striping in red, blue, or yellow, depending on exterior color. Another new Honcho feature was striping on the tailgate. The Laredo package was also revised, now including Laredo nameplates on the body and instrument panel, and body striping in silver and gray or nutmeg and bronze, depending on body color.

These were all noble efforts and, it's likely that sales would have dropped even lower if AMC had not moved to improve both the Jeep Truck's fuel economy as well as their overall appeal. But the sales of full size 4-wheel drive pick-ups experienced another free-fall in 1981:

Make	1981 Sales
Jeep	6516
Dodge	12,123
Ford	68,200
Chevrolet/GMC	81,598

The smoother roof line for 1981 is clearly seen on this 1981 J–10
Honcho. (Courtesy of author's collection)

Changes for 1982 were limited to availability of the 5-speed overdrive transmission as an option and the introduction of the new Pioneer option for J-10 and J-20 models with the Townside body. Its components consisted of, in addition to the items found in the Custom package, upper body scuff molding, tailgate stripes, "Pioneer" decals, dark argent painted grille, carpeted cab floor, Western Weave cloth and vinyl bench seat, matching door trim panels, woodgrain inserts for armrests and instrument panel, Soft-Feel sports steering wheel, painted rear step bumper, front bumper guards, full wheel covers (J-10 only), extra quiet insulation and light group consisting of lights in the cargo area, glove box, visor vanity mirror plus map lights.

Pickup Van & 4WD December, 1981, tested a J-10 in Sportside Honcho trim and described it as "an appealing machine with a hunkered down look". Although *Pickup Van & 4WD* noted that "in automotive terms it is positively antediluvian" it also noted that "in many ways we like its looks [the J-10 Honcho's] better than the Chevy Stepside that re-started the trend towards short-wheelbase sport trucks".

One trend that wasn't popular with new truck buyers was the steadily increasing cost of purchasing a new truck. In the case of the J-series Jeeps the situation since 1976 was as follows:

time, more contemporary". Among its new features were new gauges, a climate control panel and a steering wheel with column-mounted controls for the high and low beam headlight operation and windshield wipers.

As in previous years the base engine/transmission combination for the J-10 was the 258 cubic inch 6-cylinder and a manual 4-speed transmission. The 360 cubic inch V-8 and automatic transmission were standard for the J-20 and optional for the J-10. For 1986 the optional Selec-Trac 2WD/4WD system was available with a Trac-Loc rear differential. This was a short-lived feature since the next year Trac-Loc could be ordered only with the standard part-time 4-wheel drive. Other changes for 1987 included a "4 × 4" badge, similar to that found on the Cherokee, Wagoneer and Comanche models positioned on the upper rear section of the cargo box. In addition, a "V-8" nameplate was placed on the left-side of the tailgate on trucks so equipped. Three new exterior colors, Colorado Red, Grenadine Metallic and

Manufacturer's suggested retail price in dollars						
Model	1977	1978	1979	1980	1981	1982
J-10 Townside	4995	5675	6172	6874	7960	8610
J-10 Townside (131 in.)	5095	5743	6245	6972	8056	8756
J-20 Townside	5607	6324	6672	7837	8766	9766

Prices of the Jeep truck trim packages had also experienced a substantial increase:

Suggested retail price in dollars						
Package	1977	1978	1979	1980	1981	1982
Honcho	749	749	824	849	892	949
Honcho Sportside	N.A.	N.A.	N.A.	1325	1392	470
Golden Eagle	N.A.	999	1224	N.A.	N.A.	N.A.
Custom	N.A.	N.A.	126	149	157	169
Laredo	N.A.	N.A.	N.A.	1600	1680	1749
Pioneer	N.A.	N.A.	N.A.	N.A.	559	599

The 1983 J-10 was available with the Selec-Trac 2/4-wheel drive system which was standard on the 1983 Wagoneer and also optional for the Cherokee. Its standard 258 cubic inch 6-cylinder engine had a higher 9.2:1 compression ratio and the same fuel feedback and knock sensor as used in other installations of this engine in 1983 Jeeps. Except in California, the J-20 continued to have the 360 cubic inch V-8 with a 2-barrel carburetor as its standard engine.

There were virtually no changes made in the Jeep pick-ups in 1984. The only trim packages offered were the Pioneer and Laredo priced respectively at $456 and $2129. In 1985 the 119 inch wheelbase J-10 model was dropped and all models had the 131 inch wheelbase and 8 foot Townside box. The only two trim levels were base and the $475 Pioneer. Included in the Pioneer package were wheel covers (J-10 only), extra quiet insulation, Light Group, bright finish moldings, tailgate stripes, Pioneer name decals, chrome grille, deluxe door trim panels, woodgrain dash cluster overlay, sports steering wheel and hood insulation.

For 1986 both the J-10 and J-20 received an interior facelift that was shared with the Grand Wagoneer. The instrument panel was totally re-designed, said AMC, "to make it more functional and, at the same

Briarwood Metallic joined carry-over colors White, Beige, Classic Black and Dark Night Blue as the J-10/20 color choices for 1987. Pioneer trim series models now had a new, tan stripe color. Tan was also added to the 1987 interior trim selection.

Despite these changes and improvements, sales of the J-series trucks steadily declined from 1980 as this chart indicates:

Year	J-10/20 Sales
1981	6516
1982	5562
1983	4263
1984	3404
1985	1953
1986	1515

The 1986 J–10 pick-up. (Courtesy of author's collection)

The merger of American Motors into Chrysler Corporation brings the production of the J–Series Jeep trucks to a close. Although still modern in terms of technical specifications, their appearance, dating back to 1963, plus their position relative to other Chrysler products, not to mention the Comanche pick-ups, made their existence within a considerably enlarged corporate structure redundant.

AMC described their 1987 J–10 as a "workhorse utility vehicle." (Courtesy of author's collection)

Chapter 12

The Jeep Cherokees:
1974–1983

If Kaiser Jeep was out front of the 4-wheel drive field in 1967 when the Jeepster was introduced, it was caught off guard by the introduction of the Chevrolet Blazer in 1969. The Blazer, although it was essentially a bob-tailed version of a Chevrolet pick-up, represented an ambitious thrust into a new segment of the 4-wheel drive/recreational vehicle market by the country's number one automotive producer. Chevrolet was aware than there were plenty of potential 4-wheel drive buyers whose motoring needs could not be met by vehicles such as the CJ–5. This new breed needed room for four or five passengers plus plenty of room for their luggage, food and supplies. Chevrolet was by no means the trail blazer since the Jeepster/Commando was at least indirectly aimed at this market as was the Ford Bronco and the International-Harvester Scout. The latter had become more attractive when the Scout II version was announced. It had the same 100 inch wheelbase as the original model but, with another 12 inches of overall length providing much more interior space it was a far more practical vehicle.

Sales of the Blazer, Bronco, Scout and Commando in both 1970 and 1971 clearly indicated that the Commando was not participating in what would become a growth industry.

Model	1970 Sales	1971 Sales
Bronco	17,172	17,302
Scout	12,978	13,500
Blazer	10,994	18,143
Commando	7098	8511

But the Commando's lackadaisical performance was not representative of Jeep's sales momentum after its acquisition by AMC in 1970. In 1973 Jeep sales totalled almost 67,000 as compared to 30,000 units in 1970 which represented 17 percent of the 4-wheel drive market. AMC told its stockholders in 1973 that "A long range management goal is to achieve volume in related businesses which is about equal to that generated by passenger cars." With predictions that the 4-wheel drive market would grow to 500,000 units by 1976, as compared to sales of 375,000 in 1973, it was obvious that AMC was planning to drastically increase Jeep's model range as soon as possible.

Prophetically, as will be apparent, the first manifestation of this strategy, the 1974 Cherokee, was depicted as a "new entry in the multi-purpose field ... headed for highest honors." Introduction of the Cherokee to the press took place in October, 1973 on the Cherokee Indian Reservation in Cherokee, North Carolina.

In terms of physical dimensions, the Cherokee was identical to the 1974 Wagoneer. But since it was a vehicle intended to appeal to a different type of customer, the Cherokee was positioned against a different set of competing vehicles than was the Wagoneer.

The close proximity of the Cherokee to the Blazer in many of its dimensions makes a closer comparison between them useful.

	Cherokee	Blazer
Front axle ground clearance	7.8 in.	7.0 in.
Front overhang	29.7 in.	33.5 in.
Rear overhang	45.0 in.	44.5 in.
Front tread	59.2 in.	65.8 in.
Turning circle	38.4 ft.	37.6 ft.
Front hip room	60.6 in.	67.3 in.
Rear hip room	60.6 in.	50.0 in.
Front head room	38.5 in.	42.5 in.
Rear head room	37.0 in.	37.8 in.
Front leg room	39.4 in.	40.5 in.
Rear leg room	36.6 in.	44.3 in.
Cargo length		
Behind rear seat	42.0 in.	43.0 in.
Behind front seat	82.0 in.	77.0 in.

Even the most avid of the Cherokee's supporters had to concede that, on one point, at least, the Blazer was superior to the Cherokee. This involved the location of the Cherokee's fuel tank which was mounted just ahead of the rear axle's left-side where it was vulnerable to damage. In contrast, the Blazer's was positioned up under its tail. But this shortcoming aside, the Cherokee's basic design was highly regarded. For example *Pickup, Van & 4WD*, January, 1974, in its test of a Cherokee noted, "As an automotive design it is outstanding for its utilization of space ... It has the nearest thing to a 'car' look as can be found among utility machines, the kind of vehicle your wife could drive to the PTA or you could drive to a business meeting without having the feeling that you're driving up in a truck."

When a Cherokee was parked next to a 1974 Wagoneer it was apparent that both vehicles shared the same basic sheet metal. This was an obvious way to keep development costs to a minimum, but it was not at the expense of the Cherokee's loss of a distinctive appearance. The Cherokee was, for starters, a two-door wagon. This gave it a sporting look that was enhanced by the broad rear side window standard on all Cherokees. Also setting the Cherokee apart from its senior partner was its grille which was identical to that used by the Jeep trucks since 1970. At the rear the Cherokee used vertically positioned taillights rather than the wraparound units found on the Wagoneer.

The Cherokee's standard engine was the AMC 258 cubic inch, overhead valve 6-cylinder engine. With a single one-barrel carburetor and 8.0:1 compression ratio it developed 110 horsepower at 3500 rpm

	Wheelbase	Overall length	Width	Height
Cherokee	109 in.	183.7 in.	75.6 in.	66.5 in.
Blazer	106.5 in.	184.7 in.	79.0 in.	71.5 in.
Bronco	92.0 in.	152.1 in.	69.8 in.	71.1 in.
Scout II	100.0 in.	165.8 in.	70.0 in.	66.2 in.

and 195 lb.ft. of torque at 2000 rpm. Three V-8s were also available, beginning with the 360 cubic inch V-8 fitted with single 2-barrel carburetor and having an 8.25:1 compression ratio. Its power ratings were 175 horsepower at 4000 rpm and 285 lb.ft. of torque at 2400 rpm. This engine was priced at $212. For an additional $46 a 4-barrel version was available with the same 8.25:1 compression ratio. Its ratings were 195 horsepower at 4400 rpm and 295 lb.ft. of torque at 2900 rpm. The final engine offered for the Cherokee was the $295, 401 cubic inch V-8 with a 4-barrel carburetor and a 8.35:1 compression

The 1974 Jeep Cherokee was quickly identified as the leader of the sports utility vehicle class. (Courtesy of author's collection)

ratio. With 215 horsepower at 4400 rpm and 320 lb.ft. of torque it was the most powerful engine available in the Cherokee class. Shortly before the introduction of the Cherokee, International-Harvester made this engine available for its pick-up trucks and Travelall series. At that point Marv Stucky, American Motors vice president for Jeep product development reported that AMC was studying its use in Jeep vehicles.

The Quadra-Trac full-time 4-wheel drive system was standard with both the 360 engine with 4-barrel carburetor and the 401 engine. Although it was optional for the other 360 engine Quadra-Trac was not available for the 6-cylinder engine. The basic Quadra-Trac system had a single high range and was priced at $40. The unit with both high and low ranges retailed for $150.

The Blazer had first been available with a full-time 4-wheel drive system in 1973. This New Process unit, unlike the Cherokee's Warner Gear system had an "open" differential whereas the Jeep set-up used a limited slip differential. As a result, when traction was lost at one of the Blazer's wheels no power was supplied to the other wheels unless the system was in the locked position. Then the power was supplied to the front and rear wheels in equal amounts. In contrast, the Warner Gear arrangement was able to send power to the driveshaft that would not slip. Chevrolet partially closed the gap between the New Process and

Warner Gear units in 1974 by offering an optional limited-slip differential for the front axle but the consensus remained that the Warner Gear was the superior unit.

The 4-wheel drive unit for Cherokees with the base engine used a Dana 20 transfer case with a conventional in-and-out format. It could be fitted with free-wheeling front hubs for $65. A limited slip rear "Trac-lok" differential was also available for $60. All Quadra-Trac Cherokees had a standard 3-speed Turbo Hydra-Matic transmission. A 4-speed heavy-duty manual transmission was available for the 360 V-8 with a 2-barrel carburetor when used in conjunction with the Dana 20 transfer case. The standard transmission offered for the 6-cylinder engine was a 3-speed manual gearbox. Turbo Hydra-Matic was optional.

As was the case with the Wagoneer, the Cherokee used a Dana 44 open end front axle with a 6-stud wheel pattern. The same unit was found on the Blazer. The semi-floating hypoid rear axle (also a Dana 44) for V-8 Cherokees had a standard 3.07:1 ratio. A 3.54:1 ratio was optional. For the 6-cylinder version a 3.54:1 ratio was standard with 4.09:1 optional. Front and rear suspension, like the Wagoneer's, consisted of leaf springs. The front units were, like the Blazer's, of a dual leaf, tapered design and had a spring rate of 220 lbs./in. Drum brakes measuring 11 × 2 inches with approximately 168 sq.in. of effective area were standard on the Cherokee. Power front disc brakes were available for $65. In contrast, power front discs were standard on the Blazer.

This was the first year that power discs as well as variable ratio power steering was offered for Jeep vehicles. The latter unit was supplied by Saginaw. While the standard circulating ball steering had a ratio of 24:1, the power system had a ratio of 20–16:1.

The Cherokee was offered in two models, the base Model 16 and Model 17 or S (for Sport) version. The base Cherokee retailed for $3986 with the S beginning at $4549. It was not difficult to distinguish the two versions from each other. The base model had black window moldings, painted bumpers, rubber floor mats and full-width front and rear seats. The S Cherokee had fancy side body and lower tape striping, bright window reveals, chrome bumpers, flipper quarter windows, aluminum styled 15 × 7 wheels (Model 16 had small hub caps), roof rack with an "S" medallion on the rear side panel.

The Cherokee shared its interior format with the Wagoneer, which was another way of saying it had an excellent dash arrangement. Instrumentation included gauges for the ammeter and oil pressure. The S model had embossed vinyl seat trim, cigarette lighter, an instrument panel overlay, dash-mounted "S" medallion, custom door and rear side panel trim, a locking glove box, dual horns, armrest overlays, vinyl cargo mat, courtesy lights and two rear seat ash trays. A number of the features included on the Model 17 were available as options for Model 16. These included the tape trim, flipper quarter windows, courtesy lights and cigarette lighter.

In addition to the items already mentioned, numerous performance, utility and appearance options were offered for the Cherokee. A sampling included the following:

Option	Price
H78–15 Polyglas whitewall tires	$107
(F78-15-B Power Cushion blackwalls were standard)	
AM/FM radio	$137.75
Front bumper guards	$15.30
Electric clock	$16.65
Tinted glass	$38.05
Fuel tank skid plate	$51.50
Power steering	$138.10
Power tailgate window	$43.00
Air conditioning	$420.65
Tilt steering wheel	$45.10
Roof luggage rack	$71.80
Center arm rest (avail. with bucket seats only)	$39.00
Dual front shoulder belts	$29.85
Rear window air deflector	$22.80
Convenience Group (includes remote control mirror, visor vanity mirror and glove box light)	$19.65
Cargo light	$7.60

Reaction to the Cherokee by the motoring press was extremely enthusiastic. *Four Wheeler* magazine presented its First Annual Achievement Award to American Motors for "making the most significant advancement in the field of four wheeling". In its view the Cherokee "combined rugged off-road performance with superior passenger luxury and comfort in a nifty, small 2-door vehicle that can go nearly anywhere in the boondocks." *Pickup, Van & 4WD*, after testing a Cherokee in its January, 1974 issue, concluded: "Comparing the Cherokee to its direct competition, it offers the biggest, best

performing engine, the best full-time 4WD system, the best off-pavement performance, the best space utilization, the best rear seat package and is the best looking. In short, it is one hell of a fine 4WD package. In our opinion, the Cherokee is the cream of the sports utility crop."

Changes for 1975 were, in light of the Cherokee being only one year old, surprisingly extensive. The carburetors for both the 360 and 401 cubic inch engines now had smaller primary and larger secondary metering valves to improve real world fuel economy. At the same time the Cherokee's standard gross weight was increased from 5600 pounds to 6025 pounds. This allowed the Cherokee to operate on regular grade fuel since vehicles in that weight class weren't required to be fitted with a catalytic converter.

A 1975 Jeep Cherokee. (Courtesy of author's collection)

Also introduced on the 1975 Cherokee was a new electronic ignition system eliminating the usual points and condensor. This resulted in a stronger spark for improved starting and a longer sparkplug life as well as an electrical system that was virtually maintenance free in normal use.

All V-8 engines were also fitted with a new three-belt accessory drive system which resulted in a more efficient power transfer to engine accessories. Found on all Cherokees regardless of their engines were stronger engine mounts.

Replacing the F78 × 15 tires used in 1974 were H78 × 15 tires. This change was accompanied by some fairly major revisions in the Cherokee suspension. Both front and rear springs were now multi-leaf with the rear units also of a progressive design. Their dimensions were 52 × 2.5 inches (front) and 47 × 2.5 inches (rear). The Cherokee's spring rates were 200 lbs./in. (front) and 160/260 lbs./in. (rear). New longer shock absorbers were also used. Those at the rear were now mounted in a staggered position. Additional mechanical changes included quieter mufflers for all engines, a new power steering gear for improved road feel and heat shields for the muffler and exhaust pipe.

As in 1974, the base 258 cubic inch 6-cylinder engine was not available in California. Also banned in California was the 360 cubic inch V-8 with 2-barrel carburetor. In that state the 360 V-8 with 4-barrel carburetor was standard with the 401 cubic inch V-8 optional. An important development was the availability of Quadra-Trac for the 258 cubic inch engine.

No changes were made in the Cherokee's model line-up but the S model featured a new body-side tape pattern that extended around the rear deck. It consisted of a three color diamond pattern over black or white. The Cherokee name was spelled out in bold letters just behind the door. Rear of the quarter window was a new medallion in an Indian motif for the S model. The Cherokee S interior was finished in a "Desert Flower" vinyl pattern while the standard interior now had front bucket seats and a "Laramie" vinyl trim. The cargo trim panels on the Cherokee S also had the new "Desert Flower" design. The number of Cherokee interior trim color combinations was increased from three to four with carry-over black and buff joined by blue and green shades.

Added to the Cherokee's optional equipment list were a number of new items such as a stereo AM/FM radio with four speakers, Cruise Command speed control, an electrically-heated rear window defogger, a light group consisting of cargo, courtesy, glove box and ash tray lights, new cargo carpeting and insulation pad, engine block heater, 70 amp. battery and 62 amp. alternator plus a new convenience group

consisting of a remote control outside mirror, visor vanity mirror and electric clock. A stainless steel whip-type radio antenna was also available. Unlike 1974 when only a white top was offered, the latest Cherokees were available with either a black or white top.

The Cherokee, like all Jeep products, was available in a choice of ten body colors. As can be seen from the following, five of these were new for 1975:

1974 Color selection	1975 Color selection
Champagne White	Alpine White
Jetsun Blue Metallic	Medium Blue Metallic
Fairway Green Metallic	Reef Green Metallic
Fawn Beige	Green Apple
Silver Green	Pewter Gray Metallic
Mellow Yellow	Mellow Yellow
Golden Tan Metallic	Fawn Beige
Trans-Am Red	Trans-Am Red
Copper Metallic	Copper Metallic
	Raven Black

Coinciding with the introduction of the Cherokee in 1974 had been the arrival of Chrysler Corporation's entry into the sport utility field, the Dodge Ramcharger and its badge-engineered twin the Plymouth Trail Duster. This inspired a three-way test between these vehicles by *Pickup, Van & 4WD* magazine that once again left no doubt that the Cherokee remained King of the Hill. After putting all three vehicles through a rigorous test pattern that left the Blazer's fiberglass top barely attached to the body and the Ramcharger's air conditioning unit shaken loose from its mooring before the going really got rough, the

road testers had little trouble in reaching a unanimous decision. "The Jeep Cherokee", reported PV4, in its April, 1974 issue, "proved itself No. 1 of the three test vehicles. The Cherokee achieved this in an unspectacular fashion, with no heroics, no automotive histrionics. The Cherokee simply did its thing, which was everything its drivers asked of it."

Cherokee prices for 1975 were increased over 1974 levels. The Model 16 began at $4851 with the Model 17 listing for $5399. Popular options were priced as follows:

Option	Price
360 cubic inch V-8 (2-bbl.)	$201
360 cubic inch V-8 (4-bbl.)	$245
401 cubic inch V-8	$295
4-speed manual trans.	$129
Turbo Hydra-Matic with Quadra-Trac	$291
Turbo Hydra-Matic with Quadra Trac and Low Range	$396
Free-wheeling front hubs	$85
Limited slip differential	$69
Power front disc brakes	$65
Power steering	$169
Heavy duty shock absorbers	$17
Heavy duty front springs	$35
Heavy duty rear springs	$30

One point that disappointed many road test crews assigned to evaluate the Cherokee was its inability to be fitted with tires larger than L78 × 15 on 6 inch rims. In contrast, both the Blazer and Ramcharger had room for 10 × 15B tires in their wheel wells. This shortcoming was remedied with the introduction of the Cherokee Chief which made its world debut at the Detroit Automobile Show in January, 1975. The Chief package retailed for $349 over the price of a Model 17 and $649 above that of a Model 16. Regardless of whether it was based on a Model 16 or 17, the Chief was easy to identify. It had the almost obligatory special effects treatment consisting of low gloss black and a black tape for the rear deck plus bold "Cherokee Chief" lettering on the tailgate and lower body region. Interior attractions included a leather-wrapped sports steering wheel and bright trim. The Chief was available in all 1975 Jeep colours as well as special Renegade Orange and Blue. The interior could be appointed in any of the four standard colors or "Levi's" vinyl.

But the real reason for the Chief's existence was found beneath its pretty exterior where wider front and rear axles and special slot-type wheels carrying 10 × 15 Goodyear Tracker A/T tires were found. To accommodate these tires the Chief had larger front and rear wheel openings and fender extensions. Thomas J. Holmes, manager of Jeep product planning noted that "I think we have the right balance in the Goodyear tires used on the Chief. The tires do a good job off the road and they look tough, but they aren't built to tear up the environment. In addition, they perform nicely on the road."

The most important of the Cherokee's changes for 1976 was its more rugged frame with stronger cross-members and box section side rail construction. At the rear the side rails were slightly splayed to allow the rear springs to be wider spaced than in 1975. The rear springs were also of a new asymmetrical design providing a smoother ride with no sacrifice in traditional Jeep ruggedness. The front springs were unchanged in form but now had increased up-and-down

A 1976 Jeep Cherokee. (Courtesy of author's collection)

clearance. The new frame also allowed a direct steering gear mounting to be used, eliminating the need for adapter sub-assemblies. Available for the first time for the Cherokee was an optional front stabilizer bar. As in 1975 an optional heavy duty suspension was available. American Motors reported that it offered "better handling, comfort and suspension clearance than the 1975 heavy duty springs". The standard and heavy duty springs had the following specifications:

	Front springs	Rear springs
Standard	195 lb./in. (V-8: 215 lb./in.)	165 lb.in.
Heavy Duty	215 lb.-in. (V-8: 260 lb./in.)	165–265 lb./in.

Detail changes found in all 1976 Cherokees included a dual-nozzle windshield washer system and a new seat-belt warning system with a three-way lap and shoulder harness assembly. The standard Cherokee seat and door trim was a new Fairway vinyl available in black, blue, green or buff. The S interior featured a Diamond Stripe vinyl with matching door and rear quarter trim panels as well as an engine-turned instrument cluster and a forward pivoting driver's seat for easier rear seat access. All Cherokees had new graphics for the instrument panel, radio clock, heater and other controls. Cherokees with Quadra-Trac also had new 15 inch wheel covers.

Right: **The more aggressive lines of the 1976 Cherokee Chief are shown to good advantage in this view. (Courtesy of author's collection)**

Except for a new-floor-mounted lever to operate the Quadra-Trac low range, no changes were made in either the Cherokee's standard or optional drivetrain-engine combinations. Added to the list of factory installed equipment was the "Snow Boss" plow package which included complete mounting for an 84 inch Mold-board plow, hydraulic cylinders, electrical control switches and wiring, plow lights and special decals.

Total United States and Canadian Jeep retail sales in 1976 established a new record of 95,718 units. Jeep had 16 percent of the total U.S. 4-wheel drive market. But in the recreational-utility segment which included the Cherokee, Jeep held almost 40 percent.

Ever since AMC had acquired Jeep one of its priorities had been the strengthening of the Jeep dealer force. During 1976 the number of Jeep dealers increased from 1531 to 1608. The number selling both AMC and Jeep products climbed from 910 to 1049.

AMC reported to stockholders that "The 4-wheel drive market picture continues bright in the United States and Canada. The U.S. market climbed from 390,000 units in 1975 to more than 580,000 in 1976. It is expected to reach about 630,000 in 1977. Four-wheel drive vehicles are becoming a second or third family car. In some cases they are purchased as the only transportation by people who previously owned passenger cars."

Evidence that AMC was exploring just about every facet of this market was apparent in the 1977 version of the Cherokee. To appease those off-roaders who were never crazy about the Cherokee's under-the-rear spare tire location, there was a new optional, inside the vehicle, vertical spare tire mount. In addition, the power front disc brakes that had been standard for the Wagoneer and J-20 trucks were now standard for the Cherokee. Replacing the single barrel carburetor version of the 258 cubic inch 6-cylinder engine as the standard Cherokee engine was a two barrel model.

Of greater importance to the Cherokee's sales potential was the addition of a 4-door Model 18 version to its line-up. Its price of $5736 was just $100 more than that of the 2-door Model 16. Both were available with the $599 S package. The most important technical change for 1977 was a new ambient air intake system for V-8 engines.

Jeep enjoyed another banner sales year in 1977. Total sales in the U.S. and Canada reached 117,077, which for the third consecutive year represented a new record. With the new 4-door Cherokee obviously in mind, AMC told its stockholders that "Jeep is successful because

the company had developed a range of choices for customers – not just vehicle types, but a growing list of comfort conveniences and appearance options. Jeep buyers increasingly want style and individuality to go with toughness and durability. Their vehicles are used for recreation and work, and for multi-purpose family transportation."

For 1978 the Cherokee offered more of the same. Starting its fifth year of production the Cherokee was again offered in three models – the base 2-door version, the 2-door with wide wheels and tires and fender extensions, and the 4-door model. The high-line "S" package remained optional for all models, with the Cherokee Chief package exclusive to the wide-track 2-door. There weren't, except for the relocating of the fuel filler cap any exterior changes. This suited most Jeep enthusiasts just fine – the Cherokee remained a contemporary-looking vehicle. But enhancing the owner's opportunity to individualize his Cherokee was a new grille guard and 7 inch chrome-plated spoked wheels that were available as options. The latter were included in the S package, except when ordered for the wide wheel model.

Accentuating the Cherokee's appearance were three new exterior colors; Sun Orange, Golden Ginger Metallic and Captain Blue Metallic. Colors carried over from 1977 included Alpine White, Loden Green Metallic, Mocha Brown Metallic, Autumn Red Metallic, Oakleaf Brown, Brilliant Blue, Classic Black, Firecracker Red, Pewter Gray Metallic, Sand Tan and Sunshine Yellow.

No engine changes were made for the Cherokee but the ambient air intake used for V-8 engines in 1977 was now standard for all models.

More substantial changes took place in the Cherokee's interior where, due to use of a modified toe board and relocated accelerator pedal, there was 2.5 more inches of driver leg room available. The seat belts and shoulder harnesses were now color-keyed to the interior and the optional "Levi's" cloth bucket seats were available in a new beige color as well as in traditional blue.

A number of items previously listed as options were now included

Left: **1977 Jeep Cherokee. (Courtesy of author's collection)**

as standard equipment on all Cherokees. These included bright windshield and vent moldings, cigarette lighter, glove box lock and dual horns. Offered for the first time as options were factory-installed AM/FM/CB and AM/CB radios, plus an AM/FM/Multi-Plex 8-track tape system. Gross vehicle weight ratings for 1978 were increased from 6025 to 6200 pounds.

The base Cherokee 2-door now listed for $6229, the 4-door for $6335

Two views of the new 4-door Cherokee for 1977. (Courtesy of author's collection)

and the wide-wheel 2-door for $6675. The S package price was $375 for the wide-wheel version and $575 for all other applications. Additional option prices were as follows:

Option	Price
360 cubic inch V-8 (2-barrel)	$250
360 cubic inch V-8 (4-barrel)	$300
401 cubic inch V-8	$475
4-speed manual transmission	$153
Turbo Hydra-Matic/Quadra-Trac (high range only)	$366
Turbo Hydra-Matic/Quadra-Trac (high/low range)	$511
Air conditioning	$577
63 amp. alternator	$45
Locking rear axle	$82
Optional axle ratio	$17
Heavy duty battery	$36
Brush guard	$69
Cold climate group (without AC)	$91
Cold climate package (with AC)	$46
Convenience group	$49
Heavy duty cooling	$39
Cruise control	$100
Rear window defroster	$94
Free-wheeling hubs	$101
Light group	$34
AM radio	$86

AM/FM radio	$229
AM/FM stereo with tape player	$329
AM/FM/Citizens Band	$349
Fuel tank skid plate	$60
Snow Boss Package	$1165
Power steering	$212
Suspension package	$115
Tinted glass	$48
Towing package "A"	$75
Towing package "B"	$125
Power tailgate	$69
Rear quarter vent windows	$47

Left: **The 1977 Cherokee Chief. (Courtesy of author's collection)**

A 1978 Cherokee 4-door. (Courtesy of author's collection)

While sales of AMC cars dropped below 2 percent of the U.S. market in 1978, Jeep sales accounted for 34 percent of the sports-utility market. Total sales for the U.S. and Canada market moved up to a record 153,000 which was 31 percent above the 1977 total. With obvious pride AMC reported that "At year's end Jeep vehicle sales had risen over year-ago periods for 37 consecutive months."

"This reflects Jeep's prominent position in a market whose growth exceeded all industry projections and whose future is bright. Fully capitalizing on this position is a basic part of the company's plan, and development of products to meet the changing needs of the 1980s has high priority.

A 1978 Cherokee 2-door. (Courtesy of author's collection)

"The 4-wheel drive market should remain strong in the years ahead because it has become increasingly diverse, reflecting basic changes in buyer needs and preferences. Jeep vehicles were once purchased primarily for work and recreation. Now the use profile is much broader. For some young people a 4-wheel drive vehicle may take the place of yesterday's sports car. For may families it is a general transportation vehicle which provides new levels of safety and reliability in all types of weather conditions. For outdoorsmen it remains the way to travel the back country. As a result, an increasing number of former passenger car owners are turning to 4-wheel drive vehicles."

In 1979, for the first time in its five years of production the Cherokee received a new grille. Highlights of the new Cherokee "face" included rectangular headlights set within a one-piece grille of bright chrome in combination with dark argent and low gloss paint. The grille design consisted of thin horizontal and vertical dividers and an extruder center section. The center hood "beak" remained as a reminder that the basic Cherokee body was getting on in years.

Also easily noticed were the Cherokee's new one-piece chrome bumpers that were much more substantial-appearing than the units they replaced.

Adding to the appeal of the Cherokee was the introduction of the Golden Eagle package as an option for the wide-wheel 2-door Cherokee. The package included 15 × 8 inch style wheels painted gold with black striping, outline white 10 × 15 Tracker A–T tires, tubular steel grille guard, bright door frame moldings, exterior striping on the hood, cowl, body sides and tailgate, Golden Eagle decal on the hood, bronze tone tinted rear quarter windows and a black brush guard.

Comprising the interior elements of the Golden Eagle package were beige denim fabric bucket seats with a center armrest, passenger assist handle, tan carpets, tan soft feel sports steering wheel, engine-turned instrument panel cluster overlay, driver's side folding seat, carpeted wheelhouse covers and rear seat ashtrays.

The popular S model was spruced up with a new side body Indian graphic theme with either a black or white background. The Chief package had new body striping, trim and ornamentation.

Interior changes found on all Cherokees included a 4-spoke custom steering wheel, new armrest design and a new dome light. The interior of the base model, which was upgraded to approximately the level of the 1978 S model, featured Cara vinyl with accent striping. Both the S and Chief packages used a printed 'Stripe' vinyl with a coarse material known as "Western Weave" optional. This upholstery, having vertical striping and trimmed in the Cara vinyl, was praised both for its

breathing ability and its tendency to prevent the seat occupant from sliding around when the going got rough.

No longer available for any Jeep product was the 401 cubic inch V-8. Also pruned from the optional engine list was the 4-barrel version of the 360 cubic inch V-8. This just left the standard 258 cubic inch 6-cylinder and the 360 cubic inch V-8 with a 2-barrel carburetor as the only engines offered for the Cherokee. The V-8 was substantially redesigned for 1979. Primary changes included a larger carburetor, revised distributor and a redesigned ERG system which AMC claimed provided for an over 20 percent increase in horsepower at higher speed and 100 percent compensation for higher performance at higher altitudes.

New options for 1979 included an extra quiet insulation package, intermittent windshield wipers as part of the Convenience Group, a lighted visor vanity mirror as part of the Light Group, and for the high-line S, Chief and Golden Eagle trim packages a new dome/reading lamp and a soft material passenger assist handle.

For the first time all Cherokees except the wide wheel model were available with a smooth ride suspension system. This was not recommended for extended off-road use and consisted of special front springs and rear shocks plus a front stabilizer bar. This package was the direct opposite of the Extra Duty suspension which included heavy duty springs and shock absorbers. Midway between them was the standard suspension with its five leaf front and rear springs with respective ratings of 215 lb./ft. and 165 lb./ft.

Prices of the Cherokee models and their options, like those of most American cars, once again moved upward for 1979:

Model	Price
Model 16 (2-door)	$7,328
Model 17 (2-door, wide wheels and tires)	$7,671
Model 18 (4-door)	$7,441

Option	Price
S package (Model 16 and 18)	$699
Chief package (Model 17)	$600
Golden Eagle package	$970
360 cubic inch V-8	$378
Turbo Hydra-Matic/Quadra-Trac (high range)	$396
Turbo Hydra-Matic/Quadra-Trac (low/high range)	$549
Bucket seats with arm rests	$48
Convenience group	$83
Air conditioning	$586
Power steering	$226
Power tailgate window	$73
Tinted glass	$51
Roof rack	$100
Fuel tank skid plate	$69
Tilt steering wheel	$76
Cruise control	$105
AM/FM stereo radio	$241
AM/FM/CB stereo radio with tape player	$346
Heavy duty 70 amp battery	$38
Light group	$69
Front bumper guards	$25
Floor mats	$19

In order to keep inventories of the Cherokee and Wagoneer under control in late 1979 when sales began to drop off due to external economic conditions, their output at the main Jeep plant in Toledo was

reduced in July. At year's end Cherokee production stood at a disappointing 27,568.

Well shielded from public view was a new generation of Jeeps that would eventually propel sales to levels then envisioned only by the most optimistic among Jeep product planners at AMC. But to reach the point in time when they would come on stream with Jeep's market share reasonably intact required an ambitious revamping of the current models.

A new front end appearance was featured for the 1979 Cherokee. (Courtesy of author's collection)

This resulted in numerous changes for the 1980 Cherokee that significantly affected its performance. Replacing both the standard Borg-Warner 3-speed transmission and optional 4-speed transmission with their cast iron cases was an all-synchromesh 4-speed Tremec Model T-176 with an all-aluminum case. Joined to this transmission was a New Process 208 part-time transfer case in place of the Dana 20 unit previously used. This 2-speed case could also be used with an automatic transmission which for 1980 was a Chrysler TorqueFlite unit. This move wasn't greeted with overwhelming enthusiasm by Jeep enthusiasts. But in TorqueFlite's favour was its more efficient design and lighter weight.

The Quadra-Trac system now had a viscous coupling limited slip differential in place of the cone-clutch friction system used in 1979. Although it was optional, most Quadra-Trac Cherokees in 1979 had been sold with a low range. In 1980 it was an integral part of Quadra-Trac.

These changes also involved some significant changes in the Cherokee's standard gearing:

	1980	1979
First gear	3.52:1	6.32:1
Second gear	2.27:1	3.09:1
Third gear	1.46:1	1.69:1
Fourth gear	1.00:1	–

In 1979 the Cherokee's standard axle ratio was 3.54:1. For 1980 it was 3.31:1 for both 6-cylinder and V-8 engines with manual transmission. The combination of a V-8 and automatic transmission used a 2.73:1 ratio. The exception to this was the wide wheel Model 17 V-8 which used a 3.31:1 ratio. The 1979 New Process transfer case low range ratio had been 2.03:1 which resulted in a final reduction of 45.4:1 in low gear. A comparable 1980 Cherokee would have a 3.52:1 first gear rato, a 2.61:1 low range and a 3.31:1 rear axle which provided a 30.1:1 reduction. The general consensus was that the 1980 model was sacrificing a minimal amount of off-road dexterity to attain a significant improvement in overall fuel consumption.

A purposeful looking 1979 Cherokee Chief. (Courtesy of author's collection)

In addition to these gearing changes the latest Cherokee had a number of other important running gear changes. As standard equipment Cherokees with the part-time 4-wheel drive system had manual free-wheeling front hubs. Used on all Cherokees was a new propeller shaft that was in a direct line with the engine crankshaft rather then being offset as on older models. Included in the base price for V-8 or automatic transmission equipped models was a front stabilizer bar and power steering. Both of these had previously been optional. Deflection rates for the Cherokee's front and rear springs were unchanged for 1980.

A small number of changes were made in the $784 S package including an Indian head medallion, new "High Line" door and rear quarter trim panels and print strip vinyl front bucket seats.

The Chief package, available only for the wide wheel Model 17 Cherokee retailed for $799. It contained all S package features plus upper body 2-tone paint, lower body blackout striping with Cherokee Chief lettering, black and chome grille and color-keyed carpeting. Also continued for 1980 was the Golden Eagle package.

The Cherokee's version of the new top-of-the-line, $1600, Laredo package (available only for the wide wheel model) consisted of all S features plus bright drip moldings, special painted hub caps, 15 × 8 chrome styled wheels, 10R 15 Goodyear Wrangler radial tires, black and chrome grille, dual exterior remote control mirrors, full interior carpeting, special vinyl bucket seats with front folding seat backs, special door trim panels, door pullstraps, leather wrapped steering wheel, center armrest, instrument, and glove box striping, extra quiet insulation package, Convenience Group, nerf bars and visibility group.

Among the new options available for 1980 were power window and door locks, quartz digital clock and a premium audio system with a power amplifier and upgraded high fidelity speakers.

Prices of the 1980 Cherokee models and major options were as follows:

Model	Price
Model 16 (2-door)	$8180
Model 17 (2-door, wide wheels)	$8823
Model 18 (4-door)	$8380

Option	Price
Power steering	$233
AM/FM stereo radio	$245
AM/FM stereo with tape player	$355
AM/FM stereo CB radio	$495
Moon roof	$300
S package (Models 16 and 17)	$784
Chief package	$799
Laredo package	$1600
360 cubic inch V-8	$420

In spite of the improvements and innovations found in the 1980 Cherokee its sales declined dramatically in 1980 to only 11,490 units.

The changes made by AMC in 1980 to improve Jeep fuel consumption preluded additional effort for the 1981 model year. Leading the list of changes was a lighter weight version of the 258 cubic inch engine that continued to be the Cherokee's standard engine. Whereas the older engine weighed 535 pounds, its successor reported in at only 445 pounds. Contributing to this weight loss were many design changes. The engine block was now thinner with fewer flanges and webbing. The old cast iron intake manifold was scrapped in favor of an aluminum version. Similarly, both the water and oil pump housings were constructed of aluminum. Unlike the older unit the new intake manifold was separate from the exhaust manifold, making it possible for headers to be installed by owners.

Other external revisions included a nylon, rather than steel, valve cover, and replacement of the older multi-belt system by a single, six groove serpentine drive belt line.

All 258 cubic inch engines had a new emissions control system. This advance wasn't at the expense of power output. Thanks to a new cam, with slighter higher lift, horsepower remained unchanged at 115.

A 1980 4-door Cherokee "S" model. (Courtesy of author's collection)

Unlike 1980 when the 6-cylinder engine wasn't available in California, the 1981 version was the only engine installed in California bound Jeeps. These engines used a closed-loop pollution control with a microprocessor that sampled the exhaust gases and made appropriate adjustments to the engine's air/fuel mixture.

Exterior changes to the Cherokee were more than just cosmetic. A new grille of lightweight plastic was used very similar in form to the slotted unit seen back in 1974. The Cherokee also sported a front air dam just below the bumper. Its purpose was to reduce wind resistance.

Jeep continued to use Chrysler's TorqueFlite transmission in 1981. A new feature was a clutch-locking torque converter which engaged when the transmission shifted into high gear. In that situation the transmission shaft turned at the same speed as the engine's crankshaft. This provided slip-free transfer of power, less engine wear, a lower tranmission operating temperature and a marginal improvement in fuel economy.

Also contributing to that cause were new low-drag front disc brakes lacking the constant brake pad-rotor contact of earlier versions. Once again changes were also made in both the Cherokee's manual transmission and axle ratios. Essentially, the purpose of these revisions was to retain good off-road capability while incrementally improving the Cherokee's highway mpg rating.

A major shake-up of the Cherokee's trim package offerings for 1981 saw the disappearance of the S and Golden Eagle packages and the inclusion of the Chief package as standard equipment for the 4-door Cherokee. However, the 4-door version used 15 × 7 white styled wheels and P235/75R Wrangler steel radial tires instead of the 15 × 8 wheels and 10–15 Tracker A/T OWL tires found on the wide wheel 2-door. Exterior graphics of the Chief were slightly revised. The circular Indian Chief emblem previously found just ahead of the front doors

was no longer used. The rear panel tape strip now angled upward and over the rear wheel cutout.

The Laredo package was available for both the wide wheel 2-door and 4-door Cherokees. Here too, there were differences between the two versions. The 2-door used 15 × 8 wheels and 75R 15 Wrangler steel belted radial tires while the 4-door had 15 × 7 wheels and P235/

The 1980 Cherokee Laredo. (Courtesy of author's collection)

The Cherokee Chief was a new model for 1981. (Courtesy of author's collection)

75R Wrangler tires. It also lacked the wide axle and flared wheel wells found on the 2-door version. A new double shock absorber option was also exclusive to the wide wheel models.

Prices of Cherokees and their optional equipment were once again substantially increased:

Model	Price
Model 16 (2-door)	$9574
Model 17 (2-door, wide wheel)	$9837
Model 18 (4-door)	$10,722

Option	Price
AM/FM radio	$224
AM/FM stereo CB	$420
Sunroof	$369
Power sunroof	$1549
Chief package	$879
Laredo package (Model 17)	$1733
Laredo package (Model 18)	$950
Power seats	$275
360 cubic inch V-8	$345

Cherokee sales again dropped precipitously in 1981, amounting to just 5801 units. There was little that could be done to reverse this situation since the entire industry was immersed in the most severe sales collapse since the Great Depression. Referring to the sale of just eight million passenger cars in 1982, AMC observed, "These abnormally low industry sales reflected the general economic recession, high interest rates and lack of consumer confidence."

Visual changes in the 1982 Cherokee were virtually non-existent. The exterior trim element of the Chief package could be either deleted or replaced by vinyl upper body moldings if desired. For the 4-door version, Arriva black sidewall tires were used rather than the Wrangler tires of 1981.

The most important technical development was the availability of a 5-speed manual transmission. This was a Warner Gear T5 unit. Its fifth gear was an overdrive with either a 0.76:1 or 0.86:1 ratio, depending on the engine and final drive ratio selected. Also new for 1982 was a tilt steering wheel option for Cherokees with manual transmissions. Up to 1982 this feature was offered only on Cherokees with automatic transmission.

The pricing schedule for the 1982 Cherokees and selected options was as follows:

Model	Price
Model 16 (2-door)	$9849
Model 17 (2-door, wide wheel)	$10,812
Model 18 (4-door Chief)	$11,647

Option	Price
AM/FM stereo radio	$249
AM/FM stereo radio with tape player	$359
AM/FM stereo CB	$456
Cruise control	$159
Rear window defroster	$125
Luggage rack	$118
Sunroof	$377
Power sunroof	$1585
Power seats	$169
Chief package	$899
Laredo package	$1749
360 cubic inch V-8	$351

As indicated by the following comparison, the 1983 Cherokee, unlike other sports utility vehicles, failed to improve upon its poor sales record of 1982:

Vehicle	1982 Sales	1983 Sales
Cherokee	5796	4165
Blazer/Jimmy	26,851	38,456
Bronco	41,228	42,646
Ramcharger	9243	12,845
Toyota Land Cruiser	3088	4805

A 5-speed manual transmission was a new feature for 1982. (Courtesy of author's collection)

Details of the AM/FM radio option for 1982. (Courtesy of author's collection)

This situation belies the fact that the 1983 Cherokee, the last to use the basic body introduced in 1974, was one of the very best Cherokees. Appearance-wise, the 1983 model was unchanged from the 1982 version. A major revision did take place in the Cherokee's trim package offering. Standard for the 4-door model and optional for the 2-door was a new Pioneer package consisting of the following items:

1. Sun Valley vinyl bucket seats with center arm rests (Western Weave cloth optional)
2. Custom door and rear quarter trim panels
3. Color-keyed carpeting including wheel wells and cargo area
4. Soft feel 3-spoke color keyed sport steering wheel
5. Engine turned instrument panel cluster overlay
6. Bright armrest overlays with argent insert
7. Passenger assist handle
8. Dual rear seat ashtrays
9. Driver's folding seat back (2-door model)
10. Black vinyl body side moldings
11. Exterior body "Pioneer" decals
12. Chrome grille
13. Extra quiet insulation
14. P235/75R 15 Arriva radial tires mounted on argent styled steel wheels with trim rings and bright hub covers.

The Chief and Laredo packages were continued but were restricted to installation on the wide wheel model only. Overshadowing this shakeout was the announcement of what Jeep described as "The most

Two views of the 1982 Jeep Laredo 2-door. (Courtesy of author's collection)

the **JEEP** 50 year history

innovative 2-wheel drivetrain yet", Selec-Trac. This was the third major advance in the art of 2-wheel/4-wheel drive technology offered by Jeep since it was purchased by AMC. The first had been Quadra-Trac in 1973 followed in 1980 by the use of a viscous coupling.

Selec-Trac was offered only in combination with an automatic transmission for all Cherokee models. Its availability allowed Jeep to tout the fact that the Cherokee was "The only sport utility vehicle in the industry – domestic or import – to offer a system capable of full-time 4WD operation. Additionally, Jeep continues to offer part-time 4WD and thus remains the only manufacturer offering two separate transfer case systems, both capable of 4WD and 2WD operation."

It's fair to depict Selec-Trac as a conceptual offspring of the Select Drive system used by the AMC Eagle. But it had the great advantage of including a low range transfer case for added torque when needed.

The low range mode could be activated only when the Cherokee was in 4-wheel drive since a sequential lockout system within the transfer case prevented low range operation when the vehicle was in 2-wheel drive. The low range was brought into operation by a floor-mounted lever positioned next to the driver's seat.

In order to engage a Selec-Trac Cherokee for either two- or four-wheel drive the vehicle was first brought to a stop. The driver then moved a dash-mounted lever to either its "2WD" or "4WD" position. To assure that the lever could not be accidentally moved, a safety switch had to be first pulled to engage the system.

"Although the motorist with Selec-Trac sees only the movement of the instrument switch when he or she selects 2WD or full-time 4WD", said AMC, "a revolutionary mechanical system comes into play within the vehicle itself."

This process began when, for example, 2-wheel drive was selected, with the transfer case shifting into 2-wheel drive. At that point the front drivetrain was released from the freely turning front wheels by a vacuum-activated spline clutch built into the front axle assembly. This device, which was connected in 4-wheel drive mode, released torque to the left axle shaft in its 2-wheel drive mode. Since the axle differential always equalized torque between the right and left axle shafts, the release of the left axle shaft and its subsequent free-wheeling also disconnected the right axle shaft. The process to move into full-time 4-wheel drive was the exact opposite of the procedure just described.

Also included in the Select-Trac system, which was available with either the 6-cylinder or V-8 engine, was a viscous coupling providing a front-torque biasing.

The only engine change of consequence was an increase in compression ratio from 8.6:1 to 9.2:1 and the addition of a fuel feedback system and knock sensor to improve performance and fuel efficiency.

For the first time all Cherokee models had base prices exceeding $10,000:

Model	Price
Model 16 (2-door)	$10,315
Model 17 (2-door, wide wheel)	$12,022
Model 18 (4-door Pioneer)	$12,006

Option	Price
AM/FM stereo	$199
AM/FM stereo with tape player	$329
Cruise control	$184
Rear window defroster	$134
Tilt steering wheel	$106
Luggage rack	$122
Sunroof	$389
Power sunroof	$1637
Power seats	$290
Laredo package	$1128
Pioneer package (wide wheel model)	$1131

Although Jeep sales in 1983 were the best since 1979, those of the Cherokee were, as earlier noted, at an all-time low. But as far as the future was concerned this mattered little. A sensational new Cherokee was ready to go and its popularity would lead the way to a welcomed all-time sales and output record for Jeep.

Chapter 13

The Jeep Scrambler

When the Jeep Scrambler was introduced on 25 March, 1981, it was described by Thomas A. Staudt, vice president of American Motors' marketing group, as "the most versatile vehicle we've ever introduced. It has all the ruggedness and off-road capability you'd expect from a Jeep vehicle, coupled with the hauling capability of a 5 foot cargo box and the best fuel economy of any American-built four-wheeler. The new Jeep Scrambler is the perfect combination for work and recreation."

Staudt's comments and American Motors' declaration that the Scrambler was designed to combat the surge of imported mini-trucks reflected the design objectives established for the Scrambler when it was first proposed in the summer of 1979. At that time the imports had the small 4-wheel drive truck market to themselves with the Chevrolet LUV (built in Japan by Isuzu), leading the field with 33,843 sales for the 1979 model year. Close behind was Toyota with sales of 32,710, followed by the Subaru Brat of which 23,414 were sold.

American Motors wasn't about to tool up a totally new model to enter this fray, but it considered the CJ-6 as an acceptable base on which to build a small 4-wheel drive truck that could capture sales that were going by default to foreign manufacturers. American Motors had, out of economic necessity, become adept in using existing components in such a way as to produce a new product with its own distinctive attributes. Thus, with one eye on the parts bin and the other on its budget, AMC established criteria for its mini-4-wheel drive truck that included international sales appeal, ruggedness and durability, availability of numerous options, and the best fuel economy of any domestic 4-wheel drive truck.

The Scrambler program was approved by management in September, 1979 and shortly thereafter the first prototype was completed. Since this initial vehicle was based on the 103.5 inch wheelbase CJ-6, it was identified as the CJ-6S. It soon became apparent that merely converting the CJ-6 into a pick-up was not as desirable as it initially appeared. For example, the CJ-6's limited ease of exit and entry was considered unacceptable for a pick-up truck that would be available both in open and hardtop form. Gradually the Jeep pick-up became less of a compromise vehicle and more of a vehicle with its own special brand of appeal. This resulted in the CJ-8 designation being used.

This wasn't entirely satisfactory because AMC didn't want to convey the impression that its new product was a Jeep cobbled up to impersonate a pick-up. Thus when the first models came off the assembly line in January, 1981 they carried the Scrambler name. Back in 1969 American Motors had used the Scrambler name on a high performance Rambler model powered by a 315 horsepower, 390 cubic inch V-8. It was capable of covering the quarter-mile in 14.3 seconds. The Jeep model wasn't that type of performer but the Scrambler name was appropriate for a truck with excellent off-road driving characteristics and a light and lively appearance.

One of the key contributors to this look was the Scrambler's short five-foot box. The standard short-box for American trucks was six feet in length and in comparison the Scrambler's box seemed to place it at a competitive disadvantage. From an engineering viewpoint AMC had little choice but to use a five-foot box since a longer unit would have placed the load center behind the axle–not exactly the best arrangement for a well balanced road performance.

It appears, however, that box length wasn't an important factor in this market. As already noted, the Subaru Brat sold well with a scaled down box. Furthermore, the Scrambler's box length with the tailgate lowered increased to 80.75 inches from 61.5 inches. Its length and height were 36.25 inches and 10 inches respectively.

The Jeep Scrambler as introduced in February, 1981. (Courtesy of author's collection)

Like those of many other small pick-ups, this box was, unfortunately, of single wall construction which made it imperative for the driver to make certain his load didn't shift about and bang into the box sides. The spare tire mount was attached to the tailgate which, when lowered, was supported by plastic covered cables. As an option, a swing-away spare tire mount was available allowing the tailgate to form a flat surface with the box bed. Curb weight of the Scrambler was 2650 pounds with a maximum payload capacity of 1486 pounds.

From the windshield forward the Scrambler was all Jeep in appearance. In soft top form it was America's only roadster pick-up. This latter version had a base price of $7288 f.o.b. Toledo. A soft half top/steel door model was priced at $7572. For an additional $190 lockable metal doors were available. Yet another configuration with a removable hard top with metal doors was offered at $7922.

The fully boxed, reinforced frame provided a 103.5 inch wheelbase and a front tread of 51.5 inches. Rear tread was 50 inches. In most of its essential mechanical components, the Scrambler was a twin to both the CJ-5 and CJ-7. At the front were 4-leaf semi-elliptic springs with a 170 lb./in. rating, tubular shocks, a live axle with a 2200 pound capacity, free-running hubs and an anti-roll bar. At the rear a semi-floating, 2650 pound capacity axle was supported by 4-leaf semi-elliptic springs with a 185 lb/in. rate. Scramblers ordered with the fiberglass hard top were fitted with 5-leaf springs. An extra-duty suspension option consisting of heavy-duty springs and shock absorbers was available. Its price, when ordered for the base model, was $98. If desired, the heavy-duty shocks were available separately for $30.

The Scrambler had a 5 ft. long cargo bed. (Courtesy of author's collection)

The Scrambler's standard engine was the 82 horsepower 4-cylinder 151 cubic inch engine AMC was then purchasing from Pontiac. For an additional $136 the AMC-built 258 cubic inch 6-cylinder with an 8.3:1 compression ratio and 2-barrel carburetor was offered. Its net horsepower was 110 at 3000 rpm. Maximum torque was 205 lb.ft. at 1800 rpm.

The standard Warner SR4, all-synchromesh 4-speed transmission with ratios of 4.07, 2.39, 1.49 and 1.1:1 was linked to a Dana 300, 2-speed transfer case with a 1.0:1 high and 2.62:1 low range. Six-cylinder Scramblers were available with an optional Tremac T-176 all-synchromesh 4-speed manual transmission with ratios of 3.52, 2.27, 1.46 and 1.0:1. A 9.125 inch diameter clutch was used with the

151 cubic inch 4-cylinder while a 10.5 inch version was specified for the 6-cylinder engine.

Two Chrysler-built three-speed automatic transmissions, with identical prices of $350 were optional for the Scrambler. A Model 904 with ratios of 2.74, 1.55 and 1.0:1 was available for the 4-cylinder model. Scramblers powered by the 258 cubic inch 6-cylinder engine were offered with a Model 999 with ratios of 2.45, 1.45 and 1.0:1.

Standard on the Scrambler were 10.4 inch front disc brakes and 10 × 1.75 inch rear drum brakes. Power assisted front disc brakes were optional. Also offered was a limited-slip rear differential (priced at $179) and power steering with a 17.6:1 ratio in place of the standard 24.0:1 ratio. It was priced at $206. The standard equipment, 15 × 5.5 inch, wheels were fitted with H78 × 15B tires. These could be replaced with an optional tire-wheel combination of 15 × 7 wheels with either 9.00 × 15 or P235/75R × 15 tires. Additional options included a tonneau cover, wood side rails, halogen fog lamps, tilt wheel, door steps and AM or AM/FM radios.

Standard features of the base Scrambler model included 2-speed windshield wipers and washers, heater-defroster, painted front

Two views of the 1982 Jeep Scrambler fitted with the SR Sport package. (Courtesy of author's collection)

bumper, dual exterior mirrors and a folding windshield. Its bucket seats were finished in linen grain Black or Beige vinyl. Taking the Scrambler into the up-scale market were two appearance options – the SR and SL sport packages. The first included high-back bucket seats trimmed in Blue, Black or Nutmeg denim-look vinyl (which was also available as a separate option), the Convenience Group (8 inch day/night mirror, underhood light, courtesy light and spare tire lock) and the Decor group (rocker panel molding, sports steering wheel, front frame cover and instrument panel overlay). Also found on an SR Scrambler were many exterior identifications such as L78 × 15 Goodyear Tracker P/G OWL tires mounted on white styled steel wheels, wheel lip extensions and special Scrambler hood lettering and exterior graphics consisting of hood and body striping in gradations of Yellow, Blue or Red, depending on the exterior color.

Even more elaborate than the $775 SR package was the SL option which listed for $1975. Its buckets seats were finished in either Black Cara with Light Gray accents or Nutmeg vinyl with Honey accents. The steering wheel and passenger assist bar was wrapped in black leather; an interior console was installed along with a clock and tachometer. The pinstriped instrument panel, along with the indoor/outdoor carpeting was available in either Black or Nutmeg. The front grille panel, wheels, front and rear bumpers and mirror heads and arms were chrome trimmed. Goodyear P235/75R 15 Wrangler radial tires were installed as were wheel lip extensions. Exterior SL graphics in combinations of either Silver and Gray or Nutmeg and Bronze included double pinstriping for the beltline, fenders and hood. Wrapping up this option was the Convenience Group, heavy-duty shocks, hood insulation and black rocker molding.

Sales of the Scrambler in 1981 totalled 7840, a level that was destined to be its peak yearly level. Alterations for 1982 were limited to the availability of a 20 gallon fuel tank and a 5-speed, overdrive transmission as options. Calendar year sales were 7138. The 1982 Scrambler's base price was $7588. The SR package was increased to $799 with the SL moving up to $1999.

The standard mounting for the Scrambler's spare tire was relocated to the roll bar in 1983. The side graphics of the SR package took the form of a giant hockey stick. Although CJ sales had begun to recover come from their low 1982 levels, those of the Scrambler sagged to 4678 in spite of a price reduction to $6765. The SR package listed for $825 with the SL positioned at $2065. The following year, in spite of the Scrambler's adoption of AMC's 2.5 liter 4-cylinder engine which gave it EPA fuel economy estimates of 27/37 mpg, its sales dropped to 2826.

With a new Comanche pick-up ready for a 1986 model year introduction, the Scrambler's useful life as an import truck fighter was at an end and it was dropped from the AMC line at the end of the 1985 model year.

Revisions for 1985, therefore weren't extensive. They included chrome Scrambler lettering on the rear fender in place of the hood identification. Both the SR and SL packages were dropped. Their places were taken by the Renegade and Laredo options.

Interior highlights of the Renegade package included Black Garnet or Honey denim-look vinyl high-back bucket seats (standard Scrambler seats were now covered in either Black or Almond linen grain

The 1984 Jeep Scrambler. (Courtesy of author's collection)

vinyl), courtesy lights, day/night rear view mirror, glovebox lock, intermittent wipers and a soft-feel sport steering wheel. Exterior features and identification consisted of P235/75R 15 Black Wrangler steel radial tires, a "Polyspare" spare tire with cover, rocker panel molding, body graphics with Yellow, Blue or Red striping and 15 × 7 White styled steel wheels with chrome hub covers.

The Scrambler Laredo was outfitted with Celtic grain vinyl high-back bucket seats in combinations of Black and Gray or Honey and Dark Honey; a center console, color-keyed interior with removable indoor/outdoor carpeting, courtesy lights, day/night mirror, glove box

lock, intermittent wipers, leather-wrapped steering wheel and passenger assist bar, pinstriped instrument panel, tachometer and clock. The Laredo's exterior retained the SL's chromed body parts, body and hood graphics in either Silver and Gray or Brown and Gold, and P235/75R 15 White letter Wrangler tires on 15 × 7 inch styled wheels. If a soft top was installed it was available in either Black or Honey. The hardtop color choices were Black, White or Honey.

The 1985 Scramblers were available in ten standard colors of which Garnet, Ice Blue, Dark Blue, Medium Green, Sterling Silver and Dark Honey metallic paints were exclusive to the Scrambler and the CJ Jeeps. Other colors available were Classic Black, Olympic White, Sebring Red and Almond Beige.

Chapter 14

The
Cherokee/Wagoneers:
1984–1988

It was evident, just by a brief review of American Motors' 1984 Annual Report that a new era for Jeep had begun in 1984. "American Motors Corporation has reason to be proud of its performance in 1984", it began. "We positioned", said AMC, "four profitable quarters back-to-back and emerged with our first full-year profit since 1979." Part of the credit for this turnaround, which amounted to a nearly $275 million improvement in annual sales, had to go to the increased sales of AMC's Renault Alliance and Encore models. Compared to 1983 their sales were up by 16 percent to 169,601 units. But consider how well Jeep performed. Sales of Jeeps in 1984 totalled 153,801, an 87 percent increase over 1983. This moved Jeep very close to its record year of 1978 when 161,912 were sold. For the model year Jeep sales increased 100 percent over the 1983 level and totalled 139,396 – the third highest model year total for Jeep sales on record.

The reason for this sales explosion, which would soon see Jeep sales surge far ahead of the Renault sub-compact's wasn't difficult to identify – for the first time since 1962 Jeep was introducing an all-new product line. The new Jeeps carried familiar names, Cherokee and Wagoneer, but this was a limit to their connection with the 1983 Cherokee and Wagoneer models.

Since these were, in every sense, all new, state-of-the-art vehicles some industry watchers had anticipated that they might appear with equally new nameplates, perhaps even using the XJ code names used during their development. But with so much depending upon their success, AMC didn't approach this matter in a casual fashion. Joseph Cappy, AMC vice-president-marketing group, noted that "We felt it was important to get public imput in the naming of the first new-from-the-ground-up Jeep vehicles in more than 20 years. A name has a lot to do with how a person perceives the product."

AMC began the name-selection process with a list of 1000 possible names that was pared down to 50 over a period of several months. These, in turn, were presented to participants in a number of public clinics. "It became evident very quickly", explained Cappy, "that we would have two names instead of one. The people who leaned toward the sporty models favored the name Cherokee, and the people who liked the more formal 4-door wagons favored the Wagoneer name." Subsequently, American Motors explained that the 2-door models were aimed at "the more adventurous driver who may be equally comfortable in on-road or off-road environments". The 4-door versions were, AMC continued, "designed to appeal to the family-oriented buyer who wants the added security of 4-wheel drive in a station wagon with added convenience appointments". As a result the new era Wagoneer was offered only as a 4-door while the Cherokee was available either as a 2- or 4-door model. Furthermore, each model had an outward personality of their own with unique grille treatments, taillamps, exterior trim and moldings as well as interior design, fabric and trim.

Work on these new Jeeps began in mid-1979 and represented an investment in excess of $250 million in tooling and equipment that, said Cappy, was to make certain they would "have quality second to none in the 4-wheel drive field". Installed in the Toledo plant were 29 Cybotech robots as an integral part of the body framing process. Nineteen of the robots were of the gantry-type which moved on half-

tracks and reached downward to perform their welding programs. One gantry robot was used for the front structure; five were used on the underbody, seven for the bodyside framing and six worked on the Jeep's final body framing line. The other 10 robots were horizontal and reached outward to carry out their body framing welding assignments. In total, the 29 robots applied more than 1200 welds on each Cherokee/Wagoneer body.

Construction of doors for the new Jeep was totally automatic, but no robots were involved. Inner and outer door panels were welded and hemmed on a line almost identical to the door line used in the Kenosha plant on the Renault Alliance assembly line. The line was capable of producing six different doors at a rate of 300 an hour, and was designed for rapid die changes in order to be as flexible as possible. A changing of dies was completed in just 20 minutes.

American Motors' vice-president-manufacturing operations, George A. Maddox, depicted this program as the most extensive robotics undertaking in the company's history. "We are using robots for welding of underbodies, body sides and framing of the body itself … By using robots and other state-of-the-art automatic welding equipment, we have been able to build strong, precise bodies for these new, lighter weight Jeeps … We have taken a number of steps to assure the new Jeep wagons will have the highest possible degree of quality. The equipment we've installed assures precision in manufacture. It is so precise it will reject sub-assemblies and assemblies that vary even slightly from specification."

The Cherokee/Wagoneer used a new "UniFrame" body design in which a full-length boxed steel frame member was welded to the floor panel of its unitized body structure. This provided both a relatively light construction weight and an extremely rigid body as well as an optimum level of interior space utilization. The final form of this structure resulted from cooperation between AMC and Renault engineering teams. The AMC group conceived the design, while Renault engineers utilized finite element enalysis to prove the validity of the concept. By using this computerized method of designing a body structure increased metal gauge and structure could be added where needed. On the other hand, excess metal could be removed where not needed. For protection against rust and corrosion the Wagoneer/Cherokee body had one-side galvanized sheet metal on most exterior panels. The rocker panels were made of two-side galvanized sheet metal. A one-piece rear liftgate of fiberglass construction was used, which was virtually immune to corrosion.

The new Jeep's rear suspension was straightforward with semi-elliptic leaf springs and an anti-roll bar. The use of rear coil springs was considered by Jeep engineers but they were rejected because they reduced interior space. The leaf springs had very large eyes which along with a sway bar and gas-filled shock absorbers were major contributors to the Jeep's excellent ride characteristics. Up front a "Quadra-Link" suspension was a bit unusual. In order to combine a high level of off-road reliability with good handling and satisfactory on-road characteristics, AMC's vice-president of engineering, Roy Lunn, supervised development of a system combining coil springs with 4 locating arms. The latter components, which located the solid axle, were arranged in a fashion similar to that often seen on independent systems. Also used were an anti-roll bar and hydraulic shock absorbers. Commenting on this aspect of Cherokee/Wagoneer development, Lunn noted, "We began with the solid axle for its off-road ruggedness, but we refined several peripheral systems to make it as sophisticated as it is." An example of this attention to detail was the location of an inverted pinion above the center line which improved the front driveshaft angle. In adddition, constant velocity joints were used both on the front propshaft and the half shafts. Utilization of a Haltenberger steering linkage enabled AMC engineers to keep the linkage entirely ahead of the front axle and provide reasonable Ackerman angles for turning. Another advantage of the Haltenberger linkage system was a level of steering response and feel.

"We have made few compromises with these vehicles", said Lunn, "The off-road capability and ruggedness are exceptional, while the on-road and handling will be pleasantly surprising."

As part of their pre-production test program the Cherokees and Wagoneers were driven through mountain and sand-covered terrains, exposed to the temperature extremes of the polar and desert regions as well as the rigors of the Rubicon Trail in northern California.

The result was impressive. *Motor Trend*, September, 1983 concluded, "The Cherokee handles with much greater agility and stability than you expect from a 4WD truck, for it rides with astonishing smoothness for what is a relatively lightweight vehicle." Standard was Command-Trac, a new part-time system with a full-time alternative, Selec-Trac, optional.

The Command-Trac's part-time 4-wheel drive system was intended for use only in poor traction conditions. To switch in and out of 4-wheel drive the driver operated a handle mounted on the center console. It used the New Process 207 transfer case which had an all-aluminum, two-piece casing.

Selec-Trac, in addition to its viscous-clutch and limited slip center differential (a New Process 229 model) was also fitted with a differential lock in Low Range for added durability. It was suitable for full-time 4-wheel drive operation under all traction and road conditions. The transfer cases for Selec-Trac and Command Trac had the same 2.62:1 Low and 1.0:1 High Range ratios.

Three transmissions were available for the 1984 Cherokee and Wagoneers. Standard for the Cherokee was a fully synchronized 4-speed manual with a floor shift. Standard on the base Wagoneer and optional for the Cherokee was a fully synchronized 5-speed, also with a floor shift. Standard on the Wagoneer Limited and optional for all others was a Chrysler Model 904 3-speed automatic transmission controlled by a floor-mounted shifter. Their gear ratios were as follows:

American Motors devoted three years to its development and, noted Roy Lunn, "unlike most engines available today [it] was not designed for passenger cars and then adapted for trucks. We specifically developed it with our Jeep vehicles and Eagle in mind. That's the reason that performance and durability were of such prime consideration from the very beginning."

Although some components were interchangeable between the AMC 258 cubic inch 6-cylinder and the new engine, the 4-cylinder was not a cut down version of the bix six. Noted Roy Lunn, "There is some common componentry, but the 4-cylinder includes many unique items such as its own electronic systems. It also has a shorter stroke and larger bore. The valves are larger and the pistons are new."

Compared to the 258 engine's 3.75 inch bore and 3.9 inch stroke the four's respective dimensions were 3.875 and 3.188 inches for a displacement of 150.4 cubic inches or 2.465 liters. Commenting on these measurements, Roy Lunn recalled: "We wanted as much displacement – for power and torque – as possible within the confines of bore centers of the tooling. The only parameter we could influence substantially was stroke. So we picked the largest bore and stroke in order to get 2.5 liters."

The crankshaft was supported in five main bearings, hydraulic lifters were operated by an overhead valve arrangement and both the cylinder head and block were constructed of cast iron. The pistons were manufactured from Autothermic aluminum with steel struts. A relatively high, 9.2:1, compression ratio was attained by use of a double-quench combustion chamber. When fitted with base accessories the engine's dry weight was 315 pounds. When options such as air conditioning and power steering were used a serpentine belt system replaced a V-belt arrangement. In that form the engine weighed 341 pounds.

The 1980s was the decade of sophisticated control systems and the AMC engine was a state-of-the-art example. A computer-controlled electronic ignition with a breakerless distributor was used in conjunction with a knock sensor that enabled the computer to control knock without a resultant reduction in fuel economy or power. Unlike the system used on many other engines that measured knock once on average for all four cylinders, this system measured the knock each time a cylinder fired. As a result it could instantaneously retard the spark if necessary. This kept each cylinder operating at a very precise level of knock-free ignition without compromising performance and efficiency.

The single barrel carburetor with electronic fuel feedback was also computer-controlled to maintain the proper fuel mixture. It was mounted on a water heated aluminum intake manifold which also incorporated an electric "hedgehog" heater for rapid fuel vaporization

Gearing	Automatic transmission	Manual transmissions	
	3-speed	4-speed	5-speed
First gear	2.74	3.93	3.93
Second gear	1.55	2.33	2.33
Third gear	1.00	1.45	1.45
Fourth gear	–	1.00	1.00
Fifth gear	–	–	0.85
Reverse	2.2	4.74	4.74

Quite literally powering this banner Jeep year was the first 4-cylinder engine ever designed by American Motors. While not related in any way to the original L-head Go-Devil and F-Head Hurricane engines this in-line, overhead 4-four cylinder was their worthy successor.

after a cold start. An ERG system enhanced both NOx control and fuel economy. Also part of the pollution control system was a Pulse-Air, computer controlled, secondary air injection that maintained high hydrocarbon and carbon dioxide oxidation efficiency without a parasitic power loss. Also installed was a dual bed catalyst and a three-position "Solevac" vacuum/solenoid which maintained an optimum idle speed. Loss of fuel through evaporation was held to a minimum by use of a pressure/vacuum relief valve on the fuel tank, a solenoid operated fuel bowl vent on the carburetor and a charcoal cannister for unused fuel storage.

"From the standpoint of all-around technology", Lunn noted, "we feel this is as advanced as any engine in its class". This competitive position was enhanced by a durability factor that, according to the results of extensive dynamometer tests was substantially better than engines of similar size and configuration.

The new Jeep engine also excelled in absolute power output with 105 horsepower at 5000 rpm and 132 lb.ft. of torque available at 2800 rpm. "This is a high torque engine", said Roy Lunn, "and that certainly translates into a strong acceleration capability for an engine of this size."

Manufacturing of AMC's 2.5 liter engine took place at its Kenosha, Wisconsin facility where the 6-cylinder and V-8 engines were also built. Maximum output was 195,000 units annually.

All models were available with an optional (priced at $305) 173.2 cubic inch 60 degree V-6 engine supplied by Chevrolet. It was rated at 115 horsepower at 4800 rpm and 145 lb.ft. of torque at 2400 rpm. This engine was originally developed for General Motors X-cars (Chevrolet Citation, Pontiac Pheonix, Oldsmobile Omega and Buick's Skylark) that debuted in 1979 as 1980 model year cars. It was a conventionally designed but modern engine weighing 350 pounds. When it was introduced by Chevrolet it was depicted as the successor to Chevrolet's legendary small-block V-8 which dated back to 1955. Its block and cylinder head were constructed of lightweight iron castings. The exhaust manifold was nodular iron with aluminum used for the intake manifold, water pump housing, front cover and the 2-barrel Varijet carburetor. This engine was also characterized by its modified "squish" design combustion chamber, low pressure aluminum casting intake manifold and four main bearings. Regardless of the engine used, all Cherokees and Wagoneers had a standard 13.5 gallon fuel tank with an extended range, 20 gallon tank optional.

The styling of the new Wagoneer/Cherokee successfully transferred the neo-classic "Jeep Look" into the new dimensions of contemporary sports-utility vehicles. At the same time there was no evidence of slavish imitation of existing domestic or foreign products. Pure and simple, the new models were distinctive, trim and attractive. Although not shattering in the world of low drag Audis or Pontiac Firebirds, the Jeep's drag coefficient was a decent 0.54.

"Our design objectives presented us with a paradox", explained Richard A. Teague, then serving as vice-president of styling for American Motors. "First, we knew we were dealing with one of the world's most readily recognizable automotive nameplates, one whose product identity had to be retained. At the same time, the advanced engineering technology and manufacturing innovation encompassed in the new SportWagons dictated an equally modernistic styling approach. Our marching orders were clear."

Presented with a package from AMC engineering that was considerably more compact than the preceding model, Teague noted, "We examined all design possibilities, everything in our bag of tricks. We wanted to improve the vehicle aerodynamically, make it more visually appealing and yet it couldn't be too passenger-car oriented because that's not the Jeep image."

To isolate those elements that epitomized the Jeep look, AMC exterior designers selected four key points of previous Cherokee/Wagoneer models. These were: crisp, angular body lines; squared-off front and rear wheel openings; predominent slotted grilles and bold,

spoke-type wheels. These elements were supported by an interior having what AMC described as a "heavy-duty performance look".

"Combined", said Teague, "those elements represent the graphic stamp of the Jeep vehicle. Our job in designing the SportWagons was to make sure the Jeep family resemblance was retained in a whole new generation of vehicles."

To provide the Cherokee/Wagoneer with good (for a vehicle of its type) aerodynamics the AMC designers selected what was depicted as an "aircraft fuselage approach". This was characterized by body lines that were slightly rounded from top to bottom on the sides. In addition, the hood was sloped forward and down and the grille was angled back toward the passenger compartment.

Referring to the appearance of the SportWagon's passenger compartment above its door line, Teague noted, "We wanted to avoid the box-on-a-box look that some competitive products have. The lines of the SportWagons are clean and uninterrupted from the ground up."

Although it was hardly a revolutionary development, the use of curved glass for the SportWagon's front and rear windows was a first for a Jeep vehicle. In addition, the SportWagon's windshield was raked more than those of preceding Jeep vehicles.

Having a major impact upon the Jeep's front end design were the results of wind tunnel tests conducted in both the U.S. and at Renault facilities in France. Specifically influenced were its grille's contour, windshield shape, front fenders and built-in front air dam. Also reflecting the influence of these tests was the shape of the SportWagon's exterior mirrors.

These factors not withstanding, the familiar Jeep vertical grille theme continued. But, there were some significant design refinements. For example, the hood opening was now recessed from the top of the grille which was also raked back slightly. Also, headlights were more prominent with larger and bolder graphics. In tune with contemporary styling tastes, the Jeep's chrome trim treatment was very muted.

As already noted, a fibreglass one-piece rear liftgate was used on the SportWagon. Although it had a "with it" feature of two built-in audiospeakers for improved sound clarity, its full-size and rugged looking handles were part of the Jeep image. "We did that for the outdoor types," recalled Teague. "One of the tests was that you had to be able to operate the door handle while wearing a pair of heavy, snow gloves."

Three versions of the Cherokee were available; the Base, Pioneer and Chief models. Major exterior identification features of the base model (priced at $9995 for the 2-door and $10,295 for the 4-door) consisted of black bumpers, end caps and fender flares. Its grille, with a black background and an argent insert of narrow, wide-spaced bars was reminiscent of earlier models. Other distinguishing features included black and argent headlight bevels, black hub caps for the 15 × 6 inch argent-colored styled steel wheels carrying P195/75R 15 black sidewall steel-belted radial all-weather tires, Jeep lettering on the hood and lower right corner of the liftgate, Cherokee lettering on the front fenders and rear license visor, a single, black-finish driver's side mirror, a black tailgate window surround and black molding for the door window frame and vent divider and drip rail.

The design of the SportWagon interior presented its creators with the same challenge faced by their exterior body counterparts. As AMC explained, "It had to offer the comfort level and eye appeal of a passenger car, while maintaining the ruggedness associated with a sports utility vehicle."

A completely new instrument panel was used with a fully-integrated air conditioning system option, logically positioned instrumentation, an exposed stowage bin, as well as a full-size glove box. A tachometer was included for the first time along with an upshift light option (initially available only on vehicles with a 4-speed manual transmission and 4-cylinder engine).

Both the front and rear seats designs were noteworthy. Those up front utilized a pedestal format, similar to that used on the Renault Alliance. The rear seat cushion was designed to tip forward to a vertical position behind the rear of the front seat, allowing the rear seat to be folded down flush with the cargo floor. In addition, the rear seat had a quick-release feature permitting it to be removed to

The 1984 Jeep Cherokee Chief. (Courtesy of author's collection)

accomodate extra-long cargo items. All SportWagons had a one-piece headliner that AMC said provided additional headroom for passengers.

Interior appointments of the Base Cherokee consisted of a 2-spoke polypropylene black steering wheel, mini color-keyed console, black plastic door opening scuff plates, vinyl color-keyed straight arm rests, color-keyed textured vinyl trim for the passenger and cargo areas and the rear seat back, color-keyed grained vinyl covered sunvisors, black instrument cluster overlay, and a painted molded board liftgate panel. The seats (front buckets, rear bench) were finished in a Celtic grain vinyl offered in Almond or Slate Blue.

The Pioneer models, priced $1000 above their Base versions and the Cherokee Chief, which listed for $1310 more than a comparable Base Cherokee, shared the following common interior features: three-spoke sport steering wheel, "hockey-style" front armrests, 12 oz. nylon passenger area carpeting with heat and noise insulation, 14 oz. needled polypropylene cargo floor/wheelhouse/rear seat back carpeting, carpeted liftgate trim panel, four cargo area tie-down hooks, full length, color-keyed console with armrest, rear ashtray (mounted in the door handles on 4-door models; in the trim panel on 2-doors) and rear heat ducts, cloth headliner and sunvisors, bright instrument panel accent surround, electronic digital clock, gauge package (consisting of voltmeter, temperature, low fuel indicator and trip odometer) rear seat beverage holders on 2-door models, front bucket seats in Deluxe grain vinyl, tinted glass (deep tinted quarter windows on 2-door models; tinted on 4-doors), Light Group (includes ash tray light, cargo

area light, demo/map light, door switches for dome/courtesy lights added to rear doors, illuminated ring around cigarette lighter, lighted visor mirror, underhood light and under instrument panel lights), AM radio with two speakers, rear window wiper and washer (all models had a standard 2-speed windshield wiper and washer system) and a color-keyed vinyl spare tire cover.

Whereas the Pioneer shared its grille design with the base model, that of the Chief used a bright insert. Similarly, the Chief differed from other Cherokees by virtue of its black headlight bevels and 15 × 7 inch white styled spoke wheels with bright hub covers. Pioneers had white trim rings that were optional for the base model. Both the Base and Pioneer could also be fitted with the Cherokee Chief wheels at extra cost. For the Pioneer model P205/75R 15 black sidewall radial all-weather tires were specified. The Chief had P215/75/15 OWL steel-belted radial all-terrain Goodyear Wrangler tires. Added to the Cherokee lettering on the Pioneer's front fender was "Pioneer" lettering. The Chief carried special hood striping along with rocker panel identification which included "Cherokee Chief" lettering.

The Wagoneer was available in either a Base or Limited version. As expected, these were expensive (Base: $12,444; Limited: $17,076) vehicles with a considerable amount of standard equipment. Included in the sticker price of both models were front door hockey stick type armrests with bright upper and lower surrounds, four cargo area tie down hooks, a liftgate panel covered in 14 ozs. polypropylene carpet, cloth headliner, color-keyed instrument panel with bright surrounds, black plastic scuff moldings on the door openings, passenger handles

265

The base level 1984 Jeep Cherokee. (Courtesy of author's collection)

(two rear, one front), fold-flat rear seats with quick release removable bottom cushion, color-keyed vinyl spare tire cover, bright bumpers with black end caps, bright door handles, color-keyed fender flares, exterior body graphics, bright grille, bright headlight bezels, Jeep logo on driver's side of GVOP and lower right corner of liftgate, 4-wheel Drive or Selec-Trac lettering or rear quarter panels, Wagoneer lettering on front fenders and rear license visor, bright door frames, bright drip rails, bright liftgate surround, black lower bodyside with bright insert, bright quarter window and windshield surrounds, rear seat ashtrays, cigarette lighter, electronic clock with digital display, Gauge Group, glove box lamp, halogen headlights, (these were used on all Cherokees and Wagoneers), Light Group, power brakes and steering, and tinted glass.

The Base and Limited versions differed in many areas. Unlike the Base model which was equipped with the mini console, the Limited had a full length, color keyed console with armrest, rear ashtray and rear heating ducts. Door panels on the Limited combined woodgrain and leather trim with a nylon carpeted lower section and map pocket. Those on the Base were vinyl covered with a carpeted lower map pocket. Country Cord was used for the Limited's seats with leather insert having "Limited" embroidering. The Base had a Westchester cloth seat trim offered in four colors. Unique to the Limited were storage pockets positioned on the back of the front seat and a woodgrain applique on the instrument panel. Both the Wagoneer

Limited and the Cherokee Laredo had standard swing-out front vent windows. They were optional for other SportWagons and required tinted glass.

Exterior distinctions of the Limited included woodgrain bodyside and liftgate trim, dual manual remote mirrors, and 15 × 6 inch "Luxury Style" aluminium wheels, and "Limited" lettering added below the "Wagoneer" identification on the front fender.

The Limited was also equipped with air conditioning, heavy-duty battery, the Protection Group (bumper guards, floor mats, door edge guards, cargo area skid plates), AM/FM stereo radio with 4 speakers, roof rack, leather-wrapped sport steering wheel with tilt feature and Soft Ride suspension which used unique front and rear springs shock absorbers and front suspension bushings.

Both the Cherokee and Wagoneer were offered in a choice of ten paint colors. Available on both models were Olympic White, Deep Night Blue, Classic Black, Almond Beige plus the following metallic clearcoats: Silver, Chestnut Brown and Garnet. Exclusive to the Cherokee was Sebring Red and Ice Blue metallic clearcoat. Wagoneer-only colors were Nordic Green and a Cinnamon clearcoat metallic. Two-tone options for the Cherokee were Olympic White/Deep Night Blue; Olympic White/Sebring Red; Olympic White/Almond Beige; Champagne Metallic/Classic Black and Ice Blue Metallic/Deep Night Blue.

The physical size of the new Cherokee and Wagoneer contrasted sharply not only with the older models but with other contemporary down-sized 4-wheel drive competitive models:

	Cherokee/Wagoneer		Chevrolet	Ford
	1983	1984	S–10 Blazer	Bronco II
Wheelbase (ins.)	108.7	101.4	100.5	94.0
Overall length (ins.)	186.4	165.3	170.3	158.4
Front track (ins.)	59.4	57.0	55.6	56.9
Height (ins.)	66.4	63.3	64.9	68.2
Ground clearance (ins.)	7.2	7.7	6.9	6.9
Cargo volume (cu. ft.) (rear seat folded)	74.5	71.2	67.3	64.9
Weight (lbs.)	3869*	2979*	3146	3237
*4-door model				

The top-of-the-line 1984 Jeep Wagoneer. (Courtesy of author's collection)

The new Jeeps also enjoyed some significant advantages over their main domestic competitors, the Ford Bronco and Chevrolet Blazer. For example, by opting for a longer wheelbase (the Blazer's was 100.5 inches; the Broncho II had a 94 inch wheelbase) the Jeep's designers were able to position the rear seat forward of the rear wheel opening, thus creating a three-passenger seat. The Cherokee/Wagoneer constant ground clearance of 7.6 inches also was superior to both the Blazer's and Bronco II's which were identical at 6.5 inches. The Jeep's interior space, measured either in terms of room for occupants or cargo capacity, was greater than that of its two rivals.

An extensive list of standard equipment was a prime feature of the 1984 Wagoneer. (Courtesy of author's collection)

The Cherokee two-door model had front doors that were two inches wider than those of the Blazer and four inches wider than the Bronco II's.

As has already been noted, sales of the new Cherokee and Wagoneers helped push Jeep sales up to their third-best ever model year in 1984. Compared to their competition the new models also did very well in terms of calendar year sales:

Model	1984 Calendar Year Sales
Cherokee	69,057*
Wagoneer	19,886*
Chevrolet Blazer/GMC Jimmy	129,264
Ford Bronco 11	98,049

*In 1983 a total of 8729 Cherokee and 4842 Wagoneers were sold as 1984 models.

The 1984 Cherokee and Wagoneer models maintained the Jeep tradition of versatility and functionalism that appealed to four-wheel drive enthusiasts (courtesy of author's collection)

This outstanding performance was exceeded by the popularity of the 1985 models which set a new model year sales mark for the American and Canadian markets of 192,835. The previous mark had been 169,424 in 1979. In the United States sales reached 181,389, an 18 percent increase and a new record. In Canada, sales of 11,446 vehicles in 1985 exceeded the record of 7974 also set in 1979.

Production totals for the 1985 model year were as follows:

Model	Production
Cherokee	120,328
Wagoneer	10,021

Commenting on these new records, Peter G. Guptill, American Motors group vice president, North American sales and marketing, noted, "We're delighted by the continued popularity of our award-winning Jeep Cherokee. Cherokee sales increased 43 percent in 1985 ... On a sales-per-dealer basis, the Cherokee again was the top selling compact sports utility vehicle in the United States."

Certainly contributing to this sales strength was the dramatic shift in the role of women as purchasers of 4-wheel drive vehicles. Whereas in 1974, when only 7 percent of the nation's 4-wheel drive vehicles were driven predominantly by women, the corresponding figure for 1984 was over 16 percent. According to Joseph Cappy, then serving as American Motors' group vice-president – sales and marketing, the percentage was "much higher for Jeep vehicles". Indeed, one out of every five Cherokee/Wagoneer SportWagon was purchased by a woman.

Production figures for the Cherokee and Wagoneer, when compared to their domestic competitors, was even more impressive than in 1984:

Model	1985 Calendar Year Production
Cherokee	120,328
Wagoneer	10,021
GMC S–15 Jimmy	51,582
Chevrolet S–10 Blazer	231,605
Ford Bronco II	111,351

There was, unfortunately, a gray lining to this solid gold Jeep performance in the form of a near collapse of Renault Alliance and Encore model sales. Reported AMC, "the fine Jeep vehicle sales record ..., however, did not alter the fact that American Motors posted a loss of $125.3 million in 1985. The primary reason for our loss in 1985 was our dependence on the subcompact passenger car market."

None the less, AMC did note that in the second half of the year the loss was $25.8 million as compared to $99.5 million in the first half. But in spite of cost cutting measures adopted by AMC the continuing slide downward of Alliance and Encore sales would be a serious impediment to its efforts to attain a sustained level of profitability.

Although 1985 was a year of relatively minor changes in the Cherokee and Wagoneer models, AMC boasted that they would, in 1985, "put even more distance between themselves and the competition with an impressive list of new functional and convenience features." The most interesting of these changes was a 126 cubic inch

Employees at the Jeep plant in Toledo installing a 4-cylinder engine in a pilot Jeep Cherokee. (Courtesy of author's collection)

(2.1 liter), 4-cylinder turbo charged diesel engine available for Cherokees and Wagoneers sold in all states except California. Its price was $1258.

This engine was part of a family of Renault engines that from their concept had been intended to function both as gasoline and diesel designs. Included in this engine package was a water in the fuel indicator system, air to air intercooler, glow plug indicator, heavy duty diesel battery, alternator and regulator, turbo boost gauge and a diesel sound insulation package.

Far Right: **The 1985 Jeep Wagoneer was offered with an optional 2.1 liter turbocharged engine. (Courtesy of author's collection)**

Major design features consisted of a Ricardo Comet 5 pattern cylinder head, a Garrett T2 turbocharger, a Bosch EPVE fuel injection pump and a high capacity oil pump with a special release valve. Customers who selected this engine were advised to always allow the engine to idle for at least 30 seconds after start-up to allow the oil flow to be established and to also allow the engine to idle for 30 seconds before switching off the engine in order to give the turbocharger time to slow down. AMC anticipated that a turbo diesel Jeep with manual transmission would deliver an estimated 31 mpg in city driving and 36 mpg highway. Power steering was a required option with the turbo

diesel which was available with either the 3-speed automatic or 5-speed manual transmissions.

Both the 1985 Cherokee and Wagoneer were available with a new version of Selec-Trac with "shift-on-the-fly" capability. Also added to the Cherokee option list was a swing-away spare tire carrier for 4-door models. This exterior mounting was not available for the Wagoneers and required the purchase of a conventional size spare tire in place of the standard compact, limited duty spare. Both models were available with a new dash mounted "Systems Sentry" system which monitored fluid systems throughout the vehicle including automatic transmission, transfer case, engine oil reservoir, front and rear axle oil, radiator, windshield washer brake, power steering as well as front brake disc lining wear. Also debuting as a Cherokee/Wagoneer option was a keyless entry system which featured infra-red light waves, activated from a key fob that were electrically transmitted to lock or unlock the doors. This required power door locks and was offered for all models except the Base Cherokee. All 2-door Cherokees continued to be fitted with the pop-out rear quarter window vents that were introduced as a 1985½ feature. Both the Cherokees and Wagoneers had front bucket seats with headrests. Except for the Base model all Cherokees had cargo area tie-down hooks and passenger assist handles and front seats with a rocker/recliner capability.

New standard equipment installed on the Base Wagoneer included the addition of headrests and rocker/recliner capability to its front bucket seats. The Limited model now had standard power seats with a seat back recliner. Cargo area tie-down hooks were added along with three J–rail mounted passenger assist handles.

Joining the Cherokee line as a top of the line model was the Cherokee Laredo. It was set apart from other Cherokees by its front fender nameplates, bright metal trim for the headlight bezels, windshield surround and grille, black left- and right-side remote mirrors, Michelin P215/75R 15 OWL steel-belted radial all terrain tires on 15 × 7 in. cast aluminum wheels with bright hub covers, swing-out front door vent windows and body graphics which included striping along the length of the body and around the color-keyed wheel flares. The Laredo interior featured a Highland Check cloth and vinyl seat trim in Garnet or Honey. The doors were trimmed in upgraded vinyl and cloth with 18 oz. nylon carpeted lower sections. A leather-wrapped steering wheel was also installed. Additional standard equipment found on the Laredo that was not standard on other Cherokee models included 18 oz. needled polypropylene cargo floor/wheelhouse/rear seat back coverings, full length, color-keyed console with armrest, rear ashtray and rear heating ducts, instrument panel overlay of brushed pewter and a spare tire cover of color-keyed vinyl with a carpet insert and plastic, color-keyed plastic. The Laredo was also fitted with the Extra Quiet insulation package which consisted of 18 oz. nylon passenger carpet, extra passenger and cargo area insulation, underhood insulation and additional undercoating.

Commenting on this development Joseph Cappy noted that "More and more buyers are turning to 2-wheel drive sport utility wagons because they want ruggedness and durability. This is especially true in the sunbelt states where 4-wheel drive is less of a necessity."

Making sure that no one made the mistake of interpreting the new Cherokee as simply a regional model, AMC explained that its "popularity won't be limited to the South because it is an excellent alternative to conventional station wagons and vans with the cargo-carrying capacity of utility vehicles and the comfort and convenience of a passenger car."

The new model had a base price, in 2-door, 4-cylinder form of $9195 – or $1350 less than that of the 4-wheel drive version. The 4-door, 4-cylinder was priced at $9766. The respective prices of the same models with the V-6 engine were $9544 and $10,115.

The 2WD Cherokee was offered in two trim levels, Base and Pioneer and was available with the same paint and body trim as its 4WD counterparts. Thus, its color selection consisted of Classic Black, Sebring Red, Olympic White, Deep Night Blue, Almond Beige and five extra cost metallic clearcoat colors: Dark Honey, Garnet, Ice Blue, Sterling Silver and Champagne. With only a few minor exceptions, optional equipment availability was identical to the 4WD Cherokee.

Francois Castaing, AMC vice-president of product engineering and development, explained "This new Jeep vehicle will provide the same

On 12 March, 1985 Jeep stepped out of its traditional role as an exclusive builder of 4-wheel drive vehicles when it announced a 2-wheel drive version of the Cherokee SportWagon. This wasn't, of course, the first time 2-wheel drive Jeeps had been available but, not since 1969 had a 2-wheel drive model of one of Jeep's primary models been offered.

The new Cherokee was positioned in a market segment that had registered significant sales gains since 1981. At that time less than 23,000 2WD sport vehicle wagons had been sold. But in 1984 their sales reached 105,000 units of which over 40 percent were compacts.

ride, comfort, performance and rugged durability as the 4-wheel drive Cherokee ... but it will also be even more fuel efficient." On the latter point, AMC estimated it would have a two-mile-per-gallon improvement in fuel economy.

AMC's 2.5 liter 4-cylinder engine was standard with the 2.8 liter V-6 optional. The turbo diesel engine available on the 4-wheel drive models was not offered. The 2WD Cherokee's standard transmission was the 4-speed manual. Both the 5-speed manual and 3-speed automatic were optional.

Explaining the development of the 2WD Cherokee, Castaing said,

"Converting a four-wheel drive system to a two-wheel drive is not nearly as complex from an engineering standpoint as it would be going the other way." The basic alterations entailed elimination of the 4WD transfer case, the front axle gear housing and the axle disconnect mechanism. The 4WD front axle was replaced with a high-strength tubular beam axle assembly. The Quadra-Link front suspension was retained.

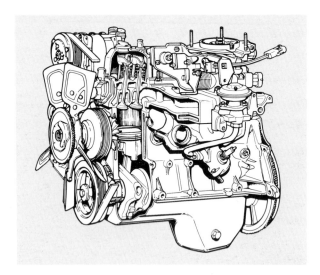

AMC redesigned its 2.4 liter 4-cylinder engine for 1985. (Courtesy of author's collection)

The 2WD Cherokee 2-door model weighed 2776 pounds – 165 pounds less than the 4WD model. The 4-door 2WD Cherokee's weight was 2827 pounds, or 166 less than its 4WD counterpart.

The specific EPA estimated fuel economy rating for the 2WD Cherokee were as follows:

	4-cyl. engine	**6-cyl. engine**
4-spd. trans.:	23 city/27 hwy.	4-spd. not available*
5-spd. trans.:	21 city/26 hwy.	16 city/27 hwy.
3-speed. auto.:	20 city/22 hwy.	16 city/18 hwy.

*The 4-speed manual was not available with the 2WD with the V-6 engine.

Summing up his perception of the 2WD Cherokee, Joseph Cappy said, "We consider the two-wheel drive Cherokee as exceptional value and expect it to provide stiff competition in the sport utility wagon market."

As far as the Cherokee's competitiveness was concerned AMC told prospective buyers that "2-wheel drive Cherokee is without peer. Perhaps you will be surprised to learn that Ford Bronco II doesn't even offer a 2-wheel drive configuration. And, when compared to 2-wheel drive Chevy S–10 Blazer well ... see for yourself.

Features	2WD Jeep Cherokee	2WD Chevy S–10 Blazer
Base engine	2.5 liter, 1–4	2.5 liter, 1–4
Base trans.	4-spd manual	4-spd. manual
Wheelbase (ins.)	101.4	100.5
Overall length (ins.)	165.3	170.3
Number of pass.	5	4

The 1985 Cherokee Chief proved far more popular than the 1985 Renault Encore. (Courtesy of author's collection)

Cargo volume (cu. ft.)		
Rear seat folded	71.2	67.3
Rear seat upright	35.3	28.8
2- or 4-door body		
Style availability	yes	no (2-door only)
Ground clearance (ins.)	7.7	7.4
Quadra-Link front suspension	yes	no
Uniframe const.	yes	no
Widest entry/exit 2-dr.	yes	no

Right: **AMC reported that women accounted for 20 percent of all Cherokee and Wagoneer SportWagon sales. This is a 1985 Cherokee Chief. (Courtesy of author's collection)**

The most impressive technical development for 1986 was the introduction of a significantly upgraded version of American Motors' 151 cubic inch 4-cylinder engine equipped with a throttle body single-point fuel injection system. This was standard not only for the Cherokee and Wagoneer but also for the new Comanche pick-up truck.

Broadening the sales appeal of the Cherokee was the 2-wheel drive version introduced for 1985. (Courtesy of author's collection)

A Jeep Cherokee competing in the 1985 Jeep Cup competition held in Canada. (Courtesy of Chrysler Canada)

273

"Our original design concept took into consideration that fuel injection would be added eventually", recalled Daniel Hittler, director of engine engineering for American Motors. "Everything was compatible for evolutionary development. We knew going in that we had more horsepower potential. The carburetor served as a cork on that power. Now we're letting it out." Also used on the 1-4 engine was a Renix fully microcomputer controlled system that regulated such engine functions as ignition, fuel injection, fuel pump, automatic idle speed control, shift indicator light and various emission controls.

A 1986 Cherokee Chief with the new off-highway package available in 1986. (Courtesy of authors collection)

The 1986 Jeep Cherokee Pioneer 2-door with 2-wheel drive. (Courtesy of author's collection)

A 1986 Jeep Cherokee Pioneer 4-door also with a 2-wheel drivetrain. (Courtesy of author's collection)

By 1986 the Grand Wagoneer was fully established as a car for the carriage trade (Courtesy of author's collection)

A 1986 Jeep Wagoneer. (Courtesy of author's collection)

The 1986 engine's maximum horsepower rating was 117 at 5000 rpm compared to 105 for its carbureted predecessor. Similarly, its torque rose to 135 lb.ft. at 3500 rpm from 132 lb.ft. at 3000 rpm. Compared to the V-6, 173 cubic inch engine from Pontiac that remained available for the Cherokee and Wagoneer the AMC 4-cylinder had more horsepower, 117 to 115 and was nearly equal in torque output, 135 to 150. The 1-4's added power did not come at the expense of fuel economy which actually was slightly improved over the 1985 EPA mileage estimates.

The use of this engine put AMC into the forefront of domestic 4-cylinder engine performance. Not only did it offer more horsepower than any other domestically-built comparable engine but its performance capabilities were equal to or better than a number of 6-cylinder engines used by competitors in their light trucks. "It's in specific horsepower ... power output per liter of displacement ... where this engine is really outstanding," noted Hittler. "Historically, the coveted goal is to achieve 50 horsepower per liter. Our engine rated at 47.6 horsepower in dynamometer testing.

"From the standpoint of specific horsepower," continued Hittler, "that would place it among the top 10 percent of conventional engines built anywhere in the world, regardless of size."

AMC adopted a 1000 hour bench dynamometer reliability test schedule from Renault that involved 500 hours of testing at peak torque rpm level plus 500 additional hours at top horsepower output. "That's about five times longer than the standard U.S. industry practice for this kind of testing," observed Hittler, "and the 1-4 came through it perfectly."

The 1986 Cherokees and Wagoneers both had minor exterior graphics and interior trim changes, but these were overshadowed by the use of a new front end appearance for the Wagoneer which further set it apart from the less expensive Cherokees. The Wagoneer now used vertically-stacked quad halogen headlights positioned at the outer edge of a grille with a bright horizontal divider and a blacked-out insert.

Both the Cherokee and Wagoneer were offered with a new premium stereo sound system; "Accusound by Jensen" with six speakers mated to a high line electronically tuned cassette radio that provided, said AMC, "the ultimate in audio reception".

In addition to its higher performance base engine and revised exterior graphics, the Cherokee was available with a new Off-Highway Vehicle package designed, in American Motors' words, "to appeal to those motorists whose recreational lifestyles occasionally take them beyond the traditional on-highway venues." It consisted of premium high-pressure gas shock absorbers (painted yellow), five P225/75R 15 OWL all-terrain Wrangler tires mounted on 15 × 7 in. white styled "spoker" wheels, skid plate package, 4.10:1 axle ratio (standard was a 3.54:1 ratio), tow hooks (2 front, 1 rear) and a high ground clearance suspension consisting of unique front and rear springs and jounce bumpers). Installation of this package required power steering and air conditioning prep. kit. Identifying Cherokees so equipped was a window decal.

Jeep's Trac-Loc limited slip rear differential was now available on all Cherokee and Wagoneer models with the optional Selec-Trac full-time 4-wheel drive system. Previously it had been offered only in combination with the standard Command Trac part-time 4-wheel drive system.

Prices of the 1986 Cherokees and Wagoneers plus those for popular items were as follows:

Model	Price
Cherokee 4WD 2-door	$10,695
Cherokee 4WD 4-door	$11,320
Cherokee 2WD 2-door	$9335
Cherokee 2WD 4-door	$9950
Wagoneer	$13,630
Wagoneer Limited	$18,600

Option	Price
Pioneer Package	$1206
Chief Package	$1700
Laredo Package	$2994
Metallic (clearcoat) paint	$161
Fabric bucket seats (Cherokee)	$65
P205/75R 15 steel-belted radial black sidewall (Cherokee)	$43
P205/75R 15 steel-belted radial white sidewall (Cherokee)	$128
P215/75R 15 OWL tires (Cherokee)	$332
P225/75R 15 OWL tires (Cherokee)	$375
2.8 liter V-6 engine	$437
2.1 liter diesel engine	$1258
5-speed manual trans. (Cherokee)	$175
Automatic trans. (Cherokee)	$670
Automatic trans. (Wagoneer)	$495
Selec-Trac (Cherokee)	$932
Selec-Trac (Wagoneer)	$757
Rear Trac-Lok differential	$255
California emission control system	$116
Air conditioning	$765
Air conditioning prep. kit.	$134
Heavy duty battery	$58
Bumper guards	$64
Cargo area cover	$67
Passenger floor carpeting (Cherokee)	$193
Digital clock (Cherokee)	$43
Cold climate group	$155
Console with arm rest	$112
Maximum cooling package	$99
Cruise control	$205
Deep tinted glass (Cherokee)	$310
Rear window defroster	$150
Extra capacity fuel tank (20.2 gal., NA with P195 tires)	$50
Extra quiet insulation package	$118
Floor mats	$28
Fog lamps	$102
Light group (Cherokee)	$88
Automatic load leveling system	$184
Keyless entry system (Wagoneer)	$119
Dual exterior remote control mirrors	$71
Dual electric remote control mirrors	$163
Dual low profile mirrors	$85
Power door locks	$194
Power door and window locks	$493
Power front seats	$386
Power steering (Cherokee)	$274
Protection group	$124
AM radio (Cherokee)	$113
AM/FM mono radio (Cherokee)	$186
AM/FM mono radio (Wagoneer)	$73
AM/FM stereo (Cherokee)	$290

AM/FM stereo (Wagoneer)	$177			
E.T. AM/FM cassette – DNR (Cherokee)	$475			
E.T. AM/FM cassette	$480			
Roof rack	$128			
Sunroof	$330			
Skid plate package	$133			
Leather-wrapped steering wheel	$86			
Heavy duty suspension package	$56			
Off-highway suspension (Cherokee)	$798	Trailer towing package "B"	$214
Tachometer	$59	Visibility group	$266
Tilt steering wheel	$118	Aluminum wheels	$246
Tinted glass (Cherokee)	$106	Intermittent wipers	$57
Trailer towing package "A"	$111	Rear window wiper/washer (Cherokee)	$136

The 1987 Jeep Cherokee Laredo. (Courtesy of author's collection)

The 1987 Jeep Wagoneer Limited (Courtesy of author's collection)

The 1987 Jeep Cherokee Laredo. (Courtesy of author's collection)

The 1987 Cherokee Chief. (Courtesy of author's collection)

While output of Wagoneers moved upward slightly to 12,800 units, production of Cherokees fell 13,103 units to 107,225.

By the mid-eighties it was apparent that the age of high performance was alive and well in the United States. Although it came too late to save the Renault Alliance from its demise, the introduction of the GTA model was just one example that virtually every nook and cranny of the automobile market would contain at least one example of a modern high performance vehicle. Admittedly not best known as a purveyor of high performance cars, AMC had offered in earlier times cars such as the Javelin and AMX that had been respected for their quick acceleration and roadability.

But even long-time AMC fans weren't ready for what AMC had in store for the 1987 Cherokee, Wagoneer and Comanche models. In short, by offering the most powerful engine in the light truck/utility sports vehicle field it added straight line performance superiority to

their long list of competitive advantages. It was, therefore, with justification, that AMC, on 8 September, 1986 announced: "With the introduction of its new electronically fuel-injected, 4.0 liter 6-cylinder engine ... American Motors is poised to deliver the most potent 1–2 power 'punch' in the light truck industry in 1987."

The superiority of this engine over its competition was so overwhelming that Chris P. Theodore, AMC director of engineering predicted that "Every aspect of this engine is so appealing, we expect Cherokee, Wagoneer and Comanche buyers will choose this option overwhelmingly. In fact, the figure could be 80 percent the first year."

The specifics of the new AMC engine were dazzling: a displacement of 242 cubic inches (larger than any other 1987 light truck 6-cylinder engine) and peak outputs of 173 horsepower at 4500 rpm and 200 lb.ft. of torque at 2500 rpm. This translated into a zero to 60 mph time of less than 10 seconds and an increase in Cherokee and

The 1988 Jeep Cherokee Limited 4-door. The first example was a mid-1987 addition to the Jeep line. (Courtesy of author's collection)

The 1988 Grand Wagoneer (Courtesy of author's collection)

The 1988 Jeep Wagoneer Limited. (Courtesy of author's collection)

Wagoneer maximum trailer-tow capacity to 5000 pounds. Among domestic trucks, the nearest horsepower to the AMC 4.0 engine was the 2.9 liter V-6 used in the Ford Ranger and Bronco II which had an advertised rating of 140 horsepower. As far as torque was concerned, the Dodge Dakota's 3.9 liter V-6 ranked closest but it was still rated only at 195 lb.ft.

At first glance, the new engine outwardly resembled the older carbureted 258 cubic inch (4.2 liter) 6-cylinder (it will be recalled that the 1–4 engine and the 258 cid 6-cylinder had common bore centers, valve locations and general front arrangements). In reality, therefore, a

A 1988 Jeep Cherokee Chief. (Courtesy of author's collection)

closer relation was the fuel injected I-4 introduced in 1986 since it utilized most of that engine's design and performance features. For example, the complete combustion chamber from the cylinder head to the piston cavity, as well as the bore center were transferred from the I-4 to the 4.0 liter 6-cylinder. In addition, the intake and exhaust port shapes from the 4-cylinder were utilized. AMC engine engineers also selected the block height of the two engines so that a common rod, piston pin and piston compression height could be interchanged between the two engines. Other parts shared included rod bearings, main bearings, oil pump, piston ring set, pistons, head bolts, rod cap bolts, main bearing caps, valve stem seals, spring retainers, keepers, rocker arms, pivots and fasteners and the hydraulic valve lifters.

The 4.0 liter engine's cast iron cylinder block was similar to that of the 4.2 liter engine which had a thin wall casting except for an increased bore diameter, longitudinal stiffening ribs, the addition of tin for improved wear and some minor boss revisions for external attachments.

A major contribution to the new engine's high power output was its increased valve area as compared to the I-4. Its intake valve diameter was 1.91 inches instead of 1.79 inches. The exhaust valve diameter was increased from 1.41 inches to 1.5 inches. In combination with high-flow intake ports these changes provided substantially higher air capacity. The cylinder head continued to be cast iron but it now had a cast aluminum cover. The head gasket was upgraded from embossed steel to a composition with tin-plated steel fire rings. Although the cam had a common profile with the 4-cylinder engine, it had increased lift and extended duration that resulted in a high volumetric efficiency at high rpm. Other details changes included an alloy sintered iron cam sprocket set and roller chain, and tri-metal (copper, lead plus overplate) instead of bi-metal connecting rod bearing. The bore and stroke of the 4 liter engine were 3.875 and 3.44 inches respectively.

The 4.0 liter had two accessory drive configurations. In base form the cooling fan was mounted on its own bracket and hub support which was engine mounted. If a heavy duty cooling system was required, the electric fan was mounted on a chassis-mounted fan shroud. Both systems used a single serpentine belt.

The electronic fuel injection system featured port-mounted, individually-sequential injectors. The microprocessor controlled engine control system had integrated function for the fuel injectors, ignition advance, on/off EGR, closed loop spark control via a knock sensor, adaptive fuel control, electric fuel pump control (mounted in the fuel tank) and closed loop idle speed control.

In preparation of its 1987 introduction the 1-6 underwent over 2 million miles of pre-production testing. In addition it was subjected to the twin dynamometer test AMC had adopted from Renault which involved 500 hours at peak torque and 500 hours at peak horsepower.

Although they were not of the magnitude of the new 6-cylinder's the power ratings of the standard 2.5 liter engine were increased for 1987 to 121 horsepower at 5000 rpm and 141 lb.ft. of torque at 3500 rpm.

Both engines were equipped with three separate "quick connect" devices controlling the vehicle's vacuum lines, fuel lines and electrical system. The most unique feature of this arrangement was the "umbilical-style" vacuum line connector that routed all vacuum lines and both the engine and vehicle harnesses through a single point.

AMC identified three important benefits of this new arrangement:

1. All vacuum line harnesses could be installed before the engine was placed in the vehicle.
2. Operator error at the factory in connecting the right hoses to the upper control was significantly reduced.
3. All vacuum line connections were easily and effectively tested on the assembly line.

Playing an important supporting role in the 1987 performance story for the Cherokee, Wagoneer and Comanche was the availability of a new wide-ratio 4-speed automatic transmission. Depicted as the "latest in high-tech engineering … the best of both worlds in performance and fuel efficiency", this transmission was an option for either the standard 2.5 liter 4-cylinder or optional 4.0 liter 6-cylinder.

Designated the Aisin-Warner 30-40 LE, this transmission was a joint venture between Aisin Seiki of Japan and Warner Gear, of the U.S. Its decidedly hi-tech features included electronic control, dual shift modes for power or comfort, an overdrive fourth gear and a lock-up torque converter. The power/comfort shift feature was controlled by a button located on the instrument panel. In the power mode, under hard acceleration, the transmission shifted at a higher engine speed, downshifted more rapidly and was more sensitive to throttle control. When operating in the comfort mode the shift schedule was more conservative, resulting in low fuel consumption.

The combination of this transmission and the standard 1-4 engine resulted in a better balance between fuel useage and performance as compared to a 1986 model with the old 3-speed automatic. When mated to the new 4.0 liter engine the 4-speed automatic helped the Cherokee, Wagoneer and Comanche models to accelerate from zero to 60 mph in 9.4 seconds.

As an added dividend, the 30-40 LE dramatically improved the noise, vibration and harshness (NVH) factors associated with either the 1-4 or 1-6 engines due to the lower engine rpm levels generated at highway speeds due to the overdrive gear.

The optional Selec-Trac 4WD system for 1987 used a new NP 242 transfer case that was considerably lighter than the older NP 228 used on Cherokees and Wagoneers in previous model years. In addition, its length was identical with that of the NP 231 transfer case used in the Command-Trac part-time system. More importantly, the NP 242 enabled all five (2WD, Hi Lock, 4WD, Neutral and Lo Lock) positions for the Selec-Trac to be controlled by a single shift lever. As a result the 2WD/4WD vacuum control switch employed on previous year Cherokee and Wagoneer models was eliminated.

A 1988 Jeep Cherokee Pioneer model. (Courtesy of author's collection)

As in 1986 the 4WD Cherokee was available in four trim packages – Base, Pioneer, Chief and Laredo. The 2WD Cherokee also continued to be offered in three trim levels – Base, Pioneer and Laredo. The Laredo package now had new interior fabrics in Hunter's Plaid available in cordovan or tan colors. The Cherokee Chief featured new blackout exterior graphics for 1987. Four new, optional two-tone paint configurations of a secondary mid-body color with a primary body color that were now standard for the base Wagoneers were also available on selected Cherokee models. The primary/secondary color combinations were; Grenadine Metallic/Sterling Silver Metallic, Classic Black/Sterling Silver Metallic, Beige/Briarwood Metallic and Champagne Metallic/Briarwood Metallic. The Cherokee color scheme differed from the Wagoneer's since the mid-body trim served as the dividing line between the primary and secondary colors.

Also now found on the base Wagoneer were new door trim panels and storage bins, new fabric wingback bucket seats with headbacks, new woodgrain instrument panel as well as the new 4-speed automatic transmission. The Wagoneer Limited now used Michelin "Tru-Seal" P205/75R 15 tires. These were also available as an option for the base Wagoneer. Joining the 10-spoke aluminum option for both the Cherokee and Wagoneer were 5-spoke versions.

As in 1986 all body colors had a clearcoat finish. The selection of colors was slightly revised. Both the Cherokee and Wagoneer were available in White, Beige Deep Night Blue, Classic Black, Metallic Grenadine, Metallic Briarwood, Metallic Champagne, Metallic Sterling, and Metallic Charcoal. Listed only for the Cherokee were Colorado Red and Metallic Medium Blue. The exclusive Wagoneer color was Metallic Dark Pewter.

The arrival of the $30,000 Range Rover from England was not greeted with stoney silence from American Motors. Instead it aggressively counter-attacked with a new top-of-the-line Cherokee Limited model listing for $22,104. The intended clientele for the Limited were, as expected, the same group of buyers Range Rover of North America hoped to attract to its Range Rover: sophisticated, image conscious individuals who were willing to pay a premium price for a vehicle combining first class luxury appointments with the flexibility of a sports utility vehicle. "Research shows these buyers", noted William E. Enockson, group vice president of North American sales and marketing, "want the rugged qualities of Jeep vehicles and the high level of standard equipment and comfort that is equated with most expensive, popular European cars. We put the most desirable features from the Wagoneer Limited in the Cherokee Limited to appeal to the young, well educated, married, financially-successful car enthusiast."

Therefore, the Cherokee Limited was a vehicle with a long list of standard features. Indeed, it was easier to identify what were extra cost items since they were only nine in number: Selec-Trac, 2000 and 5000 pound trailer towing packages, Trac-Loc rear differential, manual sunroof, cold climate group, full-size spare tire, tow hooks and metallic paint.

The Cherokee Limited was initially offered in 4-door form with a 2-door version introduced as a 1988 model. Both were available in three monochromatic exterior colors – Charcoal Metallic, Grenadine Metallic and Classic Black. Gold cast aluminum wheels carrying "Jeep"

lettering were fitted with Goodyear P225/70HR 15 tires, were joined by gold-accent striping on the upper bodyside and liftgate, gold inserts on the lower bodyside molding and on the bumper, nerfing strips. A Limited logo was integrated with the bodyside striping.

The interior of all Limited models featured leather wingback front bucket seats with perforated leather inserts; recliners; adjustable headrests and leather facings. Six-way power adjustments were standard. A plush carpeting was installed in both the passenger and cargo area. Additional Limited appointments consisted of a full-length console with armrest and rear ashtray; rear heating ducts and a leather-wrapped sport steering wheel. Special cluster graphics were also found on the instrument panel.

Standard equipment on the Jeep Wagoneer and Cherokee Limited for 1988 was the Power Tech Six engine.

The Laredo model for 1988 had new exterior trim that included bright door handles, grille, moldings, special pin striping, new lower bodyside moldings, color-keyed fender flares and a Laredo nameplate. The Laredo interior featured new trim colors as well as see-through headrests, leather-wrapped steering wheel, console, extra pile carpeting and door panels with stowage bins.

The Laredo package also had power steering, 5-speed manual transmission, swing-out front vent windows and, on 2-door models, swing-out rear window vent windows. Also exclusive to the 2-door Laredo was privacy glass, rear window wiper/washer and rear seat beverage holders.

The Cherokee Chief had many of the interior and functional features of the Pioneer model but carried more aggressive exterior graphics, P215/75R 15 tires and white spoker wheels. All Cherokee models had a new eight-slot grille design for 1988.

Optional for any model Cherokee and standard on the Wagoneer and Cherokee Limited was the wide-ratio 4-speed automatic transmission with dual shift power or economy shift modes.

Clearcoat solid colors for the 1988 Cherokee consisted of Pearl White, Bright Yellow, Coffee, Classic Black and Colorado Red. Metallic clearcoat colors choice were Spinnaker Blue, Dark Baltic, Grenadine, Sterling, Medium Bronze, Briarwood or Dover Gray. All Wagoneers had a clearcoat finish. With the exception of Coffee and Spinnaker Blue, all Cherokee colors were available for the Wagoneer.

Chapter 15

The
Comanche pick-ups

If AMC had been a trail-blazer in innovative full-time, shift-on-the-fly 4WD systems and among the leaders in developing down-sized sports utility vehicles, it had also been slow to exploit the sales potential of the light truck field. In 1984, for example, with the Scrambler and J-series trucks, Jeep's coverage in that market segment was just 0.339 percent. Furthermore, as indicated by the following, Jeep pick-up truck sales compared poorly to those of its domestic competitors:

Make/Model	1984 sales	Market share (%)
Jeep Scrambler	2826	0.154
Jeep J-Trucks	3404	0.1859
Chevrolet C/K	476,048	26.00
Chevrolet S-10	210,051	11.47
GMC C/K	121,435	6.32
GMC S-15	46,953	2.56
Ford F-Trucks	562,507	30.72
Ford Ranger	247,042	13.49
Dodge D-Trucks	160,574	8.77

By 1985 the pick-up truck market had grown to approximately 1,979,000 units of which the compact truck segment represented over one million vehicles. In 1986 AMC was projecting the entire light truck market to grow to approximately 4.2 million units of which pick-ups would take about 60 percent or about 2.5 million units. Moreover, since 1973, when approximately 215,000 compact pick-ups had been built, their popularity had quadrupled. American Motors expected the compacts to represent 52 percent or over 1,003,000 vehicles of the projected 1,963,000 pick-up market in 1986.

The largest share of the compact truck market, 71 percent, was controlled by 2-wheel drive models. Overall the Japanese producers held, in spite of the entry of both Ford and General Motors into this market in 1982 (previously both companies sold Japanese-built compacts as the Chevrolet LUV and Ford Courier) 55 percent of the compact market. When the Japanese producers were included the result showed Nissan and Toyota to be the sales leaders with Ford's Ranger in third place with a 19.8 percent market share.

American Motors, in 1986, made a belated but energetic move into this highly competitive but equally lucrative market with the introduction of the Jeep Comanche. AMC group vice-president-sales and marketing, Joseph E. Cappy, kicked off the Comanche's career by declaring; "The Jeep Comanche has so many advanced features over our competition that we expect it will be literally an overnight success... The Comanche has the Jeep heritage and shares many of the engineering innovations of our award-winning Jeep Cherokee compact sports vehicle." As far as the two- and four-wheel drive market sections of the compact truck field were concerned, Cappy noted, "The new Jeep Comanche will take on domestic and Japanese competition in both of these segments". Undaunted by the hold the Japanese had on the market, Cappy said: "We're out to change that."

Supporting Cappy's remarks were the comments of American Motors president and chief executive officer, Jose Dedeurwaerder: "The Jeep brand name has always been synonymous with rugged and durable four-wheel drive products. Now we intend to enhance that reputation by also entering the two-wheel drive pick-up market with a new product that is state-of-the-art in every respect. Concerning the Comanche's ability to be a contender for a good portion of the 750,000 sales of 2-wheel drive compact pick-ups projected for 1986, Dedeurwaerder was bullish, noting, "We firmly believe the Comanche will be a strong contender for a share of those sales."

When the Cherokee and Wagoneers were introduced as 1984 models development of the Comanche was in its final stages. "We began actual vehicle testing of the Comanche almost at the same time that the Cherokee and Wagoneer was introduced" recalled Francois A. Castaing, AMC's vice-president of product engineering and development. Explaining the relationship of the Comanche to those Jeeps, Castaing noted that "The pick-up truck derivative was part of the original design concept ... Engineering the Comanche basically focused on the rear half of the vehicle. From the cab forward, these vehicles have a large degree of commonality."

None the less a great deal of time, effort and money was committed to the Comanche's development program to assure it would be of world class quality and design. For example, nearly 100 pre-production vehicles were used to prove the integrity of the Comanche's driveline and body structure. Over the course of two years in excess of 500,000 miles of controlled testing took place at American Motors test facilities in Burlington, Wisconsin and Yuma, Arizona. This program was supplemented by another 100,000+ miles accumulated under normal highway conditions by AMC's quality and product integrity group.

When the Cherokee/Wagoneer series had been originally designed its main structural members were engineered in such a way that a joint could be eventually built into the structural side beams supporting the front and rear portions of those vehicles. This made it possible to accomodate the Comanche pick-up truck derivative which had a totally new rear sub-structure.

The final form of that sub-structure was heavily influenced by the use of finite element analysis with which AMC's partner, Renault, had gained considerable expertise by applying it to the development of the body structure for the Alliance. In essence, finite element analysis is a computerized method of designing a body structure to an optimal level of efficiency.

In the case of the Comanche, the goal was to achieve a high level of torsional rigidity; finite element analysis told AMC engineers this could be accomplished by the substitution of an X member to replace two lateral cross-members in the rear stub frame. Commenting on this development and the availability of an optional metric ton (2205 pounds) package for the Comanche, Castaing said, "The original design concept of the two side beams for Cherokee and Wagoneer made it possible to develop the new rear stub frame structure to carry that kind of payload. Additionally, all that was needed was larger wheels and tires, different spring rates and stronger shock absorbers."

Engineered into the Comanche from the outset was a load-variable brake proportioning valve as standard equipment on all models. This sensor mechanism provided a higher level of balance between front and rear wheels, depending on the vehicle's load factor. In 1986 the

Comanche was the only pick-up truck sold in the United States with this feature.

Following a practice becoming more and more common in the automotive industry, American Motors released preliminary details of the Comanche in July, 1984, more than a year before its scheduled introduction. This was done, said Joseph E. Cappy, "to begin to wet the public appetite ... This is our first state-of-the-art product in the 2-wheel drive market ... so it is very important for us to get the name and the timing out front as quickly as possible."

Obviously, it was vitally important for the new Jeep to have a name

that would associate it with both traditional Jeep virtues as well as its own unique set of credentials. This process began with a list of several hundred possible choices including over a dozen North American Indian tribal names as well as those of animals, reptiles, cities, mountains and space age objects.

These names came from many different sources including a synergetics session among AMC officials. Recalled Cappy, "The group sat around a conference table and rattled off name after name that seemed appropriate for a Jeep pick-up. In a session like this", he noted, "one suggestion almost immediately leads to another. For instance, sidewinder was followed by mongoose – a rattler and a snake killer."

Eventually the list was pared to eleven finalists for a special evaluation by 99 compact truck owners and 113 potential buyers in Dallas, Denver, Pittsburgh and San Diego. These individuals were asked to rate the names in a number of categories including appropriateness, likeability and memorability and image attributes.

Recalling the results Cappy said "Comanche was deemed the best overall name in terms of appropriateness and memorability, and conveyed a rugged, off-road image. And it ties in very well with Cherokee – a name we introduced ten years ago."

Finishing second and third in the competition were two names from Jeep history; Renegade and Commando. Renegade, it will be recalled, was used for the limited-edition CJ model introduced in 1971 that later became a regular production model. The Commando name replaced the Jeepster label after AMC acquired Jeep in 1970. Worthy of note were the fourth and fifth place finishers, respectively, Wrangler and Honcho.

"We think Comanche was a wise choice," said Cappy, "The Comanches were great hunters and warriors. They were expert horsemen – very agile and highly mobile. They travelled great distances over all types of terrain and in all kinds of weather. The Jeep Comanche for 1986 will do exactly the same."

Of prime concern to American Motors was the ability of its dealer force to effectively market the Comanche. This issue wasn't related to a lack of salesmanship on their part. Rather, the problem revolved around the restricted amount of product those dealers had been able to offer pick-up truck buyers. "Jeep previously was limited to only 4-wheel drive pick-up trucks, the J–10 and J–20", explained Joseph Cappy. "The market segment for those products is small, hence our Jeep dealers did not do a large truck volume." With so much riding on the success of the Comanche, Cappy recalled, "We wanted each of our dealers ready to hit the ground running" when Comanche production began in July, 1985.

To faciliate this fast start, AMC developed a multi-pronged "marketing game plan" including advertising, an aggressive and unique sales promotion and merchandizing activities and what Cappy depicted as "a long term program of preparing our Jeep dealers for this exciting new product". As a result the Comanche's media advertising campaign was one of the most comprehensive in Jeep history. Initially sales and marketing activity concentrated on the top 100 pick-up markets in the U.S. This blitz was then applied, in order, to the top 200 and 300 markets by the time the Comanche was introduced in September, 1985. Concurrently, a detailed sales, service and marketing plan was developed for each Jeep dealer.

The specific aspects of the Comanche's promotion exposed it to numerous and diverse groups of Americans all of whom were likely to be owners and buyers of pick-up trucks. The program began on 12 May, 1985 with a "Beach Boys/Jeep Comanche JEEPIN' SAFARI concert tour" that started in San Diego. This continued through December and in over 40 cities the Comanche was showcased to over 3 million Americans, of which the majority were considered to be prime compact truck customer prospects.

With the Comanche serving as the official vehicle of the International Professional Rodeo Association (IPRA), American Motors sponsored over 200 IPRA regional rodeos whose aggregate attendance was estimated to be over 1.3 million people. At approximately 50 rodeos the Comanche competed in a barrel race against the time of competing cowgirls on horseback.

AMC also sponsored the National 4–H Wildlife and Fisheries Awards Program as well as related activities in marine science, agriculture, fishing, ecology and environment and natural resources in which over 700,000 4–H'ers participated. Jeep Corporation presented awards of merit at the national, state and county level, thirty trips for 4–H winners to the national 4–H convention in Chicago as well as six educational scholarships for national winners. In the process, the Comanche was displayed at selected 4–H state and county fairs throughout the United States.

Additionally, the Comanche was the official vehicle of the American Bowling Association. Each ABA state champion received a Comanche as did the national Master's Champion.

Climaxing this program was a special, highly-targeted pre-launch direct mail program which reached 1.5 million pick-up buyers between June and September, 1985.

Like the Cherokee, the Comanche was available in either 2WD or 4WD form, the latter being offered in either Command-Trac or Selec-Trac. Also identical was its choice of engines. The throttle body fuel injected 2.5 liter 4-cylinder was standard with the 2.8 liter V-6 or 2.1 liter 4-cylinder turbocharged diesel optional. Three transmissions were available in either the 2WD or 4WD Comanche. The 4-speed

manual was standard. All engine/drivetrain combinations except those containing the turbocharged diesel were available with the 5-speed manual or 3-speed automatic. The diesel was offered only with the 5-speed manual.

The three trim levels for the Comanche were Custom, (base), X and XLS. The Custom model was geared to the market segment which accounted for over 60 percent of 2WD compact truck sales. Since these were mainly commercial or business customers the Custom emphasised utility both in its interior and exterior appointments. Among its standard features was a color-keyed vinyl interior with the following appointments; straight armrests, vinyl door trim panels, black textured vinyl floor covering, vinyl covered visors and head-liner, bench seat in Celtic grain vinyl trim, black plastic and a 2-spoke steering wheel.

A 1986 Jeep Comanche XLS. (Courtesy of author's collection)

All Comanche interiors were fitted with a mini console, dual dome lights (mounted on B pillars), a roof-mounted passenger-side grab handle, heater/defroster, ashtray, glove box with light and lock, utility bin (located below the glove box), color-keyed instrument panel padding in addition to a black cluster overlay with bright accents in the vent louvers plus required occupant restraint and anti-theft systems.

The Custom exterior identification included a black bumper with black end caps, black fender flares and air dam, a black grille with argent insert and black molding for the windshield surround, door window frames, vent dividers, drip rails and rear window weather strip.

The mid-series X package offered an interior with a premium vinyl bench seat, color-keyed textured vinyl floor covering, color-keyed vinyl trim behind the seat, a black instrument panel cluster overlay with bright accents on the gauge surrounds and vent louvers, and a 3-spoke color-keyed soft-feel sport steering wheel.

Unique exterior body identifications of the X package began with dual color upper bodyside strips and black lower body scuff moldings and exterior mirrors with black mounts. The X also had, like the Custom, black fender flares and air dam.

A 2-wheel drive Jeep Comanche X. (Courtesy of author's collection)

The premium XLS package contained what AMC described as "a high-line sporty exterior appearance as well as superior creature comforts." Several interior and exterior elements were shared with the X package. These consisted of that version's color-keyed hockey stick type armrests, custom vinyl door panel with a lower nylon carpeting, cigarette lighter, AM radio with two speakers, bright-finish front bumper with black end caps, bright grille trim insert and headlight bevels, headlight bezels and bright windshield surround and drip rails.

Unique to the XLS was an interior with color-keyed carpeting, for the floor and behind the seat, color-keyed molded, fabric covered sun visors, a color-keyed instrument panel cluster overlay with bright accents, a gauge containing voltmeter, oil pressure and engine temperature gauges, low fuel indicator light, trip odometer and a digital clock; bench seat with luggage fabric trim and a color-keyed deluxe 2-spoke steering wheel.

Much of the bright trim found on the X were also used on the XLS. In addition the XLS also was fitted with color-keyed fender flares, dual striping for the upper body, hood and tailgate, black lower body scuff moldings with bright inserts, dual mirrors with bright trim and bright window frames.

Prices of the Comanche and its major packages and options was as follows:

Model	Price
Custom 2WD	$7049
Custom 4WD	$8699

Package	Price
X Package	$588
XLS Package	$905
Interior Decor Group[1]	$434
Sport Decor Group[2]	$235
Metric Ton Package	$201

1: Includes reclining wingback bucket seats with headrests, upgraded door panels with fabric insert and carpeted lower area, color-keyed carpeting for floor and rear cab panel, fabric covered sun visors and headliner, color-keyed full length center console with armrest and storage compartment, leather-wrapped sport steering wheel and an upgraded instrument panel with a brushed pewter overlay.

2: Includes black grille and headlight bezels, lower bodyside black-out, black fender flares and front air dam, black bumper cover, 15 × 7 in. white styled steel wheels with bright hub covers, "4 × 4" bodyside sport decal (installed on 4WD models only), sport bodyside hood and tailgate decals (requires P205 or larger tires).

Option	Price
Clearcoat metallic paint	$161
Fabric bucket seats	$77
P205/75R 15 black sidewall steel belted tires	$43
P205/75R 15 white sidewall steel belted tires	$128

P215/75 15 OWL tires	$332
P225/75R 15 OWL tires	$375
2.8 V-6 engine	$437
2.1 diesel engine	$1258
5-speed man. tran.	$175
3-spd auto. tran.	$670
Auto. tran./Selec-Trac	$932
Rear Trac-Loc Differential	$225

With its 119.4 inch wheelbase and overall length of 194.3 inches, American Motors regarded the Comanche as a "mid-size" truck. This placed the Comanche in direct competition not with the standard

The 1986 Jeep Comanche 2-wheel drive Custom model.
(Courtesy of author's collection)

289

compact trucks from other manufacturers but rather their long-wheelbase extended cab 4-wheel drive models. The result makes for some interesting reading:

Model	Ford Ranger Super Cab	Toyota Xtra Cab	Nissan King Cab	Chevrolet S–10 Extended Cab	Jeep Comanche
W.B.	125 in.	112.2 in.	110.8 in.	122.9 in.	119.4 in.
O.A.L.	192.7 in.	184.1 in.	187.0 in.	192.8 in.	194.3 in.
O.A.W.	66.9 in.	66.5 in.	63.4 in.	647 in.	71.7 in.
O.A.H.	66.7 in.	67.1 in.	67.1 in.	63.4 in.	64.7 in.
Curb Wt.	3026 lbs.	3110 lbs.	3049 lbs.	3042 lbs.	3096 lbs.
Max. Payload.	1500 lbs.	2500 lbs.	1460 lbs.	1500 lbs.	2205 lbs.
Std. Eng.	2.9l. V-6	2.4l. l-4	2.4l. l-4	2.5l. l-4	2.5l. l-4
H.P. @ rpm.	140 @ 4600	116 @ 4800	103 @ 4800	92 @ 4400	117 @ 5000
Tor. @ rpm.	170 @ 2600	140 @ 2800	134 @ 2800	134 @ 2800	135 @ 3500
EPA Est. mpg. City/Hiwy.	18/22	22/25	19/21	22/26	23/26

As indicated by the following sales figures, although it was by no means a challenger to the industry leaders, the Comanche got off to a good start in 1986:

Model	1986 Calendar year sales
Toyota	384,150
Ford Ranger	269,490
Nissan	223,870
Chevrolet S–10	203,416
Mazda	157,127
Isuzu	88,720
Mitisubishi	34,985
Comanche	33,392

For the 1987 model year the 119.4 inch wheelbase Comanche was joined by a 113 inch wheelbase version that, said AMC, was targeted for "the buyer who wants a more personalized form of light truck transportation". This model had a six foot box as compared to the seven foot box used on the long wheelbase model.

The Comanche was offered in four trim levels for both the 2WD and 4WD models. The base model was available in both short and long box versions as was the "step-up" Pioneer model. Its primary elements included the use of exterior bright trim moldings and such interior appointments as a premium bench seat, upgraded door trim panels with stowage bins, an AM monoaural radio, bright and black instrument panel applique and a sport steering wheel.

Exclusive to the short bed models was a Comanche Chief package consisting of lower bodyside and tailgate stripes, with graduated lower door tape and a "Comanche Chief" lettering cutout which permitted the vehicle body color to show through. The Chief interior had a premium grain vinyl notched bench seat, upgraded instrument

Two views of the 1986 Jeep Comanche 4-wheel drive X. (Courtesy of author's collection)

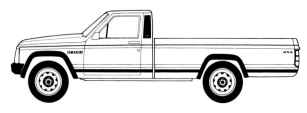

An interesting interpretation of the 1986 Jeep Comanche Pick-up. (Courtesy of author's collection)

panel trim with bright accent surrounds, passenger area carpetings, upgraded door trim panels with stowage bins, hockey-stick style armrest and a soft-feel sports steering wheel.

New for 1987 was this longbed version of the Comanche. (Courtesy of author's collection)

Long bed Comanches had a premium Laredo package with reclining wingback bucket seats finished in Hunter's Plaid cloth and vinyl, upgraded door panels with storage bins, instrument panel trim

A 1987 Jeep Comanche 2-wheel drive shortbed with the Sport Truck option. (Courtesy of author's collection)

with bright surrounds and a brushed pewter applique, hockey-stick style armrests, passenger area carpeting, carpeted trim panel on the cab back, passenger assist handle and soft-feel steering wheel. The Laredo exterior made extensive use of bright trim for the grille, front bumper, door and tailgate handles, wheel trim rings and hub covers, drip rail moldings and taillight trim. A "Jeep" decal, color-keyed to bodyside pinstripes was installed on the tailgate.

A 1987 Comanche Chief shortbed. In the background is a 2-wheel drive Comanche longbed. (Courtesy of author's collection)

The latest Comanche also had redesigned exterior graphics (including a 4 × 4 Sports Graphics package for all models except the short box base and Comanche Chief) plus all-new two-tone exterior paint combinations.

But the most perceptible features of the 1987 Comanche were its optional 173 horsepower engine and 4-speed transmission with both power and comfort modes. In the power mode, under hard acceleration, the transmission would upshift at a higher engine rpm, downshift more rapidly and be more responsive to the throttle position. The comfort mode provided normal operational conditions with a more conservative and economical shift schedule.

The gear position indicator for the automatic was relocated to the

instrument panel display cluster. Previously, it was mounted on the steering column. Details of these items are found in the 1983–87 Cherokee/Wagoneer chapter.

A 4-wheel drive Comanche Pioneer shortbed. (Courtesy of author's collection)

293

All 1988 Jeep Comanche Chief pick-ups were 4-wheel drive models with a short box. (Courtesy of author's collection)

The 1988 Comanche base pick-up. (Courtesy of author's collection)

An important addition to the Comanche line for 1988 was the high performance Eliminator model. (Courtesy of author's collection)

The 1988 Comanche line was highlighted by the new 2-wheel drive, 113 inch Eliminator sport truck. With its standard Power Tech 6-cylinder engine and five speed manual transmission the Eliminator was capable of zero to 60 mph times of under 10 seconds.

The Eliminator's special exterior appointments made certain that it would not be mistaken for anything less than a high-performance truck. Side tape treatment was applied that included Eliminator lettering on the sides of its 6 foot box, an eight-slot painted grille that matched the overall exterior body color, color-keyed fender flares and air dam, silver-painted front and rear bumpers, 15 × 7 inch, 10-hole aluminum wheels and P215/65 OWL Eagle GT steel-belted tires.

Exterior colors offered for the Eliminator were clear-coated Classic Black, Colorado Red or Dover Gray Metallic. In addition to its 4.0 liter engine and 5-speed gearbox, the Eliminator was equipped with power steering, gauge group, tachometer, fog lamps and an AM radio.

The Jeep Comanche Laredo continued to be available only with a 7 foot box. Interior appointments included wingback bucket seats with luggage cloth, upgraded door tim panels, bright instrument panel accents, full carpeting and a sport steering wheel.

The base Comanche had an improved 1475 pound payload. The step-up Pioneer models had a new bodyside decal that included the Pioneer name; new black front bumper; black bodyside scuff moldings; black windshield and drip moldings; new 6-spoke white-styled 15 × 7 steel wheels with a bright hub cover and upgraded P205/75R 15 tires.

The Comanche Chief, available only as a 4-wheel drive shortbed model for 1988 had a black colored eight-slot grille, 6-spoke 15 × 7 steel wheels lower bodyside and taillight stripes with graduated lower door stripes and Comanche Chief lettering cutout to permit vehicle body color to show through.

Standard paint colors available for the 1988 Comanche for 1988 consisted of clear-coated Pearl White; Buff Yellow; Colorado Red; Coffee and Classic Black, while clearcoat metallic colors were Medium Bronze; Spinnaker Blue; Dark Baltic; Grenadine; Sterling and Dover Gray. Many of these colors were available in two-tone combinations.

Chapter 16

The Jeep Wrangler

It was a masterful stroke of public relations – on 27 November, 1985 Joseph Cappy, executive vice-president – announced that production of the CJ Jeep would end early in 1986. Cappy set the stage for the public's response to this news when he paid homage to the status of the CJ by noting, "Completion of CJ production will signal an end of a very important era in Jeep history". Almost immediately dealers started receiving petitions from irate customers demanding that AMC reconsider its actions. Some die-hard Jeep fans went as far as to stock pile a life-time supply of CJs.

This was a dramatic, if a bit perverse manifestation of the status the CJ Jeep enjoyed. It wasn't the least bit surprising. Production of civilian Jeeps since 1945 was in the vicinity of 1.6 million units and two polls taken in 1980 … one in Japan and the other in the U.S. … concluded that "Jeep is the most popular and memorable vehicle in the world."

The universal recognition factor had been stimulated by four decades of extremely effective promotion that, even while Jeep was undergoing two changes of ownership, maintained a common philosophy. It had all began back in 1945 with the "If You Have Tough Jobs, Get A Jeep" advertising theme. In the mix-sixties the mesage was "The Original Jeep – a Work and Hobby Horse". In 1973, under American Motors ownership, came "Super Jeep – Toughest 4-Letter Word On Wheels". Five years later Jeep was telling the world that "We Wrote the Book on Four-Wheel-Drive". Then in 1984 came "Only In A Jeep". Now it seemed that all had come to an end. The ultimate manifestation of the term "Jeep", which traced its origin to the time before Pearl Harbor was gone.

But American Motors wasn't about to ring down the curtain on the single most important chapter in Jeep history without providing for a tremendous encore performance. On January 3, 1987 it announced that "Jeep Wrangler, a new-from-the-ground-up line of small utility vehicles, will be introduced." Jose J. Dedeurwaerder, president and chief executive officer of American Motors, said, "the debut of Wrangler couldn't come at a better time because interest in Jeep is at an all-time high."

Francois Castaing, vice president of product engineering, gave the press a verbal preview of the new Jeep by saying "Jeep Wrangler combines a classic, open air design with state-of-the-art four-wheel drive engineering, including 'shift-on-the-fly' capability and a tuned, smooth-ride suspension. This new generation of small sport utility vehicles will offer very comfortable and enjoyable on-highway driving and superb off-road capability."

Dedeurwaerder made it clear that the Wrangler would play a major role in AMC's goal to set back-to-back-sales records: "Our sales potential climbs with each new addition to the Jeep line-up", he said. "We have introduced new compact sports utility wagons and mid-size trucks the past two years. Now we have Wrangler as the newest addition to the Jeep family. We are confident it will help to increase Jeep's sales share in the four-wheel drive market."

On 13 May, 1986 the Jeep Wrangler was announced. While it had an outward resemblance to the old CJ, the Wrangler was, in reality, built according to a totally different set of design parameters. Explained Francois A. Castaing: "The product philosophy behind the two vehicles is completely different. Our market research told us that in recent years customers were using these types of vehicles more for personal transportation, as well as for recreational activities. For that reason", elaborated Castaing, "we learned that in any future purchase consideration they would look for everyday comfort and those special amenities that vehicles such as the CJ–7 didn't have."

The specifics behind Castaing's remarks were startling. As recently as 1978 only 17 percent of the buyers of vehicles in the Wrangler's class used them for everyday transportation. By 1986 this figure had risen to 95 percent. The flip side of this change was that while 37 percent of owners in 1978 said they frequently engaged in off-roading activities; only 7 percent did so in 1986, but this didn't mean that off-road performance wouldn't be important to Wrangler owners since 80 percent reported some off-road useage.

As a result of these factors engineers were assigned four basic product objectives when design work began on what evolved into the 1987 Wrangler. The first three were relatively easy to transform into reality. After decades of upgrading the old CJ design no AMC engineers were likely to object to having the opportunity to work on an all-new sport utility vehicle! Similarly, the mandate that it was to be a modern, open design vehicle with the traditional Jeep characteristic of rugged, durable four-wheel drive capability was not a source of discontentment among the engineering ranks. But the last requisite, that the Wrangler, in the words of AMC, "was envisioned as a sophisticated vehicle for its class with modern exterior and interior appearance, smooth highway riding performance, easy rear access and convenient soft-top fit, function and sealing, as well as being a vehicle offering the latest in corrosion resistance" was one primary reason development of the Wrangler consumed the better part of five years. The Wrangler's engineering production design program reached the "hands-on" testing stage in late 1983 with the building of 12 "mechanical mule" prototypes incorporating the new chassis and powertrains. These were used for design feasibility and durability testing.

The introduction of the Jeep Wrangler in May, 1986 was one of the most significant events in postwar Jeep history. (Courtesy of author's collection)

In the spring of 1984, another nine "skin" prototypes with the Wrangler's new exterior sheet metal were constructed. Again, they were tested extensively from both developmental and durability/reliability standpoints.

Concurrently, an assortment of packaging bucks were constructed to finalize such items as design clearances, fit/function of the tops, interior instrumentation and creature comforts.

In total, nearly 600,000 test miles were accumulated in the various stages of engineering development.

Complicating the job of the Wrangler's designers and engineers was the success of other recent Jeep products. For example, Jeep vehicles had, for three consecutive years received "4WD Vehicle of the Year" awards from major off-road publications in the United States as well as Europe. In other words, the last thing any one wanted was a Wrangler that received a luke warm reception from automotive journalists!

With Francois Castaing confidently stating that "We believe that the Wrangler will be a worthy and popular addition to the Jeep vehicle line-up", American Motors noted that not only would the Wrangler be "taking its place beside the elite of the four-wheel drive community ... [but] the debut of the Wrangler will be yet another milestone in a long list of historic Jeep vehicles."

The list prepared by AMC did indeed read like a list of Jeep "Hall of Fame" members:

1. 1946 CJ-2A
2. 1946 Model 463 Station Wagon
3. 1947 Panel Delivery and Pick-up Trucks
4. 1949 Jeepster
5. 1954 CJ-5
6. 1963 Wagoneer
7. 1967 Jeepster models
8. 1972 Hardtop CJ-5
9. 1973 Quadra-Trac
10. 1974 Cherokee
11. 1976 CJ-7
12. 1984 down-sized Wagoneer and Cherokee
13. 1985 2WD Cherokee
14. 1986 Comanche pick-up

In this context an all-important factor was the appearance of the new Jeep. Throughout the existing Jeep line there was a common styling cue of a grille that was universally recognized as the prime design feature of Jeep vehicles. Robert C. Nixon, director of exterior design for American Motors, noted that "The vertical grille is like a trademark for Jeep vehicles. It's a badge that stands for ruggedness and durability."

In terms of dimensions (if not in price) the Wrangler and CJ-7 were quite similar:

Model	Wrangler	CJ-7
Base Price	$9899	$7500
Wheelbase	93.4 in.	93.4 in.
Overall Length	153.2 in.	152.0 in.
Overall Width	65.3 in.	66.0 in.
Overall Height	70.9 in.	68.3 in.
Front Tread	55.8 in.	58.0 in.
Rear Tread	55.1 in.	58.0 in.
Front Headroom	40.0 in.	39.9 in.
Rear Headroom	40.5 in.	39.6 in.
Front Legroom	39.5 in.	39.1 in.
Rear Legroom	35.0 in.	35.0 in.

The easy access to the Wrangler's rear compartment is evident in this view. (Courtesy of author's collection)

Yet one look at a Wrangler was all that was needed to realize it was not a CJ. "We've made some subtle changes in the grille for the Wrangler", Nixon explained, "The vertical design peaks about three quarters from the top and then slopes slightly inward. But there's still no mistaking the Jeep look." Furthermore, the use of rectangular headlights plus the positioning of the parking lights at the outer edges of the grille gave the Wrangler what Nixon depicted as a "brawny" appearance.

With the exception of its doors and endgate the Wrangler, from the firewall back, used the old CJ body work. All front-end sheet metal ahead of the cowl was new, including hood, fenders, splash apron and the radiator grille guard. These changes gave the Wrangler a contemporary appearance. The hood had a bevelled edge, which combined with rounded outer edges to create a strong crisp look. Adding emphasis to this image were the standard flexible wheel flares.

A 1987 Wrangler Laredo model. (Courtesy of author's collection)

Incorporated into the Wrangler's exterior bodysides were splash shields extending approximately 10 inches back from the front fenders. As an option, a full-length splash shield running from the front to the rear fender and including a built-in body side step was available. Adding to the Wrangler's fresh look were new five-spoke cast aluminum wheels carrying the Jeep nameplate.

To achieve the required level of corrosion resistance all Wrangler exterior body panels were constructed of galvanized steel. All body surfaces received a multi-part treatment that began with a phosphate cleaning bath and included priming and sealing prior to the paint application. Body components such the hood, windshield frame, front fenders, doors and tailgate were fully immersed in a dip tank which electrostatically binded the primer coat directly to the metal. After the vehicle was assembled a protective coating was applied to the underside. The final body coat was a baked enamel finish. All bolt-on assemblies such as the hood, fenders, grille guard and windshield were also cathodic electro-coated. In addition, plastic liners were

Details of the 1987 Wrangler's built-in passenger step. (Courtesy of author's collection)

299

used in the rear wheelhouse to resist water entry into body joints and an anti-corrosive paint was used on bumpers and exposed brackets.

Almost shocking to long-time CJ devotees, who had accepted the limited weather protection of their Jeeps as a immutable fact of the off-road life, were the standard metal half doors found on the soft top Wrangler model. Aside from their contribution to the physical well being of the Wrangler's occupants, these doors also played a role in

A 1987 Wrangler in traditional, open-air Jeep form. (Courtesy of author's collection)

The Wrangler's wide-opening door provided ease of entry and exit. (Courtesy of author's collection)

With the rear seat folded, a useful cargo space was available on the 1987 Wrangler. (Courtesy of author's collection)

Although all-new, the Wrangler's front end retained the timeless Jeep look. (Courtesy of author's collection)

the Wrangler's styling. As Robert Nixon explained, "The tops of the half door are even with the rear quarter panels, while the forward parts slope upward to the door pillars to give the Wrangler more design continuity."

Both the Wrangler's soft top and its optional hard top were of entirely new design. The soft top incorporated adjustable snaps for a tight fit around the side rails and half-doors. Also helping to seal out the weather were Velcro fasteners. The soft top was factory installed and included a retention system to minimize outside road noise; this also reduced air and water intrusions. A welcomed feature was the soft top's bow structure design which made folding of the top up or down a relatively simple operation. Contributing to the open-air nature of the Wrangler were the door's easily detached soft upper halves and the "bikini-top" effect created by the removal of the side and rear windows. Side curtains were still used on the soft top but the hard top had roll-down flush glass side windows and rear tailgate glass. Also

These drawings illustrate some of the differences between the base, Laredo and Sport Decor-equipped Wranglers. (Courtesy of author's collection)

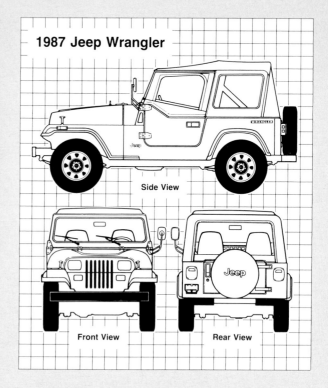

part of the hard top's design were air extractors to improve performance of the heater and standard air vents. Both versions had standard tinted glass for the windshield. The Wrangler, in either soft or hard top configuration, had a simple two-step tailgate operation. The spare tire was attached to a swingaway tailgate for convenient access to the Wrangler's rear compartment.

If Jeep fans had any lingering doubts about the veracity of the claims made for the Wrangler, a look into its interior put their suspicions to rest. American Motors boasted that "The interior of the Wrangler was designed to capture the appearance and convenience usually found only in today's upscale passenger cars." Director of interior design for American Motors, Vincent J. Geraci, explained that "We've gotten away from the 'no frills' approach that is so commonplace in small utilities because our consumer research told us people wanted more creature comforts." But concurrently, Geraci noted, "We were careful not to abandon the rugged functional look."

Key features of the Wrangler front suspension. (Courtesy of author's collection)

The 1987 Wrangler was fitted with full instrumentation. (Courtesy of author's collection)

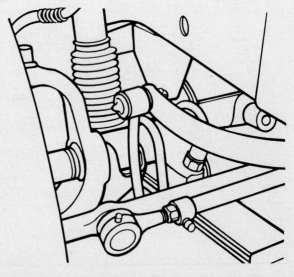

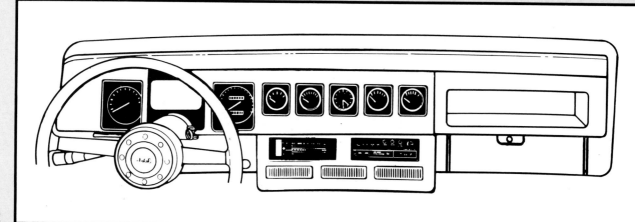

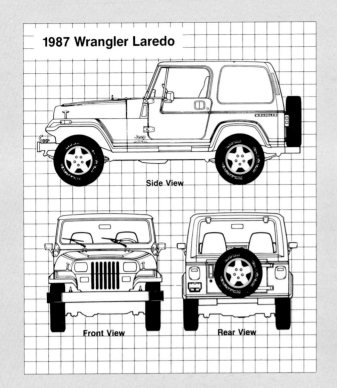

1987 Wrangler Laredo

Side View

Front View

Rear View

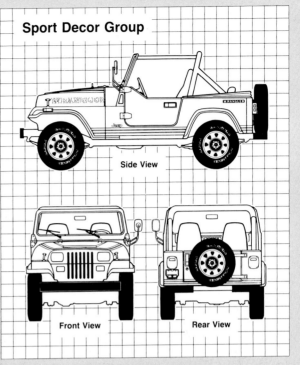

Sport Decor Group

Side View

Front View

Rear View

(Standard softtop not shown)

4WD System

An imaginative interpretation of the Wrangler's Command-Trac 4-wheel drive system. (Courtesy of author's collection)

The 1987 Wrangler's body/frame construction. (Courtesy of author's collection)

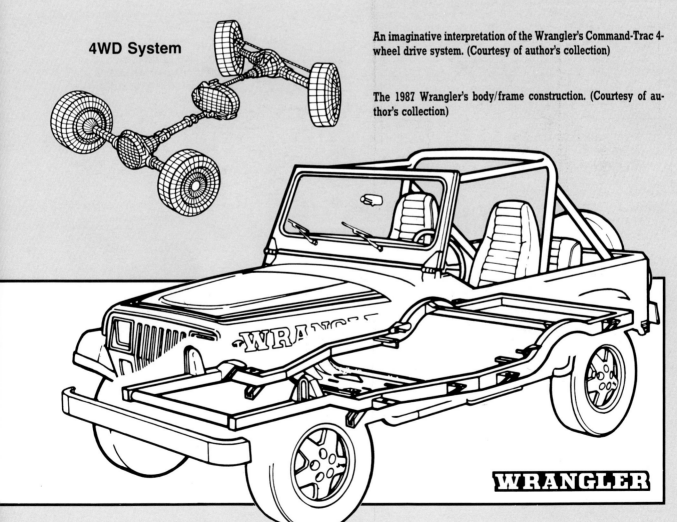

WRANGLER

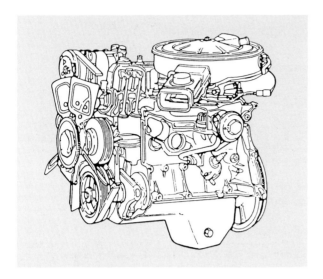

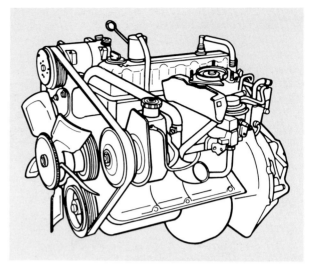

The Wrangler's standard engine was the AMC 2.5 liter 4-cylinder with fuel injection. (Courtesy of author's collection)

When equipped with the optional 4.2 liter 6-cylinder engine the Wrangler had the largest engine in its field. (Courtesy of author's collection)

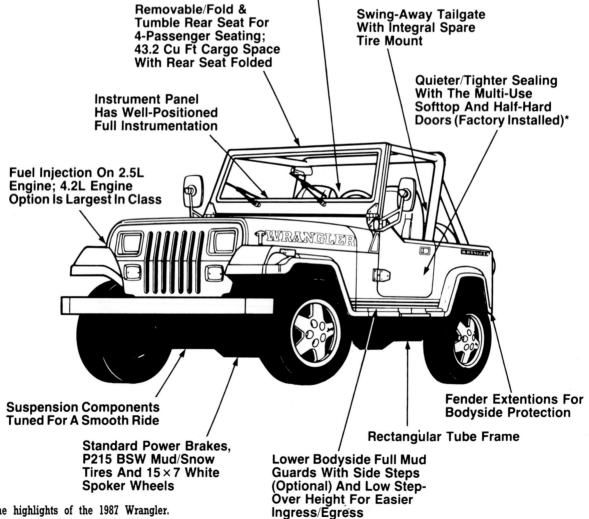

"Shift-On-The-Fly" Capabilities And 5-Speed Transmission

Removable/Fold & Tumble Rear Seat For 4-Passenger Seating; 43.2 Cu Ft Cargo Space With Rear Seat Folded

Swing-Away Tailgate With Integral Spare Tire Mount

Instrument Panel Has Well-Positioned Full Instrumentation

Quieter/Tighter Sealing With The Multi-Use Softtop And Half-Hard Doors (Factory Installed)*

Fuel Injection On 2.5L Engine; 4.2L Engine Option Is Largest In Class

Suspension Components Tuned For A Smooth Ride

Fender Extentions For Bodyside Protection

Standard Power Brakes, P215 BSW Mud/Snow Tires And 15 × 7 White Spoker Wheels

Rectangular Tube Frame

Lower Bodyside Full Mud Guards With Side Steps (Optional) And Low Step-Over Height For Easier Ingress/Egress

Some highlights of the 1987 Wrangler. (Courtesy of author's collection)

Unlike the CJ dash, which located all gauges and most instrumentation in a center-mounted panel, the Wrangler's arranged these items in a more modern ergonomical fashion. If an automatic transmission was installed the gear selection panel was positioned directly in front of the steering column. To the column's left was a circular tachometer balanced by the speedometer (which included a trip odometer) to the right-side of the column. Extending across the panel were smaller circular gauges for the temperature, fuel level, clock, oil pressure and voltmeter. Controls for the windshield washer/wiper, high beam lights, and, if installed, cruise control, were mounted on the steering column. Nicely integrated into the padded dash were the passenger assist panel, glove box and defroster ducts. The controls for the heating and ventilation systems were lever-activated. Two front high-back bucket seats were standard along with a two-place rear "fold and tumble" bench seat. Both were covered in a Denim grain vinyl. A total of 12.5 sq. ft. of cargo area was available behind the rear seat. When the seat was folded this increased to 43.2 sq. ft. If desired the seat could be removed entirely providing 53.4 sq. ft. of storage room.

Commenting on the overall effect, Geraci noted, "We've attempted to create a more comfortable interior environment for the Wrangler buyer. The interior trim is more eye appealing. It isn't just painted metal." The Wrangler used a traditional separate body/chassis

Also borrowed from the Cherokee was the Wrangler's standard transmission, a Peugeot and Aisin 5-speed gearbox. Improved shifting performance relative to the CJ resulted from the use of a new shift linkage mounted on the engine.

The Wrangler's standard engine was the electronically fuel injected 2.5 liter 4-cylinder engine with 117 horsepower at 5000 rpm and 135 lb.ft. of torque at 3500 rpm. As an option the 4.2 liter 6-cylinder was available. Its 112 horsepower rating trailed the 4-cylinder's but it produced a higher, (210 lb.ft. at 2000 rpm) torque output. A 3-speed automatic was optional in combination with the 6-cylinder engine.

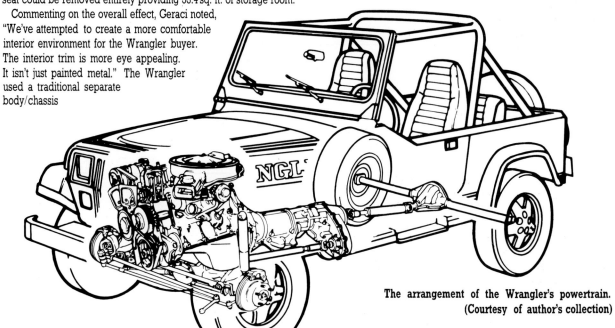

The arrangement of the Wrangler's powertrain. (Courtesy of author's collection)

arrangement with a tubular, rectangular-shaped frame side-rail design which compared favorably with the 3-sided "C" channels found on many domestic small pick-ups. This eliminated the stresses usually associated with the welding of stamped steel channels. Additionally, the section modulas were uniform throughout the side rails, thus providing the needed torsional strength and flexibility required for severe off-road use and long-term durability.

Many Wrangler chassis components were derived from the Cherokee/Wagoneer including such major components as the steering system, brake assembly, modified front and rear axles (the front unit was an inverted pinion design with a vacuum actuated disconnect; the rear axle, a Dana 35C unit, was basically the same as the Cherokee's), transfer case, manual transmission, hydraulic clutch assembly, wheels and tires. A tuned suspension system was used which included multi-leaf, longitudinal, semi-elliptical springs, 1⅜ inch shock absorbers, a power steering system with a 14:1 ratio, front and rear track bars and a front stabilizer bar. Use of a New Process 207 transfer case gave the Wrangler the same "shift-on-the-fly" capability as the Cherokee.

Both engines gave the Wrangler good acceleration. When linked to the standard transmission the 4-cylinder provided a zero to 60 mph time of 14 seconds. The larger engine, with the five-speed manual moved the Wrangler from zero to 60 mph in about 12 seconds.

Two optional suspension packages were developed for the Wrangler. An Off-Road Package included high-pressure gas charged Fichtel and Sachs shock absorbers and P225/75R 15 Goodyear Wrangler tires. These replaced the standard P215/75R15 RBL Wrangler tires. Regardless of the type of suspension used, a constant payload of 800 pounds was maintained.

The base Wrangler was available with a Sport Decor Group option that included a AM/FM monaural radio, Special "Wrangler" hood decals and striping on the lower bodyside in either silver or tan, Goodyear "All Terrain" P215/75R 15 outline white letter steel belted radial tires, conventional tire with lock and the Convenience Group. The latter contained courtesy lights with door switches, engine compartment light, intermittent wipers and glove box lock.

The interior appointments of the Laredo hardtop were decidedly upscale with Buffalo grain vinyl seat trim, front and rear carpeting, center console, extra quiet insulation, leather-wrapped sport steering

305

The Canadian version of the Wrangler was called the YJ since General Motors used the Wrangler name on a full-sized Suburban. (Courtesy of Chrysler Canada)

wheel and door panels with a carpeted lower third section and a map pocket.

Laredo exterior trim featured a chrome front bumper, rear bumperettes, grille panel headlight bezels, front bumper extensions and tow hooks. Also included were color-keyed wheel flares and full-length mud guards with integrated body sidesteps, deep tinted glass, door-mounted left- and right-side mirrors, special stripes in silver or brown for the hood and bodyside with "Laredo" cutouts in the lower bodyside stripes, P215/75R 15 Goodyear Wrangler OWL radial tires and 15×7 in., 5-bolt sport aluminum wheels.

An extensive list of options was provided for the Wrangler. Major items not already noted included the hardtop for the base model, tilt steering wheel, rear Trac-Loc, air conditioning, full carpeting, floor mats, halogen fog lights, power steering, electric rear window defogger (hardtop only), heavy duty cooling, aluminum wheels, and two other audio systems in addition to the AM/FM monaural radio; an AM/FM electronically tuned stereo or an AM/FM ETR cassette stereo with Dolby. All radios were paired with dual speakers.

Two standard colors were available for the Laredo: Olympic White and Classic Black. At extra cost three metallic colors were available; Mist Silver, Mocha Brown and Garnet. The standard Wrangler had a wider color selection that included not only those but also Beige, Colorado Red, Sun Yellow, Medium Blue Metallic and Autumn Brown Metallic. The soft and hard top colors were Black, White and Honey.

The television promotion of the Wrangler, which saw ads aired on all major networks as well as cable television, expanded the two-year old "Only In A Jeep" theme into: "New Jeep Wrangler. The possibilities are endless! Only in a Jeep." These ads corresponded with the introduction of the Wrangler on 12 May, 1986 as a 1987 model. At the same time a direct-mail campaign was launched to half a million Wrangler sales prsopects. An even more ambitious effort involved mailings to 18 million American Express card holders.

All Wrangler/YJ Jeeps are built in Chrysler's Bramalea plant. (Courtesy of Chrysler Canada)

The advantages of positioning the Wrangler as an up-scale model had the flip-side impact of leaving AMC without participation in the entry-level portion of the 4WD utility vehicle market. This was quickly filled by such vehicles as the Suzuki Samurai and Mitsubishi Montero which was also sold as the Dodge Raider.

AMC responded to this situation on 8 May, 1987 with the introduction of a new version of the Wrangler – the S model which was depicted as "an entry level sport utility vehicle aimed at new four-wheel drive buyers". With a base price of $8795, the Wrangler S was positioned to compete in between the high-line Suzuki Samurai and light four-wheel drive compact trucks such as the Ford Ranger, Dodge Ram 50 and Toyota pick-up trucks. Evaluating the nature of this market segment, William E. Enockson, group vice-president-North American sales and marketing, observed "price is the top motivating factor for the buyers in this market. But they are also looking for versatility, fuel economy and the fun associated with four-wheel drive vehicles. We

To compete with competition at the entry level of the sports utility
vehicle field, AMC introduced the Wrangler S in 1987.
(Courtesy of author's collection)

expect that approximately 25 percent of the buyers will be women who are becoming increasingly important in this segment, and like men, are attracted by the price, utility and smaller size of the vehicle."

The Wrangler S was equipped with the 2.5 liter engine, 5-speed transmission, soft top, P205/75R 15 Wrangler tires and argent steel wheels. It was available in only two exterior colors – Olympic White and Classic Black. Only four options were offered – a rear seat, full carpeting, power steering and a radio.

On the other hand AMC was also cognitive that the Wrangler was a prime model to exploit the demand for up-scale, distinctive "special edition"-type models popular with affluent buyers. One result was the Sahara model Wrangler which had its first public showing at the March, 1987 Geneva Auto Show in Switzerland, although it didn't go on sale in the U.S. until later in 1987 and in Europe until 1988.

For more affluent clients AMC offered the uniquely equipped 1988 Wrangler Sahara. (Courtesy of author's collection)

The 1988 Wrangler Laredo. (Courtesy of author's collection)

AMC regarded the Sahara as a combination of "today's 'in' products – Jeep vehicles – with today's 'in' fashion – Sahara clothing." In the view of William E. Enockson, "The Sahara will project a unique and sophisticated image that fits right in with the current trend toward exotic travel and safari-type clothing and merchandise."

The Sahara was available in two unique exterior colors – Khaki Metallic or Coffee. It also featured unique tape stripes, "Sahara" logos on the bodyside and spare tire cover, khaki-colored spoker wheels, khaki soft top (a tan hard top was optional), as well as khaki-colored interior trim appointments. Other exterior standard equipment features of the Sahara included special fender-mounted fog lights, color-keyed wheel flares and integrated body sidesteps.

The interior had a Trailcloth seat fabric in khaki with tan accents, khaki-color 20 ounce carpeting, map pouches on both door sides, a leather-wrapped steering wheel, center console with padded cover plus an AM/FM electronically-tuned stereo radio. Among the unique dealer-installed options were a brush-grille guard and a bug screen kit.

For 1988 several new appearance and convenience features were made standard on the Wrangler. These included seven new exterior colors: Pearl White, Coffee, Sand Dune Yellow, Metallic Silver, Metallic Spinnaker Blue, Khaki and Vivid Red; two new soft and hard top colors (Charcoal and Tan); two new interior trim colors (also Charcoal and Tan); a new Trailcloth water resistant seat fabric on Sahara and Laredo models; new-styled, white spoker wheels; net map pockets; plus a fore/aft adjustment track for the front passenger seat.

Chapter 17

International Operations

The combination of American Motors and Jeep in 1970 was preceded by many years of cooperative efforts between the two firms in international operations. In 1964, for example, AMC and Kaiser Jeep joined with their Mexican affiliate company to build a $7 million plant to manufacture automotive engines. Kaiser and AMC also had the same partner in an Iranian auto plant. In Argentina AMC automobiles used Jeep engines.

Jeep had established numerous overseas ties since the end of World War Two. In December, 1953 the president of the Willys-Overland Export Corporation, Hickman Price reached an agreement with Shinzo Fuji, president of Mitsubishi Heavy Industries in Japan, for Mitsubishi to produce Jeeps. In August, 1955, Mr. J.C. Delaplaine, general manager of the Willys-Overland Export Company, announced that Willys was planning to invest $8,000,000 in an Australian venture to build Jeep vehicles. This didn't take place within the original time span and as late as 1958 production had not started. In 1958 Edgar Kaiser explained "This is a big project, because we plan to manufacture the Jeep locally and not just assemble it … We would like to build at least 20 percent locally to begin with and extend the percentage as we produce. Our three-year-plan is for a 100 percent local vehicle." Eventually this effort lead to the creation of Willys Motors Australia headquartered in Brisbane, Australia.

More widely known had been the activities of Kaiser in Argentina and Brazil. Although Willys-Overland do Brazil was sold to Ford in 1967, (Today, Ford controls the Jeep trademark in Brazil. It cannot, however, use it outside that country.) the previous year Willys-Overland had produced 62,809 passenger cars and commercial vehicles in Brazil. This level of production was indicative of the size of the Brazilian operation which at one time rivaled that of Toledo. Kaiser also sold its holdings in Industries Kaiser Argentina to Renault during 1967.

Even before it acquired Jeep in 1970, American Motors had an extensive international organization including 11 assembly, 11 manufacturing plants and 250 retail outlets in 24 countries. Jeep expanded the International Division's assembly and manufacturing operations into countries stretching from the South Pacific to South America. This increased to 29 the number of countries in which AMC products were produced. Among them were three key markets – Argentina, Mexico and Iran – where AMC and Jeep had already established joint manufacturing and distribution facilities prior to the acquisition of Jeep by American Motors. This partnership strategy was expanded by American Motors to include joint ventures with foreign manufacturers. In particular, AMC noted that, "In the Far East, where exchange of products and common component parts will be the keystone of future expansion, joint ventures in selected countries will help provide a framework for such interchange."

Of at least equal significance was the solid position of Jeep in many market areas where AMC either had not been represented, or where there was considerable room for expansion. Examples cited by AMC were India, Turkey, Korea and Taiwan.

Heading AMC's international operation at that time was M.A. van Merkensteijn, who regarded Jeep as a key element of American Motors efforts to expand its overseas operations. Whereas the typical American car was not designed with an eye towards major sales in foreign markets, van Merkensteijn viewed the Jeep as well suited for sale in the world market. He even went as far as to suggest that the Jeep was better known overseas than in the United States.

International marketing activities for both Jeep and passenger cars was under the supervision of Alan F. Bethell, who was appointed divisional vice president-marketing. Previously Mr. Bethell had served as AMC's director of automotive export sales.

With the acquisition of Jeep Corporation, American Motors more than doubled the size of its operations in overseas markets. Speaking at the 1970 Paris Auto Show van Merkensteijn noted: "Sales of built-up cars to overseas markets in 1970 increased by nearly 25 percent over the previous year, and we expect this trend to continue. In all, the International Division expects to sell upwards of 55,000 passenger cars and Jeep commercial vehicles in the 1971 model year, including knocked-down units destined for assembly markets."

American Motors had an excellent year in 1973. Its domestic passenger car sales were 380,000 units, compared to 303,000 in 1972 and 253,000 in 1971. The 25 percent increase in 1973 was well above the domestic industry increase of 8.4 percent where American Motors' market share rose to 3.8 percent from 3.3 in 1972.

These domestic advances were accompanied by gains in the international market where AMC's competitiveness dramatically improved. There were three reasons for this. First, said American Motors, "increased currency values in nations of American Motors' principal foreign competitors have made the company's product prices considerably more attractive. Second, reductions in external tariffs in the Common Market and Japan have improved sales opportunities in those markets and the company is pursuing such opportunities. Third, rising income levels in many overseas countries make American-made products accessible to more people."

Sales of AMC products in Canada and other international markets in its fiscal 1973 year were $176 million compared to $148 million in fiscal 1972. Unit sales of AMC cars and Jeeps, including knocked-down units for foreign assembly rose to 67,374 from 59,251 in 1972.

The strongest sales gain was made in Canada (which was not part of international organizations) and Latin America, but a sales increase was also reported in the European market where sales to the European Economic Community rose 19 percent. Canadian passenger car and Jeep sales were 28,189, 30 percent higher than in 1972. In Mexico they rose 23 percent to 17,308 units. This total represented nine percent of the Mexican market and was accompanied by an expansion of plant capacity of the facilities of Vehiculos Automotores Mexicanos, S.A.

AMC stockholders were told in the 1973 Annual Report that, "In the Far East, where the growth rate in automotive markets is expected to be the world's highest, the company is in the final stages of new agreements in Korea and the Philippines for manufacture and distribution of Jeep vehicles."

In 1973 van Merkensteijn concluded negotiations with Shinjin Motors of Seoul, Korea to produce a variety of Jeep vehicles in Korea including the CJ-5, CJ-6, Wagoneer and Jeep trucks. "Under our joint venture arrangement", said van Merkensteijn, "Jeep Corporation will send drivetrain parts, including 6-cylinder engines from the United States and Shinjin Jeep will make bodies, components and frames locally."

This venture was on a 50/50 basis between Jeep and Shinjin. AMC, as van Merkensteijn explained, usually followed this type of arrangement in its foreign ventures. "Of the 50 AMC facilities outside the United States", he explained, "where passenger cars, commercial and utility vehicles are manufactured and assembled in subsidiary and affiliated companies and licensees, only two are wholly-owned by AMC – a passenger car plant in Ontario, Canada and a Jeep plant in Venezuela."

Although most countries experienced an economic downturn in 1975, American Motors' international business scored gains in nearly all areas. Combined wholesale sales of AMC passenger cars and Jeeps outside the U.S. and Canada reached 66,000 units, an increase of 26 percent over the same period the previous year and an all-time record.

Jeep sales abroad were 43 percent above the 1974 level. AMC proudly reported that "Since acquisition of Jeep Corporation in 1970, international sales of Jeep vehicles have more than doubled. About one-third of all Jeep units produced are sold abroad ... In countries outside the U.S. and Canada, about 31 percent of all 4-wheel drive vehicles sold last year carried the Jeep trademark."

The picture for even greater market control seemed bright. In 1974 over 200 distributors in 130 countries handled sales of AMC products and, noted AMC, "Jeep vehicles are well suited to the needs of emerging nations whose economies have been greatly strengthened by rising prices for oil and other raw materials."

An example of the former was Venezuela which in 1976 was depicted by AMC as "the world's fastest-growing four-wheel drive market." In response, the plant facilities of AMC's subsidiary, Jeep de Venezuela, was upgraded and programs were implemented to increase market penetration. As it was, Jeep was already doing pretty well, having 40 percent of the four-wheel drive market of the area covered by the Andean Pact.

Jeep sales to OPEC and other developing countries with valuable mineral resources showed continuing strength. Iran remained a strong market and AMC reported that sales in Nigeria, Indonesia and Morocco showed "encouraging growth". Directing international operations from 1975 until 1977 was Lawrence Hyde, who pursued an aggressive marketing strategy while not hesitating to shut down inefficient operations.

The setting in 1977 of an all-time sales record of 110,000 Jeeps in the U.S. was matched by the tremendous success of AMC's international operations whose profits more than doubled in fiscal 1977 to an all-time record. Stockholders were informed that "Jeep vehicles were pacesetters in international markets, with unit sales increasing 14 percent over 1976. Total international Jeep volume grew from 26,500 units in 1976 to 30,300 units in 1977."

With demand for 4-wheel drive vehicles steadily increasing, the future outlook for Jeep was excellent. AMC's international strategy continued to focus on three basic points: expand current markets and develop new ones; develop new models for specific worldwide demand; and participate in joint venture manufacturing operations.

Specific applications of these principles during 1977 included a major expansion of the Jeep de Venezuela facility at Tejerias to meet demand for the Jeep Wagoneer and CJ models. AMC described the Venezuelan market as "growing, reflecting the country's large petroleum income and a growing middle class".

In Iran, Jeep sales also grew substantially, accounting for nearly

75 percent of 4-wheel drive sales. Specifically, AMC said, "Demand for Jeep vehicles by the Iranian government continues to be strong, and in the private sector demand for Jeep high line vehicles is increasing rapidly." Of course, this was before the revolution. Once the Shah was overthrown the days of this venture – the AMC portion of which had been previously sold to General Motors – were numbered.

An important development during 1978 was completion of a joint venture agreement in Egypt to build a plant capable of turning out between 10,000 and 12,000 vehicles annually by 1981. Actually, production began in December, 1978, less than a year after ground breaking took place for the new factory. This operation, Arab American Vehicles, was 51 percent owned by the Arab Organization for Industrialization (AOI), a consortium of four mid-eastern nations (Egypt, Saudi Arabia, United Arab Emirates and Qatar), and 49 percent by American Motors.

These nations had banded together to create an arms industry that would have a good deal of civilian spin-off. Initially, production was limited to CJ-5 and CJ-6 Jeeps but eventually CJ-7 and CJ-8 models were substituted. Receiving first priority were orders from the military, but a small number of Jeeps were released for the civilian market.

Recalling that time frame, Tod O. Clare, who became Vice President-International Operations in 1978 explained, "At that time American manufacturers were being inundated with requests to build factories in the Arab world ... They (AOI) wanted Jeep, they knew the Jeep as a vehicle that could serve both a tactical and civilian purpose. It wasn't so thoroughbred that it was restricted in its applications."

At this time the U.S. military had adopted the M-151 and Mr. Clare, while noting that "The M-151 was a fine cross-country vehicle under certain conditions", explained that "it was useless in the sand because it couldn't take a big enough tire. As a result, the M-151 was rather looked down upon by people who needed a real desert vehicle. The Jeep was a very handy and inexpensive alternative. There really wasn't, in the world, any other 4×4 like the Jeep with a 16 inch Michelin tire."

The only real challenger for this contract was the Land-Rover. "The Land-Rover", Clare adds, "did its very best and we had to fight them tooth and nail."

Improving the competitiveness of the CJ Jeep in the European, Latin American and Asian markets during 1978 was the introduction of a diesel-powered CJ. The engine used in the CJ was a 2.7 liter (164.9 cubic inches) Isuzu 4-cylinder developing 70 horsepower at 3600 rpm and 114 lb.ft. of torque at 2050 rpm. The CJ Diesel was available in CJ-5, CJ-6 or CJ-7 form. Standard on all models was a 3-speed, all-synchromesh T-150 transmission. A "3 plus 1" transmission with an "extra-duty" low gear was optional.

It was apparent by 1978 that international Jeep sales were progressing along three lines. First were the advanced markets such as England where Jeep models were successfully launched in 1978 and in Australia where a right-hand drive CJ-7 received certification by the government. This paved the way for future sales expansion. In Europe, sales in 1978 doubled from the previous level. Secondly, in the Third World market Jeep continued to score advancements in such coun-

tries as Iran and Venezuela. During 1978 production capacity in Venezuela was expanded to keep pace with both current demand and to prepare for a new marketing thrust in other Andrean Pact countries.

Finally, Jeep was preparing new marketing opportunities around the world that as late as 1978 remained almost totally undeveloped.

As early as the mid-sixties the Kaiser Jeep International Corporation had made strong efforts to enter the Eastern European market for commercial vehicles. The most ambitious undertaking was a 2000 mile tour of Poland, Czechoslovakia, Hungary, Rumania and Bulgaria by a fleet of white-painted Jeep vehicles. This project had the support of the U.S. Department of Commerce and involved 15 Jeeps. Although no immediate orders resulted, Steve Girard, president of Kaiser Jeep International was both optimistic and unknowingly prophetic at a post-event new conference. "The market is big", he noted. "If we can get an initial order of 1000 to 2000 units for any one of these countries – and export approval from the Commerce Department – this could be the start of parts and assembly production that progresses into manufacturing.

Two views of a Mitsubishi-built Jeep model. (Courtesy of author's collection)

"The main purpose of the caravan was to create demand – a simple marketing development – because our product is the kind that can't be sold at a distance or out of a briefcase. It has to be demonstrated. The state buying organizations of these countries buy in big-unit lots when they buy and once we get a large order and a Commerce okay we could set up a plant in any of the European countries within a year."

No real business resulted from this drive-through although many individuals who took part later organized AMC's Latin American operations. Even today the Jeep remains a revered product name in Eastern Europe. "We still get letters from people in Eastern Europe, especially from students", Tod Clare explained, "wanting brochures, patches and any type of Jeep memorabilia."

From his perspective, Tod Clare observed that "In terms of being prepared to plow some fresh ground, Kaiser was really there and was very innovative.

"I felt very strongly that there was some sort of historical obligation – that whenever there was an opportunity to expand into a new region – that Jeep had to be involved from the very beginning. Jeep had this pioneering role to play in international business. We always felt that was borne out by our history. We were the smallest company and we had to be very aggressive, and more often than not we beat everyone to the punch in the 4-wheel drive market."

Until the CJ–7 was replaced by the Wrangler, American Motors was able to provide Jeeps for right-hand-drive markets such as the United Kingdom. Although Jeep had the product, it did not have a viable distributorship system in the United Kingdom until BMW distributors, Jonathan Seif and Christopher Tennent, took on both the CJ Jeep and right-hand drive conversions of the senior Jeep models.

This arrangement proved suitable for all parties. Formation of Jeep (UK) Ltd. provided the BMW importer with high-line 4-wheel drive vehicles while AMC, due to the 4-door availability of the Cherokee and Wagoneer exploited a market left untouched by the early Range Rover models.

Events that took place in the late 70s made Steve Girard appear more than ever a man cast in the wrong time and place. Just about 13 years later, in what really was a different time and place, American Motors announced that it was studying the possibility of producing 4-wheel drive vehicles in the People's Republic of China. Although AMC had sold about 500 Jeeps to China in 1974, this marked the beginning of what was to be a frustrating yet potentially the single most important venture into a foreign automotive market ever undertaken by an American firm.

On 26 February, 1979 American Motors reported it had reached an understanding with Beijing Automotive and Industrial Corporation to discuss the possibility of producing Jeeps in a plant currently turning out the BJ212, a 4-wheel-drive vehicle based on an old Russian "GAZ" design from the 1950s. In addition, AMC also said that it anticipated discussions involving the export of Jeeps to China to be included in the upcoming meetings.

Looking back on that situation, Tod Clare told *The Wall Street Journal* in May, 1983, "We deluded ourselves into thinking we were in the home stretch."

Not until 5 May, 1983 was a agreement signed between AMC and the Chinese government officials in the Great Hall of the People. The time between the 1979 meeting of the minds and this occasion was marked by what seemed endless meetings needed to mesh two different cultural and economic systems into a single unit capable of sustaining what would be under the best of conditions a complex business understanding. For example, Richard Swando, director of the AMC project told *The Wall Street Journal* that "We spent half a day arguing over an etc." The issue, *The Wall Street Journal* reported, was a paragraph which covered "acts of God such as fire, flood, etc". "The Chinese", explained Swando, "wanted us to spell out every act of God." Eventually the contract contained the words "beyond reasonable and foreseeable control" in place of the bothersome "etc." phrase. Later, Robert Steinseifer, director of enterprise management at the Peking Auto Works (which was soon renamed the Beijing Jeep Corporation) had to cope with the polite nature of the Chinese. All too often, Steinseifer told *Chilton's Automotive Industries*, (October, 1985), the Chinese would make a comment or criticism in such a polite manner that the Americans would miss the point. The solution was what Steinseifer called a "war room" where all sides could be as blunt as necessary.

Other areas that had to be resolved included provisions for inflation, salary levels for Chinese managers and the disposition of finished vehicles. A major concern of AMC was the availability of hard currency.

The final contract called for a new venture to be formed known as Beijing Jeep Corporation. Initially American Motors invested $16 million in technology and cash in exchange for a 31.4 percent interest in the Peking Jeep Corporation. AMC said at that point that it planned to reinvest profits in the company until it owned the maximum 49 percent possible. AMC also agreed to either purchase or cause to be purchased $70 million worth of products from Beijing Jeep Corporation (BJC) through 1990. The exportability of Chinese-made vehicles obviously hinged upon their quality and in that regard Steinseifer told *Chilton's Automotive Industries* "Any assignment I've given them, they've done in a first-class way. The prime thing for them to do is improve their productivity.

"They haven't had to do that before because their prime interest has been to furnish everybody with a job. Now their prime interest is to build a world-class car that can compete with the Japanese in the Japanese backyard (Southeast Asia) and that's quite a chore."

Plans initially called both for the doubling of the plant's capacity to 40,000 units a year and development of a new vehicle for the Chinese market based upon existing Jeep technology. This latter strategy was soon seen to involve too much time and expense. Instead the decision was made to ship Jeep Cherokees in CKD (Completely Knocked Down) form from Toledo for assembly in China.

A CJ diesel operating under extreme conditions.
(Courtesy of author's collection)

AMC wasn't the only foreign auto manufacturer setting up operations. As AMC chairman Paul Tippett remarked, "Everyone salivates when they think of the Chinese market."

Tippett was extremely optimistic about the AMC venture. After all, the attraction of very low labor costs (30 cents per hour in China compared to about $22 per hour in the U.S.) and a confidence that AMC could improve productivity at the existing plant without materially increasing the size of the 10,000 member work force were sufficient to dispell any lingering doubts about the wisdom of AMC's action. The aura surrounding low wage rates in China was dimmed by a requirement that the workers had to be paid more than six times the amount earned by other Chinese workers. Eventually this differential was scaled down to 150 percent.

Two not-so-subtle comparisons of the CJ diesel with larger diesel-powered vehicles. (Courtesy of author's collection)

Two years later, in October, 1985 the first Chinese-assembled Cherokee was completed. Although the size of the labor force was reduced to 4000 and the total output for 1985 consisted of about 2100 BJ–212s and 750 Cherokees, serious problems soon threatened to undermine the entire venture. The crisis revolved around delays and regulations concerning hard currency payment by the Chinese government. At one point AMC stopped shipment of Cherokee kits to China in mid-1986. But input from high ranking government officials from both China and the United States rescued the venture from what seemed a total collapse. The degree to which AMC was committed to its success can be gauged by the action of BJC president Don St. Pierre in writing directly to Chinese Premier Zhao Ziyang to seek his cooperation.

In May, 1986 an AMC delegation lead by Tod O. Clare went to China to meet with leaders of the Chinese auto industry including Chen Zhutao, president of the China National Automotive Industrial Corporation and the vice-mayor of Beijing, Xhang Jianmin. The joint statement issued by both sides noted that "Through these discussions, both sides agreed in principal to actions which will enable BJC to continue the Jeep Cherokee program and to accelerate localization … A comprehensive and detailed development plan will be finalized in the near future."

As a result AMC resumed shipping Cherokee kits to China in mid-June, allowing production of Cherokees to resume on August 8 after a seven week lapse. The terms of the agreement making this possible included the goal of increasing Chinese part content in the Cherokee from the current 9 percent to 25 percent during 1987. The Chinese committed themselves to the purchase of at least 2000 Cherokee kits in 1987. For each Cherokee sold at a price of $19,000 the BJC received $12,000 in foreign currency and the remainder in local currency.

By 1990 AMC planned to produce 20,000 Cherokees annually in China and to increase Chinese content to 90 percent. Future plans also called for the Comanche pick-up to be produced by BJC.

Meanwhile, overall Jeep performance in the international market continued to grow rapidly. Operations in fiscal 1979 reached an all-time high for the third year in a row. AMC noted that "This record performance was achieved of worldwide economic and political change." Although sales in the Middle East fell as a result of the Iranian revolution, total AMC unit volume increased by 12 percent, due largely to improved Jeep sales. The Egyptian assembly plant had completed nearly 2,500 units by year's end.

In Mexico, Jeep sales increased by 66 percent from the 1978 level to an all-time high. The Mexican economy was strong in 1979 and AMC reported that "The Company is well-positioned in the Mexican automotive market, and continuing improvements in sales of both passenger cars and Jeep vehicles are anticipated."

In Venezuela, AMC began a joint venture with a new partner which had the effect of doubling both its manufacturing capacity and distribution network. Jeep vehicles were now produced in Venezuela at a rate in excess of 1,000 units monthly.

In July, 1979 production started of the Llanero, a special Venezuelan version of the CJ-7 which had an all-new steel top with a vertical rear door and side bench seats. Plans were underway to offer other specialized Jeep derivatives for the Venezuelan market.

Jeep's position in Europe continued to gain strength due to increased sales of high-line luxury models as well as greater availability of diesel-engined CJ models. As a base for future expansion, the Jeep European distribution system began to utilize the Renault sales organization in key markets.

During calendar year 1980 sales and earning from AMC's International Operations were at high levels for the fourth year in a row. In most industrialized markets, including Europe, AMC faced a problem similar to that confronting it on the home market – a depressed economic climate due to high interest rates, rapidly rising fuel prices and a geneal economic downturn. This, in turn, led to what AMC depicted as "a burgeoning demand for fuel-efficient vehicles. Most of the Jeeps sold in these countries came from its U.S. plants and as Tod O. Clare explained, "International Operations was able to fill this demand quickly and efficiently. Both four-cylinder and six-cylinder gasoline and four-cylinder diesel engines were made available in all CJ vehicles for the first time on a full-year basis in 1980, and significant advertising and merchandising programs were implemented to make buyers aware of the new offerings." As a result 40 percent of the built-up Jeeps sold by International Operations had the new diesel engine.

In sharp contrast to the difficulties existing in the mature auto markets, the situation in the developing countries of the southern hemisphere provided Jeep with another outstanding year. "The Company was well positioned", said AMC, "to take advantage of strong vehicle markets as a result of local assembly and manufacturing operations in these countries."

Both in Mexico and Venezuela new records were set for both passenger car and Jeep sales. In Mexico, combined passenger car and Jeep sales totalled 30,000 units, an increase of 20 percent over 1979. In Venezuela, sales were nearly 10,000 units, with Jeep taking 53 percent of the 4-wheel drive market. An important new Jeep truck, the J-10, was introduced in Venezuela in 1980. It was virtually sold out upon its introduction. This development, plus the continuing of the Wagoneer, lead to a plant expansion program in Venezuela that added to its production capability in 1981.

In the Far East sales volume was up 105 percent in 1980. Particularly impressive was the success of the Jeep in Indonesia, where it came from having virtually no market presence to controlling 22 percent of the market despite strong competition from well-established Japanese firms.

The Jeep presence in Australia was strengthened by preparation of a new assembly program for Cherokees that was scheduled to begin operation in early 1981. In the Middle East, Arab American Vehicles once again made improvements in its operations which enabled it to reach an annual production rate of over 3500 units.

In 1981 over 100,000 vehicles carrying the Jeep trademark were sold outside the United States and Canada. This remarkable achievement represented a 13 percent increase over the level of 1980. Virtually from any angle International Operations was impressive. It had grown to include 19 production facilities and 3000 dealers in 110 countries. The only soft spot was Europe where most markets remained depressed. AMC identified the main sources of this as the combination of an economic slowdown and the increased value of the American dollar. Optimism was expressed that a planned distribution of Jeeps by Renault in France and Belgium would help to alleviate this situation in 1982.

In Latin America passenger car and Jeep sales were again at record levels, having increased 23 percent from 1980. Jeep de Venezuela, in which AMC had a 45 percent equity interest, was the largest producer of Jeep vehicles outside the U.S. Its wholesale sales of 10,000 units gave it a 50 percent share of the Venezuelan 4-wheel drive market.

The situation in Mexico was equally exciting. There, combined passenger car and Jeep sales increased 17 percent over 1980 to a new high of 35,000 units.

AMC reported that it planned to expand Latin American operations in 1981 through a new licensing and assembly agreement with a Bolivian automotive manufacturer under which volume production was scheduled to begin in mid-1982.

Compared to its 1980 level, Far Eastern operations increased 82 percent to establish a new record. Sales of the CJ-7 manufactured in Indonesia nearly doubled to control 16 percent of that country's 4-wheel drive market.

At Brisbane, Australia, a new assembly plant was opened to produce Cherokees and J-10 trucks. In the Middle East Arab American Vehicles received a government contract for CJ-6 Jeeps. Finally, in Africa American Motors entered into a partnership in Kenya – Jeep Africa – in which it had 51 percent equity. Plans called for CJ-8 and CJ-10 vehicles to be assembled in Nairobi and sold both in Kenya and other African countries.

The poor economic conditions that were experienced in many of the Jeep's prime international markets in 1982 brought its stunning sales rise to a temporary halt. Operations remained profitable, but in such areas as Latin America serious problems, not of Jeep's making, were encountered. In Mexico, for example, the devaluation of the peso had a serious impact upon motor vehicle sales. In Venezuela, a drop in oil prices caused a major downturn in sales of 4-wheel drive vehicles. Partially compensating for these setbacks was the nearly doubling of sales in France of Jeeps through the Renault dealership.

By 1984 sales in Latin American began to recover and by 1985 they were at their highest levels in four years.

Chapter 18

Merging and
converging: 1954–1987

When Kaiser purchased Willys-Overland in 1953 it was the first of three mergers between the independent automobile manufacturers that the parties involved hoped would enable them to survive the intensely competitive market of the 1950s. On October 1, 1954 Studebaker was purchased by Packard and an ambitious James Nance, with grandiose plans that envisioned Packard becoming a worthy competitor to Cadillac became the president of the resulting Studebaker-Packard Corporation. Just six months earlier, on 1 May, 1954, Nash-Kelvinator Corporation and the Hudson Car Company linked resources to create the American Motors Corporation.

Conditions at both newly created companies were fraught with difficulties. Production of all four marques, as indicated by the following chart were down drastically in 1954 as compared to 1953:

	1953 production	1954 production
Studebaker	186,500	85,300
Packard	81,300	27,600
Nash	135,400	62,900
Hudson	76,300	32,300

Although some valiant efforts ensued, the last Hudson and Nash models were built in 1957. The following year the final Packard, based on the Studebaker body shell, was assembled. For a time Studebaker, revived by the short-lived success of its compact Lark series struggled on. It's possible that Studebaker could have made a strong comeback in the mid-sixties if its strong-willed president, Sherwood Egbert, had not suffered a fatal illness that lead to his resignation as Studebaker president, in November, 1963. Egbert's vision for Studebaker included not only the restyled Hawks and new Avantis that made it into production but an entirely new range of bread and butter Studebaker sedans. Instead, Studebaker beat a steady retreat out of the car business. It stopped production in South Bend, Indiana on 20 December, 1963 and transferred all assembly work to its Hamilton, Ontario plant. Early in March, 1966 Studebaker announced that production at that plant would soon be terminated. The end of the line for Studebaker came on 17 March, 1966.

By that time American Motors had firmly established itself as a producer of compact cars. When AMC had been created it had been Nash that was acquiring the assets of Hudson. Thus it would be the president of Nash, George Mason and not Hudson's president, A.E. Barit, who would emerge as American Motors' first board chairman and president.

The Jet arrived just in time to be negatively affected by Hudson's deteriorating financial position. Not especially attractive in appearance the Jet soon was seen as a car about to become an orphan.

How different was the image of the Rambler! It never was touted as an economy car. Secondly, it was produced by a manufacturer whose other lines were, at least initially, its mainstay. Thus the company's fate didn't depend on the Rambler's success.

Most importantly, the man who succeeded George Mason as the head of AMC was a disciple of Mason – his protege and heir apparent – George Rumney. History would judge this as the single-most important factor in the survival of American Motors in the late 50s and

early 60s. Coming to Nash in 1948 after being courted by George Christopher of Packard who wanted Romney to replace him as Packard president after he retired, Romney wasted no time in plotting out a do-or-die strategy for AMC. He was, for a time, a prophet of common sense automotive design crying out in a time when opulence and excess held sway. But the tide was changing, aided by the success of the Volkswagen, social criticism of American automobiles in books such as *The Insolent Chariots* by John Keats and a growing revulsion toward contemporary automotive styling, his advocacy of the compact car gradually gained respectability. The production output of the Rambler from 1950 through 1962 indicates just how successful Romney was in attacking the dinosaurs from Detroit:

Calendar Year	Production
1950	20,782
1951	57,555
1952	53,055
1953	41,885
1954	37,779
1955	83,852
1956	79,166
1957	114,084
1958	186,227
1959	368,464
1960	434,704
1961	372,485
1962	454,784

But as early as 1961 there were signs that the Rambler era was ending. An early warning for AMC was the evolution of the Chevrolet Corvair from a ho-hum economy car into a snappy sportster. When it was first introduced in late 1959 as a 1960 model, the Corvair was promoted as a practical economy car, not unlike the Volkswagen. In that guise the Corvair was, at best, only a moderate success. In the 1960 model year its production totalled just 250,007 as compared to the Falcon's 435,676. But in May, 1960 Chevrolet began production of a sporty Monza version that quickly captured not only the public's attention, but by 1961, the majority of Corvair sales.

Mason had long-pursued the goal of unifying the independents into a single unit with the wherewithall to effectively compete against Ford, Chrysler and General Motors. This would have involved Packard, Nash and Hudson. He had removed Studebaker from this primarily because its labor costs were the highest in the industry.

Unfortunately, while he saw the independent's hefty 15 percent market share of the late 1940s as only a temporary aberration, his counterparts at the other small companies viewed it through rose-colored glasses. Thus Barit had expressed little interest in Mason's merger talk until the situation had become critical.

On 8 October, 1954, just a week after the formation of Studebaker-Packard, George Mason died from pneumonia. But before his death Mason had outlined what he regarded as the path to survival for American Motors. The key, as he saw it, was the compact car. In 1941 Nash had introduced the Nash 600 on a trim 112 inch wheelbase. The

600's trim proportions were overshadowed by its unit body construction, but when the war ended Mason encouraged further research and development at Nash-Kelvinator of a small American car.

In 1954 the Nash Metropolitan appeared. Built in England to Nash specifications and using many Austin A40 components it was the result of an earlier NXI design that had aroused considerable attention among Americans looking for a small 2-seater commuter-type car.

Far more significant was the Nash Rambler, introduced in March, 1950. This was a true compact car with a 100 inch wheelbase and overall length of 176 inches. There had been other small American cars, of course, before the Rambler. And, in the years to follow, there would be many more. Kaiser-Frazer would offer the Henry J in 1951, Willys-Overland would present its Aero Willys a year later followed by the Hudson Jet in 1953.

All three vehicles suffered from a flaw of one type or another. These weren't mechanical or design weaknesses *per se*, but rather shortfalls in their image. The Henry J appeared to be what it was – a small economy car offering little prestige at a time when the automobile's role as a status symbol was widely accepted. The Willys had much going for it – good looks, performance, fuel economy and the excellent F-head engine. Although initially uncompetitively priced against comparatively equipped models fronm Ford, Plymouth and Chevrolet, its sales in 1952 were a respectable 48,845. Unfortunately, when Willys-Overland was acquired by Kaiser in 1953 the Aero Willys' days as an American car were numbered.

The popularity of the Monza represented the discovery of a nascent market for relatively inexpensive, yet attractive and good performing "pony cars" that reached full bloom in the mid-sixties. The car that clearly defined this extremely lucrative market was the Ford Mustang. Eventually every American manufacturer followed Ford's lead with coupes of their own. AMC's first effort, the Marlin, fell well short of the mark. But American Motors did much better with the Javelin and AMX models that followed.

The public image of AMC that resulted from these efforts was mixed. Some saw it as a company that was a day late and a dollar short. The Javalin was, from this perspective a nice automobile but hardly an example of innovative design. Furthermore, its V-8 engines never seemed quite up to the standards of power established by Ford and Chevrolet. But unknown to the critics, AMC, as early as 1961, had sought to expand its operations into areas where sustainable growth was possible. In particular, Romney, before he left AMC in 1962 to run for governor of Michigan, regarded both the light truck and utility car fields as possible areas where AMC could find success. During 1960 and 1961, as a result of Romney's interest, AMC and Kaiser explored the possibility of a link-up. But while Kaiser dropped its asking price for its Jeep operations from $150 million to $110 million, it was still well above AMC's best offer of $85 million. As a result negotiations ended in early February, 1961.

Yet, the possibility that a deal still might be struck between the two parties remained alive. Helping to fuel this was the increasing level of cooperative efforts by Kaiser and AMC in Mexico, Argentina and Iran. A prime factor in its revival in 1969 was the revitalization strategy pursued by a new AMC management team, led by Roy Chapin Jr. which had come to power in 1967. Chapin, the son of Roy D. Chapin Sr., a founder of the Hudson Motor Car Company in 1908, had been one of the prime instigators of efforts to bring Jeep into AMC in the early sixties when he had served as AMC's executive vice president – finance and international. Now, as AMC's top executive, Chapin pushed hard to convince skeptics on the AMC board that acquiring Jeep still was a good idea. To be sure, the picture at Jeep wasn't

100 percent rosy. Its Toledo plant, although capable of almost an A to Z vehicle manufacturing operation was an old and relatively inefficient facility. The majority of Jeep dealers were not exclusive Jeep franchises and, in 1960, were averaging only 25 annual sales per outlet. Yet, in 1960 Jeep had produced 122,000 vehicles and held a respectable 2.36 percent share of the 6000 pound and under truck market. In the 6000 to 9000 pound class Jeep controlled six percent of the market.

Initially Chapin and AMC's new president, William V. Luneberg, were kept busy combating AMC's rather dismal public image. This wasn't easy since AMC followed up a loss of $12,648,170 in 1966 with a really impressive loss of $75.8 million in 1967. One of their first moves was to reduce the price of the least expensive Rambler American model by $234 to $1867. This placed it close to the cost of the Volkswagen. The resulting sales upturn was followed by the successful launch of the Javelin and AMX in 1967 and 1968 respectively.

Long term, Chapin and Luneberg forged a policy of diversification to broaden AMC's operational base. For example, it purchased a producer of automotive trim, Canadian Fabricated Products, in late 1968. This was followed by acquisition of Development Credit Corporation, a New York based firm financing wholesale and retail car purchases on the international market. Previously, AMC had a one-third interest in Development Credit with Renault and Kaiser Jeep holding the remaining stock.

The stage was now set for the resumption of formal negotiations between AMC and Kaiser concerning the sale of the Kaiser Jeep Corporation. By December, 1969, the basic terms were in place. AMC would acquire Jeep for what was first reported to be between $82 and $86 million. At this time Jeep's book value was $90 million. The actual cost, based on the value of AMC common stock for the 90 days prior to 30 September, 1969 was closer to $70 million. Specifically, AMC acquired Jeep for $10 million in cash, the transfer of $5.5 million AMC shares (this figure represented 22 percent of AMC common stock) which had a value of $55 million and $9.5 million in negotiable five-year notes to Kaiser. AMC also paid Kaiser about $500,000 for miscellaneous assets such as furniture and fixtures.

This make Kaiser the company's largest stockholder. With the prospect of Kaiser also having two members on the AMC board of directors (it originally had 12 members; to accommodate the new Kaiser representatives it was expanded to 14 in 1970), speculation began that Kaiser might attempt a reverse takeover. But *Business Week*, 25 October, 1969, quoted a spokesman familiar with both companies as saying "Kaiser Industries does not intend to get actively involved in American Motors management. They are acutely interested in American Motors as an investment, but there are no major plans to aggressively seek any kind of management position." Also helping to end the rumors about Kaiser's motives was a statement issued by Edgar F. Kaiser, chairman of Kaiser Industries. Declaring that he would not seek and AMC board seat, Kaiser explained that "he doesn't want anyone to get the impression that Kaiser Industries is seeking control." Eventually, Stephen A. Girard, a Kaiser Industries vice president and Roy E. Hughes, an executive vice president, were elected to the American Motors board of directors.

At the American Motors Annual Meeting, held on 4 February, 1970,

Roy Chapin dealt with the question of Kaiser influence in AMC operations. In his presentation to stockholders Chapin explained, "I want to anticipate one question that might be in the minds of some stockholders as the result of a few press reports that followed announcement of the Jeep purchase. It concerns the role Kaiser Industries might play as the holder of about 22 percent of the outstanding shares of American Motors common stock.

While Kaiser Industries will have an understandable interest in our operations, they are not in anyway seeking to control American Motors."

Of nearly equal interest to many AMC shareholders and potential investors was the status of Kaiser Jeep on the eve of the AMC takeover. The prospectus issued by Kaiser at that time was not encouraging. It reported that "Kaiser Jeep's management believes that its commercial business [which *Dun's Review* for May, 1970 stated was 37% of its sales] had not been profitable since 1964." In the first nine months of 1969 Jeep's commercial business had lost $6.4 million. As far as *Dun's Review* was concerned, AMC was purchasing a company that had been going downhill for a decade.

But Chapin countered this pessimistic view with a rosy scenario of his own in which the acquisition of Jeep was seen as a golden opportunity for AMC to get into both the recreational vehicle and light truck fields. Furthermore he was confident he could run Jeep more efficiently than it had been under Kaiser control. Specifically, Chapin saw profits resulting not only from cost-cutting moves but from some economics of scale. "Jeep's added volume", explained, "give us more leverage in dealing with suppliers." Similarly, the merging of redundant functions at the two companies into slightly larger operations was also seen by Chapin as yielding important savings.

At the Annual Meeting the vote to acquire Kaiser Jeep Corporation was 10,689,780 For and 297,142 Against. The acquisition of Jeep transformed AMC into a billion dollar corporation. Total combined 1968 fiscal sales of Jeep and AMC totalled $1.2 billion (1968 AMC sales were $791,069,780). This moved AMC up from a position as the nation's 131st largest corporation to its 75th largest.

On 1 February, 1978, just eight years after the AMC board of directors had approved the Kaiser Jeep purchase, AMC's president, Gerald C. Meyers, told an audience of about 200 stockholders at AMC's annual meeting that "We are often asked if our future includes affiliation with another company. I'm sure you have heard the rumors … The answer to those questions is yes."

The rumors that Meyers referred to told of firms including Volkswagen and Honda expressing an interest in joining AMC in some sort of partnership. There had also been speculation that a syndicate of Italian investors lead by Alejandro DeTomaso as well as a group of Arab investors reportedly with $50 million cash in hand had also indicated an interest in AMC's future.

After the annual meeting concluded Meyers, who had become AMC's chief executive in November, 1977 (Roy Chapin continued to serve as board chairman) expanded on his remarks at a press conference. Using the term "affiliation" rather than merger Meyers noted that "The door is open when the right opportunity comes along … We will consider possibilities of any type." Although Meyers also said that AMC "can live without it" (a merger), the reality was that AMC needed some sort of link-up with another company as a source of capital and technology to develop both new Jeep models and a line of fuel efficient front-wheel drive automobiles.

The point man in this effort for AMC was Chapin who had a long list of contacts left over from his days in internatonal operations at his disposal. As an answer to the obvious "What's in it for us?" question

that he was bound to be asked by interested parties, Chapin had a ready response: in the modern age the only way a European manufacturer could match Volkswagen's record in the U.S. market was with an American partner.

Not everyone had to agree with this view but there were plenty of European companies, including Fiat and Peugeot that saw in AMC's problems a golden opportunity. But in March, 1978 a joint announcement was made by AMC and Renault that they had reached an agreement under which Renault would purchase 4.7 percent of AMC common stock for $60 million. Other aspects of this agreement included the sale by AMC dealers of the Renault LeCar and the sale of Jeeps in France by Renault dealers. This was just the beginning of a growing role in AMC by Renault that saw it eventually control as much as 46.4 percent of AMC stock and provide $785.1 million to AMC for both new passenger car and Jeep models.

For a time this strategy seemed to be successful. Renault had, in the late fifties, been a major force in the American market for foreign cars. Sales of its Dauphine model, were for a time, second only to the Volkswagen. But a weak dealer network as well as quality problems contributed to make that a short-lived situation.

In 1983 AMC began production of the Renault Alliance which after a strong start soon fell into disfavor with American new car buyers. While AMC was amassing a loss of over $622 million from 1980 through 1984 Renault was also experiencing major problems manifested by losses of $1.79 billion in 1984 and $1.56 billion in 1985.

The resulting social unrest in France resulting from a government-owned company such as Renault cutting employment at home while funding what seemed a hopeless situation in the U.S. was climaxed by the assassination of Renault Chairman Greorges Besse on 17 November, 1986.

Ironically, events that would lead to Renault pulling out of the U.S. had been unfolding for nearly a year prior to this tragic occurrence. The most significant was a tentative agreement signed on 30 June, 1986 between AMC and Chrysler that would have AMC build Chrysler's rear-drive M-body models – the Plymouth Gran Fury, Dodge Diplomat and Chrysler New Yorker – in its Kenosha plant. For Kenosha this meant that 3000 workers, idled due to slow sales of the Renault Alliance and Encore, would be going back to work. A similar deal had almost been reached in 1982 which would have involved the production of Chrysler New Yorkers at AMC's Brampton, Ontario plant. But at that time Lee Iacocca felt that AMC would not be able to supply Now Yorkers in sufficient numbers to meet demand. The 1986 agreement had profound consequences for AMC and Chrysler. First came reports that they were discussing the possibility of adding the production of the Dodge Omni and Plymouth Horizon America models to the Kenosha plant. This was followed by some significant movement of AMC common stock on the New York Stock Exchange fueled by reports that such firms as Fiat, Volvo and Saab were interested in buying into AMC.

But early in November, 1986 the really big story broke – Chrysler was interested in buying AMC. Chrysler, with $3 billion in the bank and eager to acquire not only additional manufacturing space but also a part of the recreational 4-wheel drive market had by that time worked out the details that would have it acquire Renault's share of AMC stock. In addition, each outstanding share of AMC common stock was converted into a fraction of Chrysler common stock having a value of $4.50 based on closing market shares of the Chrysler common stock for the ten trading days ending five trading days before the merger.

For long-time AMC officials and loyalists the absorption into

Chrysler was a bitter sweet experience. After years of huge losses AMC was poised to finally reap the benefits of a new product line headed by the mid-sized Premier model, manufactured (along with the Wrangler) in its state-of-the art plant in Bramalea, Ontario. But as Chrysler's new Eagle Jeep division AMC lives on as the world's leading manufacturer of 4-wheel drive vehicles.

The absorption of AMC into Chrysler ended one era for the Jeep. It's also the beginning of a new one that will be ever more grand and glorious.

The new Jeep Eagle logo. (Courtesy of Chrysler Corporation)